In *Responsibility and evidence in oral discourse* twelve prominent linguists and linguistic anthropologists examine "responsibility," "authority," and "knowledge": central, but problematic, concepts in contemporary anthropology. Their detailed case studies analyze diverse forms of oral discourse – everyday conversation, conversational narrative, song, oratory, divination, and ritual poetry – in societies in the Americas, Africa, Asia, and the Pacific. The studies show how speakers attribute responsibility for acts and states of affairs, how particular forms of language and discourse relate to claims and disclaimers of responsibility, and how verbal acts are themselves social acts, subject to such attributions. The volume challenges those cognitive theorists who locate responsibility for the meaning of verbal acts solely in the intentions of individual speakers. Instead, the contributors focus on the production of meaning between speakers and audiences in particular social and cultural contexts, through dialogue and interaction which mediate between linguistic forms and their interpretations.

This landmark volume will serve for years to come as a point of reference in the study, not only of responsibility and evidence, but of reported speech, authorship, and other phenomena in the social life of language. Besides linguistic and cultural anthropologists, linguists, and folklorists, it will interest also readers from pragmatics, legal studies, sociology, religion, and social psychology.

Studies in the Social and
Culture Foundations of Language No. 15

Responsibility and evidence in oral discourse

Studies in the Social and Cultural Foundations of Language

The aim of this series is to develop theoretical perspectives on the essential social and cultural character of language by methodological and empirical emphasis on the occurrence of language in its communicative and interactional settings, on the socioculturally grounded "meanings" and "functions" of linguistic forms, and on the social scientific study of language use across cultures. It will thus explicate the essentially ethnographic nature of linguistic data, whether spontaneously occurring or experimentally induced, whether normative or variational, whether synchronic or dischronic. Works appearing in the series will make substantive and theoretical contributions to the debate over the sociocultural-functional and structural-formal nature of language, and will represent the concerns of scholars in the sociology and anthropology of language, anthropological linguistics, sociolinguistics, and socio-culturally informed psycholinguistics.

RESPONSIBILITY AND EVIDENCE IN ORAL DISCOURSE

EDITED BY

JANE H. HILL

University of Arizona

AND

JUDITH T. IRVINE

Brandeis University

CAMBRIDGE
UNIVERSITY PRESS

Published by the Press Syndicate of the University of Cambridge
The Pitt Building, Trumpington Street, Cambridge CB2 1RP
40 West 20th Street, New York, NY 10011–4211, USA
10 Stamford Road, Oakleigh, Victoria 3166, Australia

First published 1993

A catalogue record for this book is available from the British Library

Library of Congress cataloguing in publication data
Responsibility and evidence in oral discourse / edited by Jane H. Hill and Judith T. Irvine.
p.   cm. – (Studies in the social and cultural foundations of language; no. 15)
Includes bibliographical references and index.
ISBN 0 521 41515 2. – ISBN 0 521 42529 8 (pbk.)
1. Anthropological linguistics. 2. Discourse analysis. 3. Language and culture. I. Hill,
Jane H. II. Irvine, Judith T. III. Series.
P35.R45   1992
306.4′4′089–dc20   91–42610   CIP

ISBN 0 521 41515 2 hardback
ISBN 0 521 42529 8 paperback

Transferred to digital printing 1999

CONTENTS

vii

FIGURES and TABLES

Figures

Tables

INTRODUCTION

JANE H. HILL and JUDITH T. IRVINE

To say that a human being, as social actor, is "responsible" is a relatively new way of speaking in English, argues Richard Niebuhr (1963).[1] Deriving from an older notion of "responsiveness," a quality of participation in dialogue, the newer sense of "responsibility" that has emerged in the modern era indexes the development of an idea of "the continuity of a self with a relatively consistent scheme of interpretation of what it is reacting to ... [and] continuity in the community of agents to which response is being made" (Niebuhr 1963:65).

Such terms are problematic for anthropologists, who have come to recognize that ideas about "continuity of a self," and "continuity in the community of agents," are cross-culturally variable. Problematic, too, for some, would be a focus on the individual self and its scheme of interpretations as an analytic isolate, were that focus to overwhelm attention to community and situated response. The essays in this volume suggest, on the contrary, that the "quality of participation in dialogue" is a sense of the term "responsibility" that must remain central. Indeed, its importance extends far beyond the mere definition of a term.

In so arguing we take part in a recent movement in linguistic anthropology that shifts away from paradigms assigning the locus of "meaning" to the individual speaker, toward more dialogic approaches in which meanings are constructed in interactional processes (see Besnier, 1990a, Lutz and Abu-Lughod, 1990, among many other recent statements). Although dialogicality and interaction are themes of current interest in many intellectual arenas, linguistic anthropology joins these themes with a concern for cultural frameworks and linguistic structures. As some recent works in this field (Hill, forthcoming; Irvine, 1990; Urban, 1989; Silverstein, 1977) suggest, many aspects of linguistic form may usefully be seen as having interactional processes profoundly embedded in them. And though not all studies in linguistic anthropology describe "exotic" societies, all are informed by a sense of cultural variability, and ask how such variability may relate to the situated conduct of talk.

This movement toward dialogicality has several intellectual ancestries, variously drawn upon by the authors in this volume. One source is the

1

ethnography of speaking, with its focus on the speech event and the contextualization of meaning. Another part of the background to this movement can be found in symbolic interactionism and in the sociological study of conversation, with its emphasis on the negotiated and emergent quality of meanings, and its notion that social structure, institutions, and conceptions of self (or at least some aspects of these) are interactionally constructed and contingently relevant, rather than known and determined in advance. Still other intellectual sources include traditions in literary criticism and philosophy (Bakhtin/Voloshinov in particular) calling into question the authoritativeness - and even the possibility – of any strictly individual voice and point of view. Finally, although the formal investigation of discourse in linguistics has sometimes been seen by anthropologists as an irrelevant or even hostile pursuit, some of our authors find formalist concerns not only compatible with their own, but helpful to understanding how discourse structures reveal a socialized world.

Of central importance to an approach that emphasizes dialogicality and the social construction of meaning is the connection between knowledge and agency. To interpret events, to establish facts, to convey opinion, and to constitute interpretations as knowledge – all these are activities involving socially situated participants, who are agents in the construction of knowledge as well as being agents when they act on what they have come to know, believe, suspect, or opine. For this reason the topic of "Responsibility and Evidence in Oral Discourse" seems to us especially apt for furthering this new direction of work, since "responsibility" points toward the agency aspect of meaning while "evidence" points toward the knowledge aspect. But the two aspects are crucially linked, as the papers in this volume show; and both aspects are nuanced, as well.

We are of course not the first to call attention to these topics. Conceptions of responsibility and evidence, and cross-cultural variability in such conceptions, have been prominent topics in the anthropology of law. In the realm of contract, for example, Gluckman (1965) notes that a concept of accountability beyond a "general demand for faithfulness and generosity" did not exist in English law until the fifteenth century and is irrelevant to the legal system of the Barotse, where the precise terms of "good faith" differ among the various possible types of agreements. Nor do identical types of responsibility figure in the idea of criminal guilt in all societies. Gluckman argues that a doctrine of absolute responsibility (often called "strict liability"), amounting to complete inattention to the forms of intention that English speakers often consider to be "mental," must be rare; but he finds that the evaluation of "intent" may often be more a political than a psychological process, an assessment of the state of the relationships between plaintiff and defendant rather than an assessment of individuals' states of mind. Thus, among the Barotse, the attention of courts to *mens rea* spans a continuum between assumption of absolute responsibility at one extreme, and close attention to the state of mind of defendants at the other. The more distant the relationship of plaintiff and defendant, the more likely the court is to rule that liability is absolute; the closer the relationship, the more likely will be scrutiny of the defendant's motives. Barotse "responsibility" is not really a psychological notion, then, but a quality that is linked indexically to the matrix of social relations.[2]

In addition to the problem of intention as a possible ingredient of responsibility, assignment of responsibility's locus may be more or less socially diffused. Gluckman (1972) contrasts situations where what he sees as social–structural strains are assigned to individual culpability, as in the case of witchcraft accusations among the Azande, with situations where individual fault is assigned to social structure, as in the case of corporate guilt in Western law.

If ideas about responsibility and agency index ideas about social persons, relationships, and groups, then anthropologists must decompose their terms to determine which, if any, of the components thus identified may be relevant, singly or in combination, at some meaningful moment in some particular human society. We have turned the tools of linguistic anthropology to this task, for reasons grounded both in anthropology and in linguistics. Witchcraft accusations, the waging of disputes in the context of a "public" or "audience" within which persons have to claim their rights and convince others of a position, and the consultation of oracles and diviners, are topics of long standing in anthropology (see papers in Gluckman, 1972); but such discussions of the allocation of responsibility, the marshaling of evidence, and the rhetoric of claims and persuasion bear directly, too, on the analysis of language and discourse. Accusations, consultations of diviners, and the like involve verbal activities, and the available discourse patterns, genres, and linguistic options are of interest for our understanding of how and why the accusations, etc. are framed in a particular way. By such avenues we may approach, through study of the forms of talk, the forms of social engagement. But the study of language itself has also been much concerned in recent years with the evaluation of "intent." Grice's (1957) theory of intentional meaning and the theory of speech acts (Austin, 1962; Searle, 1969) are the most influential accounts of the agency of speakers that have been proposed in the present century, and much work in linguistic pragmatics has built upon their ideas. Yet linguistic anthropologists (perhaps most notably and continuously Dell Hymes [see Hymes, 1974b], but also others such as Rosaldo, 1982) have often noted that speech-act theory may not be cross-culturally portable, and have pointed out that it is rooted in a particular ideology of persons and intentions.

The papers in the present volume explore the problem of agency and responsibility within the context of communicative events. The attribution of responsible agency is seen as an interpretive process that is creative, drawing on the symbolic forms taken by the interpreted behavior, its social setting, its cultural matrix, and the motives and knowledge of witnesses.[3] Many of the papers focus particularly on communicative events in which decisions about agency are at stake: claims (and disclaimers) of authorship or spokesmanship, and decision-making about a course of action, as well as the contexts of legal (and extra-legal) dispute. The allocation of responsibility is thus a centrally important aspect of social meaning constructed in interactional processes, and our purpose is to examine closely the interactional processes and linguistic forms through which this is done. The term "evidence" as well draws us toward the interactional arena. To focus on "evidence" takes the traditional anthropological interest in culturally situated knowledge and casts it in the framework of social action, exploring how claims to knowledge (or ignorance) are made, and how such claims might be used. Attention to evidence shows clearly that culturally situated knowledge is not a matter of clearly differentiated states, of "knowing" or "not knowing," but is complex in its dimensions, and highly variable in the range of potential dimensions which may be relevant in interaction.

When we first embarked on this collective effort, our interest in responsibility and evidence had two starting-points: on the one hand, the linguistic forms relating to epistemic modality – the speaker's degree of commitment to the truth-value of a proposition, or qualification of that commitment; on the other hand, the interactional processes shaping the allocation of responsibility for authorship of a message. The sense that these two starting-points, one in linguistic structure and the other in social interaction, were intimately linked led us to explore a range of cases and materials in the present collection of papers.

In so doing, we found that a focus on responsibility and evidence provides an especially useful angle on the mutual embedding of interactional process and linguistic form. The allocation of responsibility in talk is inherently duplex, linking the attributions of agency and evidence referentially constructed in an utterance with their indexical construction in the act of speaking (and in the audience's act of interpreting). In this duplex process a wide variety of linguistic and interactional means may be invoked, a variety which the papers in this volume explore.

The analyses presented in the volume vary in method and in their particular mix of linguistic and ethnographic concerns. Some papers focus principally on linguistic structures, such as morphology or the coherence of registers; some papers analyze texts or transcripts, generated in interaction; some papers focus on the relevant properties of social settings and cultural milieux; and others explicitly foreground participant roles and interactive relationships (a consideration entering all papers to some extent).

The papers reveal diversity in the composition of social entities that may be held to account, differences in the kinds of acts (verbal or nonverbal) that are constructed as "accountable," differences in the contexts where "responsibility" or "evidence" is relevant, and differences in the communicative means by which responsibility may be claimed, diffused, or evaded. All share the aim of focusing on the rigorous specification of these communicative means, and on the cultural contextualizations by which they are made meaningful. Where the analyses converge, finally, is in highlighting the importance of participation frames in articulating social context with linguistic form. All papers find themselves considering, more or less explicitly and in greater or lesser degrees, structures of participant roles whose laminations are key to the dialogic process.

The contributors to the volume also explore various nuances of our core concepts of *responsibility* and *evidence*. Although the concept is not absent from other papers, those contributors focusing most explicitly on *evidence* are Bendix, Philips, and Maranhão. While Bendix presents the linguistic encoding of evidentials, Philips considers properties of a social setting – the trial – and its management, cross-culturally; and Philips and Maranhão each take up the question of cultural and subcultural differences as to what forms of discourse (and nonverbal signs) are admissible evidence of knowledge. It is also useful to juxtapose these studies with Du Bois' paper on the discourse of divination, a situation where diviners and clients, much concerned about the truth-value of a proposition about the future, focus their attention on divinatory responses as available evidence. Note, however, a further line of comparison. In contrast with the studies by Bendix, Philips, and Du Bois, which in their various ways treat cases where the truth-value of statements is of paramount concern, other papers in the volume play down the question of truth-value as not necessarily what is most at issue for the significance of a particular type of discourse (Shuman, Bauman, Irvine, Maranhão).

Regarding *responsibility*, the papers severally invite us to see many different dimensions of talk and of situation for which a participant can take responsibility or seek to evade it. Some of these dimensions concern acts or states referentially constructed in the discourse. Philips, Kuipers, Duranti, Du Bois, and Hill and Zepeda consider occasions of talk that discuss events of high social or personal import, such as the commission of a crime or the occurrence of calamity. Responsibility for the crime, or for the calamity, is allocated through the discourse in the event at hand, be it trial, ritual, political forum, divination, or narrative. For Du Bois, Bendix, and Philips, the truth-value of an uttered proposition is much at issue, while for Duranti and Chafe, what is more important are the utterance's consequences. Other dimensions of responsibility concern the act of speaking itself. Irvine and Shuman consider the allocation of responsibility for taking on the participant role of utterer or reporter; Bauman, Besnier, and Maranhão discuss how (and whether) a participant assumes responsibility to an audience for a display – of verbal technique or dramaturgical persona (Bauman), of affect (Besnier), or of knowledgeability (Maranhão). In addition, both Maranhão and Philips move onto an analytical meta-level by considering responsibility for determining the ground rules for discourse management in a particular social setting or genre. For Maranhão, the management of discourse in ethnographic writing is itself of concern. Finally, Hill and Zepeda, Irvine, Besnier, Duranti, and Du Bois consider cultural variability in concepts of agency and of the responsible self, and relate these concepts to discourse genres and forms of participation.

While the contributors examine the nuances and complexity of the volume's core concepts, they also explore ways in which responsibility and evidence are linked. A good example of the link is the question of how discourse comes to be seen as authoritative, a question considered by several papers in the volume. Establishing the authoritativeness of discourse – a particular type of discourse, or particular statements or texts – is particularly important when the discourse serves as the basis for a judgment or a course of action having serious social or personal consequences. Thus some authors discuss the discourse that occurs in cases of divination (Du Bois, Kuipers) or of disputation (Duranti, Philips, Irvine, Shuman). The question of authoritativeness arises, too, in cases where a speaker's personal identity or social position is somehow insufficient as a guarantee of a statement's truth or authenticity. A question of authenticity may arise under many different kinds of circumstances: if a speaker is young or low-ranking (Irvine); if a statement has ritual significance and governs the well-being of an entire community (Chafe, Kuipers); if a statement's value depends on its being perceived as handed down from earlier generations (Bauman); or if an ethnographer expects "knowledge" to be displayed in one discourse mode rather than another (Maranhão).

One of the principal ways in which utterances come to be seen as authoritative concerns speakers' ability to create "double-voiced" utterances (to use Bakhtin's term) that manage to add the moral weight of other voices to their own. Many of the papers in the volume thus concern reported speech. In some cases, the ultimate source of the reported speech, or the ultimate guarantor of a statement's authenticity, is located outside the ordinary human world – in deceased elders or ancestors (Bauman, Kuipers), in the spirit world (Chafe, Du Bois), or even in impersonal forces, such as the Zande poison oracle (Du Bois).

In other cases, however, the function of the reported speech is not so much to enhance the utterance's consequentiality, as to distance the speaker from an utterance deemed somehow reprehensible (Besnier, Irvine, Hill and Zepeda). Here speakers seek to evade responsibility by invoking additional sources for an utterance, rather than seeking to augment their own utterances' force.

Reported speech is an example of a way a speaker claims, in effect, that an utterance has already been co-constructed. Some papers in the volume focus explicitly on the process of co-construction of meaning, and its relation to participant roles in interaction (Duranti, Irvine). In other papers a similar process enters in more implicitly. Even in Bendix's discussion of "evidentials" in Newari morphology – of all papers in the volume the one dealing most specifically with linguistic form and the only one relying principally on linguistic elicitation techniques – it turns out that informants supply reportive frames and presupposed dialogue to account for the grammaticality of the evidential morphology.

Reportive frames and "double-voiced utterances" thus lie at the heart of our concern with the display of evidence and the attribution of responsibility in discourse. Notice the importance of reported speech in the linguistic analysis of evidentials (Bendix), and in the criteria for evidence at trials (Philips), in "taking sides" in a factionalized world (Shuman), in the construction of genre conventions (Chafe, Kuipers, Irvine, Bauman), and in ethnographic reportage (Maranhão). The papers also reveal the complexity such frames can have – what one might call the "laminations" of participant role structures. On the one hand, as Hill and Zepeda show, responsibility for an utterance's occurrence may be divided among a variety of voices co-present in a speaker's text, so that the speaker splits (as it were) into a variety of presences, and her utterance looks toward a story-world as well as a world of ongoing interaction. On the other hand, as Irvine shows, responsibility for an utterance may be socially distributed over many persons participating in a social occasion. We suggest that these kinds of cases, despite some obvious differences, have much in common.

Intentionality and authoritativeness in discourse

We begin our volume with papers by Alessandro Duranti and Jack Du Bois, who argue that theories of meaning in the philosophy of language and linguistic pragmatics must be revised, reoriented away from an ethnocentric psychologism and toward recognizing the social and cultural dimensions of communication. In particular, these contributors focus on Grice's (1957) theory of intentional meaning and the theory of speech acts, introduced by Austin (1962) and elaborated by Searle (1969, 1983). Attempting to detach the "meaning of 'meaning'" from its classical definition in terms of truth-conditions, Grice took the verb "to mean" as transitive, presupposing an intention of a speaker who, in "meaning," tried "to produce some effect on an audience by means of a recognition of this intention" (Grice, 1957:442).[4]

Searle's development of Austin's speech-act theory gives a central place to intention, and assumes some speaker "S" who has wants and intentions that are indexed performatively. These wants and intentions are, for Searle, specifically mental states, essentially devoid of social content:

> What is crucially important to see is that for every speech act that has a direction of fit the speech act will be satisfied if and only if the expressed psychological state is satisfied, and the conditions of satisfaction of speech act and expressed psychological state are identical.
>
> (Searle, 1983:11)

Searle has even proposed that these psychological states can be reduced to the biological level, an account that puts intentions not only beyond sociological inquiry, but beyond psychological inquiry as well. Intentional states, says Searle, are states of the brain: "Intentionality is a biological phenomenon and it is part of the natural world like any other biological phenomenon" (*ibid*:230).

As Duranti and Du Bois point out, an anthropological critique of this analysis of intention has been developing for several years because of its limited applicability to non-Western modes of communication. In an influential article Michelle Rosaldo (1982) argued that the Ilongot of the Philippines are little concerned with "truth" or "sincerity" and do not evaluate the felicity of speech acts in terms of the mental states of some person in isolation from relations with other persons. Instead, the successful accomplishment of the prototypical Ilongot speech act, the *tuydek* (roughly, "command"), requires particular differences in social rank, which in turn derive from other qualities of persons achieved in social action, such as a knowledgeable heart. To *tuydek* indexes relationships, not internal psychological states. Criticisms of speech-act theory and the intentionality model have come also from sociologists and linguists working in conversation analysis, who have pointed to the difficulty of identifying speech acts and intentions independently of the socially constructed interaction in which an utterance occurs (e.g. Goffman, 1979, 1983; Levinson, 1983).

Duranti's discussion of the Samoan theory of speaking is a particularly important development of this "antipersonalist" critique of speech-act theory. "Interpretation" in Samoa does not attempt to determine private meaning. Instead, Duranti writes, "Samoans practice interpretation as a way of publicly controlling social relationships." Words often do not emanate from "individuals" in the Western sense, but instead from the locus of a positional identity, such as a particular noble title. Certain types of speech acts require the participation of certain types of audiences. For instance, the closest Samoan equivalent to English "promise" – the speech act Searle examines most closely – is the action designated by the verb *folafola*, which designates a commitment or acknowledgment made in public. Words are evaluated according to their consequences, and it is on the basis of these "new realities," publicly constructed, that speakers are rewarded or punished. As Duranti emphasizes, "for Samoans meaning is seen as the product of an interaction (words included) and not necessarily as something that is contained in someone's mind." Examples are given in which, *contra* the intentionalist theory of speech acts, Samoans hold speakers responsible not for intentions that might be imputed to them by their acts of speaking, but for the social consequences of those acts.

This Samoan ethno-theory of pragmatics thus draws our attention to the co-operative work between speaker and audience in constructing the meaning and relevance of utterances. Where the intentionalist theory of speech acts defines meaning in terms of subjectivity, Duranti looks toward intersubjectivity and its linguistic mediation.

Du Bois similarly criticizes the intentionalist theory of meaning on the basis of ethnographic examples. His paper argues that there are forms of discourse regularly occurring in many societies in which the presupposition of "intention" is specifically excluded. The cases cited concern divination and the consultation of oracles, a widespread activity whose particular genres and techniques vary, and may include nonverbal as well as verbal signs. The Zande poison oracle, for example, operates through the medium of a chicken whose behaviors (and possible demise) are observed by a diviner who has administered the poison to it. The oracle is treated as a participant in the verbal discourse: questions are put to it by the diviner, to which it reacts with a meaningful (and unpredictable) response – its influence on the chicken – a nonverbal sign translated and interpreted verbally by the diviner. The oracle is utterly impersonal, more like a catalyst in a chemical reaction than like a personalized being, and its impersonality is the reason for consulting it. It is a responsible agent in the sense that it creates meaningful signs in response to dialogue, but *not* in the sense that any intentionality can be attributed to it.

The discourse of divination also illustrates a complex structure of participant roles, as the diviner, conversing with the client and (sometimes) manipulating objects, casts himself in the role of reporter and interpreter of the oracular communication. By "creating" the oracle as author or original source of his words, the diviner shifts responsibility for them away from himself. Developing themes proposed in an earlier paper (Du Bois, 1986), Du Bois considers, as well, linguistic devices used in divination to shift responsibility away from the speaker. These include the use of rhythmic and versified speech, language supposed "archaic," figurative language, formulaic expression, repetition and parallelism, and distinctive tones of voice to produce what he calls "apersonal authoritative meaning."

Similar findings emerge in cases examined by Wallace Chafe and Joel Kuipers, who also consider the problem of authoritative discourse. Chafe distinguishes three styles of speaking in Seneca, an Iroquoian language of the United States: conversational style, used in everyday interaction; preaching style, used in recitations of the "Good Message" of the prophet Handsome Lake; and chanting style, used in thanksgiving rituals. The three styles exhibit a continuum in four dimensions: prosodic freedom, formulaicity, sentence integration, and epistemological certainty, which are icons for the location of authority. Conversational style, which locates authority in the speaker, exhibits high prosodic freedom, and the highest scores on the other dimensions. Preaching style is intermediate. In this iconic manner, Chafe proposes, the styles progressively represent a detachment from immediate involvement in the pragmatic present and suggest remote participants – Handsome Lake and the messengers sent him by the Creator – who are ultimately responsible for what is said and for its effectiveness.

Joel Kuipers' paper examines a lengthy ceremonial process of atonement among the Weyewa of Indonesia. Weyewa oratory functions to mediate a complex structure of authority relations, bridging communicative "gaps" between transgressing living people and angry ancestors. The organization of power in Weyewa is modelled by an image of a tree, and speech must flow properly from the "trunk," the center of ancestral power, to the "tip." When speech contains many quotatives, the multiple "tips" of the tree are profiled – a multiplicity of statements and opinions. At a relatively early point in the ceremonial process, while presenting this multiplicity in the form of multiple instances of reported speech, the orator is not disclaiming or diffusing responsibility, but is representing a troubled and disorderly state of affairs. Later in the process, when speech is direct and quotatives disappear, the image evoked is one of smooth relationships, of "trunk" and "tip" in proper alignment. The orator claims, not personal authority, but proper representation of the ancestral voice. The ancestral voice is now so dominant that no explicit differentiation of it from present participants (as would occur, for instance, with quotative verbs) is any longer necessary or even appropriate. Kuipers uses the notion of "entextualization," proposed by Bauman (1987b) and others,[5] to capture the ideological significance of this practice, which the Indonesian government has taken as creating an illegal counter-government; thus Weyewa oratory is now forbidden.

Reported speech and participant roles

The papers discussing "authoritativeness" in discourse show how speech can come to be seen as reported – deriving in some respect at least from a source other than the actual speaker – even if it contains no overtly quotative forms. These observations recall Erving Goffman's discussions of participation frames and the relationship between report and responsibility (Goffman, 1974, 1979; see also Levinson, 1988). Goffman distinguishes several possible realizations of a "speaker": as an "animator," an "author," an "addressing self" or "principal," and a "figure." The "animator," as the party who physically transmits an utterance, need not be responsible for its wording or intent. The "author," who composes the utterance's wording, need not be responsible for content. The "figure" is a protagonist in drama. Only the "principal" is a legally committed entity, "responsible" in some sense for the position attested to by the utterance's content. While these speaker components can be linked, they are often separated, even in perfectly ordinary communicative events. When the US Food and Drug Agency sues over a false claim ("Miracle Bread builds strong bodies") it is the manufacturer who is the defendant, not the advertising agency or its copy-writers.

Goffman derived the source of this complexity within his dramaturgical theory of social interaction. When narratives are recounted in conversation, for example, the listener knows that the teller before him has access to the denouement of an anecdote, and may grow impatient. Thus to maintain narrative suspense the teller must separate the "principal," her or his morally accessible and responsible presence, from an earlier self, who did not know what would happen. The goal of this separation is, Goffman says, "reduction of responsibility," a suspension of access to knowledge. While Levinson (1988) has pointed out that Goffman did not systematically develop his decomposition of speaker and hearer, Goffman's work is essential in demonstrating that the indexical reference constituted in the speech signal must be relativized to a participant structure that is constructed in the speech event, in the interactional space "beyond the sentence."

The papers included in this volume reveal that, cross-culturally, a variety of concerns about different types of responsibility can be managed through such a construction of complex participant structures, and especially through reported speech. Judith Irvine's discussion of genres of

verbal abuse among the Wolof of Senegal illustrates a case where the
distribution of responsibility in a communicative event may exploit
literal, not figurative, third-party participants. In *xaxaar* insult poetry,
women in the family to which a new bride has come hire griots –
professional verbal artists – to chant outrageous poems insulting the
bride, her relatives, and other members of the community. The insults
performed in the *xaxaar* are potent. They can destroy careers, and
offended parties have tried to restrict these performances. But *xaxaar*
continues, suggests Irvine, because it is a wonderfully safe device through
which to vent affect. The employers of the griots evade responsibility
because the words of the insults are not theirs. The griots avoid responsibility because they perform only for hire. Audience members who repeat
the insults later evade responsibility because they only report what they
heard. The locus of responsibility for insult, then, is diffused or distributed, laminated away from individual human beings into an intersubjec-
tively constituted realm of community consensus. For Irvine, the lesson of
xaxaar when compared with verbal abuse in conversational and quasi-
legal settings, is that meaning does not inhere so much in the content of
verbal acts as in the calculus of their relationship with metacommunicative frames and contexts. Moreover, a hierarchical society like that of
rural Wolof villagers distinguishes different types of "self" – and different
levels of responsibility – within a community of speakers. The utterances
of a griot never bear the same responsibility as would the utterances of a
higher-ranking person, because the nature of their ranks presupposes
different participations in decision-making and in dialogue.[6]

While *xaxaar* performances are highly ritualized, many responsibility-
distributing devices, among Wolof and elsewhere, exhibit less rituali-
zation. Amy Shuman's study of American teenagers shows how stories
about fights often have as their goal that the story should be carried by a
third party to a potential opponent, who will then know that the original
teller wishes to fight. Yet, this being the case, the role of messenger then
becomes somewhat dangerous, since some responsibility for instigating a
fight may "leak" from the message onto its bearer. Thus the semiotic
impact of the reported speech used in the adolescent fight stories turns on
a fundamental ambiguity about the relationship between the speaker and
the source of reported speech. Is the speaker a mere "reporter," and thus
innocent in conveying a challenge? Or does the speaker manifest the voice
of one allied with the challenger, and share in the responsibility for the
move? In a world of pervasive factionalism and shifting allegiances,
"talking," points out Shuman, "is a part of fighting." Her study shows
that reported speech in the telling of fight stories is an important locus for
the negotiation of "entitlement" (a term Shuman takes from the work of
Harvey Sacks): the right to recontextualize – and report – both experience

and knowledge, and the experience of hearing speech about these. Such recontextualizations manipulate the state of relationships between interlocutors, and highlight the reporter's responsibility for taking on the reporter role, as distinct from (and, here, often more important than) responsibility for the truth-value of the message.

The possibility of "leakage" from reports is a common and important phenomenon, occurring when some participant in the speech event "sees through" (or is permitted, or invited, to see through) the framing of a report. Because of leakage, we prefer to say that reported speech, and other responsibility-framing devices, "distribute" responsibility, thinning out and socializing its central focus, rather than absolutely relocating it at a distance from the animator. Such distribution or socialization of responsibility through leakage is perhaps an informal analogue to Moore's (1972) notion of the public assignment of "collective responsibility." The most famous type of "leakage" of responsibility, of course, is when the recipient of a speech act "shoots the messenger," the result feared by the adolescents Shuman describes who refuse to carry fight stories. An excellent example attesting to leakage comes from Hill's own field materials. In the passage below, a Mexicano-speaking woman is discussing one important reason to speak Mexicano: to understand and respond to the obscene insults that Mexicano speakers use to guard the boundaries of their towns:

Porque quēmaniān āmo nicmatīz de ōme, hasta nēchtēhuīcaltilīz in nonāntzīn, pero in āmo nictendēroa tlen nēchilia, hasta nēchilīz, "Chinga tu madre," con perdón de Dios, quēn nicmatīz tlen nēchilia?

Because if I didn't speak two languages, someone might say something about my mother, but when I don't understand what he is saying to me, even if he says to me, "Fuck your mother," begging God's pardon, how would I know what he is saying to me.

Here, even though the obscenity is assigned to a third party, the speaker has still uttered it in her own voice; in Goffman's terms, she has "animated" the utterance. Yet clearly she does not see herself as morally neutral in this role; she must ask God's forgiveness for the obscenity, even though it is not "hers."

It is useful to compare our contributors' perspectives on reported speech, participation frames, and "leakage" with linguistic work on the "speaking subject" – an entity more analytically interesting and contextually enriched than is the "speaker" of speech-act theory. Linguists who have carefully investigated the problem of the speaking subject have, at least, generally abandoned naive psychologism. In what Lyons (1982) called "post-Saussurean phenomenological structuralism," developed most notably by Emile Benveniste, the speaking subject is not "in nature" but "in culture," constructed through the indexical trace of deixis in the moment of speaking. The deictic field created by the speaking "I" of Benveniste's *discours*, "I–you" speech, indexes a subject at a moment of space–time inextricably linked to the speech act (Benveniste, 1971. (Such a coherent subject is also assumed by speech-act theory, but without the phenomenological argument that the "I" is constituted in interaction.)

Linguists in the "phenomenological structuralist" tradition have confined analysis largely to the level of the sentence, neglecting discourse situated in communicative events. In addition, they have been concerned almost exclusively with material from Western literary tradition (mainly in English and French), and especially with the novel, with its well-known association with the ideology of "individualism" (Watt, [1957] 1964). Thus linguistic analysis, like speech-act theory, has led to a "psychological" account, an elaboration of the "types of consciousness" of a speaking subject, rather than attention to how such a subject is embedded in social context. Yet the syntactic study of "point of view" (Chafe, 1976) has developed important lines of evidence for the decomposability of the indexical reference to the consciousness of a speaking subject. Kuno (1976) and Banfield (1982) argue that "point of view" is syntactically constrained: a single sentence cannot have more than one. Banfield uses this insight to argue, using evidence from literary discourse, that "point of view" must be decomposed into several types of "subjectivities" that do not co-occur in the relevant syntactic domain.

The phenomenon of reported speech in novelistic discourse, as well as novelistic styles such as the *style indirect libre* ("free indirect style"), are central to Banfield's analysis. On syntactic grounds, she argues, the "subjectivity" manifested in certain types of constructions is not the same entity as the speaker "S" of pragmatics. SPEAKER and SELF must be distinguished, and some sentences, those in free indirect style, are "speakerless" (Banfield, 1982:97).

Although the syntactic approach has thus led to some useful insights, many authors have disputed the position that only one type of subjectivity can be represented in a single clause, arguing instead for a "dual-voice" theory of novelistic discourse as distinguished by its capacity to blend the voice of the author with the represented subjectivity of novelistic figures. The idea that the distribution of subjectivity is constrained formally by the structure of language itself and is thus outside of history is challenged, for instance, in the work of Bakhtin and his circle (Bakhtin, [1929] 1984), Voloshinov, [1930] 1973), and by many modern critics, who argue that the literary sentence in fact represents a complex intertwining of "voices."

Evidence presented by papers in this volume suggests that "double-voiced" utterances are not restricted to novelistic discourse. If, instead of restricting ourselves to sentence-level syntactic analysis, we examine the use of reported speech in context, we find many examples of this phenomenon. To understand the relationship between talking and fighting, as described in Shuman's paper, requires a double-voice theory. Similarly, in Niko Besnier's account of reported speech in Nukulaelae, a double voice is manifested. In representing the emotions and attitudes of those whose speech is reported, the Nukulaelae speaker claims to be in part constituting their subjectivity. Yet the pragmatic force of these reports, Besnier argues, is precisely to convey an attitude held by the reporter, which it is inappropriate to represent directly. Special keying devices in Nukulaelae reported speech are used to manage an ideology which de-emphasizes individual thoughts, intentions, and emotions in favor of collective authority. One should not attribute thoughts, emotions, or intentions to other persons. One can, however, avoid blame for making such attributions by representing these in reported speech attributed to other persons, or through deictic adverbs, prosodic features, and other aspects of rhetorical style that are of low metapragmatic salience.[7]

Traditional linguistic accounts of reported speech that insist on the presence of but a single point of view in each clause ignore leakage. They also present an oversimplified view of the kinds of responsibility that are at issue in the use of this rhetorical device. Thus Leech (1978), in a discussion of the semantics of reported speech in English, proposed that while the speaker of a speech act was responsible for truth and sincerity, the "reporter" of the direct-discourse reported speech act of a second speaker was "responsible" only for "fidelity": the accurate representation of form and content of the quoted speech. In indirect discourse the speaker is responsible only for content, not for form. But this account neglects phenomena associated with quotation that are familiar to English speakers, and it cannot handle cross-cultural diversity. Even in English, the responsibility for "fidelity" in representation of reported speech clearly is not absolute, but varies according to context. Different types of responsibility are at stake when an author quotes a written source in a scholarly essay, when a speaker reports a remark in the presence of a person who is quoted, and when a parent constructs dialogue in retelling "Goldilocks and the Three Bears" (the nursery audience may, in fact, be the most demanding, insisting on exact repetition of well-known speeches by members of the Bear Family). In much reported speech fidelity is irrelevant. As Tannen (1988) has pointed out, direct-discourse reported speech is "constructed dialogue," a trope for speech, not a copy of it, and may function more to maintain the hearer's involvement in a story than to be "faithful" to a source. Tannen's claim is supported by Shuman, who emphasizes in her paper in the present volume that many adolescent fight stories are in no sense representations of real events – there are far more fight stories than there are fights. The major functions of fight stories are not representational, but are attempts to shape potentials within the social arena in which their tellers operate.

Thus far we have examined cases where the responsibility at issue involves the content, form, or source of communication. Richard Bauman's paper shows us another important possibility, that of responsibility for performance. Indeed, Bauman uses "responsibility" as a key term in the definition of performance: "I understand performance as a metacommunicative frame, the essence of which resides in the assumption of responsibility to an audience for a display of communicative competence." Bauman argues that analysts of performance must therefore investigate cases where the issue of responsibility is foregrounded, the case of performances that are "hedged, ambiguous, negotiated, shifting, or partial." In "yarns" Bauman collected from an elderly speaker in the La Have Islands off the coast of Nova Scotia, negotiation about responsibility for performance appears repeatedly. Such disclaimers take several forms: appeals about the ability to sustain narrative (Well, uh, I get kind of worked up, and I can't think what to say), appeals about the ability to "tell a story" (I can't tell any story about it. But uh, I know ... I know I heard the story ...), appeals about knowledge of "what happened" (But I don't remember ... I don't know what to tell you – what he done when he left). The speaker's own performance ability remains implicit, "leaking" through his report, rather than explicitly claimed. Bauman explores the significance of such disclaimers for an understanding of narrative, and for the analysis of the elements of narratives which contain them.

Oral narrative, as a genre, is also examined in the paper by Jane Hill and Ofelia Zepeda, who show how double-voiced utterances in a personal narrative provide the opportunity for a speaker to split into many presences, as it were, and so diffuse responsibility among them. The narrative text they analyze comes from an interview with an O'odham (Papago) woman, who uses reported speech to manage an account of a "trouble": her youngest son, at age 19, has yet to graduate from high school. This "trouble" is problematic for her presentation of a valued identity as an up-to-date, urbanized, education-oriented Indian parent who has succeeded against all odds in putting several children through school. Hill and Zepeda argue that the semiotic properties that make reported speech in direct discourse (prominent in her tale) appropriate to her disclaimer of responsibility are predicted by the structural position of this reported speech in a hierarchical discourse structure. They argue further that, since narratives that "distribute" responsibility across a social field of reported speakers are very common (especially among working-class speakers, see Hill, 1989), the vernacular view of identity and responsibility in the West may be more sociocentric than is generally acknowledged by scholars, who have focused on egocentricity and individualism.

Responsibility for knowledge: evidentiality in context

If reported speech has been central to the contributions we have discussed so far, it is no less so for the remaining papers in the volume. These papers turn to an explicit concern with the problem of evidence, in the sense of speakers' assumption (or evasion) of responsibility for knowledge, and various levels of linguistic and interactional organization at which the allocation of responsibility for knowledge can be examined.

The first paper in this group, Edward Bendix's analysis of evidential morphology in Newari, a Tibetan language of Nepal, examines evidentiality at the level of linguistic structure within the sentence. Bendix's analysis must be compared with other linguistic work on similar problems of morphology and syntax, since a number of linguists have recently been intrigued by the devices whereby the state of "evidence" is marked in language. Such research on "evidential" elements has emphasized that these index a "natural epistemology," specifically, "human awareness that truth is relative" (Chafe and Nichols, 1986:vii). Chafe and Nichols hope that exploration of evidentials in language will reveal the universal dimensions in terms of which such relativity can be organized: for instance, that the speaker's knowledge is not based on first-hand evidence, that an action, event, or entity does not match some prototypical manifestation, or that some knowledge is different from what might have been expected.

Evidential elements obviously function in the manipulation of responsibility for knowledge. But Du Bois (1986) has suggested that it is misleading to think of evidentiality in the strictly cognitive or epistemological terms preferred by "personalist" accounts. "Knowledge" is instead a social phenomenon, an aspect of the social relations between people. This state of affairs is even indexed linguistically in the famous ambiguity of the English modal "must" between so-called epistemic modality, where "must" indicates certainty of knowledge, and deontic modality, in which "must" constitutes a directive. Furthermore, the decision about which is meant requires interpretation by the hearer, drawing on evidence from context.

The possibility for deploying apparently "epistemic" evidential elements to achieve a variety of subtle social effects is illustrated by Bendix's paper in this volume. Newari grammar requires that speakers use a set of evidentials, which appear as suffixes on verbs. What this obligatory set does is, in effect, to grammaticalize contrasting points of view on a reported event: an internal, self-aware, point of view expressing one's intention or control over an action (INTERNAL evidence); an external point of view expressing an observer's assessment of evident appearances and the contingent properties of an action (EXTERNAL evidence); and an observer's vaguer report that merely associates or characterizes the subject of a proposition with its predicate (CHARACTERIZING evidence). Along with point of view, the evidentials can also be used to mark "control" or responsibility for action.

Bendix finds that Newari evidential particles permit a variety of marked usages which express social distance and challenge, insincerity, skepticism, and other effects deriving from special features of context and requiring the participation of the hearer in the assessment of the implicature. Examination of this bit of morphology has implications, therefore, for how meaning is constructed. It is constructed, Bendix argues, through a process of pragmatic reasoning in which an audience supplies the necessary inferencing steps, inferring what evidence the speaker might have had (including evidence based on self-awareness) as a basis for uttering the sentence. This paper thus coincides with Duranti's in emphasizing the co-construction of meaning, although it is based on a very different methodology. Indeed, for Bendix the use of a linguistic elicitation method, in which the precise semantic roles of grammatical units are not assumed but rather questioned, shows how inescapable the processes of pragmatic reasoning and co-construction are.

(Note, by the way, that although Bendix refers to pragmatic reasoning and to "intention," his analysis does not rely on Searle's speech-act theory. "Intentionality," though probably helpful as a component of meaning in Newari, is not assumed as universally implicated or as part of a theoretical model. Nor does Newari "intention" necessarily bear the same aura of subjectivity and self-consciousness as it might have in English, Bendix suggests.)

Just as this analysis points up the co-construction of meaning, it also shows – again despite the elicitation method or perhaps more emphatically because of it – the importance of dialogic contexts in evidentiality. Question–answer pairs and reported speech frames, it turns out, are central to understanding this grammatical phenomenon. Even where such frames are not obvious in the syntax nor in the tasks given to the Newari consultant, Newari-speakers supply such frames when asked to interpret unusual examples. This study thus provides an apt illustration of the mutual embedding of interactional processes and linguistic form, and an illustration of the link between referential and indexical constructions of agency and evidence.

Unlike Newari, English does not require that speakers mark the evidential status of utterances. A statement like "It's raining" is evidentially vague. We do not know whether the speaker heard rain on the roof, saw it out the window, heard that it was raining from a third party, or has inferred that it is raining from other evidence, like wet tracks on the floor. But English speakers can accomplish evidential coding, such that the marked absence of evidentials can create special perlocutionary effects. Thus, if Irvine, about to make a trip, asks Hill (here in Tucson, Arizona) "What's the weather like in Seattle?" and Hill answers "It's raining," unless Irvine knows that Hill has just heard the weather report she will take this as a joke about Seattle weather. But an evidentially marked sentence, like "It's probably raining, since that is what it does most of the time," would not be funny.

The lack of compulsory morphological encoding of evidentiality in English does not mean that English speakers are uninterested in the nature of evidence. Instead, as Susan Philips shows in her paper, they make evidential distinctions through other means. In the context of court proceedings in the United States, constraints on the nature of "evidence" (having as their purpose "fairness") are highly codified and specific. They include rules about how to present evidence (through adversarial questioning), rules about what can be presented (witnesses must have directly observed what they report, with "observation" meaning, literally, that they must have seen it, not heard it), and rules about who can present it (people who have directly observed relevant events, and experts who control relevant specialized knowledge). The rules of evidence include also restrictions on what types of inference are permitted (jurors are permitted to use only what they learn in the courtroom; they are allowed to consider the demeanor of witnesses). The goal of these constraints is the determination of "what happened." The idea that "what happened" is uncertain, can be demonstrated through the presentation of "evidence," and will, upon being so demonstrated, carry moral implications that will be apparent to any fair-minded person, is, Philips points out, not universal. Many dispute management procedures, as among the Barotse, begin with consensus about "what happened." Legal proceedings function to determine the moral implications of these happenings: what they should imply for social relationships. Philips' observation that the standards of evidence used in US courts lack correspondence not only to what can be observed to be typical cross-culturally, but also to everyday "common-sense" categories used by jurors, is significant as we consider whether American trial procedures in fact achieve the universalistic "fairness" that is their goal.

Tullio Maranhão's paper in this volume develops yet another complication of "evidentiality": that certain discursive forms may be quite relevant to one type of evidence, yet irrelevant for another. He discusses his interactions with fishermen in the north-east of Brazil during research on what might be called "ethnoichthyology." For Maranhão – at the time of the fieldwork – the evidence of knowledge was located in discursive fluency; for the fishermen, it lay in practical evidence. For the fishermen, "text," which took the form of heroic lays, was a vehicle for the representation of virtue, not knowledge, the latter being best represented through "doing." Maranhão expected that knowledge would be "defined by its potentiality to be congealed in a text," specifically one to be constituted through dialogical inquiry. But this was, he admits, a peculiar form of dialogue, since as questioner he had no interest in persuading or in disagreeing. The fishermen found such inquiry puzzling, insulting, or at best suspicious, since possible answers to questions about such matters as the colors of fish were "self-evident." Maranhão's recounting of his experiences as a youthful anthropologist are often very funny, and constitute a potent critique of the metapragmatic assumptions of "ethnoscience" and other text- or discourse-centered approaches in anthropology that exclude practical evidence and do not adequately recognize the cultural values attaching to modes of communication. Maranhão relates his concerns with the distribution of evidence across texts to venerable philosophical questions about the relationship between will and knowledge, truth and textuality, and the place of writing and authority in anthropology today. The problem of authority will not be solved merely by giving the "natives" a voice in "dialogue," if the terms of distribution of knowledge, virtue, and evidence across text and action are entirely established by the anthropologist.

Conclusion

The papers collected in the present volume barely scratch the surface of the relationship between the devices that manage responsibility, the local cultural understanding of responsibility and evidence, and the nature of social identity revealed by their management. Important areas of investigation are neglected. For instance, on the theoretical front, Du Bois' and Duranti's papers in this volume suggest that the anti-personalist critique might well be extended to Brown and Levinson's (1978, 1987) much-cited theory of universal strategies of politeness, since their work depends heavily on intentionalist speech-act theory and on the Gricean theory of conversation (Grice, 1975), which is also vulnerable to the anti-personalist critique, since it requires psychologically situated "intentions." We have not been able to include a paper on irony; it seems likely that the Sperber and Wilson (1981) account will not accommodate cross-cultural variation, and a study of the distribution of this trope both cross-culturally and across contexts invites investigation.

On the descriptive front, the complexity of even well-known examples invites linguistically informed research. For instance, in the legal system of the United States responsibility is relative to age and to "insanity"; this and similar diversity in the possibilities for "personhood" within a society have received attention by ethnographers, and close linguistic investigation can contribute to the study of this problem. Vernacular theorizing about the structure of persons and responsibilities that is revealed in mythic texts also merits consideration. Ellen Basso (1987, 1990) has pointed out, for instance, that trickster stories may explore the ways that action might be "disclaimed." Thus the integrity of the body of the actor as the locus of responsibility can be questioned, as in Winnebago trickster narratives recorded by Radin, where tricksters change themselves into single body parts (disembodied penises are popular in trickster stories around the world).

The social organization of displaced responsibility is of great interest. The studies included here show that the distribution of responsibility onto literal third parties can involve a wide variety of "other" persons. In many communities young children may be used to perform minor but socially awkward tasks, such as asking the neighbors to turn down the radio, or requesting the loan of small items. Ochs-Keenan (1974) has pointed out that the Malagasay men, who are supposed to speak only very indirectly, may have women, who are noted for their direct speech, perform such offices. The distribution of responsibility onto third persons cross-culturally seems often to proceed from more powerful to less powerful people. Wolof griots are low-status people in their society, and perform only for people who rank higher than themselves. Duranti points out that in the Samoan *fono* low-ranking titled men, not the highest-ranking nobles, are chosen to articulate potentially controversial positions. Even though it is well-known that they speak for a high noble, the lower-ranking speaker stands to be blamed if the position turns out badly. Among the Kuna of Panama, chiefs speak in a high language, supposedly understood by nobody, which is spoken again in more ordinary language by an official of lower rank (Sherzer, 1983). The status of journalists, who publish "leaks" of confidential information is probably lower than that of the government functionaries who "leak" to them. This tendency for high-status authors of messages to shift responsibility "down" in the social order to lower-ranking utterers (and, similarly, for low-ranking speakers to shift responsibility for the authorship of their utterances "up" to higher-status authors, ancestors, or supernatural beings) may exploit a likelihood that lower-ranking people will be less significant in the relevant complex of relationships. Lower-ranking people may have less to lose, and their loss may not be as important to the community as a loss by a high-ranking member. A child conveying a parental opinion might be scolded for insolence, but this would not constitute a permanent stain on the child's reputation. Disruption to the career of a low-ranking young noble might be less important to a Samoan community than a serious challenge to the reputation of a senior noble.

We do not mean to suggest that the distribution of responsibility simply correlates with some pre-existing system of social ranks; rather, we suggest that responsibility distribution may be a key site for the production and reproduction of rank and "significance," inviting the close analysis of discourses in which responsibility is at issue. Duranti's (1990) analysis of the use of ergative marking in attribution of agency by speakers of Samoan exemplifies what might be done in this regard.

Important also for future study, and relatively neglected in the present volume, is the ethnography of the use (as opposed to the linguistic patterning) of grammaticalized evidential systems of the type discussed by the authors in Chafe and Nichols (1986). Bendix's paper in the present volume hints that a discourse-centered study of the negotiation of power and knowledge by speakers of languages with such systems might be an important site for untangling the complex intersections between these terms.

Investigation of the representation of "responsibility" and "evidence" in oral discourse, then, can open the way to rigorous description of the way ideas about knowledge and authority are developed in particular societies, and may ultimately yield a more theoretically productive conceptualization of the realms of human activity glossed by these terms. Knowledge, responsibility, and authority are central issues in modern anthropology. We hope that the papers in this volume show that research on language in context is essential in exploring them.

NOTES

1 The earliest citation of this sense of "responsible" listed in the 1971 Supplement to the Oxford English Dictionary is from 1691, in a discussion by Locke on contracts.

2 Moore (1972) rejects the evolutionary component of Gluckman's argument, in which absolute responsibility is held to be more characteristic of tribal than of state society. She cites many legal situations involving "absolute responsibility" in Western law. More recently, Moore's point is highlighted in a 1989 decision of the US Appellate Court in San Francisco in the appeal of the conviction of members of the Sanctuary organization for smuggling illegal aliens into the United States. Both the district court judge and the Appellate decision held that the Sanctuary defendants, who had argued that they acted for compelling humanitarian reasons to bring Central American refugees into the United States, could not present evidence of their motives. They were held, instead, to a standard of "strict liability."

3 See also Irvine, 1982b.

4 In English (as in most languages; see Hopper and Thompson, 1980), the prototypical scenario associated with transitivity involves a volitional agent. Thus Grice's philosophical result may be a piece of linguistic ideology (Silverstein, 1979), a conclusion uncritically drawn from English usage.

5 In this regard Bauman 1987b draws on ideas developed in a working group on "Text and Discourse," held 1986–9 at the Center for Psychosocial Studies, Chicago. A volume of papers from the group is in preparation, edited by Michael Silverstein and Greg Urban.

6 See also Duranti, this volume: "We could say that, in Samoan society, the higher their rank the more individualistic people are allowed to be ... [A high chief] can 'own,' as it were, the meaning of his own words and expect others to comply with his own interpretation."

7 On the concept of metapragmatic salience of linguistic forms, see Silverstein, 1976, 1981.

I

INTENTIONS, SELF, AND RESPONSIBILITY: AN ESSAY IN SAMOAN ETHNOPRAGMATICS

ALESSANDRO DURANTI

Introduction

In this chapter I criticize theories of meaning that are predominantly based on the reconstruction of the speaker's intentions, and argue for the importance of the role of responsibility in the interpretation of speech in social interaction. On the basis of an ethnography of communication of a particular Samoan speech event called *fono* (see below) and a number of ethnographic accounts of other aspects of Samoan social life and ethos, I shall suggest that Samoans typically see talk and interpretation as activities for the assignment of responsibility rather than as exercises in reading "other minds." Thus, for instance, Samoans rarely engage in discussions about speakers' motives or their inner psychological conflicts. More typically, they publicly engage in interpretation as an overt attempt to assign responsibility to someone for his words. In such activities, participants provide interpretations of words as deeds on the basis of a variety of socially available criteria which often start from the consequences, rather than the premises, of one's words, and include an attention to public identities and dramatis personae as well as to social relations between speaker and referent(s) or between speaker and audience. In this sense, the Samoan local theory and practice of interpretation are very akin to the sociology of C. Wright Mills for whom "rather than fixed elements 'in' an individual, motives are the terms with which interpretation of conduct *by social actors* proceeds" (1940:904). Overall, the main concern for a Samoan interpreter is not the speaker's psychological state of awareness of certain contextual conditions, but rather the responsibility speakers must assume (or be forced to assume) for the state of affairs created by their own words. Another of Mills' definitions well captures Samoan interpretive practice: "Motives are names for consequential situations, and surrogates for actions leading to them" (1940:905).

Although mainly drawing from my fieldwork experience in one community, a traditional village in Western Samoa, my discussion will be comparative in nature. The case-study presented in this paper is offered as a contribution to a general theory of ethnopragmatics. It is here assumed that, to the extent to which pragmatics is concerned with the meanings implied or instantiated through relationships between signs and the context of their use, it must study the local theories and the local practices of particular speakers as heirs of specific cultural traditions. In this perspective, ethnography becomes an essential element of the analytical process. Furthermore, once we start thinking about speakers as social actors and carriers of cultural traditions, we are compelled to relate the meaning of their individual utterances to the larger contexts those utterances help sustain (or challenge). In our case, the words said by titled individuals in a village council meeting must be continuously projected against the background of village politics and the management of local hierarchies. Through ethnography, we can easily show that speakers' daily dealings with one another's opinions, promises, stances, and complaints are always embedded within a logic of social relations and social order that is in turn challenged and reproduced throughout acts of speaking as social deeds.

The role of intentions in current theories of meaning

The view of communication as an exchange of individual intentions through a particular code is still very common in the Western tradition of linguistic studies. In speech-act theory, for instance, meaning is often identified with the speaker's intentions to express certain beliefs or bring about certain changes in the world (see Searle 1983). In this perspective, meanings as intentions coincide with certain psychological states and it is implied that the meaning of an utterance is fully defined in the speaker's mind *before* the act of speaking. Despite the many cases in which words achieve (or don't achieve) certain ends because of the audience's work at making a given context possible (or impossible), many speech-act theorists have chosen to concentrate on the speaker's intentions as their main object of inquiry (see Clark & Carlson, 1982b:4). In this framework, other elements of the speech event are largely ignored. Thus the addressee is usually seen as a passive spectator whose only job is to guess what the speaker has in mind. The larger social activity in which language is used is taken into consideration only when the analysts' intuitions suggest that conflicting interpretations may be possible.

This view is clearly at odds with any kind of interactively oriented approach to the study of language and social interaction (see C. Goodwin, 1981; Gumperz, 1982; Griffin & Mehan, 1981; Psathas, 1979; Schenkein, 1978; Schegloff, 1982; Streeck, 1980). It also appears too limited or overtly ethnocentric to anthropologists and linguists who have been looking at non-Western or (within the US) non-mainstream modes of communication (e.g. Caton, 1985; Kochman, 1983; Morgan, 1991; Ochs,

1982; Ochs, 1984; Ochs & Schieffelin, 1984; Paine, 1981; Rosaldo, 1982; Silverstein, 1977; 1979; Verscheuren, 1983). The work of these researchers suggests that the relevance assigned to the speaker's intentions in the interpretation of speech may vary across societies and social contexts. On many occasions, what speech-act theorists might call "perlocutionary effects" and hence classify as not conventional (see Austin, 1962) can be shown to be an acceptable criterion for the assignment of responsibility to a speaker. This is possible because the conventionality of certain interpretations is partly defined by the kind of norms and social world that the participants in the interaction are able to evoke at a given time and place. There are many cases in daily life in which the meaning of a given act is not defined until the recipient of that act has replied. Gift exchanges (Bourdieu, 1977) and ritual insults or indirectness among African–Americans are well-known examples of such cases (Kochman, 1983; Mitchell-Kernan, 1972; Morgan, 1991).

In this paper, I shall continue within the ethnographically-oriented tradition by presenting a Samoan case-study that should help make the following points: (1) the personalist view of meaning (i.e. meaning as defined by the speaker's intentions or reconstructed psychological state at the time of act of speaking) fails to explain certain apparently successful uses of speech among adult Samoan speakers; (ii) the relative reliance upon the individual *vis-à-vis* the participants in the speech event for determining the force of a given speech act is closely related to local theories of self (or person) and task accomplishment; (iii) the role of the audience in shaping utterances and (re)defining meanings must be an integral part of any model of verbal communication.

To make these points, I shall illustrate how Samoan speakers view meaning and practice interpretation as a collective affair, in which the individual's ability to convey certain meanings is manifestly dependent on his addressees' response and social behavior.

By discussing several examples from transcripts of audio-recordings of politico–judiciary meetings, I shall argue that the Samoan ideology and practice of doing things with words cannot be explained on the basis of the notion of "intentional meaning." The Samoan local theory of interpretation in fact mirrors the Samoan theory of task as a co-operative, albeit hierarchically structured, enterprise. Rather than taking words as representations of privately owned meanings, Samoans practice interpretation as a way of understanding and controlling social relationships, not as a way of figuring out what a given person "meant to say." Once uttered in a given context, words are interpreted with respect rather to some new reality they help fashion than to the supposedly intended subjective content. This is related to two facts: (i) the assessment of the consequences of a given act are often more important to Samoans than the understanding of its original circumstances; (ii) given the emphasis on social relations in Samoan society in general, it is often dramatis personae rather than individuals who are seen as producing meaningful speech acts. As a consequence, the individual actor is much less in control of the possible interpretation of his words.

After suggesting that the Samoan theory of meaning and interpretation is grounded in local theories of knowledge, self, and task which are different from mainstream Western epistemologies and theories of social action, I shall suggest that the Samoan and "Western" theory represented by the notion of intentional meaning can perhaps be reconciled within the larger theoretical context of sociohistorically oriented approaches to cognitive processes and within dialogically oriented approaches to meaning.

To illustrate these points, I have chosen to discuss the ways in which the speaker's responsibility is contextually and co-operatively defined in politico-judiciary meetings in a traditional Samoan village. Although my analysis is based on one particular type of event, the Samoan theory of interpretation presented here is consistent with other accounts of Samoan language, culture, and society based on participant-observation and extensive recordings of Samoan daily interaction across a number of contexts. In particular, my description and understanding of Samoan interpretive procedures is consistent with Shore's (1982) ethnography and with the work on Samoan language acquisition and socialization carried out by Ochs (1982; 1984; 1988).

The *fono*

All the examples of Samoan speech acts in this paper are taken from transcripts of the verbal interaction in speech events called *fono*, which I studied in one village, Falefā (Upolu), during my first fieldwork in 1978–9 (see Duranti, 1981a; 1981b; 1983a; 1990). There are many different kinds of *fono* or formal meetings in Samoan society (see Larkin, 1971). The kind I shall be discussing in this paper is the special convocation of a delibera-tive assembly of title-holders or *matai* – chiefs and orators – which, as typical of similar events in other "traditional" societies (see Comaroff & Roberts, 1981), acts both as a high court – concerned only with crimes involving *matai* – and as a legislative body. *Matai* gathered in a *fono* can thus make, ratify, and abrogate laws (at the village level) as well as discuss the policy to adopt with respect to a new problem or potential conflict.

Although the particular discourse organization typical of a *fono* dis-cussion is, in many ways, unique (see Duranti, 1981a, b, 1983a), the speech genres used, the social relations among participants, and the modes of strategic interaction found in a *fono* are also found in other speech events that characterize the daily life of a traditional Samoan village. In fact, given the emphasis on political modes of interaction in

Samoan communities, the *fono* is emblematic of much of Samoan adult life. Although participation in it is restricted to *matai*, a *fono* is a rather "public" context in the sense that people can be held accountable for their words and political stands at some later time. A *fono* is always embedded in a larger "social drama" – in the specific sense given to this term by Turner (1974). This means that a *fono* is a highly antagonistic arena in which different powerful groups and individuals try to control one another's political actions. Hence it is hard for participants to predict what the final outcome of a meeting will be. In such a context, it is often convenient to be cautious, humble, and vague. At the same time, there might be reasons for a speaker to be forceful and direct, as when his role in the proceedings prescribes that he be the one to make certain announcements or accusations, or when he might want to try to gain in prestige or material goods.[1]

Although I recorded a total of seven meetings in 1978–9 and several others in my two subsequent field trips (1983, 1988), most of the examples discussed in this paper are taken from one meeting. I hope in this way to help the readers orient themselves in the midst of the fairly complex events and issues that characterize any debate within a *fono*.

Announcing the agenda: sharing responsibility for changing the world with words

The first point I want to make here is that Samoans are quite aware of the power of words, especially in public settings. By this I mean that in public events a great deal of energy and skill is spent to find the most appropriate way to present someone's view or to report on someone's actions. In Samoa, as in other places in Polynesia, a special class of people, the *tulāfale* – variously translated as "orators," "talking chiefs," etc. – has the right and duty not only to represent others ceremonially and verbally in public events such as rites of passage and gift exchanges, but also to act as spokespersons and mediators in political conflicts and crises. The position that a given orator takes on a given issue is likely to be remembered. If things turn out differently from what an orator implied or suggested on a given occasion, he might get in trouble. This system protects the dignity of chiefs and other high status parties by allowing them to withhold their views or wait to make a decision until many of the issues are either solved or at least sufficiently debated to give participants a sense of whether a consensus might be reached and in which direction. The chiefs, in turn, are expected to reward an orator who has worked and spoken on their behalf in public arenas. Things are made more complicated by the fact that the same orator may have allegiances to different chiefs or different descent groups in the village or by the fact that the chief who should protect him may not be very active or forceful. All of these factors make it difficult to predict at any given moment what the preferred strategy is going to be. Whereas it might be fruitful in some cases to be outspoken, in other circumstances it is wiser to be indirect. Thus, when we look at actual talk, we find that Samoan orators adopt a variety of strategies for dealing with the potentially dangerous power of words, with their performative, context-creating force. In a *fono*, one way of protecting oneself against retaliation, punishment, or blame is that of avoiding public commitment to a given cause either by avoiding saying anything compromising or by being very vague (Duranti, 1990). An orator may simply avoid talking in any detail about what he considers a dangerous topic or a delicate issue. There are cases, however, when the speaker's role in the proceedings or his positional identity in the village may force him to mention names and events. An example of this sort is discussed below.

At the beginning of a *fono*, after the opening *kava* ceremony, an orator from a particular section of a village delivers a formal speech, called *lāuga* (Duranti, 1983). In this speech, there is a part, toward the end, dedicated to the announcement of the agenda of the meeting (*matā'upu o le fono*). The same orator who might "show off" his knowledge of oratorical formulas and ancient metaphors in other parts of his speech tends to be very brief and vague in the announcement of the agenda. In some cases, the first orator might even leave out one (or all) of the topics of the day, in which case the senior orator Moe'ono (M), who acts as chairman of the meeting, might remind him, as shown in excerpt (1) below:

(1) (*Fono*, 7 April 1979. The orator Loa has just concluded the introductory speech leaving out the mention of the agenda)

359 Loa; *maguia le aofia ma le fogo!*[2]
    Good luck to the assembly and the *fono*!
360 ? *mālō!*
    Well done!
        [
361 M; *'o ā makā'upu o le fogo?*
    What are the topics of the *fono*?
362 (1.)
363 *fai mai makā'upu o le fogo.*
    Tell (us) the topics of the *fono*.
364 Loa;   [*o makā'upu o le aofia ma le fogo*
                            The agenda of the assembly and *fono*
365 Moe; *fai mai (?)*
    Tell us (?)
        [
366 Loa;   *ia e fa'akakau kogu lava i lo kākou Falelua*[3],
            Well it's really about the two subvillages,
367 (CLEARS THROAT)
368 *oga pau gā 'o makā'upu,*
    those are the only topics,

369   (1.5)
370 M;   *oi!*
        Oh!
371   (1.)
372 Loa; *e ā?*
        What?
373 M;   *'o le isi makā'upu o Savea*
        The other topic of Savea
374 Loa; *ia 'o le isi fo'i makā'upu e uiga i le –*
        Well the other topic is about the –
375   (.5) *le afioga iā Savea ogo'o: –*
        the honorable Savea 'cause –'
376 M;   *(Fa'amakuā'igu,*
        (Fa'amatuā'inu)
377 Loa; *'o le lā- (3.) mea fo'i ma Fa'amakuāigu,*
        The – thing also with Fa'amatuā'inu,
378   *go 'ua kukulu Savea i – (1.) i le mālō,*
        given that Savea has complained to – the Government,
379   (.5) *ia'*
        well
380   *go 'ua ka'ua gi fa'akosiga Fa'amakuā'igu i le paloka,*
        given that some illegal campaigning of Fa'amatuā'inu
        during the elections has been said (to occur)
381   (1.)
382   *ia 'oga pau gā 'o- 'o makā'upu o le aofia ma le fogo,*
        Well, those are the only – topics of the assembly and the *fono*,
383   *-hh iai fo'i gisi makā'upu*
        -hh (if) there are other topics,
384   *o lo'o lē maua,*
        I am not getting to,
385   (.5) *ia la'a maua i luma!*
        Well they will be brought to the front!
386   (1.5)
387 ?;   *mālō!*
        Well done!
388 Moe; *mālō fekalai.*
        Well done, the (honorable) speaking.
389 ?;   *mālō fekalai.*
        Well done, the (honorable) speaking.
390   (...)
391 Moe; *ia fa'afekai aku Kafiloa. (...)*
        Well, thank you Ka(o)fi(ua)iloa ...
392   *'ua 'e fa'amaga le fogo*
        for starting the *fono*
        [...]

The fact that a vague reminder such as "the other topic about Savea" is
sufficient for the first orator Loa to remember Savea's case, suggests that
he might have known but did not want to be the one to initiate the
announcement.[4] His reluctance can be better understood once we interpret

pret the announcement of the agenda not simply as a statement *describing a fact* about the world, but also, in Austin's (1962) terms, a *performative*, that is, *a conventional verbal act through which the world is changed.* The new reality is defined as one in which the ideal social harmony or "mutual love" *(fealofani)* of the village is in danger or already disrupted. The announcement of the agenda puts the orator in the different position of having to define the actions of a higher-ranking chief as causing such a state of affairs. The orator's way of handling this difficult task is to involve someone more powerful, the senior orator who acts as chairman of the meeting, in jointly performing the act. No-one would then be able to scold him for having announced the wrong agenda or having reported unfounded accusations. This strategy is particularly effective in light of other potential outcomes. Thus, for instance, as we shall see below, it is possible for an orator to be reprimanded for being too direct or for expressing an opinion that can be defined as "wrong" or "inappropriate" in the light of later developments.

Getting reprimanded for speaking one's mind

Later on in the same meeting (7 April), as announced in example (1), there was a debate about whether the young chief Savea should or should not pursue his court case against the district MP, Inu. Most members of the village council felt that to confront the MP directly in the cntral court would have seriously damaged the already precarious relationship with the nearby village of Lufilufi where the MP lived. However, the orator Fa'aonu'u, the highest ranking orator from Savea's subvillage, spoke in favor of Savea's decision. Here is the crucial passage from his speech:

(2) (*Fono*, 7 April, speaker: orator Fa'aonu'u)

2332 F;   *'o lea lā 'ou ke fa'a – (...) malulū aku ai*
         Now I would like to ex–...cuse (myself)
2333   *i lau kōfā le Makua Moe'ogo (...)*
         with your highness the Senior Orator Moe'ono ...
2334   *ia e fa'apea fo'i 'Āiga gei ma kagaka o le kuiākua, (...)*
         as well as the families (of chiefs) and the
         people of the King of Atua (= the orators) ...
2335   *ka'akia ia le makā'upu a Savea ma – (...) le kōfā iā Igu*
         do drop this issue of Savea and ... the honorable Inu
2336   *lā ke ō i le Malō (...)*
         let them go to court ...

Later on in the meeting, however, the chief Savea, under pressure from important members of the assembly, agreed to reconsider his decision to go to court. In his concluding speech, at the end of the meeting, the senior

orator Moe'ono, who had been the primary advocate of a "traditional"
(i.e. out of court) settlement, takes the opportunity to scold Fa'aonu'u
for not having shown moderation and for having hastily expressed an
opinion which was eventually contradicted by the chief's later decision.
Moe'ono's opening remarks about Fa'aonu'u's rare participation in
village affairs – due to his job in the capital – reveal an ethic of public
speaking in which one may speak his mind on an issue only if he is a
full-time member of the village assembly and not just an occasional
one.

(3) (7 April, speaker: Moe'ono)

3541 M;   *ma: – (. . .) ou ke kaukala aku fo'i Fa'aogu'u iā ke 'oe (. . .)*
          And – . . . I am also talking, Fa'aonu'u, to you
3542   *mea lea e leaga ai le – le alualu i galuega*
          this going away (from the village) to work
3543   *sau fo'i ua- (. . .)*
          coming back to – (speak up) is bad
3544   *pei o agaleilā o le ā koe aga'i kua lo'u kāofi. (. . .)*
          as for before, my opinion is going to reach back
          (i.e. to what you said before)
3545   *'o le – o le makā'upu ua fikoikogu i loukou faleakua (. . .)*
          as for the – the topic that concerns your subvillage,
3546   *kaofiofi le i'u maea. (. . .)*
          moderate yourself . . .
3547   *ae aua le luaiga lālā mai fa'amaka o Avi'i lou kāo –*
          and don't show off your op(inion) like the crab that
          has eyes that stick out
3548   *a'o lea ua aliali gei,*
          now it looks like
          [. . .]
3550   *ua fausia e Savea le – le figagalo lea e fai aku iai*
          Savea has agreed to say that
3551   *iga ia kākou feiloa'i ma Lufilufi. (. . .)*
          we should meet with Lufilufi . . .
3552   *KO'A! le fa'aukaga. (. . .)*
          HOLD (IT)! the advice . . .
3553   *ko'a le fa'aukaga. (. . .)*
          hold the advice . . .
3554   *e leai fo'i se isi Fa'aogu'u 'o oe*
          there is no other Fa'aonu'u but you
3555   *ga'o 'o oe ā 'o Fa'aogu'u. (. . .)*
          only you, you are the Fa'aonu'u . . .

The orator is here reprimanded for having said something that was *at a
later point* contradicted by the chief Savea. This incident also illustrates
the above mentioned hypothesis that one of the reasons for having
orators speak first or on behalf of a chief, a fairly common practice in
Polynesia (Firth, 1975), is that of allowing the chief to change his opinion

without loss of face. The chiefs' "wrongs" are assumed, in the public arena, by the orators who spoke on their behalf. The source of authority and wisdom represented by the chief is protected by having the lower-ranking orator expose himself to potential retaliation and loss of face. The complementary relationship between chiefs and orators (Shore, 1982), however, allows the orator to "get back" at his chief in other contexts, given that it is the chief who is responsible for materially supporting his orators and any payment or retaliation suffered by the orators will call for the chief's contribution.

The next case will show that in defending or simply presenting a chief's (or for that matter anyone's) position, an orator makes himself vulnerable to the subsequent doings of the party he represents. In these cases, then, the speaker's beliefs or intentions at the time in which he produced his speech acts are not relevant.

The role of personal intentions in the assessment of responsibility

As shown in the previous example, a Samoan orator may get in trouble and risk retaliation if things turn out differently from what he had assumed or let others believe. Thus an orator can be held responsible for having announced something on behalf of a higher-ranking *matai*. Retaliation may take place against him if people cannot have direct access to the original "addressor" of the message. In such cases, the grounds on which an accusation is made may be the practical consequences of his words as well as the relationship between the orator and the party he is seen as representing. The orator's beliefs or personal motives may well be irrelevant. As shown in this case, under these circumstances Samoans do not evoke "good will." Without openly rebelling, they must accept the responsibility of having taken part in a particular social act which was not fulfilled, e.g. a public commitment to doing something, or which had an unfortunate outcome, e.g. a political defeat or a loss of face. This attention for the consequences of actions is repeatedly stressed in Shore's lucid ethnography: "... when I questioned informants about the relative seriousness of different misdeeds, their tendency was to base their evaluations on the results for the actor of the action rather than on any intrinsic quality of the act" (Shore 1982:182).

This means that in Samoa a speaker must usually deal directly with the circumstances created by his words and cannot hide behind his alleged original intentions. As in the African–American speech communities discussed by Morgan (1991), in Samoa, a speaker cannot rely on excuses such as "I didn't mean it." In fact, such a phrase is literally impossible in the Samoan language. The need to deal with the reality created by speech means that the distinction between the sender and the addressor sometimes is not as sharp as expected in those Western contexts where it is assumed that a messenger should not be held responsible for what he says.

An example of the way in which Samoans act in these circumstances is provided below in an excerpt from a meeting in which one of the two highest-ranking orators in the village, Iuli, proposes to fine the orator Loa for having announced, a few weeks earlier, that the newly re-elected district MP, Fa'amatuā'inu (shortened to "Inu" in example (4) below), was going to present some goods to the village assembly. Iuli argues that, since the MP did not come to share food and goods with the village, Loa should be considered responsible and heavily fined, perhaps even expelled from the village:

(4) (*Fono* 7 April, speaker: Iuli (Iu))

3362   *'o le makā'upu gei e uiga iā Loa.* (...)
          This topic now is about Loa ...
3363 Loa; *(mālie)*
          Well said.
            [
3364 Iu;   *kusa o le aso ga – pokopoko ā lo kākou gu'u*
          About the day our village gathered together
3365   *e fa'akali le faipule.* (...)
          to wait for the M.P. ...
3366   *'o mea fa'apea 'o se luma o se gu'u.*
          Things like that are a humiliation for a village.
3367   (...)
3368 Loa; *mālie!*
          Well said!
            [
3369 Iu;   *ula e – ua ka'uvalea lo kākou gu'u.* (...)
          Bad to – our village is ridiculed ...
3370   *'ua fiu le kākou gu'u e kakali.* (...)
          Our village was tired of waiting ...
3371   *leai se faipule e sau.* (...)
          There is no M.P. who comes
3372   *'a e se'i gofogofo Loa*
          but Loa just sits there
3373   *alu amai se mea e kaumafa ma le gu'u.*
          (instead of) going to get some nourishment for the village
3374   (...)
3375 Loa; *mālie!*
          Well said!
3376   (...)
3377 Iu;   *'o lo'u lea kalikoguga,* (...)
          This is what I believe, ...
3378   *(ka)kau ga sala Loa.* (...)
          Loa should be fined ...

3379	*'o le makuā ma makagā le mea*
	The thing is extremely ugly
	[...]
3388	*'ae kakau oga fai maukigoa*
	and (he) should have made sure
3389	*auā e 'āiga Loa ma – ma Igu, (...)*
	because Loa and – and Inu are related, ...
3390	*āfai ua fai age iā ia,*
	if he said that to you,
3391	*sa kakau oga makuā ma'oki (...)*
	one should have been very clear about it ...
3392	*gi mea e fa'akaumafa ai le gu'u*
	something to feed the village
3393	*ga – ga amai lā'ea*
	(Loa) should have brought
3394	*pe'ā lē sau le faipule (...)*
	when the M.P. doesn't come ...
	[...]
3400	*mea lea ua fai e Loa. (...)*
	this is what Loa did. ...
3401	*'a le povi, (...)*
	whether a cow, ...
3402	*uā e kokogi fo'i e le mākou pikogu'u o le s – 'o Sagogu*
	our village of Sanonu will assign the fine.
3403	(SOFT LAUGHTER)
3404 ?;	*mālie!*
	Well said!
3405 Iu;	*'a le povi,*
	Whether a cow,
3406	*ia(a) Loa ma le selau kālā,*
	from Loa and 100 dollars,
3407	*alu 'ese ma le gu'u!*
	get out of the village!
3408 Loa;	*mālie!*
	Well said!
	[...]

Iuli's arguments for holding Loa responsible are the following: he created a situation that ridiculed the village *matai*; when he saw that the M.P. was not coming, he should have done something to remedy the village's loss of face; finally, he is related to the MP Loa's conventional agreements *mālie!* "Well said" throughout Iuli's speech are not ironic. They rhythmically exemplify Loa's preoccupation with the potential seriousness of the accusation.

The orator Fa'aonu'u, who was not present when the events recounted by Iuli took place, asks for more information about the case. Is Iuli saying that Loa lied to the village? Or what else did Loa do? (See Duranti, 1990, on the use of reported speech in this particular case.) Iuli reconstructs the events more clearly:

(5)
3467	*'o Loa ua sau kala'i le kākou gu'u*
	Loa had come to summon our village
3468	*e fogo – ma pokopoko*
	to have a *fono* and gather together
3469	*la'a sau le faipule – e amai oga momoli (...)*
	the M.P. was going to come – (and) bring his gifts ...
3470	*ia' oga – pokopoko lea o le kākou falefiku,*
	Well then – our seven subvillages get together,
3471	*leai se isi e o'o iā Fagaloa ma Falevao*
	there is no one who doesn't come from Fagaloa or Falevao
3472	*ma kagaka uma o le kākou – gofoaala (...)*
	and all the people of our – four subvillages ...
3473	*pokopoko ua fiu ua alu legā aso o kakali*
	get together (we/they) are tired of waiting the whole day
3474	*leai se faipule o sau ma se mea (...)*
	there is no M.P. who comes with anything ...
3475	*ae se'i gofogofo*
	and (we) just sit and sit
3476	*fu'e mai fo'i le suāvai a kaulele'a (...)*
	The untitled men prepare the food ...
3477	*ia' savalivalia'i fealu –*
	there he walks wand –
3478	*fealualua'i Loa pei e lē – e le popole i le mea lea.*
	Loa wanders around as if he didn't – worry about this.

After this clarification, Fa'aonu'u speaks again asking Iuli to forgive Loa. In his words, Loa's behavior is *'ese*, that is, "unusual, strange, wrong" (Milner, 1966) given that he and the MP are relatives. In this case, as in other ones that I witnessed, the relationship between social actors is foregrounded and used as a means for assessing responsibility.

The discussion of the case is eventually tabled by the chairman, Moe'ono. The reasons adduced for temporarily suspending the case, however, are procedural (*viz.* the case had not been properly announced at the beginning of the meeting) and pragmatic (the village is about to meet with the MP and this matter may then be solved along with other problems). No-one challenges Iuli's accusation by introducing the issue of Loa's motivations or his possible intentions. Only the chairman Moe'ono, who often took issue with Iuli's positions (see Duranti 1981a and below on their antagonism), rejects the relevance of Loa's family ties with the MP. He does agree, however, that Loa made a mistake by making the announcement to the assembly. The meeting ends with the prospect of a meeting at the MP's village where the members of the *fono* will have a chance to ask him whether in fact he did tell Loa to announce his gift to the *fono* members. Given the ranking differential between Loa and Inu, no-one questions the implied procedure: the words of the higher-ranking *matai*, Inu, will be taken as the "truth." If they contradict Loa's statements, he will be punished.

If we broaden our perspective to include some background events to this exchange, we may gain some insights into the role that such a discussion has in playing out various important themes in the community. We can then appreciate how speech acts are indeed "deeds" as Austin taught us, but of a much more complex nature than any ordinary language philosopher ever suggested.

It is relevant here to know that, at the time of the meeting in which Iuli brings out the accusation against Loa, the village has just come out of a controversial political campaign during which three important members of the assembly (Iuli, Moe'ono, and the chief Savea) have competed with one another in trying to gain support against the incumbent MP, Inu, from the nearby village of Lufilufi. Inu's victory has left the village in a serious crisis. Not only have Falefā's leaders fought against, rather than supported, one another; not only have they lost the election; they also broke an earlier agreement with the *matai* from Lufilufi to vote for the incumbent Inu. Furthermore, by accepting the "Western way" (*fa'apā-lagi*), that is, the secret ballot, they have damaged their relationship with Inu and his village – a serious breach of the relationship with the village of Lufilufi, which, according to the history recorded in their genealogy and ceremonial phrases of polite address and *kava* announcements, they should protect. People belonging to the different factions in the village are still resentful of one another and looking for ways to air some of their anger. In this context, it is not unreasonable to think of Loa as a scapegoat. By getting Loa in trouble, Iuli can get back at Inu (Loa and Inu are related and Inu might have to take care of Loa if the latter gets in trouble) and at Moe'ono (there are rumors that Loa helped Moe'ono in the campaign). Furthermore, by keeping the relationship with Inu problematic, Iuli can also upset Moe'ono's plans to end quickly the crisis caused by the elections and bring back harmony (*fealofani*) in the district. Maintaining the tension might be advantageous to Iuli if he intends to run again against Inu, or if he decides in the future to ally himself to the younger chief Savea (the third contender).

If these speculations are legitimate, we should expect Loa's fate to be contingent on the relationship between the *matai* in Falefā and Inu. The ensuing events confirm this hypothesis. The next week, when the *matai* from Falefā, led by Moe'ono and Iuli, go to meet with Inu and the other *matai* from Lufilufi, their conflict is, at least momentarily, ended. After a long exchange of speeches, some of which review the history of the crisis, Inu generously presents his traditional donation of food to the Falefā *matai*. At this point, Loa's case ceases to exist. Inu's later actions have

once more redefined prior acts. Since Inu has presented his contribution
to the village, Loa's words become "true" and the case against him is
dropped.

Group identity, individuals and dramatis personae

In a *fono*, opinions are often framed as delivered on behalf of a group.
Thus we often find speakers shifting between the first-person singular "I"
(*'ou* or *a'u*) and the first-person plural exclusive "we" *mākou*. The use of
mākou defines the speaker as the representative of a contextually defined
group, e.g. his subvillage, his family, the orators (as opposed to the
chiefs). Here are a few examples:

(6) (7 April, II, p. 22)

... *mea fo'i lea mākou ke – ...*   *'avaku ai fo'i se vaimālū.*
  thing also that we – EXCL TA   give + DX Pro also ART soothing water
... [as for] that thing we are ... [trying to] soothe (you).
Or
... [as for] that matter we are ... advising you not to be hasty.

(7) (25 Jan., I, p. 80)

Tui: *a'o legei fo'i 'ua mākou fa'alogologo aku*
     but this also TA we–EXCL listen   DX
     But now we have just listened

     i lau vagaga Moe'ogo.
     to your speech Moe'ono
     to your (honorable) speech, Moe'ono.

The plural form is used more often at the beginning of the discussion,
when each orator, in his first speech, is seen as speaking on behalf of his
high chief and his subvillage, than later on in the meeting, when alliances
may shift and the referent of "we" might be problematic. "We" is also
used more often by lower-ranking orators than by higher-ranking ones.
These facts suggest that the use of (exclusive) "we" is a potentially useful
strategy for sharing responsibility or presenting one's own opinion not as
an individual's stand but as a group's stand. There are cases, however, in
which the speaker cannot or does not want to speak on behalf of a group.
Thus, for instance, in the village of Falefā, the two highest-ranking
orators, Moe'ono and Iuli, usually speak in the first-person singular: they
are clearly the leading forces of the local polity and people are concerned
with what *each of them* thinks.

    As in the case of a personal accusation, there are also situations in
which a speaker may not be allowed to speak on behalf of a group. An
example of this is provided in (8) below, where the orator Vave (a

pseudonym) tries to defend himself from the accusation of using offensive language toward the village council:

(8) (*Fono*, 17 March, 1979, pp. 46–7)

Vave: '*Ou ke fefe ma 'ou maka'u.*
  I am afraid and I fear

> '*O le ā le agasala a le gu'u iā ke a'u?*
> What is the sin by the village because of me?

> '*O lea 'ou gofo ai fua ma fa'aleaga le gu'u,*
> Now I would just sit and give a bad name to the village,

> '*ou ke iloa a'u mea ga fai . . .*
> I know what I did . . .

> '*O lea 'ou ke kalosaga aku ai ma le agaga vaivai,*
> I hereby implore (you) with a humble spirit,

> *e mamā Vave e le ai saga 'upu fai fa'apegā*
> Vave is clean. There are no words of that sort that he said

> *pei oga silafia . . .*
> as it is known (to you)

The line before the last provides an example of a third-person referent used for referring to oneself. This is not uncommon in the *fono* speeches, but not found in ordinary conversation. Another example of this is provided in (9) below:

(9) (25 Jan., I, p. 28. In explaining his role in the present crisis, the senior orator Moe'ono tries to convince the rest of the assembly of his trustworthiness)

Moe'ono: '*Auā 'o 'upu a Moe'ogo e lē alo,*
  Because Moe'ono's words do not dodge.

Given that all speakers in a *fono* are *matai*, the name they use coincides with their *matai* title. The speaker's reference to himself through his own title frames his words as originating from his positional role. Given that a title can be held by more than one person at the same time and is defined as deriving from a mythico–historical figure and his descendants, the use of the title in talking about oneself can be seen as a strategy to recreate a relationship, a groupness when the circumstances would seem to call for an individual commitment. In fact, the tendency to obscure the individual in favor of the public and positional role a person is embodying is quite common in Samoa across all kinds of situations. As noted by Mead:

> This separation between the individual and his role is exceedingly important in the understanding of Samoan society. The whole conception is of a group plan which has come down from ancestral times, a ground plan which is explicit in titles and remembered phrases, and which has a firm base in the land of the villages and

districts. The individual is important only in terms of the position which he occupies in this universal scheme – of himself he is nothing. Their eyes are always on the play, never on the players, while each individual's task is to fit his role.

(Mead, 1937:286)

Such a separation between the individual and his dramatis persona is of course not restricted to Samoa. Thus, for instance, in discussing the notion of self in Bali, Geertz (1983:62) writes:

... there is in Bali a persistent and systematic attempt to stylize all aspects of personal expression to the point where anything idiosyncratic, anything characteristic of the individual merely because he is who he is physically, psychologically, or biographically, is muted in favor of his assigned place in the continuing and, so it is thought, never-changing pageant that is Balinese life. It is dramatis personae, not actors, that endure; indeed, it is dramatis personae, not actors that in the proper sense really exist.

In the Samoan case, one way of explicitly evoking the contextually appropriate dramatic persona is to use one's title in talking about oneself.

Toward an anti-personalist view of meaning

The ethnopragmatic approach implemented in this study shares with much contemporary cultural anthropology the assumption that local theories of meaning should be described and analyzed in the context of local theories of person and social action (Geertz, 1983; Myers & Brenneis, 1984; Rosaldo, 1982; Shore, 1982). This means that how people think about themselves and how they do things together has consequences for the model of communication to be used in analyzing their talk. Thus the speech-act theory distinction between sender and addressor is tied to a particular socioeconomic model whereby people should be held responsible only for those acts (and words) that can be clearly seen as reflecting their own individual intentions. The latter perspective is explicitly adopted by those speech-act theorists who, as pointed out by Rosaldo (1982:204), "think of 'doing things with words' as the achievement of autonomous selves, whose deeds are not significantly constrained by the relationships and expectations that define their local world' (Rosaldo, 1982:204). This view corresponds to what Holquist (1983) calls the "personalist" theory of meaning: "This view holds that '*I* own meaning.' A close bond is felt between the sense I have of myself as a unique being and the being of my language. Such a view, with its heavy investment in the personhood of individuals, is deeply implicated in the Western Humanist tradition" (Holquist, 1983:2). This "heavy investment in the personhood of individuals," however, is not shared by Polynesian cultures. Thus, for instance, in discussing the Hawaiian concept of self, Ito (1985:301) writes:

The Hawaiian concept of self is grounded in affective social relations [...] This conceptualization of self is a highly interpersonal one. It is based on the reflexive relationship of Self and Other and on the dynamic bonds of emotional exchange and reciprocity. For Hawaiian, Self and Other, person and group, people and environment, are inseparable. They all interactively create, affect and even destroy each other.

In similar fashion, Shore (1982) describes the Samoan theory of person in the following way:

Not only are there in Samoan no terms corresponding to the English "personality," "self," or "character," but there is also an absence of the corresponding assumptions about the relation of person to social action. A clue to the Samoan notion of person is found in the popular Samoan saying *teu le vā* (take care of the relationship). Contrasted with the Greek dicta "Know thyself" or "To thine own self be true," this saying suggests something of the difference between Occidental and Samoan orientations. Lacking any epistemological bias that would lead them to focus on "things in themselves" or the essential quality of experience, Samoans instead focus on things in their relationships, and the contextual grounding of experience.

...When speaking of themselves or others, Samoans often characterize people in terms of specific "sides" (*itū*) or "parts" (*pito*) ... By parts or sides, Samoans usually mean specific connections that people bear to villages, descent groups, or titles.

(Shore, 1982:136–7)

Given such a contextual and relational theory of person and social action, it should not be surprising that in Samoa meaning is *not* conceived of as owned by the individual; rather, it is closer to what Holquist (1983) characterizes, following Bakhtin (Voloshinov, 1973), as a "we relationship," that is, as a co-operative achievement. For Samoans, *meaning is seen as the product of an interaction (words included) and not necessarily as something that is contained in someone's mind.* In engaging in interpretation, Samoans are not so much concerned with knowing someone else's intentions as with the implications of the speaker's actions/words for the web of relationships in which his life is woven.

Samoans thus do not share what Michael Silverstein (1979) typifies as the "reflectionist point of view," that is, the idea that language is mainly used for classifying and describing some pre-existing reality (either "out there" or "inside of someone's head"). It is not accidental that the Samoan word *fai* means both "say, tell" and "do, make," and that the word *uiga* means "meaning" and "behavior" (Milner, 1966:297). The examples I have discussed so far should have shown that, for Samoans, words are indeed actions. Such actions, however, do not belong to a single actor. Meaning is a mosaic that no-one can compose by himself.

In this sociocultural context, the distinction between the illocutionary and the perlocutionary force may be problematic at times, if not

irrelevant. Such a distinction implies several beliefs about human nature
and social action which are not shared by Samoans. In particular, the idea
that one can always distinguish between the intended meaning and the
effect of someone's words implies that speakers/actors have control over
their actions/words *independently* of other people's recognition of those
actions/words as having a particular, conventionally defined goal. After
offending someone, an American can say "I didn't mean it." This cannot
be done by Samoans, given that part of what one meant *is* what the other
person understands as meant. In Samoan, one does not say "you mean
x?" but "is the meaning of your words x?" The latter phrase de-
emphasizes the view of meaning as defined by the speaker's state of mind
and accentuates instead a view of meaning as a conventional load carried
by words in a given context.

Correspondingly, from the point of view of Samoan ethics, people
cannot really know whether they have done wrong until someone else says
so – viz. the Samoan saying *e lē iloa se tagata lona sesē* "a person does not
know his own error" (see Shore, 1982:176). It is the community, others
recognized and organized as institutions (*viz.* particular kinship relationships, committees, local courts, ceremonial settings) that provide social
control, not the individual. More generally, this view of ethics relates to
the Samoan notion of task. Samoans do not see task accomplishment as
an individual achievement; instead, they see it as a joint, collective
product. This point can be illustrated by the important Samoan notion of
tāpua'i "supporter, sympathizer." As discussed in Duranti & Ochs (1986),
Samoans always see people as needing someone else to sympathize with
them, to give them some support or feedback on their accomplishment.
The role of the supporter is in fact institutionalized and routinely symbolized by what we call the "*mālō* exchange." When someone does something, his supporter recognizes that doing as an accomplishment by
saying *mālō*. The person who performed the action or accomplished the
task answers back with another *mālō*. The relationship between the actor
and the supporter must thus be understood as reciprocal. The first *mālō*
acknowledges the doing and the second *mālō* acknowledges the acknowledgment. This exchange implies that something is an accomplishment
because of and through the recognition that others are willing to give it.
In Samoan society, if a performance went well it is to the supporters'
merit as much as the performers'. Thus, for instance, if the performer
receives a prize or some previously established compensation, he will have
to share it with his supporters.

All of these facts imply a belief in interpretation as a practical activity
to be prototypically performed in the public rather than in the private
sphere of self-evident rational thought. Such a belief comprehends the
cognitive, the social, as well as the moral realm. "Knowledge of one's

actions must be public to some extent for one to be responsible" (Shore, 1982:175). Thus, for instance, in Samoan there is no precise translation for the English term *promise*. Milner, in his thorough Samoan dictionary, translates the English *promise* with the Samoan *fōlafōla* (1966:416). When we look at the English translation of *fōlafōla*, we find that it means; (i) announce (publicly); (ii) acknowledge (a gift) by public announcement; (iii) promise (Milner, 1966:68). The act of promising is thus characterized as a public commitment associated with particular social settings, in front of witnesses. The speaker's commitment to some future act is constituted in and by the presence of others and not simply by the speaker's intentions as represented by his words. Similarly, the noun *māvaega* which is also at times translated as "promise" – or "parting promise" in Milner's diction-ary (1966:142) – refers to words said by a party before leaving and in some cases in a solemn moment. Thus it is typically used in referring to the last words pronounced by a chief before dying ("the chief's will") or to an agreement made by two parties. In the latter case, *māvaega* would be characterized as an act performed by both parties, hence a reciprocal commitment rather than a promise from one to the other. Once again, as in the *mālō* exchange mentioned above, the underlying ethos is one of joint venture and reciprocal recognition rather than unilateral, individual intentionality.

Conclusions

One obvious issue at this point is the extent to which what I have discussed about Samoan verbal interaction is restricted to political arenas or instead is pervasive across social situations. This is an important question because recent work on political language has stressed the *constitutive* or context-creating nature of political language (Myers & Brenneis, 1984; Paine, 1981). What I discussed in this chapter might then be a potentially universal yet context-specific type of relationship between words and deeds rather than a more general range of phenomena indexing the fundamentally social nature of speech. However, the local theory of meaning I have presented on the basis of political speech seems consistent with other accounts of Samoan society and culture. In par-ticular, as demonstrated by my extensive quotes from Shore (1982), my description and understanding of Samoan interpretive procedures are consistent with Shore's ethnography and with the work on language acquisition and socialization carried out by Ochs (1982; 1984; 1988). Thus, for instance, Ochs (1982) has shown that Samoan caregivers do not engage in the kind of interaction typically observed in middle-class Anglo households. Samoan caregivers do not assign intentions to the infants' acts or vocalizations, which are instead "treated more as natural reflexes or physiological states (e.g. hunger, discomfort, pleasure)." Furthermore, more generally, Ochs (1984) argues that across a variety of social situations, *Samoans display a dispreference for explicit guessing*. At the same time, the highly stratified nature of Samoan social life forces lower-ranking individuals to be more attentive to higher-ranking individuals' goals. To put it in our own epistemological jargon, we could say that, in Samoan society, the higher their rank the more individualistic people are allowed to be. Thus, for instance, whereas most Samoans have no exclusive access to any of the goods available within the household, a high chief can "own" certain clothes or commodities. Similarly, he can also "own," as it were, the meaning of his own words and expect others to comply with his own interpretation. While no time is usually spent to reformulate a child's possible motivations outside of the most obvious and conventional ones, people may be forced to try to guess what is going through a chief's mind. In fact, in the political arena, the act of engaging in guessing about someone else's wishes or decisions is of itself an admission of that person's authority.

Let me stress at this point that my main goal in this paper is not to argue that for Samoans the recognition of the speaker's intentions is not a legitimate route to understanding. I imagine that it could be demonstrated that there are contexts in which it is. My point is that it is not the *only* route and furthermore in some contexts the dispreferred one. Instead, Samoan social actors seem more eager to act upon conventions, consequences, actions, public image, rather than upon individual intentions. Given that human action, and speech as one aspect of it, is goal-oriented, Samoans, like any other people in the world, must interpret one another's doings as having certain ends with respect to which those doings should be evaluated and dealt with. The problem – for us, and, I would like to suggest, for them as well – lies in the extent to which, in interpreting one another's behavior, Samoans display a concern for the actors' alleged subjective reality. The fact that a society can carry on a great deal of complex social interaction without much apparent concern with people's subjective states, and with a much more obvious concern for the public, displayed, performative aspect of language is, in my opinion, an important fact which any theoretical framework concerned with the process of interpretation should take into account.

The almost exclusive concern for a subjectively defined meaning typical of some speech-act theorists and the Samoan emphasis on an intersubjective and context-minded notion of verbal communication can be reconciled only in a theoretical framework in which both the subjective and the intersubjective, the cognitive and the social aspects of communication and interpretation of reality are acknowledged, represented, and integrated. In particular, we need a theory of pragmatics that would recognize not only the speaker's knowledge, needs and wants but also the praxis-producing co-operative work between speaker and hearer in making utterances relevant and meaningful. The notion of "recipient design" in conversation analysis, for instance, comes close to the kind of analytic tool we need in discussing these phenomena (see Goodwin 1981). Some more recent contributions highlight the work that the "audience" performs in redirecting and influencing the speaker's decisions, sometimes helping an idea or story to come out but in other moments undermining a possible narrative frame (cf. C. Goodwin 1986). Furthermore, as shown by Haviland (1986), not only do we speak *to* others and *for* others, we also speak *through* others. In some cases, certain "secondary" or "indirect" meanings of a given utterance or speech can exist only through the work that an audience would do to elaborate, report, or speculate about such implicit meanings (see Brenneis, 1986).

Such compelling phenomena and interpretations call for a theory of mind that systematically links intrapsychological processes to interpsychological ones; a theory in which language is seen as both representing and changing reality; a theory in which the individual and the social context can be seen as two sides of the same coin. The sociohistorical approach to cognition, as originally developed by the Soviet psychologist Lev Vygotsky and his colleagues Luria and Leontyev, seems to be a good candidate for such an enterprise. One of the basic tenets of this approach is that higher psychological processes in the individual have their origin in social interaction (see Vygotsky, 1986; 1978; Leontyev, 1981; Laboratory of Comparative Human Cognition, 1983; Wertsch, 1985). Also relevant, from the point of view of our discussion, is Vygotsky's definition of language as a psychological tool: that is, an object that mediates either interpsychologically (between social actors) or intrapsychologically (within the same person). A sign, e.g. a word, a sentence, etc., is used by people to affect behavior (Vygotsky, 1978:54): "... speech not only accompanies practical activity but also plays a specific role in carrying it out" (1978:25). In this approach, speech is seen as a mediating activity that organizes experience (Vygotsky, 1986:125) rather than as a symbol of an already constituted world (whether out there or in the speakers' minds). This idea is consistent with (and probably inspired by) Marx's definition of language and consciousness as arising "from the need, the necessity, of intercourse with other men" (*The German Ideology* [1845–6] 1978:158).

Within philosophy, the Samoan theory and practice of communication has striking similarities with what is known as "hermeneutic philosophy": that is, with the view that any form of understanding is an activity which cannot consist simply in the reconstruction of the sender's original intentions and his cultural milieu, but must also consist in a constant negotiation between past and present, sender and receiver, history and consciousness (see Gadamer, 1976). Indeed, I can't think of anything more appropriate for characterizing the Samoan view of words and social action than Gadamer's statement that "understanding is an adventure and, like any adventure, is dangerous" (1981:109–10). If you have doubts, just ask a Samoan orator, next time you meet one.

NOTES

Acknowledgements: this chapter is a revised version of a paper published with the title "Intentions, language, and social action in a Samoan context" in the *Journal of Pragmatics*, vol. 12, pp. 13–33. I would like to thank the four anonymous reviewers and the two editors of this collection for their suggestions and encouragement to revise or expand several parts of the earlier text.

The research on which this paper is based was conducted between June 1978 and June 1979 and between March and May 1981 in the village of Falefā, on the island of Upolu, in Western Samoa. Without the kindness and co-operation of the people of Falefā, my research on Samoan language and culture would have been impossible. Special thanks go to Rev. Fa'atua'oloa Mauala and his wife Sau'iluma for having accepted our research group as part of their extended family and to the many people in the village who worked with us transcribing and interpreting all kinds of potentially unintelligible utterances. From them I learned that interpretation is a joint adventure and one always goes home with more than one started with. With Elinor Ochs and Martha Platt I shared, in the field and after, funny combinations of Samoan, Italian, and American cuisine, and long hours of discussion about many of the ideas I present in this paper.

The following agencies and institutions gave financial support to my fieldwork and research on Samoan language and culture: the National Science Foundation (grants no. 53–482–2480 and BNS–8608210), the Australian National University (Research School of Pacific Studies, Department of Anthropology), and the Consiglio Nazionale delle Ricerche (Rome, Italy). While working on the first draft of this paper (1983–4), I was supported by a postdoctoral fellowship from the Center for Human Information Processing, at the University of California, San Diego. Invaluable comments on earlier drafts came from my colleagues at UCSD and later on at Pitzer College. In particular, I would like to thank Don Brenneis, Michael Cole, and Peg Griffin for their efforts to educate me on a number of subjects including political anthropology and Soviet activity theory.

1 Although some *matai* (hence *fono* participants) are female, the large majority are male.

2 *Transcription conventions*: I have used traditional Samoan orthography to transcribe actual speech: the letter "g" stands for a velar nasal and corresponds to what in other Polynesian languages is transcribed as "ng." The inverted apostrophe (') stands for a glottal stop. Three dots (. . .) indicate untimed pause, three dots between brackets ([. . .]) indicate that some material was left out, and

material between parentheses should be taken as additional information provided to ease interpretation of the text. Further information not directly available in the text is added between brackets ([   ]). The examples with line numbers are taken from computerized transcripts produced with a program ("SCAN") for personal computer written and kindly made available by John B. Haviland. In examples (6) and (7) I have used the following *abbreviations*: TA = tense/aspect marker; ART = article; DX = deictic particle; EXCL = exclusive; pro = pronoun.

3 The phrase "the two subvillages" refers to two nearby villages in the Fagaloa Bay, whose *matai* are being accused of *not* having maintained their original commitment to one of the Falefā candidates.

4 Further, more systematic evidence can be found in other transcripts where subsequent speakers all avoid repeating the agenda of the meeting in the introductory speeches (see Duranti, 1990).

2

MEANING WITHOUT INTENTION: LESSONS FROM DIVINATION

JOHN W. DU BOIS

Introduction

In this chapter I wish to examine a certain way of using language, most dramatically evident in rituals of divination, which presents a serious challenge to the view that intention is a necessary criterion of meaningful language use. Certain ways of speaking actively subvert the expression of intention in the speech event, producing meaning without intention, and even without responsibility. Indeed the production of meaning independent of the intentions of a responsible speech actor is, I shall argue, the motivating goal of much of ritual procedure. Because these workings are revealed with particular clarity in divinatory rituals, it is the language of divination that will be the primary focus here. Ultimately, intentionless meaning extends well beyond divination to make its subtle presence felt in numerous domains of social life. Its implications for theories of meaning and language use are broad, and occasionally surprising.

Speech-act theory and ritual speech

To speak of responsibility necessarily brings out, if only indirectly and covertly, our conceptions of the nature of action and of actor – as well as of certain auxiliary notions, which for many will include intention. Thus an actor will be judged responsible or not responsible for an action; and this judgment will depend in part, perhaps, on his or her intention. In the domain of language, the theory which puts itself forward in this connection is that of speech acts, as developed in the well-known work of Austin (1962), Searle (1969), and others. From the outset many saw in this theory an opportunity to shift attention from language as an abstract system or descriptive device toward speaking as an action in the social world, an action for which an actor (the speaker) was responsible. Given commonplace conceptions of action and responsibility, it is not surprising that soon enough the notion of the actor's intention had taken up a prominent place in the theory. Intention, though it appears in Austin's work, first took on its critical role in speech-act theory through the work of Grice

48

(1957) as adapted and developed by Strawson (1964), Searle (1969, 1976, 1979), Bach and Harnish (1979), and others. Illocutionary intention continues to play a key role in theories of meaning, as evidenced in recent statements by Sperber and Wilson (1988), Grice (1989a, 1989b), Levelt (1989), Bach (1990), Jones (1990), Morgan (1990), Perrault (1990), and many others (see also Searle 1983, 1990).

Among the many who began to make immediate application of performative theory, students of ritual were especially keen. This is no accident, perhaps, given that the first two utterances which Austin selected to illustrate his theory were drawn from the rituals of marriage and ship-christening (Austin, 1962:5). Speech-act theory seemed expressly designed for ethnographers of ritual speaking, to judge by their ready adoption of it. Tambiah invoked Austin's categories to conclude that

> ritual acts and magical rites are of the "illocutionary" or "performative" sort, which simply by virtue of being enacted (under the appropriate conditions) achieve a change of state, or do something effective (e.g. an installation ceremony undergone by the candidate makes him a "chief").
>
> (Tambiah, 1973:221)

Studies of ritual speech (or of ritual in general) which were influenced by speech-act theory include those of Finnegan (1969), Ravenhill (1972), Ladrière (1973), Tambiah (1973, 1985), Foster (1974a), Rappaport (1974, 1976, 1979), Martinich (1975), Gill (1977, 1987), Witherspoon (1977:34), Ahern (1979), Isambert (1979), Wheelock (1982), and Aune (n.d.), among others.

But the extent to which the full dimensions of speech-act theory were drawn on, or even taken account of, varied considerably. Some scholars, in making use of the implicit license provided by the theory to elaborate lists or taxonomies of indigenously labeled (or unlabeled) speech acts, either left the rest of the standard Searlean speech-act theory implicit in their application of it, or perfunctorily repeated those elements which they saw no reason not to endorse. Among the foundational assumptions of Searle's theory which sometimes came into play by this route was that of intention, the intention which was supposed necessary to undergird the speech act – and now, the ritual act. For example, Wheelock concludes that ritual speech acts are "those speech acts whose intention is to create and allow the participation in a known and repeatable *situation*" (Wheelock, 1982:59). In this, as in many such cases of the invocation of speech-act theory, the use of the word "intention" seems almost incidental. Often enough it could easily have been factored out through a paraphrase (for example by substituting the word "function") without losing whatever real insights had been gained in the application of speech-act theory. Nevertheless, even when intention was not explicitly mentioned, it was often implicit in the reliance on the concept of the responsible speech *actor*, a role which is naturally hard to avoid if one is using speech-act theory.

The speaker's volition, or something like it, has been around for a long time as an ingredient of linguistic meaning.[1] Sapir cited the involuntariness of inarticulate cries (as of pain or surprise) as grounds to exclude them from the domain of language, placing them on a par with clouds as portents of rain (Sapir, 1921:5). Intention took on its current central role for meaning in the theory of "meaning$_{NN}$" ("nonnatural meaning") put forward by Grice (1957) (see also Grice, 1968, 1969, 1989a; Wetterström, 1977; Cohen, Morgan and Pollack, 1990). If a speaker A produces an utterance x, according to Grice, "'A meant$_{NN}$ something by x' is (roughly) equivalent to 'A intended the utterance of x to produce some effect in an audience by means of a recognition of this intention'" (1957:442). Even the meaning of expressions (as opposed to utterances of them) is thought to be grounded somehow in intentions, though here Grice evinces doubts: "'x meant something' is (roughly) equivalent to 'Somebody meant $_{NN}$ something by x'" (1957:442). Even in the case of a red traffic light indicating that traffic should stop, Grice says tentatively, "there seems to be *some* sort of reference to somebody's intentions" (1957:442).

Searle, though he made important modifications to Grice's theory of meaning$_{NN}$, continued to give central status to intentions (Searle 1983, 1990). Upon posing the question, "What is the difference between regarding an object as an instance of linguistic communication and not so regarding it?", Searle observed:

> When I take a noise or a mark on a piece of paper to be an instance of linguistic communication, as a message, one of the things I must assume is that the noise or mark was produced by a being or beings more or less like myself and produced with certain kinds of intentions. If I regard the noise or mark as a natural phenomenon like the wind in the trees or a stain on paper, I exclude it from the class of linguistic communication, even though the noise or mark may be indistinguishable from spoken or written words.
>
> (Searle, 1969:16–17)

It is instructive that Searle should select, as a challenging case, a disembodied and decontextualized mark or sound, cut off from any obvious connection with an intending actor. But even here, according to Searle, if no actor is immediately present we must postulate one, in order to be able to interpret the phenomenon as a linguistic communication at all. Austin, Grice, and Searle are all committed to the view that linguistic communication (effectively, linguistic meaning in use) is always part of an act. The disembodied word (or proposition) does not of itself constitute a meaningful message: it does not communicate.[2] Following Austin (1962:138), Searle states that "The unit of linguistic communication is not, as has generally been supposed, the symbol, word, or sentence, but rather the production or issuance of the symbol or word or sentence in the performance of the speech act" (1969:16).

Grice does actually allow for a kind of meaning without intention, what he terms "natural" meaning. The English word "mean" can be used in sentences like "Those spots meant measles," where an interpreter observes that someone has spots, and draws significant conclusions. There is no question of involving intentionality here; the verb "mean" is predicable of subjects quite incapable of intending anything. Though Grice quickly enough set aside such uses of the English verb "to mean" as not constituting "meaning$_{NN}$," the word's polysemy – paralleled in other languages – may hint at some significant commonality.[3] That discriminable signals as "found" phenomena in nature (or in culture) should commonly be said to mean is not without significance.

Although speech-act theory was soon widely embraced, it was not long before some linguistic anthropologists began to question certain of its tenets – asking, for example, whether the posited framework of speech-act types and roles was intrinsic to human speech, and whether it was applicable to all cultures. Silverstein argued that even the role of "speaker," being indexically created by the instance of speaking (e.g. of the word "I"), partakes of a "theory of the types of roles in types of events socially recognized in a society" (1977:142), a theory necessarily belonging to social anthropology. Rosaldo, who aptly qualified speech-act theory as "at once my inspiration and my butt" (1982:203), emphasized that both the taxonomy of speech acts and the social principles underlying them must be subject to open-ended ethnographic inquiry in each new culture. Where Searle took the performative verbs of English to be guides to "something like a universal law" (Rosaldo, 1982:228), in fact a culture's assumptions about how language works are likely to reflect local folk theories of human agency and personhood (Rosaldo, 1982:203, Silverstein, 1979). Critics of personalist theories of action mounted persuasive ethnographic evidence to demonstrate the culture-boundness of the intentionality criterion (Rosaldo, 1982; Ochs, 1984; Duranti, this volume), showing that for certain non-Western societies intention is relatively unimportant to the social interpretive process of construing meaning (see also Irvine, 1979, 1982b; Streeck, 1980; Bourdieu 1975; Levinson, 1983; Bauman and Briggs, 1990:62ff). If intention operates as a factor of interpretive procedure more in some cultures (e.g. white middle-class Anglo-American) than in others (e.g. Ilongot, Samoan), this would seem to cast doubt on its status as a theoretical constant.

The question of intention often leads to that of responsibility. Though connected, the two are mutually independent. Searle points out that we "hold people responsible for many things they do not intend and we do not hold them responsible for many things they do intend" (1983:103). While discourse in the Samoan *fono* downplays intention (as Duranti shows, this volume), speakers remain responsible – for the *consequences* of their words. But there exist ways for speakers to reduce even responsibility for their own utterances, as Goffman has argued (1974:512ff). As we shall see, a striking characteristic of divinatory language is that it is capable of going beyond suppression of intention to the actual elimination of speech-actor responsibility.

Intention in literature?

Intentions have been debated far longer in literary than in linguistic or speech-act theoretical circles, and a brief glance in this direction will be profitable at this point.[4] Some literary theorists have argued the need to determine what the author intended or "meant" in writing a particular poem or novel, while others have sharply challenged the usefulness of this line of inquiry to interpretation. In their famous thesis attacking the "intentional fallacy," Wimsatt and Beardsley argued that critical judgments of a literary work cannot properly be based on the author's intention, since "the meaning of a work resides within the work; no judgment of intention has relevancy unless corroborated by the work itself, in which case it is supererogatory" (Beardsley and Wimsatt, 1942[1953]:232; also Wimsatt and Beardsley, 1946). Stallman concurs, reiterating the objective character of the literary work: "Once the work is produced, it possesses objective status – it exists independently of the author and of his declared intention" (Stallman, 1974:399). But Hirsch challenges this position, insisting that "A text can represent only the *parole* of a speaker or author, which is another way of saying that meaning requires a meaner" (Hirsch, 1960 [1971]:193). Knapp and Michaels claim, in terms echoing Searle's, that, for a sentence to be recognizable as a sentence, "we must already have posited a speaker and hence an intention" (Knapp and Michaels, 1982:726). Language without intention is not really language at all, but only resembles it. Hirsch sets as a key task of literary interpretation "the imaginative reconstruction of the speaking subject" (Hirsch, 1960 [1971]:193) as implied in the literary work (Dowling, 1983:788; Foucault, 1977:125; Ricoeur, 1971:534). For Olson (1980:190) a match of literal meaning to authorial intention is supposed to guarantee constancy of meaning across contexts and hence authority.

   Once speech-act theory began to be invoked in the study of literary discourse (e.g. Öhmann, 1971; Pratt, 1977, 1981; etc.), this naturally suggested a framing of the author's role as a speech actor. But Searle has rejected the view that a "writer of novels is not performing the illocutionary act of making an assertion but the illocutionary act of telling a story or writing a novel" (1979:63), concluding rather that "the author of a work of fiction pretends to perform a series of illocutionary acts, normally of the assertive type" (Searle, 1979:65; see also Öhmann, 1971). On this view, meaning in literary works still derives from speech acts performed by speech actors, if only in a world of pretense.[5]

Protagonists in the intention debate have returned again and again, consciously or not, to the dictum formulated by Hirsch: "meaning requires a meaner." But the dichotomous terms of this debate have tended to obscure some fundamental questions. Can discourse genres (e.g. poetry and conversation) differ in their intentionality? If so, why two such contrasting types of meaning? Are some meanings "deliberately" intentionless? If so, what is the function of intentionless as opposed to intentional meaning? If the intention debate is to move forward it must ask not only whether intentionless meaning exists, but also what it can do.

Intention in ritual speech?

Is ritual speech intentional? Ironically, while ritual utterances of a certain type (marrying, christening) have been favorite performative examples among speech-act theorists, it is precisely in this domain that a few anthropologists and sociocultural linguists, even those most sympathetic to speech-act theory, have begun to question the speech-act theorist's reliance on intentionality. In "trance speaking," as Becker (1979:232f) has pointed out, the utterer of the shifter pronoun is "speaking involuntarily or nonintentionally" – and thus, paradoxically, in another sense is not "speaking," if we understand by this acting as a responsible speech actor. Tambiah (1985:127) maintains that in conventional rituals like marriage, the sacrament remains valid even if one is being forced to marry for having made one's partner pregnant, or if the ceremony is performed by a drunken and immoral priest – as long as appropriate conditions such as the ordaining of the priest have been met.[6] In formalized ritual, he says, convention will tend to outweigh intention. Yet, while Tambiah raises questions about applying the intentionality criterion to ritual, he nevertheless fundamentally accepts the philosophers' conception of the performative act. He even toys with the possibility of retaining intentionality, through attributing to the ritual actors a set of conventionalized and culturally defined intentions. But applying the word "intention" to such conventionalized attitudes would seem to beg the question.[7]

The divinatory mode of meaning production

Meaning without intention is most readily apprehended in the language of divination. It is especially clear in mechanical divination (as opposed to "mental" divination, in which the diviner may speak in the role of an inspired or entranced medium).[8] Viewed literally, divination is a process for obtaining information which is (typically) unavailable by ordinary means, that is, which cannot be gotten by the usual techniques of indigenous practical epistemology, such as seeing, hearing, being told by another person – the commonplace categories of evidential coding systems (Chafe and Nichols, 1986). Viewed in its social aspect, however, divination is not so much a means of obtaining information as a means of establishing social facts, facts which command a consensus and can form the basis for legitimate, recognized social action. Nevertheless, the crisis which leads to divination typically presents itself in epistemological terms: an illness lingers inexplicably, game cannot be found, crops fail unaccountably, a venture is entertained whose outcome is uncertain. Ordinary evidence is unavailable to support propositions about the case, such as "So-and-so (or such-and-such) is responsible for this situation." In the absence of such evidence, help is sought in securing (or socially establishing) the facts of the situation at issue, as well as in determining what is to be done about it in the way of ritual or other act. In mechanical divination, the meanings arrived at are determined by something other than a volitional, human act. Admittedly, because the oracle cannot in a direct sense vocalize, it may be left to the diviner (or the petitioner) to carry out the uttering of the words. But which words are selected, and which meanings, are in principle outside the utterer's volitional control. To show this, I now examine three cases of the use of language in divination.

Sixteen Cowrie divination (Yoruba)

For the Sixteen Cowrie divination of the Yoruba of Nigeria, a diviner shakes a flat basket containing sixteen small cowrie shells (Bascom, 1980). The number of shells that come out facing mouth up (i.e. from zero to sixteen) defines a named figure, which has several divination verses associated with it. These verses are then recited by the diviner in sequence, until the client finds the one that is appropriate to his or her case (or additional cowrie throws can be used to select further among the verses). For example, if six of the sixteen cowries come face up, this defines the figure called Ọbara, for which the first divination verse would then be recited as follows (cited in Bascom's orthography):

> *K'á kó'lé kotó d'ajé;*
> *K'á y'òdèdè'lè d'orò;*
> *K'á r'aso tuntun'lè d'omo àmódún*
> *Dá f'Ólòbàrà*
> *Tí nl'oko àlorò odún.*
> *Òsà w'pé on pé ire ajé;*

On pé ire omo,
Nibi t'á gbé dá àgbàgbà méfà
L'órí àte.

"We should build a storehouse for money in advance;
"We should make a verandah for riches in advance;
"We should buy new clothes for next year's child in advance"

Cast for Obara
When he was going to his year-round farm.
Orisha says that he says, "A blessing of money;"
He says, "A blessing of children,"
Where we cast Six Elders
On the tray.

(Bascom, 1980:494–5)

The recitation continues for another 101 lines, and there are eighteen more verses corresponding to the divination result of six cowries. A different number of cowries facing up will select a different set of divination verses. For example, if five cowries come face up, the figure is called Ọ̀ṣẹ́ and the first verse begins:

A ṣ'erin ja'ri agada;
A ṣ'agada ja'ri erin;
A ṣe'gi oko ma wẹ̀ ọkọ̀
Dá f'Ọ̀ṣẹ́
Ti ńlọ tọrọ'wà gbogbo l'ọ̀wọ́ Olódùmarè.

"The iron that will spoil the sword;
"The sword that will cut the iron;
"The tree in the farm that can swim like a canoe"
Cast for Oshe
When he was going to ask for all destinies from Olodumare."

(Bascom, 1980:388–9)

The language employed for Yoruba divinatory utterances is distinctive. The texts are recited in short verses, and contain allegedly archaic words and formulas, whose meanings are in some cases unknown even to their reciter (in this case, a diviner knowledgeable enough to recite for Bascom more than 10,000 lines of divination verse). The verses are often highly figurative, appearing, to the outsider at least, as opaquely metaphorical in places: "the tree ... that can swim like a canoe." Some portions are parallelistic: "We should x a y for z in advance," iterated thrice; "the p that will/can q", thrice; etc. The verses incorporate a great deal of ostentatiously marked quotation: "Orisha says that he says ..." These quotations are generally ascribed to myth figures and deities, or to divinations performed for these individuals in myth times: "Cast for Oshe / When he was going to ask for all destinies from Olodumare." The mythical instance of divination acts as a "precedent" for the current divination, constituting a lamination of speech roles within a total laminated speech event:[9] the role of the ancient diviner–speaker is laminated onto the current diviner, as the role of the ancient client–addressee is laminated onto the current client. All of these features are such as to locate the ultimate origins of the speech in a distant place and time, and to emphasize its separation not only from everyday life in the present moment, but from the diviner's own ordinary mode of speech, as expressed in the ordinary persona which he or she presents outside the divination context, in the role of neighbor, etc. (Du Bois, 1986).

Regarding intentionality, clearly these utterances are outside the control of their utterer in at least two respects. First, they are traditionally specified texts, memorized from the oral teachings of a senior diviner over the long years of study required to master such a large corpus of divination texts. Second, the verse that the diviner utters on a particular occasion is specified by the aleatory mechanism of the cowrie toss, whose result is quite outside the control of the diviner. Although the client selects among the several verses presented the one which he or she considers relevant to the case, what is relevant for our purposes is that the diviner's recitation is governed by an aleatory mechanism.

Similar features also characterize the other major Yoruba oracle, the Ifa divination (Bascom, 1969; see below), though its techniques are rather more complex.

Poison oracle (Azande)

Among the Azande of the Sudan, the most revered and authoritative of all oracles is *benge*, the poison oracle (Evans-Pritchard, 1937). The poison, derived from a certain creeper by ritually specified processes, is administered to chickens kept specifically for divination purposes. Great care is taken to ensure that the oracle is operating properly, which is to say, it is discriminating enough to kill some fowls and let others live. Evans-Pritchard assured himself, after much close observation and participation in actual divinations, that the outcome is not manipulated. After the chicken has been forced to swallow some of the poison, the questioner addresses the poison oracle inside the fowl for as long as five minutes, if the fowl lives so long, explaining the background of the matter he has come to consult about, and reiterating the question so as to be clearly understood. In this speech, presented in a style special to oracle-questioning, he will incorporate a specific proposition whose truth he links verbally to the death of the fowl, and an opposite proposition whose truth he links to the survival of the fowl. For example, a man who wished to marry a certain woman sought to find out if his project would go well, or if the woman would die should he marry her. Upon administering the oracle poison to the chicken he addressed the oracle as follows:[10]

Poison oracle, that woman, since I intend to marry her, she is my wife? We will make a homestead together? We shall count the years together? Poison oracle, listen, kill the fowl. It is not so, mine is the weariness of piercing boils – a man pierces a boil and can eat nothing – such is the affair of that woman. I must do without her and may not marry her, poison oracle, listen and spare the fowl.

The addresser continues, framing again the pair of opposed propositions, and again linking them to the death or survival of the fowl:

It is not so, poison oracle, refuse to be deceived; you are marrying her to me, she is truly my wife. I will praise this verdict of yours, poison oracle, about that affair of my wife. Straight be your utterance like Zakiri, like Moragböndi. Poison oracle, kill the fowl. It is not true, poison oracle, she is not my wife; although you are as fierce as Gbudwe if you see that that woman will not be my wife, poison oracle, spare the fowl.

(Evans-Pritchard, 1937:298)

(The questioner goes on in this vein.) Because of the way the questioner has linked propositions and oracular outcomes here, the fowl's death will be interpreted as meaning that the marriage will go well, while its survival will mean that the new wife will die. The speech employed to address the poison oracle must be adaptable in order to frame the question currently at hand, so that it cannot consist entirely of traditionally specified text. But it does have distinctive stylistic characteristics. The address to the oracle characteristically employs a "special phraseology" and incorporates "traditional refrains, pieces of imagery, compliments to the oracle, ways of formulating a question," etc., usually including many "analogies and circumlocutions" (Evans-Pritchard, 1937:297–9), such as "making a homestead together" and "counting the years" for marrying happily. Speakers from myth times (e.g. Zakiri and Moragböndi, ancient Zande kings) are invoked as models for the current divination.

The question arises as to how the fowl's "answer" attains the specific meaning[11] ascribed to it. Considered in illocutionary terms, the oracular response indeed presents a curious aspect. Clearly the petitioner, in uttering the divinatory propositions (whether expressed as questions, assertions or conditionals), has left open the question of their truth, and cannot be said to have provided the fowl's answer with any specific illocutionary force. The decision as to which of the uttered propositions is true is rendered by an event outside the petitioner's control: the death or survival of the fowl. Divination participants take the binary divinatory signal (life-or-death) as tantamount to a "yes-or-no" answer: in effect, "Yes, she is your wife" or "No, she is not your wife." But would speech-act theory impute speech-act status to a binary signal that counts as no more than a "yes" or "no"? Searle has long held that even a simple "yes-or-no" response can, in appropriate contexts (such as following a "yes-no" question), commit its speaker to a full-fledged speech act – one that in another context might have been performed using a full sentence, such as the assertion "Yes, I am going to the movies" (Searle, 1969:19). The problem in applying speech-act theory here derives not from the simplicity of the binary divinatory signal, but from the manifest absence of personal intention and speech-actor responsibility. As with any "yes-or-no" answer, the divinatory signal accrues its *propositional* meaning by anaphorically incorporating the appropriate proposition as previously formulated by the diviner; but its *pragmatic* backing – backing of a sort usually thought to require an intending speech actor – here derives from a semiotic mechanism which is apersonal, mechanical, and aleatory.

Symbol-spinning (Sisala)

Among the Sisala of Northern Ghana, a divination session begins with the diviner opening a bag from which he takes out several ritual instruments (Mendonsa, 1982). He then utters an invocation of gods and ancestors in a distinctive tone of voice, while slowly shaking a ceremonial rattle:

God! What have I called? Savai [an ancestor] is the god. Which gods should I call? I should call Jevaha and Forkorbawie. They should call Gominabaah and Navrije. They should call Salfuo and Jallo. Jallo should ask Janawia, the eldest river, and he should ask Dajare. Dajare is the eldest farm, and he should ask grandfather, who will ask God.

(Mendonsa, 1982:121)

(The diviner continues.) For the divination proper the specialist removes, one by one, each of a set of symbolic figures contained in his divining bag, each of which has a specific meaning associated with it. The diviner suspends the symbolic figure by two strings that are attached to it, rubs the strings together in his palms to make the object spin round, and watches to see where it points. The two knots in the string are said to be "eyes," and if these end up pointing to the client, the symbol is indicated as potentially pertinent to his case. Symbols which "look" away from the client when spun are set aside as irrelevant. (Further divination using another technique may be used to select among the objects picked out by this procedure, as well as to choose between pairs of opposed propositions framed by the client, etc.) In one seance, among the symbols picked out by the spinning technique were the following:

(1) a notched piece of gourd with two protrusions, carrying the traditional signification, "You knew the truth but spoke in two different ways" (that is, "you lied");

(2) a dried black fruit from the *bubinga* tree, signifying "It will be a black (bad) thing if you continue";

(3) a single cowrie shell, signifying "You made a promise to a shrine and asked it for some things, but now you have forgotten your promise."

(Mendonsa, 1982:124)

These words are uttered by the diviner to the client, in accordance with whichever figures have pointed to the client. The diviner's statements are thus selected by the symbol-spinning, an aleatory process which puts the result – at least apparently – outside the control of the diviner.

Again, if we consider this speech event from an illocutionary standpoint, we must find ourselves reluctant to ascribe to the diviner the responsibility of a speech actor exerting volitional control over a series of assertions. Propositions are indeed being uttered, but apparently without support of, or dependence on, personal intention of the illocutionary sort.

A word on the issue of control is in order here, as some readers may remain skeptical even when ethnographers present evidence that a divinatory signal is outside the diviner's control (against this skepticism, see Boyer, 1990:61–3). The real issue, though, must be kept sight of: not actual control (as skeptically evaluated by an outsider), but the indigenous client's *belief* regarding control over the divinatory process. It is the client's beliefs rather than "the facts" as posited by a foreign skeptic that will enter into the actual meaning construal process. Divination clients commonly hold that a *legitimate* divination (as opposed to fraudulent or ineffectual ones, which are not to be trusted) has the capacity to produce a definite signal by means other than personal volitional control, and this may become a basis for imputing meaning. Divinatory devices are often selected precisely because they provide the appearance, at least, of such independence. The challenge to pragmatic theory comes when the divination client construes an utterance which he or she believes is *not* backed by a personal illocutionary intention to have the pragmatic backing needed for instantiated meaningfulness.

For the present, these three cases will be sufficient to illustrate the use of language in divination. I turn now to problems of interpretation.

Apersonality

What matter who's speaking, someone said,
what matter who's speaking.
Samuel Beckett (1974:16)

Speech-act theory, confronted with the aleatory mechanism's apparent intention-suppression function, might hope to rescue the criterion of intentionality by recourse to an imagined intender behind the oracle. Surely, one must reason, if oracle users believe they have received meaningful information about their present affairs from an oracle, *they* at least must assume that this information was communicated by someone, by some speaker or addresser – perhaps a deity, spirit, or other such anthropomorphic figure. This deeply ingrained reaction on our part, reflecting the strength of the personalist ideology of language use, was experienced already by Evans-Pritchard when he would try to present to his countrymen the Zande view of the poison oracle:

> I have described to many people in England the facts [about how the Azande employ oracles] and they have been, in the main, incredulous or contemptuous. In their questions to me they have sought to explain away Zande behaviour by rationalizing it, that is to say, by interpreting it in terms of our culture. They assume that Azande ... attribute a personality to the oracle, a mind that judges as men judge, but with higher prescience ...
>
> (1937:313)

If we could but believe that the Azande personify their poison oracle, perhaps we could then comprehend their faith in it: "Given a mind the Zande oracle is not much more difficult to understand than the Delphic Oracle."[12] But, Evans-Pritchard insists, "they do not personify it." While it might seem to us that they must take the oracles to be personal beings, since they do address them directly, this question appears absurd when framed within the Zande language. The poison oracle "is not alive, it does not breathe or move about. It is a thing. Azande have no theory about it; they do not know why it works, but only that it does work." Oracles work, now as always, simply because that is their nature (Evans-Pritchard, 1937:320).

The Azande are not alone in their reluctance to seek a personal or personified source for the meanings derived from divination. In his analysis of divination among the Tiv, Bohannan (1975) evinces some frustration in his attempt to apply a "communication model" (a Jakobsonian variant received from Sebeok, 1964) that assumes, along with message, code, referent, and channel, the existence of an addresser and an addressee. He calls divination "a sort of quasi-communication" (1975:151) at first, but has doubts:

> To call the "interaction" between the diviner and his oracle a "quasi-communication" because diviners like Koson cock their heads and "listen" may be to interpret the Tiv point of view a little too literally.
>
> (Bohannan, 1975:166)

Divination might be better compared, says, Bohannan, to the use of an artificial extension of the senses, like a Geiger counter. The "addresser" that the communication model asks for cannot be validated in native terms: "the Tiv do not and will not speculate about the nature of any thing, person, or force that 'sends' the message" (1975:166). As with the

Azande, the refusal to personify genuinely confounds our attempts to apply either a speech-act model or a standard Jakobsonian communication model, given their insistence on speech actors and addressers.

To be sure, some traditions do posit a more personal figure behind divination, associating its procedure in some way with a particular deity or set of deities, who may be more or less anthropomorphic. For example, the Quiché Maya diviner invokes a long list of deities and other powers in order to ensure that a seance goes well (Bunzel, 1952; cf. B. Tedlock, 1982), as do the Ixil Maya diviner (Colby and Colby, 1981:278ff.), the Sisala diviner (Mendonsa, 1982:121), and many others. But such figures often turn out to function simply as patrons or "supervisors" of the divinatory process. Often they are not specific to divination, and would be invoked in performing other kinds of ritual or magic as well, to serve as a generalized source of undifferentiated power or epistemological efficacy. In general there is no indication that any of the beings invoked is thought of as the actual speaker of the divinatory message.

But in the Ifa divination of the Yoruba, a closer relationship is indicated (Bascom, 1969). Ifa is the name not only of the divination process, and of a major Yoruba cult, but also of the deity "responsible" for divination. Before the first divination of the day, the diviner invokes Ifa "to make sure that Ifa supervises the divination and sees that the correct figure is selected" (1969:37). According to Bascom, the divinatory mechanism is designed to enable reception of a message "which Ifa wishes the client to receive" (1969:30). But supervising is not speaking. There remains some question whether the Yoruba ascribe the character of a speech actor responsible for intentions underlying the specific divination "message" to a deity speaker addressing the diviner and client – however much we might think such conclusions logically necessary. Certainly, many of the traditional Ifa divination texts explicitly present some statements as quotations from Ifa: for one example among many, in the fourth divination verse for the figure *Ọyẹku Ogbe* (corresponding to palm nut throws 2, 2, 2, 2; 1, 1, 1, 1), a demand for a sacrifice is attributed to Ifa: *Ifa ni ki ẹni-kan ru-(ẹ)bọ nitori oye ti a njẹ ni idile rẹ* "Ifa says someone should make a sacrifice because of a title that is to be taken in his lineage" (Bascom, 1969:232-3). But the appearance of a personal source is tempered by several considerations. First, because these are fixed traditional texts, the participants (including the client) know that this same text may have been uttered the day before to some else. Second, the directness of contact is mitigated by the fact that a significant portion of Ifa divination verses consists in a quotation of utterances made by some myth-time diviner – a hero or deity – to another myth-time personage. In such "protodialogic" speech event laminations (Du Bois, 1986:321; 1989), a prior (postulated) speech event is presented as precedent to the present divination. In this context there is often ambiguity as to whether the attribution of saying refers to a present saying or to the original myth-time saying. This ambiguity is anything but accidental, of course, and is indeed actively cultivated. Third, ambiguity about who is speaking is again heightened when the words "Ifa says ..." are seen to alternate, seemingly interchangeably, with the indefinite attribution "they say ..." (e.g. Bascom, 1969:233).[13]

Even where speaking is indicated it may not be volitional speaking, that is, speech in which choice exists – for example, the choice between telling the truth or lying. Magic, in some views at least, *coerces* rather than entreats action from gods and powers; as Mauss observes, the demons invoked in a demoniacal rite "are not free agents" ([1950] 1972:105). Typical explanations offered for a failed divination would be that witch-craft interfered with its procedure, or that the correct question had not been made sufficiently clear to the oracle, but not that an oracular "speaker" chose to lie. Given Bascom's materials, Ifa must be recognized as a rare case where a relatively personified, if not necessarily free-willed, "speaker" is postulated for at least part of the fixed divination texts given by tradition. But in most divination traditions, any associated deities or powers are at most patrons or supervisors of the divination procedure.

To draw an analogy from a Western context, a scientist who supervises a medical laboratory might fulfill an important function in ensuring that all equipment works and that tests are appropriately carried out by laboratory personnel, but we would not as a result take him or her to be the author of the diagnostic "messages" derived from the chemical reactions in the tests.[14] Bohannan's apt comparison of Tiv divination to a Geiger counter – a mechanism which will supply useful information if used properly by trained personnel – points in the right direction for understanding the character of divinatory technique, and the role of a supervising deity therein.

Mauss, in his discussion of the place of "spirit beings" in a general theory of magic, concluded that such figures were never in themselves sufficient to account for the beliefs about magic (a category which, in Mauss' usage, would encompass divination). He emphasized that, even where such spirits were invoked by native theory, there was always something left over unexplained:

The idea of spirit beings is not a sufficient representation of anonymous general forces which are the basis of a magician's power, the strength behind his words and actions, the power of his looks and intentions, spells and death ... the idea of spirits ... cannot explain either the existence of the ritual or its special features – sympathetic actions, magical substances, ritual prescriptions, private languages, etc.

Even in a demoniacal rite, Mauss says, "the idea of spirits is necessarily accompanied by an impersonal notion of efficacious power" (Mauss,

1950:105; Durkheim, 1915). It would not be too much to say that in divination, the apersonal is primary, and is present whether or not any secondary invocation of spirits is made.

Functions of intentionless meaning

The question of divinatory function can be raised on several levels, from the basic level of technique where we might speak of the aleatory generation of distinctive signals, to higher-order functions where we might speak of such things as social integration. While the highest levels cannot be attended to here, we do need to probe beyond the level of mechanical function if we are to understand *why* intentionless meaning should be so widely sought after, and so highly valued.

On one level, divination establishes "facts" without recourse to ordinary evidence, which may become the basis of a course of action undertaken by an individual or a group. Often a divinatory client faces several alternative courses of action whose relative merits cannot readily be determined (e.g. to build a house on this site or that, when either seems suitable; to go on a journey or stay home, etc.). What human source could provide assurance that ill fortune will not befall one in a house built on this site? In such circumstances, any well-defined course of action may serve as well as the next, even if determined aleatorily, so long as it can be confidently and resolutely followed. "Even tossing a coin can end indecision and lead to positive action" (Bascom, 1969:70). But this is likely to be effective only when it is possible to believe that the result is more significant than is mere "chance." To base a large undertaking on what one believes to be an accident would certainly require a curious cast of mind; and this is not the cast which is found among users of divination. Bascom points out that

when decisions are left to divine guidance rather than chance, the individual has far greater assurance that he is following the correct course of action. He can proceed with greater confidence; and, accordingly, in some cases he probably has a greater chance of success.

(Bascom, 1969:70)

From the perspective of the group, facts need to become not only "known" but socially legitimated. This is especially true for facts that bear on relations between individuals, or which involve concerted action by the group. But in the face of crisis the location of social responsibility for decision-making can become an embarrassment. Among the Tiv, for example, distrust of authoritarian roles makes it difficult for one person to impose a decision if that person has to be singled out as responsible for it:

Without the divining apparatus, the Tiv mode of group decision making could not be utilized so effectively – someone would have to take the authoritarian position of "dictating" the answer. Sometimes influential elders can and do merely "tell" their juniors what *akombo* [roughly, supernatural forces] are involved and occasionally even what relationships are to be "repaired." But such authoritarianism is both rare and distasteful to Tiv.

(Bohannan, 1975:166)

Divination means that no-one will have to be the personal source of decision. Rather than taking on the role of speech actor, one can defer to the apersonal divinatory source. And impersonally authoritative decisions can more readily attract consensus, by virtue of the fact that they cannot be attacked as proceeding from some interested person or faction (Bloch, 1975, 1989). As Park observes, "divinatory procedure, whether 'objective' in quality or merely inter-subjective, constitutes a technique for establishing an effective consensus upon a rather particular project" (Park, 1967:240; Fortes, 1966). It does this by the suppression of personal agency and hence responsibility:

it is the peculiar property of the diviner's role that he is able, in the public conscience, to remove the agency and responsibility for a decision from the actor himself, casting it upon the heavens where it lies beyond cavil and beyond reproach.

(Park, 1967:236)

Because divination "brings to light and so dispels the quarrels and grudges in the social group" (Turner, 1975:245), it may function, in concert with any ritual it prescribes, to resolve interpersonal conflicts (Beattie, 1967:231; Mendonsa, 1982:9).

The truth-discovering capacity of divination gives the diviner special access to otherwise private domains within the group. The Tiv diviner can ask his clients for any information he needs to carry out his work – about kin's health, grudges, political personages, etc. – including information that would ordinarily be closely guarded and might otherwise remain unaired. Petitioners readily answer these questions, saying "the oracle cannot tell you the truth if you lie to it" (Bohannan, 1975:152; see Herskovits, 1938, cited in Bascom, 1969:68).[15] Retel-Laurentin (1969) emphasizes that the Nzakara rubbing-board and poison oracles, with their vaunted infallibility, function as an effective "truth serum" in court cases. Discourse under compulsion to honesty can of itself serve important psychological and sociological functions, even where its participants treat it as merely ancillary to securing the divinatory response.

Divination addresses not only fact and action but emotion as well, fulfilling psychological functions beyond the more apparent epistemological and sociological ones. The client is often led to delve into thoughts and feelings of deep concern; and the structure of symbolic materials and potential explanations which are offered up by the divinatory tradition is likely to point in directions linked with emotion.[16] This interpretive activity is carried out in a psychologically protected environment, since the consulter is not responsible for backing the various propositions with any particular illocutionary force: as in the Azande poison oracle, the propositions are entertained rather than asserted. In this respect the entertained propositions resemble the psychoanalyst's category of primary process language, characterized by Fenichel as (among other things) "lacking in any identification of linguistic mood (*i.e.* no identification of indicative, subjunctive, optative, etc.)" (Bateson, 1972:139) – and, we might add, of illocutionary force.

What remains constant through all of these functions is the thread of reliance on apersonal authoritative meaning. The aleatory process suppresses intention, but it does so within an interpretive matrix which allows attribution of significance to the resulting signals, constituted as authoritative but apersonal validations of instantiated meanings, which can be put to a wide variety of uses in social life.

Moore ([1957] 1979) proposed a different explanation of the function of the aleatory in divination, arguing that the introduction of randomness into human behavior through divination can, under certain circumstances, have a positive survival value, and that this is what is accomplished by randomness-generating mechanisms like Naskapi scapulimancy. But Park (1967) points out that an odd crack in the heated shoulder blade would not lead its users to set off in an obviously unproductive direction on its account; this oracle was not entirely random in actual interpretive consequences. Rather, the value of its chance mechanism lay in its impartiality and impersonality. While Moore is entirely correct in stressing the nonintentional aspect of divination, his conclusion that its function is to introduce randomness into human behavior seems at most partially correct. Randomness is needed to drive the intention-suppressing function of divinatory technique, but the consulter's consequent actions and interpretations need not be random.

To say that the language of divination lacks intention is not to say that it is without function. It is ironic, no doubt, that the very intentionlessness of a process should allow it to serve its characteristic function – that devices for generating random outcomes should figure in a process said to be useful. But in the end there is neither contradiction nor paradox in the intentional pursuit of intentionless meaning.

Intention and the speech act reconsidered

We are now in a position to assess the implications of divinatory language for speech-act theory. But first it will be useful to look back and see what it was that speech-act theory initially had to offer, and where it went wrong. In its time, performative theory promised an escape from the prevailing idealist model of pure form, abstracted away from the living world of action. It moved in concert with the larger contemporaneous movement (e.g. Hymes, 1962) that sought to take language out of the Platonic world of ideal structure assumed by many structuralists (including generative structuralists) and place it in the world of social life, which encompasses notably social action. In departing from theories of "rules acting on forms" (of themselves, it seemed), the new focus on action and intention promised to align well with the re-emerging interest in the dynamics of function in language. In contrast to static structure-oriented theories that treated meaning and "the world" as belonging to separate spheres, correlated only by processes with names like "mapping" or "verification," the new theories placed meaning and language in the same world with persons, goals, intentions, and actions. Words now had consequences: something was said, and the facts of the world changed. To commit oneself to a view that meaning was necessarily linked to action was to make a place forcefully not only for actors but for their goals and contexts. For anyone whose primary frame of reference had been limited to the then prevailing idealist theories of language, speech-act theory pointed to the possibility of a theoretical understanding of language use. It can now be seen as part of a broader resurgence of action-oriented theories of language within pragmatics, sociocultural linguistics, and linguistic anthropology (Hymes, 1962; Bauman, 1977b; Silverstein, 1977; Becker, 1979; Friedrich, 1979), ultimately unfolding in the present dramatic efflorescence of dialogic approaches to discourse as culture (Friedrich, 1986; Holquist, 1983; Hill, forthcoming; McNeill, 1985; Hickmann, 1987; Haviland, 1988; Urban, 1989; Bauman and Briggs, 1990; Besnier, 1990a; etc.). Though many now rightly point to the early seminal work of rediscovered (or rehabilitated) ancestors like Bakhtin/Voloshinov (Voloshinov [1929–1930], 1973, Bakhtin, [1934] 1981, Vygotsky ([1934], 1986), and Malinowski ([1935] 1978), the view from linguistics cannot overlook the deglaciating role of Austin, Grice, and Searle.

The success of this movement cannot be doubted: no informed linguist or philosopher would now seriously propose returning to a theory of meaning which could not take into account context, including action in the social world. To know only the uttered linguistic form and its grammatically associated system-meaning is to have access to but a limited portion of the semantic process, which may involve reference, many would argue, to the speaker's manifest intention, on at least some occasions in some cultures.[17] But the apparent contribution of intention in one class of cases led to exaggerated estimations of its importance, and even reification within the speech-act model as a necessary component of all language use. To the extent that this theory mirrored and reinforced the common-sense folk theory of action, the two conspired to obscure the full range of language uses.

The challenge to the centrality of intention offered here parallels that posed by the anti-personalist critique (as mounted by Rosaldo, Duranti, Ochs, and others), but it also contains an additional ingredient – or rather lacks one, that of speaker responsibility. However attenuated the role of intention in Samoan *fono* speech, for example, the speaker's *responsibility* clearly remains – with this difference, that the Samoan speaker is responsible for the consequences of words rather than the intention behind them (Duranti, this volume).[18] In contrast, divination represents speech for which there is in principle no speaker responsible – neither for personal intentions behind the words, nor for the selection of the words themselves, nor for their consequences. This is of course no accident, since what divination seeks is precisely the absence of human responsibility for either intentions or consequences.

Regarding an apparent case of limited speaker involvement, intention, and responsibility, Strawson observed:

a speaker whose job it is to do so may offer information, instructions, or even advice, and yet be overtly indifferent as to whether or not his information is accepted as such, his instructions followed, or his advice taken. His wholly overt intention may amount to no more than that of making available – in a "take it or leave it" spirit – to his audience the information or instructions or opinion in question; though again, in some cases, he may be seen as the mouthpiece, merely, of another agency to which may be attributed at least general intentions of the kind that can scarcely be attributed, in the particular case, to him.

(1964:614)

But an intention to "make available" in a "take it or leave it spirit" will not satisfy the needs of illocutionary theory. Obviously even diviners presumably act in accordance with *some* sort of intention, such as the intention to follow the correct ritual procedure, or the intention to pronounce the ritually prescribed words precisely. But these kinds of intentions, though perfectly valid, are largely beside the point (*pace* Nuyts, 1989:115f), since they are not the kind of intention that can provide the *pragmatic backing* for a specific oracular utterance: a backing specific enough to distinguish between "she will die" and "she will not die," when both propositions have been uttered with equal force by the diviner. Speech-act theory never made much of the intention to perform the utterance act, and for good reason; although it clearly exists, the real power to shape meaning in speech-act theory derives from a higher level, i.e. the illocutionary intention. (Nor will Strawson's move of attributing "general intentions" to some agency behind the mouthpiece succeed in the case of divination, as we have seen.) Diviners are responsible for many things – integrity, correct procedure – but not for the one thing that matters most to the petitioner: the pragmatic backing of the oracular utterance.

Conclusions

Highlighting intention throws personality into relief; obscuring it lets individuality fade into the sociocultural background. Divination's achievement is to extract contingent, contextualized, applicable meanings from apersonal domains and in the process to imbue them with authority.

To interpret the indigenous process of producing meaning through divinatory procedure as just another speech act, with the implications of intending speech actors, would be to miss the lesson which divination offers. A truly encompassing theory of meaning-in-use must recognize that in social life there exist roles for several radically different kinds of meaning to play. Does divination refute the role of intention in language use? Not at all. There may well be good reason to recognize at least some ways of speaking in some cultures that demand for their interpretation a reference to the intentions of speech actors, which become fair game for theory to the extent that local interpretive practice actually *uses* them. But there exist also sharply contrasting language use types, not dependent on speech actors, which are yet equally consequential in the world of social action. In speaking of language use divorced from responsible actors, we are in no danger of reverting to the time when hypothesized language structure was a pure "object" of study divorced from action. But by now it is clear that not all phenomena in social and linguistic life need be actions, and not all meaningful use of language need be interpreted as engendered by speech actors.

Divination might at first seem like an exotic, obscure, or isolated case, a genre scarcely visible among many groups, such as the highly educated segments of industrial societies. But divination will prove to be far from unique as a representative of intentionless meaning. Though it presents the most visible challenge to existing assumptions, the same mechanisms of meaning construal can be witnessed, in subtler form, in phenomena ranging from calendrical ceremonials to ordinary proverbs to gaming and gambling. Nor is intentionless meaning restricted to "primitive" or "exotic" cultures; it is prominent in all cultures including our own, if not always in transparently recognizable form. Its hallmarks can be recognized not only in actual divinations like the flower petal-pulling that accompanies the child's refrain, "She loves me, she loves me not . . .," but also in secular forms of playful, aesthetic, and authoritative action, from a game of poker to the enjoyment of poetry or mystery narratives to the invoking of official rules or "the dictionary" in a dispute. Intentionless meaning is interwoven throughout much of social life in all cultures; but that is a matter for another essay.

Speech-act theory erred in taking intentionality to be a constant, but it would equally be problematic to exclude all reference to it. Such a move would actually make it more difficult to understand divination, given its striving after the aleatory. Intentionality does in fact seem to be a central concern of many human beings – so much so that on occasion they pay it the high compliment of directing great resources to its suppression. Ironically, it is only within a theory that recognizes the role of speech actors that one can fully appreciate the significance of their effacement. This understanding puts us in a better position to assess what it is that intention genuinely does contribute, whenever it is verifiably present in the meaning process. The real lesson from divination is not that intention should automatically be disregarded as a factor in the process of construing meaning; rather, the dynamic of invocation and suppression of intention carries social meaning in itself.

NOTES

In addition to the original presentation as a paper at the session on "Responsibility and Evidence in Oral Discourse" at the 82nd Annual Meeting of the American Anthropological Association in 1983, earlier versions of this chapter were presented as papers in colloquia at UCLA and UC Santa Barbara in May 1986, and published in Du Bois (1987). (The present chapter represents a significantly revised version of that paper.) I thank the participants at all three meetings for their stimulating comments. For their comments on several issues addressed in the present chapter, I thank Alessandro Duranti, Charles Goodwin, Jane Hill, Judith Irvine, Joel Kuipers, Paul Schachter, Sandra Thompson, Elizabeth Weber, and the anonymous reviewers for this volume. The research as presented here was supported in part by a UCLA Career Development Award, and by a UCLA Academic Senate Research Grant, which I gratefully acknowledge.

1 In discussing the role of intention for meaning, it is important to distinguish two meanings of "meaning." For many traditional language scholars, meaning meant first and foremost dictionary meaning (plus, perhaps, propositional or system-sentence meaning), both of which pertain to the language as system, i.e. Saussurean *langue*. But more recently, growing awareness of pragmatic issues has focused attention on pragmatically grounded instances of language use, subsuming, among other things, what has been called speaker's meaning. Now obviously the traditional theories of system-meaning were never founded on intentions, since no-one supposed that dictionaries (or language systems) had them. Only in the domain of language *use* has intention been put forward as a key factor, and only here does the possibility of intentionless meaning become interesting.

2 However, in dealing with quotation, Searle allows for a special status for the quoted proposition, from which the speaker has distanced himself or herself in relevant ways, an issue which I treat elsewhere (Du Bois, forthcoming).

3 Grice has recently concluded that natural and nonnatural meaning do share "a single overarching idea" (1989b:349; cf. 1989a:291f), but his proposal, that "if x means y then y ... is a consequence of x" (1989b:350), is probably too broad to capture it. From the (manticist) *interpreter's* point of view, what natural and nonnatural meaning share is the seemingly inherent significance of the semiotic phenomenon, from which meaning can apparently be extracted.

4 For a fuller discussion of the literary debate on intention, see Du Bois (1987:87–90).

5 Postulation of a special illocutionary act of divination would naturally be heir to the weaknesses which Searle pinpointed in claims for special literary acts. Instead, the very applicability of the notion "speech act" to divination will be called into question below.

6 Compare Wierzbicka (1985:500).

7 The role of intention in divination has also been challenged by Boyer (1990:51ff), in remarks which in part parallel the views put forward in Du Bois (1986:330ff), and the present work.

8 For a distinction between mechanical and mental divination, see Reynolds (1963:118), Mendonsa (1982:119); also Rose (1928). Park classifies divination procedures as mechanical, ritual, or emotive (Park, 1967:244); but a separate category of ritual divination seems of doubtful value, since it appears that mechanical and emotive divination are also in general ritual (see also Zeusse, 1987:376). Trance divination, like mechanical divination, also incorporates intentionless meaning. But to demonstrate this would require a different line of argument, which limitations of space preclude my developing here.

9 I have described the phenomenon of speech-role lamination elsewhere in terms of the "duplex speech event" (Du Bois, 1986:321) and "protodialogue" (Du Bois, 1989). Similar conceptions of multiple voice and related ideas can be found in Voloshinov ([1930] 1973), Bakhtin ([1934] 1981), Goffman (1974), Irvine (1982b), Clark and Carlson (1982a), Hill (forthcoming), Haviland (1988), Urban (1989), and others.

10 Although Evans-Pritchard originally recorded this in the Zande language, he published it only in translation.

11 Here I am speaking of use-meaning as opposed to system-meaning. (A standard framing of this opposition would be as between system-meaning and "speaker-meaning," but the latter construct is of doubtful application to the present case, as will be seen.)

12 It is interesting to note that the *authentic* divinatory utterances of the famous Delphic oracle – those proved to be historically genuine – have more in common with the African oracles described by Evans-Pritchard and others than they do with the dramatically clairvoyant, but apparently fictionalized, prophecies of Delphi in Greek literature and legend (Fontenrose, 1978).

13 Commonplace usages in many languages (such as English "what your behavior says to me is ...," "the dictionary says," "those spots mean ...," "Scorpio

rising means . . . ," etc.) urge caution in positing authors based on statements containing verbs of saying or meaning.

14 The aptness of the experimental analogy for divination was already recognized by Evans-Pritchard (1937; see also Zuesse, 1987).

15 In contrast, the Yoruba reject on principle the frank approach that characterizes the probing divinatory investigations of many other groups, preferring that the diviner not even know the nature of the client's problem, lest he "twist" Ifa in seeking to please (Bascom, 1969:68). As a result, little in the way of revealing dialogue is likely to take place during the selection of the traditional divinatory text. This may be linked to the prominence of the fixed text, particularly in the initial stage of the Ifa session, which is especially suitable for the essentially projective function which Ribeiro and Bascom have posited for the individual's process of text selection and interpretation. In contrast, divination systems which concentrate on securing specific new information via spontaneous propositions (e.g. about which neighbor's anger is causing one's child's sickness, etc.) may tend to correlate with a commitment to frank discussion.

16 Some divination procedures, while specifying a set of traditional texts, leave it to the individual to decide which is relevant to his or her case, creating a sort of projective technique like the Rorschach test, as Ribeiro observes regarding Ifa divination (Ribeiro, 1956:18–19, cited in Bascom, 1969:69).

17 To cite only one standard example, the satisfaction or non-satisfaction of context-based felicity conditions, including those grounded in illocutionary intentions, may shape utterance interpretation (Searle, 1969; Bach and Harnish, 1979; etc.).

18 Nuyts notes that even in Western culture there are times when responsibility takes precedence over intention, i.e. when individuals are held responsible for results they did not intend or even cause (1989:125). Conversely, Duranti acknowledges that, outside the *fono*, in certain kinds of everyday language use, intention may be taken into consideration even in Samoan culture (Duranti, this volume and [1984:17]).

3

SENECA SPEAKING STYLES AND THE LOCATION OF AUTHORITY

WALLACE CHAFE

Introduction

Seneca is a Northern Iroquoian language presently spoken by about two hundred people on the Allegany, Cattaraugus, and Tonawanda Reservations in western New York State. (A partial description of the language is available in Chafe, 1967.) In observing the range of uses of this language, one notices three quite different styles of speaking that are in common use today. (Other styles, such as that used in story-telling, are less often encountered at the present time.) One of these styles is that of normal conversation, one is a style that I have labeled "preaching," and one a style that I have called "chanting" (Chafe, 1961:147–8). These labels are for linguistic identification only. So far as I know, Seneca speakers have never given names to these styles, nor are they consciously aware of their existence. I believe that they would, however, immediately recognize the inappropriateness of a style that was used in the wrong situation.

The three styles are, of course, associated with different aspects of Seneca life. The conversational style is used in casual, everyday interaction. The preaching style is used especially in recitations of the *káiwi:yo:h*, or "Good Message" of Handsome Lake, the Seneca prophet (Parker, 1913; Wallace, 1970). This four-day ritual, the gospel of the Longhouse religion, used to be performed annually (though now less often) on Seneca and other Iroquois reservations in the United States and Canada, the performer belonging to a small number of highly gifted orators who make a circuit of "Six Nations Meetings" assembled for this purpose. The chanting style is characteristic of the several important rituals of thanksgiving: the ubiquitous *kanǫ:nyǫk* or "Thanksgiving Speech" which opens nearly every Seneca ceremony, the *konéoǫ?* or "Thanksgiving Dance," and the *kayę?kǫthwę:?* or "Tobacco Burning," the latter two rituals having a more restricted occurrence within the cycle of calendric ceremonies (Chafe, 1961; Foster, 1974b). These three thanksgiving rituals require, roughly, from twenty minutes to an hour for their performance. Since they are in that respect less demanding than the Handsome Lake recitation, the number of qualified orators has been somewhat larger.

The three styles show different degrees of prosodic freedom, formulaicity, sentence integration, and epistemological certainty. These stylistic properties reflect iconically the speaker's location of the authority for what is being said. There is a stylistic continuum with conversation at one end, preaching in the middle, and chanting at the opposite end, and this continuum reflects a decreasing responsibility of the speaker, or an increasing responsibility of a remote authority for the content being expressed.

The continuum in question can be understood within a framework for the analysis of ritual speech that has been provided by Du Bois (1986). Du Bois distinguished between a "proximate speaker" – the person who actually utters the language in question – and a "prime speaker" – the person ultimately responsible for what is said (often no acknowledged person at all). When the proximate and prime speakers are not identical, as in quoted speech or ritual language, Du Bois identified a correlation between the degree of proximate speaker responsibility and a range of linguistic features that express a greater or lesser reliance on the proximate speaker's contribution. At one end of the scale lie those features associated with the presentation of a speaker's own firsthand knowledge in a conversational style. At the other end of the scale, "in the utterance of the ritual practitioner, the prescribed form of speech tends to obliterate the indexing of individual personality. In place of distinctive voice, intonation, hesitation, rhythm, sentence structure, is a voice made uniform and intonationally inexpressive, a pauseless automatic flow of ritual syllables within given structures, where any imposition of proximate speaker control is checked at every hand ... The groundwork is thus laid for a belief that the ritual practitioner channels words derived from, at best, the nebulous ancestors, or more simply, from nowhere" (Du Bois, 1986:333). My purpose here is to show how this correlation of speaking style with responsibility is manifested in the three different ways of speaking Seneca.

Prosody

It is useful to view the prosodic characteristics of the three speaking styles on a continuum from maximally free to maximally stylized or constrained. The conversational style shows considerable intonational variety, along with expressive uses of volume, timing, and voice quality. It is in conversation that speakers exploit the prosodic richness of their language to the full. The other two styles have a more limited prosodic range, with the chanting style showing the most extreme limitations:

Table 3.1. *Prosodic range*

< free prosody > ------------------------------------ < stylized prosody >
< conversation > ------------- < preaching > ---------------- < chanting >

I will not try to describe here the prosody of Seneca conversational speech. For our purposes it is sufficient to mention that it is what we might perceive as a "normal" prosody, with varying pitch contours, hesitational phenomena, changes in volume and tempo, and perhaps an unusually strong admixture of laughter. On the other hand, I will try to describe in some detail the properties of the two more restricted styles: preaching and chanting.

Speakers of all three styles produce their language in the kind of spurts that I have been calling "intonation units" (Chafe, 1987). These intonation units tend to consist of only two or three words in Seneca (as contrasted with five or six in English), perhaps because the language is polysynthetic and thus tends to pack more information into a word than English does (Chafe, 1985). The following excerpt from a conversational narrative shows something of the nature of Seneca intonation units. The acute accent mark (á) indicates an accented or high-pitched vowel. Two dots indicate a brief break in the flow of vocalization, three dots a perceptible pause, and four dots an unusually long pause. The comma indicates a non-falling clause-final pitch contour, the period a falling sentence-final contour. I have translated only those particles whose functions are easy to approximate in English:

(1) ... *tá:*   *wa ʔakwakéhi:yá ʔk,*
        and so we spent the summer

   "and so we spent the summer"

(2) * kę̇:s*   *hikę̇:*   *né: ʔ*   *ǫkwá:yakwę̇h,*
    repeatedly that   we are picking berries

   "picking berries"

(3) ... *akwáta:yá:ni:nǫ́h,*
        we sell berries

   "we sold berries"

(4) ... *a:yę̇: ʔ*   *kę̇:s*   *ne ʔhó*   *nǫ̇:*   *né*
        it seems repeatedly there   I guess

        sę̇   *nǫ ʔo:tá: ʔ,*
        three   that many days

   "it seems we were there for I guess three days"

(5) ... *onę   áe?   wa?akwatyé?nít,*
       then again we got enough,

"then we got enough"

(6) *ta   onę   áe?   wa?akwatké:onǫ?,*
   and so then   again we went peddling,

"and so then we went peddling"

(7) *né:wá?   kanǫtakǫ́:   wa?a:kwé:?,*
   this time in town   we went

"this time we went into town"

(8) ... *wa?akwat?ashækéhta:t,*
        we put baskets on our backs

"we carried backpacks"

(9) *o?tyakwayá:ya?k.*
   we crossed over

"we crossed over"

(10) .. *skęhǫ:tí:kwá:h,*
        to the other side of the river

"to the other side of the river"

(11) .. *nękho   kwa: sę?ę   nǫ?kę́hǫtí*
        this   toward because which side of the river

       hikę: néh,
       that

"because it was on this side of the river"

(12) .... *ne?hoh ... akwanǫtayętáhkwak.*
         there   we were camping

"where we were camping."

The more constrained prosodies of the Seneca preaching and chanting styles are both best described in terms of intonation units, and especially in terms of the patterns that affect the prefinal and final syllables of these units. I can illustrate the preaching pattern with the beginning of one section of the "Good Message," transcribed below.

Here, as above, I use the acute accent (á) to indicate a high pitch. In addition I use the wedge (ǎ) to indicate a rising pitch, and the circumflex (â) a falling pitch. The rise or fall extends over an entire long vowel or vowel sequence; for example, over the entire sequence *â:o* in intonation unit (14), even though the mark is only on the first vowel.

When a falling pitch occurs within an intonation unit, as in (14) and (15) below, it does not fall as far as it does at the end of an intonation unit, as in (16), where it falls to its lowest point. Intonation units (16), (18), (21), (23), and (25) end in a sentence-final falling pitch. Sentence-medial and sentence-final intonation units are marked with commas and periods respectively.

The five-dot pause preceding intonation unit (13), during which the speaker presumably recalled the content of the entire upcoming section of the recitation, was a very long one, lasting more than ten seconds. The four-dot pause before (14) lasted about two seconds, the three-dot pause before (15) a little less than a second, and the two-dot pause before (16) less than a tenth of a second. The initial pauses in the remaining intonation units were of similar lengths, as shown by the dots. In general, the delivery was noticeably slow and deliberate:

(13) ..... *ta   oné̜   wa:ení̜ʔ,*
         and so now   they said

"and so now they said"

(14) .... *o:né̜h   .. e̜kwâ:owíʔ,*
        now   we will tell you

"now we will tell you"

(15) ... *né:ʔ   e̜shê:owíʔ,*
           you will tell them

"you will tell them"

(16) .. *né   shéno̜:ksho̜ʔ.*
         your kinsmen

"your kinsmen"

(17) ... *né:ʔ ... yako̜:kwe̜h,*
           woman

"there was a woman"

(18) .. *yé:wátsíyæ:ye̜ʔ.*
        she has a family

"who had a family"

(19) .... *né:ʔ tí né wâ:se̜:ʔ,*
              it is new

"it first"

(20) .. *oʔtyohathéʔ,*
        it gets light

"became light"

(21) .. *nę:*   *hé*   *yǫ́ętsátêˀ.*
             on the earth

"on the earth"

(22) .... *o:nę́h*   .. *ne:ˀ*   *oˀtyę́ˀnyaę̌ˀ,*
      now   she tends to it

"then she attended to"

(23) ... *nę̌:*   *néh*   .. *yéáˀtánǫ́:wę̂s.*
                food

"food"

(24) .... *nę̌:h*   .. *ęǫtiáˀtanǫ̂wę̌ˀ,*
             they will eat it

"for them to eat"

(25) ... *nę̌:h*   .. *hǫwǫtiáwákshǫ̂ˀ.*
             her children

"her children"

Intonation unit (13) does not typify the prosodic pattern of the preaching style. It would not be out of place in a conversation, where it is typical for a sentence-medial intonation unit to end with a simple high pitch.

Intonation units (14) through (16), however, illustrate well the prosodic pattern that is typical of this style. Each begins with a high-pitched particle (*o:nę́h, né:ˀ,* or *né*). There follows, sometimes after a brief pause, the major content word. The pitch assigned to that word differs according to whether the intonation unit is sentence-medial, for example (14) and (15), or sentence-final, for example (16). In sentence-medial intonation units there is a falling pitch on the penultimate vowel or vowel sequence, and a rising pitch on the final vowel or vowel sequence. Thus we have *ękwâ:owíˀ* and *ęshê:owíˀ.* The point where the pitch begins to fall, at the beginning of the vowel or vowel sequence, constitutes the highest pitch of the entire intonation unit. The pitch then falls to a relatively low point, from which it rises during the final vowel to a point that does not, however, reach the height of the beginning of the fall. In Chafe (1961:148) I mentioned that typical fall–rise contours were 523, 423, and 412, where the higher numbers represent higher pitches.

Intonation unit (16) shows the pattern that is typical of sentence-final intonation units in the preaching style. The content word has high pitch throughout, with a sentence-final fall to a maximally low pitch on the last vowel: *shénǫ́:kshǫ̂ˀ.*

We see these patterns repeated in intonation units (17) and (18). The sentence-medial intonation unit (17) shows the fall–rise pattern on *yakǫ:kwĕh*. The sentence-final intonation unit (18) shows a high pitch that is sustained up to the sentence-final fall on the last vowel in *yé:wát-siyǽ:yę̂ʔ*.

The sentence composed of intonation units (19) through (21) is not quite as faithful to this pattern. After the typical sentence-medial pattern in (19), ending with the fall–rise contour in *wâ:sĕ:ʔ*, (20) departs from the preaching style in favor of a more conversational pattern of rising pitch on the last syllable. The particle that begins (21) has a low pitch, but otherwise that intonation unit conforms to the sentence-final preaching pattern, with *hé yǫ́ętsátê ʔ* exhibiting a sustained high pitch and then a fall.

The sentence composed of (22) and (23) is again typical. The same can be said of (24) and (25). In this last sentence it is noticeable that the intonations of the content words in both (24) and (25) were influenced by the position of the intrinsic, morphological accent on the third and fourth vowels in both *eǫtíáʔtan ǫ̂:wę̂ʔ* and *hǫwǫtíáwákshǫ̂ʔ*. In (24) these intrinsically accented vowels received the same high pitch they would normally receive in isolation. In (25) the sustained high pitch of a sentence-final intonation unit does not begin before the morphological accent. (It happens that the content words in sentence-final (16) and (18) have no intrinsic morphological accent.)

In summary, the prosody of the preaching style follows a fairly regular pattern, characterized by a fall–rise at the end of a sentence-medial intonation unit, and a sustained high pitch and then a fall at the end of a sentence-final intonation unit. The effect is that of a distinctively stylized prosody, a prosody that one would never mistake for conversational. At the same time it is a prosody that shows a certain amount of pitch variation, of rising and falling pitches during the course of an intonation unit, particularly one that is sentence-medial. It is also a prosody that allows a certain admixture of conversational patterns, as in intonation units (13) and (20). Though unquestionably stylized, it remains nevertheless somewhat flexible.

The prosody of the chanting style is simpler to describe. The following is an excerpt from the Thanksgiving Speech, the beginning of the section that gives thanks for the earth:

(26) .... *ta   onę   wai   nyo:ye:ę́h,*
       and so now   indeed he did it

    "and so now indeed this is what he did"

(27) .. *hotyę:noʔktaʔ*   *hê tyǫheʔ.*
    Our Creator

    "Our Creator"

(28) ... *hawe:ʔǫ́   waih,*
       he decided   indeed

"indeed he decided"

(29) *ękǫętsa:tá:t,*
      I will establish the earth

"I will establish the earth"

(30) .. *neʔho   tęyakotaʔǫ:ǫtyéʔ,*
       there   they will come to be standing

"where they will be standing"

(31) .. *ne   wa:sé:ʔ,*
       the new (ones)

"the new ones"

(32) .. *ne   ʔǫ:kwéh,*
       the people

"the people"

(33) .. *hęǫwe   ęyǫętsa:tê:k.*
       where   the earth will be there

"on the earth"

(34) ... *ne:ʔ ti ne   kanǫ:kshǽʔ,*
        it is the kinship relation

"it will be a kinship (term)"

(35) .. *no:nę   ne   ęyǫthyonya:néʔ,*
       when   they will talk about it

"when they talk about it"

(36) .. *ęyǫętsa:té:k,*
       the earth will be there

"the earth"

(37) .. *ne:ʔ   nę:nǫtǫ́:ǫk,*
        they will say

"they will say"

(38) .. *akhinoʔę   teyǫkwę:hsiʔtakęʔsǽhkǫh.*
       our mother she is a support for our feet

"our mother who supports our feet"

One thing that is immediately apparent here is the regularity of the pauses. At the very beginning of this section there was a pause of about two seconds. The intersentential pauses, before (28) and (34), were about one second long. All the other pauses lasted only about a tenth of a second. The effect is one of great fluency, even though the precise wording of this speech differs each time it is performed.

The pitch patterns are completely regular. Again we can distinguish between intonation units that are sentence-medial and those that are sentence-final. Sentence-medial intonation units are chanted monotonously on a low pitch up to the final vowel or vowel sequence, where the pitch is high. Sentence-final intonation units follow the same pattern, except that the final vowel or vowel sequence falls from maximally high to maximally low. The need for a minor qualification of this last statement is illustrated in (38), where there is a high pitch on the penultimate syllable as well. That word in isolation would be pronounced *teyǫkwę:hsi²tak-²sǽhkǫh*, with an intrinsic morphological accent on the penult. That penultimate accent was retained, and the final falling pitch of the chanting style was added.

We have seen how the varied prosody of normal conversation is considerably limited by the preaching style, and limited to the highest degree by the chanting style. We can look now at some other respects in which conversation, preaching, and chanting line up in the same way.

Formulaicity

One other continuum of this sort involves formulaic expressions – memorized phrases and intonation units, as well as certain sequences of intonation units. As we move from conversation to preaching to chanting we find formulas used with increasing frequency, as well as formulas of increasing length.

It would of course be wrong to suggest that formulas are absent from conversational language. Fluency in conversation undoubtedly stems in part from repeating prepackaged word sequences that are standard items in the speaker's repertoire. There are, for example, a number of conversational formulas consisting of sequences of particles, among them *onę ae²* "then again" and *ta onę ae²* "and so then again," which appear in intonation units (5) and (6) above. In contrast to the preaching and chanting styles, however, conversational language shows the largest proportion of creatively produced, non-memorized word sequences.

Intonation units (13–16) show a formula that occurs over and over in the Good Message, at the beginning of nearly every one of Handsome Lake's ethical prescriptions. The formula begins with a statement by the speaker himself (13), who reports a statement by the three messengers sent by the Creator to Handsome Lake (14), who in turn direct Handsome Lake to pass the message on to his people (15–16):

(13) ..... *ta: oné   wa:ęní?,*
     and so now   they said

"and so now they said"

(14) .... *o:nę́h   .. ękwâ:owí?,*
      now   we will tell you

"now we will tell you"

(15) ... *né:?   ęshê:owí?,*
        you will tell them

"you will tell them"

(16) .. *né   shénǫ́:kshǫ́?.*
        your kinsmen

"your kinsmen"

Each ethical section closes with a two-line formula confirming that both the messengers and Handsome Lake performed their roles properly:

(39) ... *ne?ho   wáih   .. nǫ̂:ti:yě:?,*
         that   indeed   they did

"that indeed is what they did"

(40) .. *ne?ho   waih   .. nyá:yéhâk.*
        that   indeed   he used to do

"that indeed is what he used to do"

But formulaic language dominates even more completely the chanting style of the Thanksgiving Speech. As in the Good Message, each section of this speech begins and ends with a formula. The beginning formula appears as (26–8):

(26) .... *ta   onę   wai   nyo:ye:ę́h,*
          and so now   indeed he did it

"and so now indeed this is what he did"

(27) .. *hotyę:no?kta?ǫ   hê   tyǫhe?.*
        Our Creator

"Our Creator"

(28) ... *hawe:?ǫ́   waih,*
         he decided indeed

"indeed he decided"

The formula that ends each section of the speech is as follows:

(41) *ta: ne?ho   wai   nęyo?tę:ǫ́k,*
     and so that   indeed it will continue to be so

"and so indeed it will continue to be so"

(42) *nǫkwaʔnikǫ̀ęʔ*.
     our minds

     "our minds"

But between these opening and closing formulas there are numerous
others involving the particular item for which thanks is being given. For
example, the following is a formulaic way of referring to the future
generations of people who will walk about on the earth:

(30) .. *neʔho tęyakotaʔǫ̀ǫtyéʔ*,
     there   they will come to be standing

     "where they will be standing"

(31) .. *ne wa:séːʔ*,
     the new (ones)

     "the new ones"

(32) .. *ne ʔǫ̀:kwéh*,
     the people

     "the people"

(33) .. *hęǫwe ęyǫętsaːtêːk*.
     where   the earth will be there

     "on the earth"

In this section, as in some of the others, explicit recognition is given to a
formula that the Creator himself ordained:

(35) .. *noːnę ne ęyǫthyonyaːnéʔ*,
     when   they will talk about it

     "when they talk about it"

(36) .. *ęyǫętsaːtéːk*,
     the earth will be there

     "the earth"

(37) .. *neːʔ nę:nǫtǫ̀:ǫk*,
           they will say

     "they will say"

(38) .. *akhinoʔę teyǫkwęːhsiʔtakęʔsæ̀hkǫ̂h*.
     our mother   she is a support for our feet

     "our mother who supports our feet"

On the scale of formulaicity, then, there is a progression from the least
formulaic conversational style, through the moderately formulaic preaching style, to the maximally formulaic chanting style.

Sentences

A third continuum of this sort involves what I have called the integration of sentences – the degree to which sentences present complex and coherent structures that go beyond the relatively loose fragmentation of typical sentences in conversation. When conversational speakers put together sentences quickly and perhaps for the first time, as illustrated in (1–12), they lack the capacity to plan the complex structures that are more easily achieved with language that has been rehearsed many times, both openly and silently. Though (1–9) constitute a single sentence on intonational grounds, the connections between its parts are only loosely indicated. Even the intended boundaries of sentences may be problematic. Thus, for example, the sentence-final intonation at the end of (9) seems, with hindsight, premature:

(9) *oʔtyakwayáːyaʔk.*
we crossed over

"we crossed over"

(10) .. *skęhǫːtíːkwáːh,*
to the other side of the river

"to the other side of the river"

(11) .. *nękho   kwaː   sęʔę   nǫʔkęhǫtí*
this   toward because which side of the river

hikęː néh,
that

"because it was on this side of the river"

(12) .... *neʔhoh   ...akwanǫtayętáhkwak.*
there   we were camping

"that we were camping"

As the speaker was creating this piece of language, he chose first to end the long initial sentence by saying "we crossed over." But then he must have thought of the difference between the two sides of the river and the direction of the crossing, thoughts which led him to add (10–12) in a form that might, from a retrospective point of view, be regarded as somewhat illogically attached to what preceded.

On the other hand, the preaching sample shows short, neat, well-constructed sentences. The first and longest expresses a sequence of related events:

(13) ..... *ta   oné   waːęníʔ,*
and so now they said

"and so now they said"

(14) .... *o:nę́h* .. *ękwâ:owíʔ*,
now   we will tell you

"now we will tell you"

(15) ... *né:ʔ ęshê:owíʔ*,
you will tell them

"you will tell them"

(16) .. *né shénǫ́:kshǫ̂ʔ*.
your kinsmen

"your kinsmen"

The second introduces a referent and then predicates something of it:

(17) ... *né:ʔ néh* ... *yakǫ́:kwĕh*,
woman

"there was a woman"

(18) .. *yé:wátsíyǽ:yę̂ʔ*.
she has a family

"who had a family"

Another contains an initial predication followed by an elucidation of one
of its arguments:

(22) .... *o:nę́h* .. *ne:ʔ oʔtyę̂ʔnyǎęʔ*,
now   she tends to it

"then she attended to"

(23) ... *nę̂: néh* .. *yéáʔtánǫ́:wę̂s*.
food

"food"

While simple, these and the other sentences in this excerpt are tightly
constructed, their constituent intonation units combining in more integrated ways than those of the conversational example.

When we look at the sentences of the chanting style, we find them
generally longer and more complex than those of the preaching style.
The second sentence in our excerpt, for example, contains a long
embedded complement of the verb "decide" in (28): first the simple
statement in (29), followed by the spatial adverbial predication in (30),
to which a series of arguments is attached in (31–2), with a final spatial
adverbial in (33):

(28) ... *hawe:ʔǫ́ waih*,
he decided indeed

"indeed he decided"

(29) *ękǫ̨etsa:tá:t,*
I will establish the earth

"I will establish the earth"

(30) .. *ne²ho tęyakota²ǫ:ǫtyé²,*
there   they will come to be standing

"where they will be standing"

(31) .. *ne wa:sé:²,*
the new (ones)

"the new ones"

(32) .. *ne ²ǫ:kwéh,*
the people

"the people"

(33) .. *hęǫwe ęyǫętsa:tê:k.*
where the earth will be there

"on the earth"

In short, we find the loose structuring of sentences in the conversational style replaced by a tighter, but relatively simple structuring in the preaching style, which in turn gives way to the longer and more complex structures of the chanting style.

Epistemological stance

Finally, there is a similar progression in the attitude of the speaker toward his knowledge in each of the three styles. Not atypically, the conversational sample above contains expressions of uncertainty regarding what is being said:

(4) ... *a:yę̨:²*   *kę̨:s*   *ne²hó nǫ̨:*   *né*
it seems   repeatedly there   I guess

sę̨   *nǫ²o:tá:²,*
three   that many days

"it seems we were there for I guess three days"

The particles *a:yę̨:²* "it seems" and *nǫ̨:* "I guess" are common indicators of uncertainty in Seneca conversational speech.

The Good Message is conspicuous in its freedom from epistemic particles. There are none in the excerpt quoted above, which is typical of this style.

In the Thanksgiving Speech, however, there is an explicit contrast to

the conversational style in the repeated use of the particle *wai(h)*
"indeed" or "for sure," which occurred above in (26) and (28):

(26) .... *ta   onę   wai   nyo:ye:ęh,*
     and so now indeed he did it

     "and so now indeed this is what he did"

(28) ... *hawe:ʔǫ   waih,*
     he decided indeed

     "indeed he decided"

Although it was not present in our excerpt, there is a verb form *tkaye:iʔ*
"it is a fact" that plays a similar role. It is often accompanied by *wai* in the
formula:

(43) *ta: ne:ʔ   wai   ne   tkaye:iʔ,*
     and so   indeed   it is a fact

There is, then, a continuum which extends from particles of uncertainty in
the conversational style, through an absence of epistemic particles in the
preaching style, to a prevalence of particles and verbs of certainty in the
chanting style.

Locating authority

We have seen that conversation, preaching (as illustrated by the Good
Message of Handsome Lake), and chanting (as illustrated by the Thanksgiving Speech) sort themselves in parallel ways on four dimensions as
shown in table 3.2.

Table 3.2. *Dimensions of style*

	Conversation	*Good Message*	*Thanksgiving Speech*
Prosody:	Free	Somewhat stylized	Highly stylized
Formulaicity:	Low	Moderate	High
Sentences:	Fragmented	Somewhat integrated	Highly integrated
Epistemology:	Uncertain	Unexpressed	Certain

The array of the three styles on these four dimensions reflects another,
functional dimension: the extent to which the speaker is himself or herself
the authority for the knowledge being conveyed, or, conversely, the extent
to which that knowledge is attributed to a remote authority.

In ordinary conversational speech of the kind quoted above, speakers
relate events in which they themselves were direct participants. The

knowledge they verbalize arose from their own experience. They are their own authorities.

In the Good Message, the actual speaker was not a direct party or witness to the knowledge being conveyed. The specific authorities for what is said, as is repeatedly explained in the beginning formula of each section (13–16), were the three messengers sent by the Creator to Handsome Lake. The messengers themselves were supernatural beings, but they appeared to Handsome Lake, a historical personage. The authority for the Good Message lies in a set of partly historical, partly supernatural events known or believed to have occurred almost two centuries ago in a location that can still be identified (although since the 1960s it has lain at the bottom of a reservoir).

The Thanksgiving Speech, however, conveys knowledge that is remote in every way. The authority for this kind of knowledge is distant from everyday experience in every respect. In fact, the question of where the knowledge originated does not even arise; to ask it seems absurd.

These Seneca styles and their uses thus support Du Bois' finding that an increasingly remote authority for what is being said is likely to be indexed in a variety of identifiable, gradient linguistic features, features that serve in several ways to remove the language from its conversational roots in the proximate speaker's firsthand knowledge. Whereas the prosodic richness of conversation reflects the speaker's richly variable involvement, doubts, and expectations, its absence distances the speaker from personal responsibility. Increasing the measure of formulaicity is, of course, a way of facilitating the recall of an oral tradition, but it also expresses the kind of immutable stability one associates with things that are heard over and over again. The elegant, worked-over quality of integrated syntax, less common in the spontaneous world of conversation, conveys in still another way the solid reliability of a well-established authority. Finally, markers of epistemological certainty are nothing less than explicit signals of that same authority. The effect of combining these features is to present a voice that is unified in transferring responsibility from the proximate speaker to a remote, unquestionable source of truth.

4

OBLIGATIONS TO THE WORD: RITUAL SPEECH, PERFORMANCE, AND RESPONSIBILITY AMONG THE WEYEWA

JOEL C. KUIPERS

Introduction

In the Weyewa highlands of the eastern Indonesian island of Sumba, elders say that, long ago, the ancestors gave their descendants their "word, voice" (*li'i*). The enduring wisdom and valued knowledge of these words is embodied in a poetic couplet style of "ritual speech" (*pan-ewe tenda*). In exchange for periodically re-enacting and fulfilling the promises and obligations these words entail, Weyewa are blessed with prosperity, fertility, and well-being. When such "words" are inevitably neglected and misfortune ensues, specialist performers of ritual speech are hired to recover it through a culturally recognized and indeed admired "path" of atonement and feasting. Spokesmen begin with divination, then re-state the neglected promises or "words" in placation rites, and finally fulfill these promises in celebration and house-building feasts. This ritual acknowledgment of responsibility to maintain, reproduce, and abide by the "words of the ancestors" (*li'i marapu*) is a key symbol of Weyewa collective life.

Over the course of this prolonged ceremonial process of atonement, speakers of this couplet style gradually transform the highly situated, dialogic discourse of the initial divinatory inquiries (*urrata*) into relatively de-contextualized, monologic accounts of mythically established order (*we'e maringi*). Reported speech is particularly frequent in the earliest stages of the healing process, in which it serves to individuate, particular-ize, and situate discourse; in the later stages, however, reported-speech frames become less frequent as the speaker constructs an image of mono-logic, authoritative "words of the ancestors." The result is a stretch of talk which appears to be detached from the immediate "here and now" of performance, even though in many ways it is not. This process of "entex-tualizing" discourse (Bauman, 1987b) is depicted in Weyewa ritual ideol-ogy with botanical and genealogical imagery as a relation between multi-form "tips" and a single, authoritative "trunk" of knowledge.

In ritual contexts, the use of reported-speech verbs ("locutives") indexes the nature of responsibility for the "word." In divination, locutives frame the individual voices of particular spiritual agents of calamity, as well as isolating and identifying the neglected words of promise made by forgetful descendants. The absence of these verbs of reported speech when directly transmitting the words of the ancestors in the final stages of the atonement process, on the other hand, collectivizes the speaking voice, assigning the responsibility for the "words" to the source of all tradition: the "ancestral spirits" (*marapu*).

Ethnographic setting

Until the last decade, the Weyewa notions of responsibility and obligation were organized primarily around traditional kinship ties, and sanctioned by the ancestral spirits and their "words." In part because economic opportunities on the island were limited largely to subsistence cultivation of rice, corn, and root crops, and some livestock breeding, the Dutch, and later the Indonesian bureaucracies maintained a relatively low profile on Sumba. Christian missions, despite nearly a century of effort, could claim only about 20 per cent of the population as converts in 1980. As a consequence, these "modernizing" influences did little to establish new lines of obligation to written laws, formal bureaucratic regulations, and foreign religious beliefs, or any of the rights those might engender.

But while the island of Sumba was spared most of the extreme depredations of the Dutch colonial system, the responsibilities and obligations of the ordinary Sumbanese under the kin- and village-based system can be demanding and even harsh. The poor, the marginal and the weak are often deeply obligated to various "big man" figures, self-appointed leaders whose charisma, economic strength, and high status permit them to extract tribute in ritual feasting. Indebtedness to these men – usually by giving one's "word" of promise in exchange for cattle, land or protection – can lead to a lifetime of subordination and dependency. Regarded as sacred covenants, these exchange obligations are fulfilled in the context of ceremonial exchanges of goods and verbal performances. Neglected exchange responsibilities are passed down according to a rule of agnatic descent. Weyewa men often find themselves held responsible for damages, commitments, or obligations engendered by their fathers and grandfathers.

Weyewa regard the failure to fulfill one's word of promise as a breach of morality, a neglect of tradition, and a cause for supernatural retribution. For them, living up to one's promise is not simply an expression of a reliable personality; in ritual contexts it is depicted as "following in the path, following in the tracks" of the ancestors. To fail to do so is to deviate seriously from that inscribed path. The inevitable misfortune that results from such deviation is represented with metaphorical imagery depicting the isolation, vulnerability, and exposure felt by those who pursue individual interests. Myths, folktales, and daily admonitions relentlessly drive home a point about the dependency of children and their responsibility to follow the words of their ancestral forebears.

Ritual reproduction of the "Words of the Ancestors"

When Weyewa experience sudden and shocking calamities such as a flood, a devastating fire, or an untimely death, the misfortune is believed to occur as a result of a broken promise, or "word, voice" (*li'i*). "Divination" (*urrata*) is the first stage of atonement in which specialist speakers try to identify the broken "word" or promise to the ancestors. The second stage, if the victims have the feasting resources and the determination, usually occurs a few hours or weeks later, and is an all-night ritual dialogue in which the broken promise is reaffirmed and reproduced, although not actually fulfilled. The final, climactic stage is when the promise to feast in honor of the ancestors is fulfilled and some components of the charter myth of the founding of the agnatic clan are told. It is here that the "true voice of the ancestors" is revealed.

These performances are conducted in "ritual speech" (*panewe tenda*). This poetic style consists of conventional couplets in which the first line parallels the second line in both rhythm and meaning. The specialist spokesman draws from a stock of thousands of these traditional couplets, and links them together according to the appropriate genre conventions in particular situations. Speakers engaged in performance accept responsibility for the fluent, accurate reproduction of these couplets, as well as for the suitable organization of such units according to discourse conventions. Failure to do so properly may result in a fine of a cloth or knife or animal, or even supernatural retributions.

Although most Weyewa adults claim some competence in ritual speech, not everyone in Weyewa society has equal access to, skill or interest in, these verbal resources. Since this style is required for all communication with the ancestral spirits, specialist ritual spokesmen are regularly hired, particularly for events involving prolonged public performance and communication with the spirits. These mediators are typically males, in their forties or older, and they are hired for the purpose of speaking on behalf of someone else. The couplet phrase used to describe this role is:

(1) *a kandauke kambu wiwi*   he who talks beneath the lips

   a panewe kambu nganda   he who speaks beneath the mouth.

This may be glossed as meaning "one who speaks under the auspices of someone else." In rites of misfortune, marriage negotiations, litigation, even courtship, this role may be invoked to permit the reporting of one's speech to another party. These specialists are traditionally compensated with a large portion of meat from whatever ritual sacrifice follows the ceremony. Additional gifts may include a knife, a bolt of cloth, and a small, live piglet.

The job of the spokesman is to report the speech of not only his client, and sponsor, but also the ancestral spirits. In both cases, the "source" of information is represented as a "trunk" (*pu'u*). The word *pu'u* itself is richly polysemous, and also means "center." For instance, another way of referring to the source of speech is "lord of the center" (*mori pu'u*); such usage can be further expanded in couplet terms:

(2) *pu'u-na wazu*　　　　　　　trunk of the tree

　　mata-na we'e　　　　　　　well-spring of water.

For Weyewa, this "source" imagery is the idiom for a broader ideology of communicative interaction which explains differences in authority. For them, authority is represented as a source, a place, a central foundation, from which derivative, secondary, and subsequent components (or "tips") develop. Their ancestors are the ultimate "source" (source of the water, trunk of the tree), and the authority of the descendants is measured in a kind of spatial relation to the source. Thus ancestors are identified with particular holy places, say the ruins of a particular ancient village, and descendants trace their relationship to that ancestor as a kind of migration outward from it, towards the "tip."

In general, people who claim a direct line to that source have the most "authority." In the Sumbanese context, this might be defined as a quantity of legitimacy which imbues certain persons, places, and performances with a right to define and construct certain historical, political, and religious realities in a particular way and have those constructions accepted as true. In Weyewa, such definitions are usually played out in the context of ceremonies I describe below.

Such authority implies certain liabilities regarding the propriety and efficacy of the verbal performances. One is the requirement that such performances be appropriately carried out. Errors in performance – failure to complete the speech event, inaccurate recitation of names of people and places, failure to reach consensus – all can result in a call for the invalidation of the event and requests that it can be repeated. In extreme cases, errors may result in supernatural retribution against those responsible – the sponsor and performers. More generally, the "sources" and/or originators of ritual performance may also, to varying degrees, be responsible for the efficacy of the event. If a ritual speech event does not result in fertility, prosperity, health, or at least cessation of calamity, then the sponsors or "sources" may be accused of leaving out some crucial detail. On one occasion, for instance, a man staged an expensive feast following the sudden death of his wife and daughter. While his crops improved the next year, several of his cattle died. He suspected that his ancestral spirits had not been forthright with him during a divination performance, and that some outstanding word of promise had been kept hidden from him, causing continued calamity. Other participants in the event suspected that he had neglected some critical element of the performance.

Divination

The first step on the "ladder" to atoning for neglect of the word is "divination." Cognate with the Indonesian word for "letter" (*surat*), the Weyewa term *urrata* "divination" stands for a verbal performance in which specialist speakers attempt to inscribe and thus "fix" the uncontrolled, disorderly communication between humans and the spirit world so that the source of misfortune can be identified, and the true "word" of promise to the ancestors can be reaffirmed and fulfilled. By using a rhetorical strategy emphasizing segmentation, differentiation, and contrast, Weyewa diviners attempt to sort out the lines of responsibility for this communicative breakdown, narrow down the number of relevant "voices," and arrive at a single "path" which explains how the victims arrived at their present predicament (Kuipers, 1990:81).

Although there is only one human performer, Weyewa explicitly describe divination as a dialogue. It is an effort to regulate and normalize communicative exchange between humans and the spirit world. In ritual speech, Weyewa vividly depict the dreadful state of emptiness and loneliness following misfortune, when they feel singled out and isolated from communication with their ancestral spirits. It is an experience they liken to that of an abandoned or orphaned child attempting to communicate with its parents. The diviner seeks to rectify this situation by reconstructing a dialogue.

In example (3) below, a specialist spokesman proposes to the ancestral spirits scenarios which would account for a misfortune, in this case the serious injury of a man struck by a motorcycle driven by a Javanese civil servant. By stretching his arms along a spear which is stuck into the ancestral house-post, the diviner receives responses to questions he poses to the spirits. He keeps his left hand tightly gripped on the handle of the spear while he stretches his right hand towards the post. If he is able to touch the post, this is taken as a positive sign, and confirmation of the scenario; otherwise it is a negative response.

In example (3) below, the spokesman begins by proposing a scene: during a "chicken and rice" feast (staged by the clients in the previous week), perhaps certain portentous signs were overlooked:

(3) *Noto-ngge hiti manna-na*   perhaps last week
   bana muttu-na manu   when the chicken was roasted
   ángu tollu kaddo ngguku-ko-wa   maybe the egg omen was not positive
   hitti manna-na   last week
   ba na-mummu-ni ngge nga'a   when the rice was cooked   5
   ángu manu ngguku wewala   perhaps the augury was not earnest

But the interesting but very characteristic thing is what he does next: after providing this scenario, he quotes the ancestors as claiming responsibility for the speech (lines 7–8), and then asks them whether they agree (line 9):

"lunggu   "I say [that]   7
lunggu-nggu"   I say [that] to you"
lummu takka-wu?   Do you say that?

Having posed the question, he gets a positive response. The "yes" he frames as a quotation as well:

"O-O," ba   "yes" if that is said   10
   lummu takka-ngga   truly by you to me
"O-O," ba   "yes" if that is said
   lummu takka-ngga   truly by you to me
wa'i takka-ko-ngge   there really is
   a zele ngadi ngara   a complicated path   15
wa'i takka-ko-ngge   there really is
   a ndeinda tungga ndara   a tangle in the horse's mane;

In lines 10–17, the diviner explains that, like a tangled horse's mane, and like a complicated path, the route to discovering the source of responsibility for the broken "word" of the ancestors is difficult. To sort out this complexity, the diviner represents himself as differentiating, sifting, and selecting among a variety of possible explanations and voices. By identifying the components and structure of participation in the calamity, he seeks to construct a dialogue which will lead to reconciliation.

To understand how the diviner has constructed the image of dialogue, it is important to examine his use of reported speech. As V.N. Voloshinov ([1929–30] 1973:117) has remarked, the "productive study of dialogue presupposes ... a profound investigation of the forms used in reported speech, since these forms reflect basic and constant tendencies in the active reception of other people's speech, and it is this reception, after all, that is fundamental for dialogue." Deborah Tannen (1986) observes that such encoding of another's speech through quotation is a way of creating and maintaining involvement in narrative discourse rather than making an exact copy of what was said. Reported speech, she argues, is in fact "constructed dialogue" (Kuipers, 1990:66).

An important verbal device through which these attributions of responsibility for discourse are acomplished in Weyewa is a category of verb I have come to call a "locutive." These verbs frame an utterance as directly reported speech: e.g.

(4) *"kako-nda" hinna-ngge Mbulu*
     "let's go," said Mbulu.

These reported speech phrases are also a way of talking about intentions. In the example above, the sentence implies that Mbulu plans to depart.

These locutives contrast with the "quotatives" described by Whorf (1956:119), which refer to a distinct class of uninflectable particles whose import is to collectivize the responsibility for speech rather than individuate it; e.g. "they say [i.e. the ancestors, not I]." Unlike Weyewa locutives, quotatives do not usually attribute agency. Nor can Weyewa locutives be considered evidentials in the sense described by Chafe and Nichols (1986). Their use does not depend on the nature of the evidence on which a statement is based, nor on the sensory modality through which the information was received. Choice of whether to use a reported-speech frame in Weyewa is not related to whether the speaker received the information through hearsay, or through visual, olfactory, or tactile cues.

An important feature of choice in the use of Weyewa locutives is inflection for speaker and hearer:

(a) inflected for speaker:
    lunggu "I say"
    lummu "you say"
    hinna "he, she it says"
    limma "we (excl.) say"
    hinda "we (incl.) say"
    limmi "you (pl.) say"
    hidda "they say"

(b) suffixes for hearer/recipient
    -ngga "me"
    -nggu "you"
    -ni, -na "him, her, it"
    -ma "us" excl.
    -nda "us" incl.
    -minggi "you all"
    -ndi "them"

A sample inflection: *lummu-ngga* "you say to me"

This form of locutive is usually postposed to the statement which is being quoted. In most contexts, it can be glossed "say," or "will." This verb is optionally inflected for hearer, or recipient.

Regarded as the "words of the ancestors," ritual speech creates an interpretive frame in which utterances are seen as issuing ideally not from the actual sender, but from a collective source – the ancestral spirits. Thus to employ locutives in ritual contexts is, in some respects, situationally and culturally marked. The use of these verbs of speaking calls attention to the issue of responsibility for communication, and makes problematic the nature of communication. Rather than collectivizing discourse the way many Amerindian *verba dicendi* do, the import of Weyewa locutives in ritual speech contexts is to particularize and individuate it. This particularizing has the effect of heightening the connotation of personal responsibility for discourse.

The high frequency of reported speech in divination suggests an image of dialogue in which participants are not in a state of consensus. It connotes fragmentation into particulate components, lack of complete uniformity and unanimity, with multiple performers expressing unique, subjective perspectives in the context of interaction. While in some circumstances, such dialogue is positively valued, (e.g. *mbyali monno mbyali*; "one side then another [speaks]"), as in litigation, marriage negotiations, and in the *zaizo* case below, dialogue can also be a sign of disorder. I recorded one placation rite in which the sponsor warned before beginning it that he did not want "each man to speak his mind" (*tekki dou, tekki dou*) back and forth in a dialogue fashion. A common image for a lack of unity is dialogic genres of song and riddling used in the neighboring districts of Lawonda and Wanukaka:

(5) *ndau kedeka Lawondakana*   do not make riddles like Lawondans
    ndau lawiti Wanokakakana   do not sing [cryptic] Wanokakan songs

Dialogue often accompanies conflict and disagreement.

In ritual contexts, dialogue is a ceremonialized form of interaction associated with instability and change in human–spirit, and human–human relationships. Dialogue does not occur in situations that emphasize completion, solidarity, or resolution but rather those that emphasize transition. Ritual dialogues, however, always seek to move *toward* solidarity. Inasmuch as the constructed dialogues of divination imply individuation and differentiation, it is something to be overcome in the search for stability and order. But dialogue is better than no communication at all. Talking to oneself is an image of utter desolation among Weyewa, a sign of total despair or even insanity. Thus dialogue, constructed through locutives, is a necessary first step toward the unification of different perspectives and voices.

Rites of placation (*zaizo*)

Following the approximately one-hour-long divination performance, the next stage is a "placation rite" (*zaizo*). These complex, all-night performances reaffirm the commitment of the clients to fulfilling the broken "word" discovered in the divination performance. To carry out these events, several specialist orators gather in the house of the victim. They make sure there is consensus on the allocation of responsibility and blame for the calamity, verbally expel the hostile spirits, and invite the ancestors back into their village and home. Like the diviner, they speak in couplets, but their rhythmically spoken accounts unfold in approximately twenty ten-minute-long speeches. At the end of each of these brief forays, a small orchestra consisting of four tuned gongs and two tuned drums strikes up, and a "singer" (*a zaizo*) sings an accompanied version of the preceding monologue up to the spirits.

The example below is typical of the orations:

(6) *ho zaizo!*	hail singer!	
mbyali monno mbyali	on each side	
a kandauka wiwi-na	the lips have talked	
a panewe nganda-na	the mouths have spoken	
"'a mattu mata	"'all the faces	5
a tanga wiwi	all the lips [agree]	
nda'iki bongga kedu ate	there are no coy dogs	
nda'iki manu basa koko'	there are no puffed-up cocks'	
lunggu"	it is said by me"	
ba limmi-ngge,	if you say that,	10
na tena.	it is true.	
ne be hinna ne	Right now	
"nda ku tura tana pamba	"I don't cultivate new rice fields	
nda ku poka ala omba	I don't clear new jungle	
tana oro leduna inna waika	this is land trod by Grandmother,	15
rutta oro iwwuna ama umbu"	this is grass trod by Grandfather"	
ka paukku Byenge Moddu-ko	[thus it is] according to the custom of Byenge Moddu	
ka papata Lero Dinga-ko	[thus it is] according to the tradition of Lero Dinga	

In this speech, after greeting the singer, the speaker goes on to register his agreement with a claim he attributes to the singer, namely, that all the other participants to the event (i.e. "faces" and "lips"; lines 5–9) believe there to be consensus – i.e. there are no coy dogs or arrogant puffed-up cocks. He quotes the singer as taking responsibility for that claim, and says he agrees with it. Indeed, he argues, the discourse here is nothing new ("I don't cultivate new rice fields, I don't clear new jungle"), and ultimate responsibility for this discourse belongs not with him, but with their collective ancestor, Byenge Moddu, Lero Dinga.

Table 4.1. *The frequency of quotatives
in three genres of Weyewa ritual speech
(average number of occurrences in sample 100-word texts)*

Divination	5.67
Zaizo	2.50
Blessing	0.00

In this second stage of the atonement rites, the reporting of speech is increasingly associated with consensus, harmony, and cosmic order. What they seek to overcome is individualized speech, and spontaneous, novel discourse. When locutives are employed, they are used to frame the speech of another participant to the actual speech event; when ancestral speech is reported, however, it is typically framed not with a locutive, but with an elaborate phrase such as "[thus it is] according to the law of Byenge Moddu" (e.g. lines 17–18).

The use of reported speech in placation rites differs from that in divination in several respects. First of all, it is apparent that locutives are significantly less frequent in these *zaizo* placation rites than in divination ceremonies. This impression was borne out by statistical comparisons and word counts of several sample, 100-word texts (see Table 1). Furthermore, while a variety of reported speech frames are represented in rites of placation, there are certain types which are more common than in other genres of ritual speaking associated with atonement, namely couplet-type quotatives such as the one framing the quote on the last two lines of the example above.

In general, these two observations seem to be related to the fact that in placation rites, the focus is not so much on finding out *whether* something was said, but on *agreeing* as to what was said, and legitimating what was said. The speakers do this by using reported speech phrases which suggest a traditional, authoritative source, and by linking their discourse to general, collective categories, not by discovering new ones. They do this not so much by attributing speech to specific individuals in the speech context (as in the rites of the divination), but assigning it to a distant ancestral spirit shared by all, or to the group of participants as a whole.

The importance of this focus on consensus can be glimpsed when we realize that the stakes of placation rites can be quite high. Following these events, a large number of cattle and pigs are slaughtered; who contributes these animals, and who must repay the debt, depends to a significant degree on whose neglect of the ancestral spirits is considered to blame for misfortune, and how that blame is interpreted.

In one series of ceremonies I attended, two rival factions of a single agnatic clan presented interpretations on consecutive nights of the neglect which caused the collapse of the temple headquarters. Singers and orators sought to expel the calamity-causing "hot" spirits from the village and invite the alienated ancestral spirits back in. An ancestral sign of approval in a bowl of ashes laid at the base of the newly rebuilt house was to indicate whose placation rites had been successful.

The sign not only meant financial responsibility, but also rights to farm rich, collectively-owned rice fields, a rare commodity on this dry island. After nine hours of singing and oration, the first night was considered unsuccessful – there was no sign. On the second night, although I confess I did not see any difference in the configuration of ashes, with a different speaker and singer, success was claimed by the sponsors and participants. While the reasons given for this success were complex, one factor consistently mentioned was the speaker's and singer's oratorical prowess. I compared the transcripts of the first and second night, and found differences not so much in the content of the discourse, but in the style of establishing the discourse's authority. The first night, the speaker's interpretation focused on the events of neglect, while in the second night, the speaker stressed the conventionality and authority of the interpretation. To do this, the latter made copious use of couplet-type locutive phrases.

Blessing song

If the sponsor of the ritual of atonement is sufficiently determined, and has the economic and political resources for it, he and his relatives may attempt to fulfill the *li'i* "word, promise" to the ancestral spirits by staging an elaborate feast. The three most important rites of fulfillment are dragging a tombstone (*téngi watu*), building an ancestral house (*rawi umma*) and staging a celebration feast (*woleka*). They are all elaborate feats of organization, involving complicated exchanges of labor, food, and material resources. None of these feasts is obligatory, and indeed only a few wealthy, ambitious, and status-seeking men manage to perform all three in a lifetime.

In these rites of fulfillment, ritual specialists re-enact a sacred lineage charter myth known as *kanungga* or "migration narrative" (Kuipers, 1990:138). These closely guarded genres consist largely of a list of place and personal names which evoke the tale of the settlement of the Weyewa homeland and its current social order. The example below is a short excerpt from one such narrative delivered in the context of a "blessing song" associated with a house-building ritual. In the final stage of the feast, just prior to the slaughter of the animals for the dedication of the houses, a spokesman – usually a clan elder – stands in the middle of the village courtyard at mid-day, and sings a song, unaccompanied by gongs or drums. At the end of each stanza, the singer prolongs the last vowel of the last word, and a chorus of young men sings the formulaic phrase "cool water ooo-ooo," at which point the singer begins again:

Nyakka-na lolungo malawo-na	Therefore they proceed like rats in a row	
nyaka-na burungo tawewe-na	Therefore they parade like a phalanx of pheasants	
ngara ndukka ole inna-nggu	all of my Mothers	
ngara ndukka ole ama-ngguuu	all of my Fathers	
Chorus: *We'e Maringi O-oo*	Cool Water O-oo!	5
Nyakka-na pa-zama-ko-ngge lawi-na	therefore the tip is matched	
nyaka-na pa-mera-ko-ngge pu'u-na	therefore the trunk is parallel	
newe wolo inna-ngge	_ these deeds of the Mother	
newe rawi ama-nggeeee	these works of the Father	
Chorus: *We'e Maringi O-oo*	Cool Water O-oo!	10
teda-mu-ni nawwa-ngge	wait for this one [named]	
Mbulu Nggolu Wola-ngge	Mbulu Nggolu Wola	
a longge-na kadippu runda rangga	whose hair is silver *dewangga* cloth	
kadippu mbali mbonu-ngeee	a piece of gold from abroad	
Chorus: *We'e Maringi O-oo*	Cool Water O-oo!	15
a mángu kangango aro umma	who has a spirit altar in front of his house	
a mángu kátoda tillu natara	who has a skull tree in the courtyard ...	

It is clear from even this short excerpt from an hour-long performance that this is a highly formalized presentation. There were no locutives or reported-speech frames, but many neatly paired couplets. It is mostly monologic, with few opportunities for the audience's voice to intrude, and challenge or modify the authority of the text (see Jakubinskij, [1923] 1979). Even though a chorus ratifies the singer's speech, and helps to highlight the stanza structure of the song, the content of the singer's discourse is not contingent in any way on these responses.

But while Weyewa describe this performance as an ancient text, the "voice of the ancestors," in fact, it too is linked to its immediate context of performance, but in subtle ways. For instance, the speaker uses particles such as "therefore" and "so" and "this" in ways that presuppose audience understandings of prior discourse contexts. More importantly, performers often elaborate on the couplet names of certain key ancestors with whom the sponsoring family can trace a close connection, so as to emphasize the close relation between them and the source of authority.

In one performance I witnessed, for instance, the singer juxtaposed the name of the ancient mythical ancestor of all of Weyewa ("Lende Nyura

Lele") with the name of his own more recent ancestor. As he described the social order of the village in which he lived, he emphasized the role of his own ancestors in its establishment, thus neglecting the names of the ancestors of a number of people in the audience. Complaints immediately arose: some critics grumbled that his account was not "true" (*nda hinna takka-ki*).

Despite such apparent creativity on the part of the singer, these monologues typically contain many disclaimers of individual responsibility for the discourse, and assurances of the ancestral origins for the speech. In one chant I witnessed, for instance, the singer employed a couplet which assured the audience that no-one was "goofing off" and no-one was "playing around," i.e. engaging in playful repartee or joking. Instead, he sang, the discourse was following in the "tracks of the Mother, the trail of the Father." The responsibility for the "words" in these final stages of performance is supposed to lie with the ancestral spirits.

While the performances of the *li'i marapu* "words of the ancestors" in the final stages of rites of fulfillment are the most authoritative forms of ritual speech among the Weyewa, this claim is not based on the exact and precise replication of the "actual words" attributed to the ancestors. To claim to do so, one ritual spokesman told me, would be regarded as an arrogant usurpation of ancestral authority. Speakers cannot claim to *be* the ancestors, but they can claim to be *close* to them by performing their words. Speakers sometimes reluctantly admit that omissions or additions do occur in these performances; one singer who heard himself mispronounce the name of an ancestor during a playback of my tape recording of his performance suggested that he might have been temporarily bewitched. He would not, however, willingly lay the blame for the error on himself.

Responsibility to ancestral "words"

In Weyewa ritual ideology, the paramount responsibility of all members of their society is to the "words of the ancestors." Only by living up to, fulfilling, and re-enacting the promises those words embody can the disorder, neglect, and calamity be held in check. Those words and promises, in their broadest sense, represent the whole of the Weyewa tradition: the obligations that persons in that society bear to one another as members of a common culture. *Li'i inna, li'i ama* ("words of the Mother, words of the Father") is an expression describing the whole of Weyewa customary practices handed down from one generation to the next. In some very real ways, by reneging on these words, an individual is not just risking misfortune. It can be viewed as an act of turning one's back on what it means to be a Weyewa.

The dominant imagery of Weyewa notions of responsibility in this ritual context are the idioms of verbal performance and gift exchange. The use of linguistic imagery extends well beyond the attribution of "words" to the ancestral spirits. The responsibilities of specific spirits and individual descendants in rites of divination are explicitly framed as acts of speaking through the use of locutives. A diviner, for instance, typically reports his client's excuse for neglect to the spirits as follows: "'I received no message from my forebears,' he said." Not only is the excuse reported as an act of speaking but the reason given for the neglect itself is the lack of a communicative act ("no message"). The way to re-establish responsibility is to renew the reciprocal exchange of acts of speaking: "May you respond to my pleadings, may you answer my arguments." To describe the client's acknowledgment of his responsibility, Weyewa draw once again on the imagery of verbal expression: "He remembers the old song."

In Weyewa ritual ideology, responsibility is not a personality trait of an individual so much as an act of exchange *between* persons. When assessing responsibility, Weyewa do not dwell on a psychological vocabulary of motive or a legalistic idiom of liability; the prevailing metaphors draw from the domain of economic transactions. The "word," prosperity, health, indeed, life itself are gifts from the "trunk" of all Weyewa – the ancestors. This generosity requires a countergift from the descendants or "tips." When forgetful descendants neglect their responsibilities, the exchange relation is severed. Diviners attempt to mend the relation by establishing verbal exchange dialogue. By identifying the angry parties, and the source of neglect, they seek to establish a structure of responsibility for the creation of exchange relations. In *zaizo* placation rites, dialogue gives way to more harmonious forms of interaction. In these, singers and orators use music and narratives to expel the harmful "hot" spirits from the village, and in exchange, invite the alienated ancestral spirits back home.

The final stage of atonement is when the promise is fulfilled with an elaborate feast. By clarifying the structure of participation and responsibility through divination, and reaffirming commitment to the "word" in *zaizo* placation rites, Weyewa are able to give the "words of the ancestors" back to the spirits in unified and monologic form, at the same time as they provide them with offerings of the meat of water buffalo, cows, and pigs. In these celebrations, the focus is not on once and for all completing a deal and thus resolving the relationship, but on setting limits to the disorder that plagued the exchanges with the spirits. By reciting the "word" in the form of the charter myth and thus sending it back, they are not expunging their responsibility, but re-enacting their commitment to its orderly reproduction.

The "fixing" of responsibility: entextualization

In ritual contexts, Weyewa are preoccupied with the fleeting and transient nature of valued sociocultural knowledge symbolized by the "word." The effort to gain control of that knowledge by "fixing" it is a process Ricoeur has called "inscription" (Ricoeur, 1976:26–9). By this he means something considerably more than the literary activity of writing with a pen or the artistic one of etching into bark, or steel, or stone; the diviner's effort to gain control of the diverse points of view following misfortune, and to assign a structure of responsibility to the human and spiritual participants to the event, might also be called inscription in these terms (note that *urrata* "divination" also means "to etch, to carve"). Likewise, when singers and orators in *zaizo* placation rites and blessing songs describe their speech as following in the "tracks" and "spoors" of the ancestral spirits – ancestral "markings," as it were – they can be seen as trying to inscribe that ancient wisdom through their speech. In short, they seek to "fix" and stabilize the responsibility for the "word."

Since this process involves an active, creative relation between discourse structures and social practices, I refer to this conversion process as *entextualization* (Bauman, 1987b; Briggs, 1988). This term refers to the ideological and linguistic process by which texts come to be more thoroughly patterned linguistically and rhetorically at the same time as they are increasingly detached from their pragmatic context of performance, such that the resulting text is viewed as somehow transcendent, or separated from the vagaries of the immediate "here and now," even though in many ways it is not. It is a performance which denies its situated character.

This process of extracting, incorporating, and objectifying words has relevance well beyond eastern Indonesia (see Kuipers, 1989). In societies in which religious ideology draws on the authority of an earlier period of revelation and cultural grandeur, and in which privileged spiritual knowledge is believed to have been communicated in a special style of language, then the concept of entextualization is useful in explaining the extraordinary convergence of textual structures and religious authority. Among the Chamula of highland Chiapas, for instance, there is a "continuum of style" in speaking resources, in which the most formalized texts are those believed to be the most ancient and authoritative (Gossen, 1974). Briggs describes a similar arrangement among the Mexicanos of New Mexico, for whom the endpoints of formality are fixed texts of hymns, prayers, and rosaries believed to have been "handed down verbatim from the generations of *los viejitos de antes* [elders of the bygone days]" (1988:327; and see also papers by Du Bois and Chafe in this volume).

The entextualization process attempts to remove the responsibility for discursive meanings from the immediate situation of performance and to reassign them. For Weyewa ritual speakers, the process of creating formalized texts representing the "words of the ancestors" is an act of reassigning personal responsibility for discourse and "fixing" it with the ancestral spirits. By calling attention to the form of their language through repetitive structures and formal patterns, they evoke earlier forms of discourse, and suggest that their current performance merely follows the "tracks" and "spoors" of the ancestral spirits.

New responsibilities

As the Indonesian government advances its modernization programs, new responsibilities are increasingly demanding the attention of the Weyewa. Over the past ten years, school attendance has become mandatory, taxation has become more efficient, and participation in government-sponsored agriculture programs is often required. At the same time, there is a declining authority for the obligations attached to ancestral "words." Many new government programs in education, agriculture, and health directly and indirectly challenge the traditional ways embodied in the "words." When the local Indonesian government built a new irrigation facility at a sacred gushing spring, this device permitted a five-fold increase in irrigable rice fields, as well as double cropping. This posed an indirect challenge, because, as some young people told me, there were no "words" of the ancestors to guide the complex new responsibilities associated with the administration and organization of this new facility; the Indonesian government official instead stepped into the breach. A much more direct affront occurred in December 1987, when most of the ritual speech events considered in this paper were officially banned by the regent of West Sumba as "wasteful" and "backward." It is still too early to assess the precise impact of this ban on ritual speech.

The new structures of responsibility do not appear to be organized around a verbal idiom or that of dialogic exchange. In classroom exercises and political treatises, Sumbanese who are trying to learn how to be citizens in this new Republic are urged to take *personal* "responsibility." This is a trait of individuals, which can be taught in schools, and expressed in public duty. It is not primarily a matter of exchange, nor something assigned in ritual contexts as a verbal act.

Since the ban on the most prominent ritual speech events, other forms of ritual speech, associated primarily with women's discourse, are acquiring a new poignancy. These spontaneous, expressive, and personal songs (*lawiti tana dawa*) are not concerned with reproducing the ancestral "word" but with evoking emotional experiences of loss, alienation, and ambivalence toward figures of authority. Often drawing on the imagery of "orphans," the songs are notable for their absence of reported speech. Although narrative in character, changes in speaking voices are generally not framed with locutives or other reported speech frames. Such ritual speech songs are not represented as part of a dialogic exchange.

The Weyewa case suggests that notions of responsibility, discursive practice, and social and historical processes are closely interrelated. Since the ban on the performance of the "words of the ancestors," some officials of the regency of West Sumba have suggested to me that it might be well to preserve the beauty of this ritual speech style in the form of elementary school textbooks for the children, or as part of folkloric performances for visiting dignitaries. This folklorization and estheticization of ritual speech, if it occurs, implies a radical agenda of compartmentalizing the "word," severing it from the social, ritual, economic, and political responsibilities it engenders. As this chapter demonstrates, verbal and ceremonial acknowledgment of those responsibilities are central to the collective life of this eastern Indonesian people.

5

INSULT AND RESPONSIBILITY: VERBAL ABUSE IN A WOLOF VILLAGE

JUDITH T. IRVINE

Introduction

Acts of verbal abuse and defamation of character provide a special opportunity for the study of responsibility and evidence in talk. Anthropologists and sociologists have long noted that a society's principles of conduct may often be most clearly revealed in the breach – through violations and disruptions of normative forms of conduct and social relations, and through negotiated claims about those violations. In acts of verbal abuse, there are two levels at which conduct is questionable: the reprehensible behavior or condition alleged to be the case and predicated of someone other than the speaker; and the speaker's act of making the allegation, an act that might itself be reprehensible under some circumstances. Thus defamatory statements bring to the fore the relationship between the referential and the pragmatic dimensions of an utterance. In which dimension is the violation or ignominy to be located? If in both, which is to be taken more seriously? How is responsibility for disreputable acts, including acts of speaking, to be allocated? As one tries to understand how a particular community attends to these problems and how its members manage and interpret particular occasions of talk, one must also consider the contexts – cultural, linguistic, and situational – that might be relevant to understanding local instances of evaluative discourse.

This chapter explores some problems in the analysis of insults and verbal defamation in a Wolof village in Senegal (West Africa). Three questions about insults are addressed. What kind of statement can count as an insult? What difference does it make how the insult is composed and phrased? How and when can speakers get away with it, i.e. vilify others without exposing themselves to retribution?

A pertinent exemplar for this kind of study, especially in an African context, is Evans-Pritchard's paper on the Zande concept of *sanza*, oblique ways of speaking that are usually spiteful or abusive. Evans-Pritchard writes ([1956] 1962:348): "How far one goes in *sanza* and what words one uses depend on the situation in which one is speaking, and most importantly, to, or about whom one speaks it. The great thing, however, is to keep under cover and to keep open a line of retreat should the sufferer from your malice take offence and try to make trouble." In other words, the forms of malicious speech are governed by the social consequences of offending, and the ways in which responsibility for a verbal message is allocated or evaded.

In examining some forms of verbal abuse and their social context in another African society I shall be following a similar line of argument. But I depart from Evans-Pritchard where he narrows the scope of his material to a particular form of malicious speech – circumlocutory and metaphorical insult – and explains it by referring to the type of society in which he observed it to occur. Zande society, according to Evans-Pritchard, has an authoritarian pattern of social relationships, and pervasive witchcraft beliefs that foster jealousy and mutual suspicion among the subjected; these social features, he proposes, account for the malice and its oblique form of expression.[1] But although Wolof society resembles Zande society in these respects,[2] verbal abuse among the Wolof is not always circumlocutory. Sometimes it is baldly explicit.

The question is: *when* is Wolof abusive talk circumlocutory and when is it explicit, and why? Keeping open a line of retreat is just as important for Wolof speakers as for the Azande. But circumlocution and metaphor are only one line of retreat among several. Others are provided by interactional strategies that manipulate participant roles and discourse frames. In other words – as I shall try to show – there is a trade-off among speech forms, participant roles, and discourse frames, such that obliqueness in one or two of these permits directness in another. Because Wolof speakers sometimes have other means of evading personal responsibility for a message, they can then phrase an abusive message boldly and still get away with it.

One of the themes of this chapter, then, concerns the notions of "directness" and "indirectness" in speaking, familiar to us not only from works like Evans-Pritchard's but especially from work in linguistics and the philosophy of language. There, "direct" and "indirect" are often treated as a simple dichotomy applied to whole speech acts, and relating to the act's politeness (or lack thereof). The material to be considered here suggests, however, that one cannot characterize a verbal act as a whole as either "direct" or "indirect," but only particular aspects.[3] The *intersection* of those aspects results in the complex evaluative judgment that deems an act "insulting" or "polite," and endows it with social consequences.

A related theme concerns the kinds of contextualization necessary to understand the communicative effects of evaluative talk. One kind of context involves the social setting of the talk in a social occasion with a particular location, actors, biographical background, and so on; another kind involves a cultural framework of moral assumptions, conceptions of the person, and notions of responsibility. Some of the recent linguistic literature on politeness has taken a universalistic approach to this second kind of context, invoking a rational-actor model to explain the relevant intentions, motivations, and responsibilities of speakers and addressees (see, in particular, Brown and Levinson, 1987). I assume a greater, though not limitless, cultural variability.

I begin by considering some general questions about verbal abuse. How can we identify examples of insult, or discover the boundaries of a domain of verbal abuse? Indeed, to what extent should we even try to do this? The next section of the paper briefly examines some features of rural Wolof society that bear upon the relationship of the speech participants and the motives and responsibilities of the insult-utterer, as constituted within the framework of a Wolof cultural system. I then turn to a particular Wolof verbal genre, a public poetry of abuse, which has a special importance in village-level politics of reputation. This poetic genre is compared with insults and abuse in Wolof conversational genres, in order to examine the relationship between the wording of the abusive message, its metacommunicative frame, and the structure of the social occasion in which it takes place. I conclude by turning briefly from insults to politeness and a more comprehensive view of socially evaluative discourse.

What can count as abuse?

Perhaps the most basic question about forms of verbal abuse is how to recognize them as such. What kinds of statement can count as insult or verbal abuse? How much does one need to know about the statement's context, cultural and situational, to assess this communicative effect?

These questions are both substantive and methodological. They are substantive because we may wish to inquire why certain utterances have the effect that they do (i.e. why they are abusive); and they are methodological because they concern the delimitation of data. Suppose, for instance, that one wanted to collect a corpus of insults, or a set of transcripts of interactions in which insults occurred, how would one know what to collect? Should one even try to do this?

One approach, sometimes found in the literature, would be to focus on the semantic content of utterances. Even without knowing anything about Wolof social life one might guess that statements like (1) are likely to be insults:

(1) (a) *J-S-, yaa jabaru mbaam; wàr ci suba, wàr ci nggoon, tàkkusaan nggai wiccax geen.*
J-S-, you are a pig's wife; mounting in the morning, mounting in the afternoon, at 5 o'clock prayers you're wiggling a tail.

(b) *Doomi taxaw sebben, kenn takkul sa ndei.*
Child of people who stand up to piss, nobody married your mother.

Along these lines Edmund Leach (1964:28) has suggested that the language of verbal abuse falls roughly into three categories: "(1) 'dirty words,' usually referring to sex and excretion; (2) blasphemy and profanity; (3) animal abuse – in which a human being is equated with an animal of another species." These types, Leach proposes, are to be found in most languages around the world, though with differences in the particular animal species involved, of course.

I do not question the likelihood of these types of statements being widely found and, where they are found, of their being abusive. Still, this categorization does not answer the question of what can count as an insult, because, clearly, it does not exhaust the possible range and variety of insulting statements. It does not, for instance, include statements like (2), although these look like good candidates for insults:

(2) *yaa xoogurló.*   You're hunchbacked.
     nyaw ngga.   You're ugly.
     ab saaci ngga.   You're a thief.
     yaa di borom digé fomm.   You're a master at promise-breaking.

It will not reveal what insults are more serious than others (compare (1) and (3)):

(3) *X-, yow, doomi gaana, sëtub dëmm yi.*
     X-, you are the child of lepers, grandchild of witches.

and it will not predict that the statements in (4) are abusive at all:

(4) (a) *J-, mbaa jaar ngga K-M-; nun kat xamu nu njaq.*
J-, maybe you passed through K-M- (village name); *we* don't know how to make gargoulettes (type of jug).

(b) *X-S-, du ma ko xas. Mbokk la.*
I'm not insulting X-S-. She's kin.

For these we need to know some cultural and situational specifics. For example, (4a), addressed to a professional potter,[4] suggests that J- has associated with potters in a different village, who happen to be of a lower rank. The ranks of potters (something like subcastes) are distinguishable by the types of jug they produce. In (4b), X-S- is of much higher rank than the speaker, so it is insulting to X-S- for the speaker to claim kinship with her.

What these examples illustrate, perhaps unsurprisingly, is that verbal abuse involves evaluative statements grounded in specific cultural systems of moral judgment. Identifying what kinds of statements are insulting depends on knowing what those moral systems are – although there may be some features in common to all or many of them as Leach's three categories suggest. Among Wolof villagers, Islam, kinship, and caste (as the system of social ranking found in the western Sudan is called in the ethnographic literature) dominate the moral framework of social action. Within this framework, a conflict between values of community and competition brings fears of witchcraft in its train.

The problem of identifying which statements are insults does not end here, however. Even with a detailed familiarity with cultural context, there can still be no hard-and-fast semantic criterion distinguishing statements that are abusive from statements that are not. That (4b) is an insult depends not on the content of the utterance itself but on the identities of its speaker and addressee. If both had been members of the same caste the statement might have been innocuous.

The situational features that can turn an innocuous statement into an abusive one also include the discourse sequence into which the statement is placed. Consider (5), illustrating the strategic use of a proverb:

(5) K.   (request to borrow a radio)
    JTI. (refusal, in which I claim I need to listen to the news very
          soon)
    K.   (moving off) *borom tubéy, ku ko nyaanee sol.*
          When somebody asks for trousers, their owner puts them
          on.

Here K draws on a standardized, epigrammatic piece of ancestral wisdom, irreproachable in itself, to call me (as we might put it) a dog-in-the-manger – someone who claims to need something just to keep others from having it. The effect depends, of course, on the listeners' construction of an equation between the trousers and the radio, and so on. But the equation itself is left to the imagination; and I am rebuked in a way I cannot challenge.[5]

(In my own defense, I must point out that the request which, in (5), I am rebuked for refusing was excessive – and not just in my own judgment. I knew, and the requester knew, that "borrowed" radios are not usually returned, since "borrowing" among Wolof implies social dependency more than it implies impermanence of the transfer. We both knew, too, that there were other villagers having stronger personal claims on my largesse. No-one was really surprised that I refused; but the thwarted requester neatly turned the moral tables on me by responding with a proverb.)

Just as the effect of the proverb depends on constructions that are never explicitly stated, so insulting someone does not necessarily require *any* verbal statement or even any overt act. The effect may depend, instead, on the absence of something expected. There are insults of omission as well as insults of commission, and it is hard to see how a corpus could conveniently represent them.

What these last examples indicate is that insults are not simply a set of statements, or a type of content inherent in statements. Instead, insult is a communicative effect constructed in interaction – constructed out of the interplay of linguistic and social features, where the propositional content of an utterance is only one such feature. In fact, the content could even look like a compliment, were it examined in isolation. For example, a certain griot (praise-singer) was hired to sing praises of a family from the Leatherworker caste. He thought they had not paid him enough, so during his performance he praised them in an exaggerated way with allegations everyone knew to be untrue, such as calling their ancestors kings and queens. The audience recognized these statements as insults, but there was nothing the Leatherworker family could do about it. How can one object to being extravagantly praised?

Conceivably, any utterance, or even silence, could have the perlocutionary effect of insult if enough other interactional features suggesting it are brought into play (or if the hearer is in a mood for paranoia).[6] Moreover, speakers routinely create and exploit ambiguities as to whether they are being abusive or not. This is one of the principal ways of "getting away with it." The problem of whether an utterance is an insult is not only an investigator's problem, then, but inevitably a members' concern as well. For these reasons we shall never be able to collect a clearly bounded set of instances of verbal abuse.

Still, a means of identifying *some* instances is to focus on native categories for forms of speech, and to invoke informant commentary that applies these labels to particular examples of discourse. One type of category is the distinctive, named genre in which insult, abuse, or challenge is composed according to special rules of poetic form. (See, for example, the literature on genres such as "playing the dozens" [Labov, 1972b, Kochman, 1983], Fiji Indians' song challenges [Brenneis and Padarath, 1975], and so on.) It is along these lines that I shall describe below a Wolof genre of insult poetry, called *xaxaar*. *Xaxaar* poems are identifiable by their form; and because they are abusive by definition, they permit us to discover how and why some of their contents are considered insulting by Wolof villagers even where the insult is not obvious to an outsider at first hearing (such as accusing someone of knowing how to make a particular type of water-jug).

But while Wolof insult poetry is interesting in its own right, an adequate account of verbal abuse must not be limited to special genres. Those genres do not exhaust the domain of abuse; and they may have a play or ritual quality making them not count as truly abusive. One must also consider everyday (not "ritual") insults and conversational examples, and seek native categories that apply more to effect (i.e. abuse) than to form. The most general Wolof label would be *saaga* "insult" (see example (8)), a term that can apply to prose and conversation as well as to poetry. There are also related terms such as *xas* "swear, reprimand," *tam* "accuse of witchcraft," *dóóral* "talk about someone untruly behind their back," *nàngamétaneko* "insult indirectly," and so on. Indeed, what insult is like in a particular society is affected by that society's full range of available forms and avenues of verbal aggression, including whether it is possible to make a public, legal accusation of, say, witchcraft.

Invoking informant labeling of this sort is essential if we are not simply to import our own notions of defamatory content and find them everywhere. Another reason, however, for considering informant commentary is that defamation is fundamentally an audience effect. It requires some listener(s) who consider the target of abuse to have been defamed or insulted. Even if this audience is limited to the target person himself or herself, some recognition of defamation as such, or at least that the target's "face" has been jeopardized, is a crucial part of what defamation is.

Despite the importance of eliciting native categories and informant commentary, however, their definition of abuse will still not necessarily include all instances. In the first place, native categories may not exactly parallel the concept of abusive, defamatory talk that we might be looking for. The Zande label *sanza*, by Evans-Pritchard's account, has more to do with indirectness than with abuse *per se*. (So, to assume that all Zande verbal aggression is indirect, or all circumlocutory speech aggressive, would be a mistake.) Moreover, regardless of how elaborately informants can discuss a category and its boundaries in the abstract, whether they are willing to label particular pieces of discourse uttered by their kin and neighbors as "abuse" is quite another question. The act of labeling might be considered abusive in itself. Finally, as mentioned earlier, even if the conceptual boundaries between categories were clearcut, the boundaries between instances need not be.

In sum, creating an ambiguity as to whether what you say is insulting or not is one of the best ways to get away with it. Another way, as we shall see, is to create an ambiguity as to whether it is *you* who are being insulting – whether you are the person who has responsibility for a particular insulting statement.

The cultural constitution of persons: hierarchy, reputation, and responsibility in Wolof society

Let us turn to the social and cultural system in which abusive talk takes place – the system in terms of which the insult-utterer, target, and audience are bound together, and which defines responsibility for acts and for utterances.

The material presented here is drawn from a Senegalese village of some 1200 people, who identify themselves ethnically as Wolof. As societies studied by anthropologists go, Wolof society is relatively large-scale and complex. The largest ethnic group in Senegal, the Wolof number over two million people. Before the French colonial conquest in the late nineteenth century, they were politically organized in a set of kingdoms whose history traces back to the thirteenth century, when a Wolof state first emerged within the Empire of Mali. The Wolof economy is based on farming, but it has also traditionally included a variety of professional specialists, such as blacksmiths, leatherworkers, fishermen, soldiers, woodworkers, weavers, musicians, Muslim clerics, and professional speechmakers. These various categories are organized in a complex system of social stratification which the ethnographic literature on the region refers to as a system of "castes."

Wolof today include urban as well as rural populations, élite as well as peasant. Their society is not static and never has been. Still, the traditional system of caste ranking, with its emphasis on endogamy and ancestry, remains important on the rural scene, including the community I have primarily lived in while in Senegal.

There are two aspects of this social system to call attention to. One is the importance of social hierarchy, birth, and ancestry, which go together. By and large, Wolof villagers take it for granted that hierarchy is both inevitable and right, deriving from a moral hierarchy based substantially on ancestry. (They may question a *particular* hierarchy or its incumbents – such as the legitimacy of the modern state, or the last kings of the old kingdoms – but not the *principle* of hierarchy.) In the traditional view, you are what your ancestors made you, at least to a large extent. Your place in society, which follows from theirs, is a place in a chain of command and an order of precedence. Notions of personal responsibility, whether in talk or in any other activity, must be seen in the light of this cultural pattern. They are not absent, but they are qualified by the hierarchical framework.

The other aspect of this social system to be specially noted is that speechmaking – that is, any elaborated or public discourse – is a caste-linked occupation.[7] The castes who specialize in this, the griots, rank low, even though they make a good income from their verbal activities. Like advertisers and public relations people in our own society, whom they resemble in some ways, griots usually do their public speaking on other people's behalf. They serve as spokespersons and intermediaries for people of higher caste, who pay them for publicity and communication services which, for the most part, they could not appropriately perform themselves. Although one of the griot castes, the *gewel*, specializes in praise-singing, griots can also be hired to insult people, as we shall see.[8] The effectiveness of the insults rests not only on their composition, at which griots are said to be more skilled than other people, but also on the supposition that a griot's talk involves a wider public – just as an advertiser mobilizes other people's opinions, or as a spokesperson represents other people's views.

The griots' activities as spokespersons, and their frequent use of "traditional" (*cósaan*) discourse forms that derive from, and invoke, ancestral forebears, illustrate the ambiguities of personal responsibility in a hierarchical society. A spokesperson is not individually responsible for the general import of a speech made at someone else's behest, nor for the general outlines of its form if the speech is cast in a traditional genre. Although individual griots build professional reputations for their verbal activities, what they are personally responsible for is the skill and faithfulness with which they execute a verbal task, not for the task's existence. Analogous statements could be made for other activities and other persons in a Wolof community, even for political leaders, whose positions and tasks are largely seen as deriving from some external higher authority. Hierarchy, therefore, as a pervasive feature of Wolof society, is to be found in the organization of many kinds of activities, including the management of verbal abuse.

Actually, it is through examining verbal interactions of this sort that some of the subtleties and complexities of Wolof social life can be discovered. The evaluative statements people make to and about their neighbors are important parts of the conduct and organization of social life. They are the stuff of reputation, on which depends so much of social success or failure – such as acquiring political offices, and contracting marriages (or losing them), as cases to be described below will illustrate. Moreover, the act of making an evaluative statement about someone is itself a social act subject to evaluation. Speakers who vilify others risk injuring their own reputations by injuring someone else's, unless some means can be found for dissociating the speaker from the act.

What injuries are possible, however – what risks a speaker runs in threatening another's "face," say, and what "face" there is to be threatened – are not identical in all social and cultural systems. In a culture of hierarchy, persons of different social positions differ in the import of what they say, and the degree of politeness, insult, or threat it represents. They are not just morally equivalent individuals occupying different social slots, but, according to that cultural framework, different moral persons; and whoever they are, they derive much of their moral authority from outside themselves. The ideology is thus a primary context affecting the social consequences of an utterance, because it frames the moral identity of the speaker (and addressee too). In terms of the Wolof system, for example, a griot may utter at least some kinds of insults to a noble with relative impunity, but also with less threatening effect unless the griot can manage to imply that some wide public is involved, as source and/or audience for the message.

I noted above that one way of "getting away with it" is to create an ambiguity as to whether it is *you* who are being insulting. In a hierarchical system, responsibility for an action is so often seen as emanating from outside the actor, that this ambiguity is probably more easily created than it would be in a system with a more morally egalitarian ideology. The implication that responsibility for an insult really rests with someone other than its utterer arises most readily in regard to low-ranking speakers, especially griots, who are spokespersons for others virtually by definition. Still, other features of the interaction are also relevant to creating these ambiguities in the allocation of responsibility for talk, as we shall see in the following discussion and comparison of the Wolof genre of public insult poetry, *xaxaar*, with conversational modes of derogation.

Xaxaar: the poetry of abuse

It is in the *xaxaar* genre, with its poetic framework and its legitimacy as a traditional discourse form, that some of the most outrageous insults can be uttered. As regards their propositional content many *xaxaar* utterances do not look ambiguous at all. Examples (1)–(3) above, which come from recordings of these performances, illustrate the point. In *xaxaar* sessions, one finds explicit insults and accusations about serious matters: graphic descriptions of sexual deformity and misbehavior; accusations of uncleanness, poverty, stinginess, thievery, violations of the rules of caste, and other crimes, including murder; and, perhaps worst from a Wolof point of view, allegations of witchcraft. How is it that people can get away with saying things like this to and about their fellow villagers? *Xaxaar* insults are *not* all merely conventional, untrue, playful or painless.

Xaxaar is the name both of a poetic genre – a kind of epithalamium of blame – and of the speech event in which that genre occurs. Its occasion is part of a Wolof wedding, celebrated when a bride moves into her husband's household. Usually the *xaxaar* session takes place during the morning after the bride's first night there with her husband. (This is not her first sexual contact with him, although the poems may speak as if it had been.) Sponsored by other women who have married into the household, especially the bride's own co-wives if any, the *xaxaar* session consists of a public performance of poems vilifying the bride and, through her, her kin. The groom and his kin may be derogated as well. Women of the whole village are invited, although in practice people attend only weddings of their own and higher castes. While men are not officially invited, many find some excuse to wander by and listen to the insults.

The co-wives who sponsor the event do not normally perform in it.[9] Instead, they engage women of lower rank, especially griot women, to perform on their behalf. Some of the poems are composed beforehand in collusion between one of the higher-ranking women and one of the griot women. Others are composed by the performers themselves. In the actual performances there are few clues as to whether a performer composed her own poem, or how much in advance she prepared it. The only exception comes at the end of the session, when a concluding verse is recited in unison by a crowd that includes both performers and sponsors.

Xaxaar sessions last about two hours and comprise some twenty poems. A poem begins when a performer steps into the arena (center of the encircling crowd) and teaches a short couplet to a group of drummers, who are to accompany her, and to a section of the audience. The rest of the performance takes the form of a solo–chorus alternation, with more and more of the audience joining in on the couplet refrain. At first the soloist merely repeats the refrain, but once the chorus has thorough command of it she inserts solo verses. At the end the drummers shift to a more rapid rhythm and the soloist concludes her performance with a little dance, sometimes perfunctory but sometimes sexually explicit. Meanwhile the bride, at whom all this is addressed, must sit with downcast eyes and deadpan expression, virtually not moving a muscle. No more than one of her kinswomen may be present to sit with her and lend her support.

In some ways this looks like a form of ritual insult, where the insults are set off by a ritual frame and do not quite count as true abuse. They are performed in a jocular manner, and their occurrence and many aspects of their delivery are hallowed by tradition. Although the co-wives get a chance to express any hostility they feel for the newcomer, that expression is also a compliment to her because it implies that she is a genuine rival for male attention and respect. And because the bride maintains her rigid deadpan no matter what is said, she is set off in a positive way from the other women. *They* are the ones engaging in questionable behavior; *she* displays utter self-control. Moreover, the hostile relations between bride and co-wives expressed during the *xaxaar* session are reversed in later parts of the wedding ceremonies.

Some of these "ritual" aspects of the *xaxaar* session provide a rationale for the occasion. For example, although *xaxaar* can be said to insult the bride, it is also claimed that the session is held in order to greet her. What would really insult her is if this were *not* done, since it would imply that she had absolutely no importance. But these aspects of the activity do not go very far toward accounting for the enormous public interest occasioned by *xaxaar*, or for the many things that are said in the poems that have little to do with the bride personally. A great deal of the subject matter of *xaxaar* poems concerns not the bride herself but the activities of her older kin and connections, who, because they are older, are more prominent members of the community. Of course, these remarks do constitute insults to the bride too, since her rank and reputation are affected by the misdeeds of her kin. But *xaxaar* poems often stretch this point, taking off into flights of derogation about local notables only distantly connected with the bride. In this sense the *xaxaar* session seems to serve more as a forum for defamation and gossip about third parties than for insulting the bride, although the two purposes cannot be separated.

The text transcribed below (example (6)) illustrates how *xaxaar* poems dwell on the scandalous histories of prominent persons. It was recorded in 1971. At that time M- G-, the bride's classificatory mother's brother, was a wealthy villager holding an important political office which he had obtained in about 1960. A few years later he had embarked on two affairs with married women, both of whom eventually divorced their husbands in order to marry him. (Although he had several wives already, he joined a Senegalese Muslim sect which permits a man to have more wives than the usual limit of four.) One of these women, A-, had been married to M- G-'s cousin Maka (the name also means Mecca) for many years. Indeed, she had five children by Maka. But during Maka's absence on a long business trip to the Ivory Coast, she became involved with M- G-, and she was so taken with him that she eventually divorced Maka – though it is relatively rare for a Wolof woman to leave a husband by whom she has had several children. The scandal attaching to these middle-aged goings-on and the attendant disruption of families and alliances did not end when M- G- actually married A-, for one of his previous wives, F- G-, angry at the situation and at having A- for a co-wife, then divorced him.[10] Eventually M- G- repudiated A-, but F- G- did not return.

(6) *Xaxaar* text:[11]

Choral couplet:

| M- G- né na, baalal ma Maka — | M- G- said, Forgive me, | { Maka
Mecca } – |

| — sa xaj gi demul. | your pilgrimage didn't go. |

Soloist:

M- G- né na, baalal ma Maka,   M- G- said, forgive me,   { Maka } –
                                                           { Mecca }

— na ma jeegal.   —let me   { have a woman   }
                                           { lease something }

(*Chorus*)

Soloist:

M- G- moo jénaxi tookër; lan   M- G-, he's a bush-rat; whatever

la mu gis jàppéwaan ni ca cop. he saw, he grabbed, to climb up
                                   on it (and spoil it).

Du ko laaj — mu dajéwoon.   He didn't ask – he just coupled.

(*Chorus*)

Soloist:

Waatal naa: moo jénaxi tookër; lan   I have caused it to be sworn: he
                                       is a bush-rat; whatever

la mu gis, jàppéwaan ni ca cop.   he saw, he grabbed, to climb up
                                       on it.

Du ko laaj -- mu dajéwoon.   He didn't ask – he just coupled.

(*Chorus*)

Soloist:

Waacal ma, alor! Boo reewee,   Beware of me, then! When you
                                      laugh,

A! Bul keeku. M- amul àndub daaw.   Ah! Don't laugh too hard. M- had
                                      no friends last year.

(*Chorus*)

Soloist:

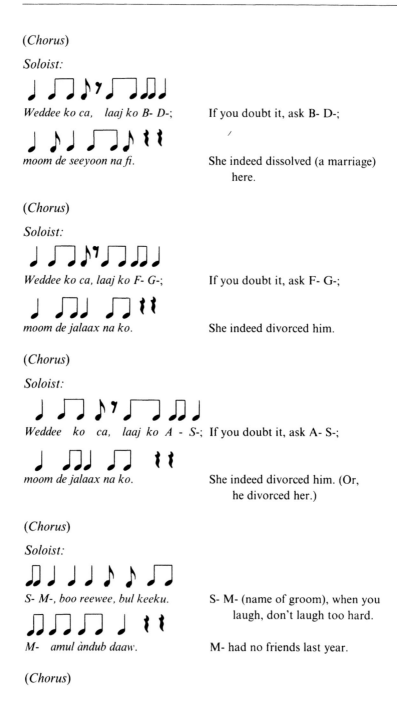

Weddee ko ca, laaj ko B- D-;	If you doubt it, ask B- D-;
moom de seeyoon na fi.	She indeed dissolved (a marriage) here.

(*Chorus*)

Soloist:

Weddee ko ca, laaj ko F- G-;	If you doubt it, ask F- G-;
moom de jalaax na ko.	She indeed divorced him.

(*Chorus*)

Soloist:

Weddee ko ca, laaj ko A - S-;	If you doubt it, ask A- S-;
moom de jalaax na ko.	She indeed divorced him. (Or, he divorced her.)

(*Chorus*)

Soloist:

S- M-, boo reewee, bul keeku.	S- M- (name of groom), when you laugh, don't laugh too hard.
M- amul àndub daaw.	M- had no friends last year.

(*Chorus*)

Notice the line in the poem saying, "Beware of me ... When you laugh, don't laugh too hard; M- (G-) had no friends last year." This is no idle threat. The *xaxaar* plays an important part in the mobilization of public opinion and the politics of reputation; one ignores it at one's peril. It is a session of public shaming, and a focal occasion for criticism of people like M- G-, A-, and Maka. At any wedding involving any connection of these parties their scandalous history can legitimately be discussed in *xaxaar*. People even look forward to these particular weddings and talk about what suitable subject matter the poems will have to work with. During the performance, the audience (in its role as chorus) memorizes part of each poem; and afterwards, people continue to repeat the poems and discuss them. Long after the wedding is over, they speculate about the details of the case, especially if a poem includes novel allegations. Even years later, a *xaxaar* poem can serve as the starting-point for conversational gossip about the people mentioned in it ("Do you remember the one that went ...?").

The characters in our particular drama, M- G-, A-, and so on, were not unaffected by the turn of public opinion against them. To try to rebuild his reputation M- G- undertook a pilgrimage to Mecca, a proof of piety few Wolof can afford. People say, however, that ten trips would not be enough and he might as well not have bothered. His political career has suffered too. Although the office he held was not taken away from him, in 1970 most of its powers were transferred to another office, which he did not succeed in obtaining. Nor has he received other offices or duties that might have passed to him, given his caste rank, his genealogical position, and his financial standing. By 1975 some villagers claimed that he had only bought his title in the first place, although it ought to have been awarded on the basis of genealogical rank and moral virtue. Had an occasion arisen when the holder of this title had to do anything really important, they said, the office would have had to be taken away from him, even though there is little precedent for doing so.

Of course, the *xaxaar* as such is not what altered M- G-'s political fortunes. That role belongs more properly to the scandal itself, of which the *xaxaar* poems are only the public expression. Other factors, too, such as M- G-'s involvement in village factionalism, have doubtless played a part. Yet several villagers remarked to me that, were it not for the *xaxaar*'s constant reminder, the scandal surrounding M- G-'s affairs might have been forgotten and forgiven long ago. In *xaxaar*, the story of M- G-'s misdeeds has taken on a life of its own that his subsequent acts cannot erase.

A-'s fate was still more unhappy – a personal breakdown which, whatever its etiology in Western psychiatric terms, villagers attributed to the intensity of criticism of her in *xaxaar* and in the gossip sessions inspired by *xaxaar* performances. A- died in 1975 after wandering off distraught into the bush.

I have gone into this example at some length in order to show that being insulted in *xaxaar* matters. To be the subject of discussion in *xaxaar* poems is not only to be defamed in public but also a guarantee of being talked about in private as well. The ritual insult of the bride is, in a sense, only a façade for a public gossip session that "counts" in a way that the insult to the bride does not. In *xaxaar*, abusive gossip is crystallized and endowed with a longevity uncharacteristic of the ephemeral utterances of casual talk. Thus in 1975 villagers could recall word for word some of the *xaxaar* poems I had recorded five years earlier.

Presumably, part of a *xaxaar* poem's longevity is due to its poetic form, which contributes to making its content memorable. The poetic structure is based on a strict metrical pattern, performed in rhythmic counterpoint with a percussion ensemble of three drums, some mortars and pestles used as percussion instruments, and hand clapping. Rhyme, alliteration, and vivid imagery also contribute, though less systematically. But besides making a stretch of discourse easy to memorize, the poetic structure of *xaxaar* can help to insulate some aspects of the message from criticism. An expression that might be deemed "too nasty" if it occurred in isolation can be buttressed by a poetic organization supporting the use of this expression rather than another. Apparently the constraints of form help to deflect complaint; "the meter made me do it," one imagines a performer claiming (though I never heard anyone actually say this).

The *xaxaar* text in example (7) shows some of these poetic characteristics especially clearly. As in the previous example, the meter of the spoken text is indicated in musical notation above the text (the rhythm of the percussion accompaniment is not given). Lines 1–4 are a good illustration of the use of imagery, while lines 9–14 rhyme *ràggal/yàggal* and *gat/sat/xabat*. Lines 15–16 use alliteration (*sa giir gee gënn sopp góór*). Puns, near-puns, and close parallelisms occur in several places: *ràggal* "scrub" / *ràgal* "be afraid" (line 9), *giir* "family" / *giir* "bucket" (line 15), *sab ci seru ndeiëm* "crowing in her mother's skirt" / *sob ci saru ndeiëm* "peering in her mother's bed" (lines 4, 8), and so forth. A particularly striking expression supported by the poetic form is the verb *xabat-xabatja* "move (as liquid) slishy-sloshily", a somewhat novel word-formation that brought shrieks of laughter from the audience.

(7) *Xaxaar* text:

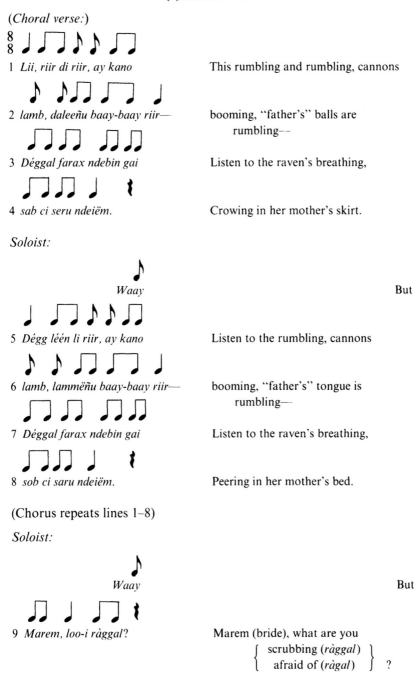

(Choral verse:)

1 *Lii, riir di riir, ay kano*   This rumbling and rumbling, cannons

2 *lamb, daleeñu baay-baay riir—*   booming, "father's" balls are
                                                                  rumbling—

3 *Déggal farax ndebin gai*   Listen to the raven's breathing,

4 *sab ci seru ndeiëm.*   Crowing in her mother's skirt.

Soloist:

Waay   But

5 *Dégg léén li riir, ay kano*   Listen to the rumbling, cannons

6 *lamb, lammëñu baay-baay riir—*   booming, "father's" tongue is
                                                                  rumbling—

7 *Déggal farax ndebin gai*   Listen to the raven's breathing,

8 *sob ci saru ndeiëm.*   Peering in her mother's bed.

(Chorus repeats lines 1–8)

Soloist:

Waay   But

9 *Marem, loo-i ràggal?*   Marem (bride), what are you
                                                    { scrubbing (*ràggal*) }
                                                    { afraid of (*ràgal*) } ?

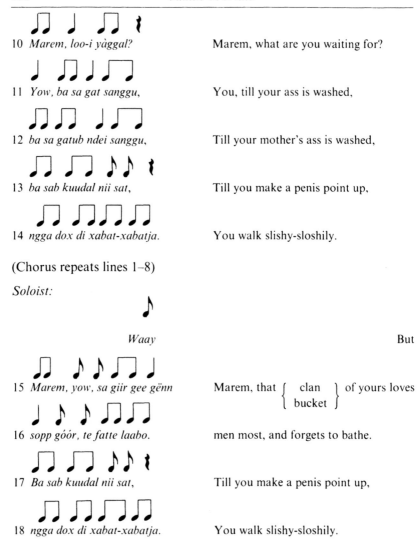

10 *Marem, loo-i yàggal?*   Marem, what are you waiting for?

11 *Yow, ba sa gat sanggu,*   You, till your ass is washed,

12 *ba sa gatub ndei sanggu,*   Till your mother's ass is washed,

13 *ba sab kuudal nii sat,*   Till you make a penis point up,

14 *ngga dox di xabat-xabatja.*   You walk slishy-sloshily.

(Chorus repeats lines 1–8)

Soloist:

                              Waay   But

15 *Marem, yow, sa giir gee gënn*   Marem, that ⎧ clan   ⎫ of yours loves
                                                          ⎩ bucket ⎭

16 *sopp góór, te fatte laabo.*   men most, and forgets to bathe.

17 *Ba sab kuudal nii sat,*   Till you make a penis point up,

18 *ngga dox di xabat-xabatja.*   You walk slishy-sloshily.

With this discussion of poetic structure we return to the central question:
how is it that *xaxaar* performers can get away with what they say? People
do get angry at having their private lives detailed in public, and at
allegations that they have committed this, that, and the other misdeed.
Yet there is little recourse or retribution, and little sense that a particular
performer could be vilified herself for having said what she did. One
woman who gave vent to anger at a *xaxaar* performer for having insulted
her became the target of even more gossip, both for the angry behavior
itself and for its implication that the insulting allegations – previously
only rumored – were really true.[12] "If she was afraid of being insulted, she

shouldn't have let her daughter get married," remarked the performer's brother to me on recounting this story – and pointing out, by implication, the inevitability of insult in *xaxaar*.

Several aspects of the *xaxaar* genre, it seems to me, protect a performer or composer from retribution. Firstly, the esthetic dimension mentioned above lends linguistic support to the use of particular insult expressions and marks the discourse as poetry, contrasting with the conversational discourse of everyday life.

Secondly, a ritual context (in effect a discourse frame) identifies the discourse not only as poetry but as *xaxaar* in particular. The genre is associated with "tradition" and occurs at a point in the wedding ceremonies that allows it to *appear* to be only mock insult of the bride, rather than real insult of other persons connected with her. These aspects of the *xaxaar* session are explicitly mentioned as rationales when the activity is criticized. In 1974, some of the local notables – men who are prime targets of *xaxaar* defamation – went to the village chief to complain about the *xaxaar* as an institution and ask him to prohibit it. But when he discussed the matter with the leaders of the village women's organizations, the women countered that the *xaxaar* session is part of tradition. It was done by their grandmothers and greatgrandmothers, so who was he to say it should be stopped? And besides, the *xaxaar* performance is a way of welcoming the bride to her new home. These arguments carried the day (though whether the chief could have successfully prohibited an activity strongly supported by the women's political organizations is somewhat doubtful, whatever rationale were given).[13]

Finally, another aspect of *xaxaar* that tends to protect speakers of insults is to be found in the social organization of participation in the performance event, in particular the diffuseness of responsibility for authorship of the message and the diffuseness of its perlocutionary target. The performers of *xaxaar* insults are at least partially absolved from responsibility because it is the co-wives who engaged their services who are the "real" senders of the insult message. The performers are only carrying out orders. As for the co-wives, even though they have arranged to hear their rival insulted they can claim not to be accountable for the specifics of what the performers say. Although the sponsoring co-wives may take part in the composition of some *xaxaar* poems, and although some individual performers may receive special gifts, it is not usually clear to an audience which woman sponsored which poem. Most of the payment is done as a group contribution, all the in-married women contributing *en masse* to all the griots. Thus no-one bears full authorial responsibility for all aspects of a defamatory statement.

Verbal abuse in conversational contexts

Let us now turn to some other kinds of discourse with which *xaxaar* insults might be compared. Can any of the "lines of retreat" identified for *xaxaar* be found in other forms of Wolof discourse?

It is useful to begin by considering what happens if speakers do *not* provide themselves with escape routes. Bald statements of abuse can be articulated without retribution in *xaxaar* only because of the mitigating factors provided by the structure of the discourse and the structure of the social occasion. Should the same or similar statements occur in ordinary conversation, with no such mitigations supplied, they would be actionable, as the following two examples illustrate:

(8)[14]

SG: *Toog léén foofu.*	SG (adult woman): Sit there (pl.).
Toog léén foofu ca	Sit there by the radio.
rajó. Bul dem, Coro,	Don't go, Coro, sit. Come,
toogal. Kaay, Koddu.	Koddu.
Koddu: *Coro, xoolal.*	Koddu (age 16): Coro, look. Yes, sit
Waaw, toogal fi.	here.
Coro: *Daa la noq de!*	Coro (age 4): Screw you!
Adults: *A! A!*	Adults: Ah! Ah!
FT: *Kooku de saaga na!*	FT (adult woman): That person has
	insulted, indeed!
Other child: *Mëcal, mëcal*	Other child: Make her chew it.
ko.	(i.e. make her take it back?)
FT: *Mu né yaa ko wax de.*	FT: She says, "*You* were the one who
	said it."
SG: *Demal toog fee.*	SG: Go sit way over there. Sit.
Toogal.	

Example (8) shows children and adults talking in the courtyard of an extended family's household on an ordinary afternoon. The adults are performing household tasks, chatting with the researcher and one another, and minding the children. The highest-ranking woman, SG, tells the children to be quiet and sit down. Trying to control a particularly unruly four-year-old, Coro, SG enlists the aid of her teenage daughter Koddu, who also exhorts the little girl to sit down. But the child reacts angrily, with an utterance that elicits expressions of surprise and disapproval from the adults, one of whom labels Coro's remark as an insult. In the end SG punishes Coro by sending her a little way from the group.

In example (9), an adolescent girl named Mati has been hauled up before a family tribunal on suspicion of having called someone a leper.

(Since lepers are supposed to have a special relation to witches, this insult comes close to calling someone a witch, perhaps the most serious accusation in the Wolof repertoire.) Notice that the girl is also suspected of stealing, or at least intending to steal, millet from the Bajaan's granary. But so serious is the insult charge that it, rather than the theft, is the main focus of the inquiry. Mati manages, however, to convince her interrogators that the insult was uttered by someone else – her companion Fatu Turé, a younger child who was always getting into trouble:

(9)

Mati: *Xanaa, yaay. Ngënte noo ànd, dem dagai Mbajaan, di – di fob ay màtt – xam ngga né –*

Mati (age 13): It was like this, mama. We [Mati, Fatu Turé, and Ndei] were walking together, going to the Bajaans' granary – uh, gathering firewood – you know –

BB: *Booba xaleu jom! – booba sabaar bi nggai wax.*

BB (elderly woman, related to the Bajaan family): This shameful child! – Millet sheaves, you mean. (i.e. stealing them.)

SG: *E, baayi ko ba mu yeggal rek. Nggai di naa lan?*

SG (middle-aged woman, political leader): Hey, just let her finish. You were saying what?

Mati: *Ndei né ko, bu la Benn Sarr jappee, di na la noq. Kii né ko, gaana gi. Fatu Turé ne ko, gaana gi – ak sa tàngk gu ñëppërël.*

Mati: Ndei said to her, if Benn Sarr catches you, she'll screw you. *She* said to her, "Leper." Fatu Turé said to her, "Leper – with your stinking feet."

(pause)

(pause)

SG: *Fatu Turé mi! Lammëñam dëfë mel né jaasi.*

SG: That Fatu Turé! her tongue is like a sword.

Eventually Fatu Turé got spanked for the offense, while Mati got off with a lecture about having allowed Fatu, later, to provoke her into a sharp response.

Notice that, although Mati utters a shocking insult here, the quotative form protects her from being held responsible for it. It is the author of an insult, not the speaker *per se*, who is to blame. In conversation, then, quotation can serve ends similar to those that are served in *xaxaar* performances by the use of intermediaries: dissociating speaker from author. Actually, Wolof use intermediaries quite often, not only in *xaxaar* sessions but also for many public or important statements. For instance, commands or requests are frequently conveyed through intermediaries even when the sponsors of those utterances are physically present (see example (10)). Although the intermediary *par excellence* is the griot, any person junior to or lower-ranking than the sponsor and addressee will do.

(10)

(a) (Visitors have arrived at the household of a high-ranking elder. Present are the elder and his son, a young man in his twenties. The elder is seated, the son and the visitors are standing.)
Elder: (mumbles inaudibly in the direction of his son. Waves his hand in a vague pointing gesture.)
Son: *Mu né, ngga toog fii.*
He says, you should sit right here.

(b) (Boy, requesting eye medicine for his aunt. The aunt is present but says nothing:)
Boy: *Daa soxlo – kii bi.*
She needs – this thing.

Also similar to the use of quotative speech and intermediaries is the use, in conversation, of proverbs (see example (5)) and other "traditional" sayings, with fixed text or structured format, which can be assumed to have been handed down from ancestral times. Again, this is a type of quotation dissociating the speaker from authorship of a message.

The use of traditional sayings – or at least the avoidance of novel ones – can also be seen in conversation (11), where one high-caste man teases another for speaking inappropriately. In this conversation, which took place early in my fieldwork (when I knew little about what made speech appropriate or inappropriate, in the Wolof view), I had persuaded S- to tell a folktale – a mode of discourse usually performed by griots, women, or children, *not* by mature high-ranking men. Traditional in some respects, folktales are improvisational in others, including the rhetorical devices and dynamic aspects of performance that are the griots' specialty. S- agreed to tell a tale but, as will be seen in the transcript below, he was then teased as a stammering loudmouth by M-, another high-caste man, S-'s patron and former brother-in-law.[15] Also present besides myself was A-, another American visitor, who did not speak Wolof. A- set up a tape recorder:

(11) (Utterances in French are represented in small capitals)

M-:	(laughs) *am piil –* PAS BESOIN DE PILES, CE MACHIN.	M-:	(laughs) Batteries – you scarcely need batteries for that thing.
A-:	PARCE QUE C'EST TRÈS SENSIBLE.	A-:	Because it's very sensitive.
S-:	AH OUI.	S-:	Ah yes.
A-:	C'EST TRÈS SENSIBLE.	A-:	It's very sensitive.
M-:	EH BIEN, *dëfë am doole, dërëm, bu mu jogé sa gëmmiñ.*	M-:	Well, because his stammering will provide the power, when it comes out of your mouth. (Spoken with broad smile and laughing tone)
	(Pause)		(pause)
S-:	*A, lééb. Lëb. Amoon na fa. Daan na am.* (pause)	S-:	"A story." "Tell!" "Once it was, somewhere else." "It used to be." (pause)
S-:	*heh-heh. Jeex na.*	S-:	heh-heh. "The end."

Having been insultingly rebuked, S- produces only the opening and closing formulas of Wolof folktales – the Wolof equivalent of "once upon a time ... and so they lived happily ever after." He quotes both the tale-teller's formulas and those that are normally provided responsively by an audience; and he omits the more improvisational tale-telling itself altogether. It is as if he were talking about story-telling rather than doing it.[16]

Some other "lines of retreat" can be seen in this conversation also. For example, the form of M-'s rebuke of S- turns what might have been a serious insult into mere teasing. One of M-'s mitigation strategies involves metacommunicative keying: smiling and laughing while delivering the rebuke marks it as non-serious. Another strategy is to separate addressee from perlocutionary target. Thus until the end of the rebuke M- is ostensibly talking to A- about S-, rather than addressing S- directly. That S- *is* the target, however, is made quite clear by M-'s switch from French, which S- controls only marginally, into Wolof, which S- speaks while A- does not. At the end of his utterance M- also switches pronominal forms, from "*his* stammering" to "*your* mouth," both referring to S-.

This conversation somewhat resembles the Barbados genre of "dropping remarks" (described by Fisher, 1976), where insulting allegations are made or implied about persons who are present but not directly addressed. The target is supposed to overhear what is said but, being excluded from the conversation, cannot easily protest. Though similar in structure, however, the Wolof use of this device (as in (11)) seems to be less institutionalized. It probably relates more closely to the much more systematic Wolof use of intermediaries, where messages are relayed through third parties. (Either way, the participant role structure in (11) is distinct from that which occurs in the type of gossip where there is no particular intention that the persons gossiped about should learn that they have been spoken of. Of course, this type of gossip is found among Wolof too, as it probably is everywhere. The distinction among these structures of participant roles rests on whether the principal perlocutionary target is someone other than the addressee.)

Finally, in ordinary conversation as elsewhere, it is always possible to shift the expression of verbal abuse away from bald assertions by using semantic mitigations and circumlocutions: euphemisms, metaphorical constructions, and forms of ellipsis or avoidance of the actual defamatory assertion, which is implied rather than stated (e.g. instead of "So-and-so is a witch," one says, "I heard that so-and-so has been seen walking around at night"). Since these strategies are essentially similar to the Zande *sanza* circumlocutions described by Evans-Pritchard, I shall not detail them further here.

Summary: insults in *xaxaar* and in conversation

In sum, then, some of the protective devices we see in *xaxaar* performances have analogues in the performance of conversational insults. One kind involves manipulating participant roles: dissociating speaker from author, and dissociating addressee from target. Ways of separating these roles include the use of intermediaries (a structure virtually built into *xaxaar*, when griot women utter insults sponsored by co-wives, and address the bride with poems about her kin and connections), and quotative forms of speech (especially frequent in conversation). In addition, both forms of discourse may (for *xaxaar*, must) use metacommunicative devices and contextualization cues to frame the discourse as something special, set off from everyday talk and not fully counting as serious. In *xaxaar* sessions this is accomplished through poetic conventions and the setting of the performances as part of a ritual sequence; in conversation it is done more often with paralinguistic phenomena (gestures, intonation, smiles, and laughter). These metacommunicative devices do not necessarily render an insult painless, just deniable.

Both modes of discourse, too, may make use of semantic obliqueness (euphemism, metaphor), circumlocution, and ellipsis. But since the *xaxaar* genre always involves a special discourse frame and a special role structure, some degree of mitigation is built in. The performer is protected from having to assume full personal responsibility for authorship of an abusive message even if it is harshly and explicitly worded. In conversation, speakers can be similarly protected only if they invoke some other devices of mitigation. If, instead, they utter explicitly abusive messages, they make themselves vulnerable to retribution.

This is not to say that Wolof villagers never do make boldly defamatory assertions in conversation, but that when they do, they take on a responsibility for those assertions that the mechanisms I have just been outlining would serve to displace. The occasions when villagers are willing to take that responsibility are governed by the hierarchical pattern of Wolof social relations, for speakers do not need "lines of retreat" in relationships where they have sweeping presumptive rights over their addressees. An adult may scold a child of the same household, for example, in terms that would be unforgivable in a peer relationship. The relevant presumptive rights are not only those one has over a dependent or a person inferior in rank, however. They include also the dependent's right to express annoyance if a request for goods, money, or protection is not granted and there is no reasonable excuse.[17]

The construction of successful insults, and the problem of getting away with them, thus concern a complex set of features of talk and context: the cultural basis of evaluative judgments; the social relationships in which they are embedded and which they influence; the forms of statements in which they are made; the metacommunicative frames and the discourse contexts that surround them; and the interactional structures in which they are performed. An account of abusive talk must consider all of these. "Lines of retreat" are to be found not only in euphemism or circumlocution, but also in other kinds of ambiguities, such as ambiguities of authorship and target, and ambiguities of metacommunicative framing (whether the insult counts as "real," or only as "ritual" or play). And in some relationships a speaker needs no lines of retreat at all, for the relationship itself provides one.

To understand an insult's success, then, we must not privilege its linguistic form to such an extent that we ignore other aspects of its delivery and setting. Though we might characterize the linguistic form as "direct" or "indirect," we cannot presume that we have thereby characterized the statement's communicative function. Some other aspect of the performance, such as its role structure, might provide a mitigation, obliqueness, or ambiguity lacking in the form of the insult statement itself. These other avenues for "indirectness" can allow such tactics as complicating the message's route from source to utterer, and from utterer to target – circumlocution in a social, rather than semantic, sense – as well as routing the message through complicating or "non-serious" frames. The trade-off among these various aspects of an insult performance implies – as I suggested at the beginning – that one cannot characterize a verbal act as a whole as either "direct" or "indirect," only particular aspects of the act. The politeness or insultingness of the act as a whole is a more complex evaluative judgment taking all aspects of the act into account.

Why call this relationship among the dimensions of an insult perform-ance a "trade-off," when in some ways the various forms of obliqueness are cumulative rather than alternative? It is true that speakers who provide themselves with as many safety nets as possible will probably be that much less vulnerable to anger or retribution from the targets of their defamation. Even *xaxaar* performers occasionally veil their insults, adding obliqueness of linguistic form to the mitigations already present in the *xaxaar*'s role structure and metacommunicative frame. But if they do so the insult loses some of its effectiveness. One such performer was booed out of the ring because her poem was "boring," and village commentary termed some similar poems "too respectful – not good *xaxaar*." Some aspect of the act must be sufficiently direct for an insult to be effectively abusive.

Outside the realm of *xaxaar*, this most direct aspect does not have to be the linguistic form. The several aspects of a defamatory act vary independ-ently, and the relationship among them is complex. For example, a man who remarked in conversation that "a great many of so-and-so's relatives have been sick lately" effectively defamed that person as a suspected witch, because the role structure and framing of his utterance were direct and "serious" even though its linguistic form was circumlocutory. Con-sider, in comparison, the (mildly) abusive utterance of a woman who laughingly teased her stout brother-in-law for being "fat and lazy as a pig" ("non-serious" metacommunicative frame, directness otherwise), and the insult offered by a griot who accused a noble woman of stinginess but addressed the accusation to her companion (oblique participant role structure, directness otherwise). Each of these examples shows a different combination of aspects that are direct and aspects that are oblique.

As I have suggested, then, our notions of "directness" and "indi-rectness" can be useful in the study of abusive talk, as long as we apply them to the various aspects of the communicative act, considered jointly, rather than applying them only to linguistic form and assuming we have thereby characterized the act as a whole. However, the question of an insult's directness hardly exhausts all there is to say about verbal abuse. In particular, to focus only on "lines of retreat" may leave unanswered some important questions about effectiveness, engagement, and interest – such as why *xaxaar* poems command so much attention, why some instances of insult and teasing are especially effective, and why some insults are repeated and remembered. From the perspective of effectiveness and engagement, rather than that of the allocation of responsibility, one might say that the various aspects of the communicative act provide many possible avenues for defamatory creativity. Choosing the right moment, the right frame, and the right interactional vehicle for an insult can be choices as creative as is the choice of its wording.

Insult and politeness

Why should one study insults, anyway, rather than forms of politeness? This paper should not be taken to imply that Wolof insult one another or gossip about one another more than do most other peoples of the world, or that all their talk is of this kind. Indeed, a great deal of Wolof talk consists of compliments and eulogy, including elaborate performances of public praise-singing (see Irvine, 1978, 1989, and 1990). A full appreciation of the evaluative dimension of Wolof discourse would have to include the positive as well as the negative. I have not attempted so full a picture here. Instead, I have focused on insults for two reasons: as a counterbalance to the proliferation of studies of linguistic politeness; and because conventions of appropriateness and sociability may emerge most clearly in the discourse of social criticism.

Much has been written in recent years about forms of politeness in language and speech (e.g. Brown and Levinson, 1978, 1987; Leech, 1980; Lakoff, 1974; and much of the literature on "indirect speech acts," such as papers in Cole and Morgan, 1975). Less has been said about insult and abusive talk, except as the absence of politeness markers, or as marginalia (cf. *Maledicta*). Some authors apparently equate *impoliteness* with *lack of politeness* on the basis of a social theory in which aggression is the unmarked condition of human relations (Brown and Levinson, 1987:1): "From a gross ethological perspective, perhaps we can generalize somewhat: the problem for any social group is to control its internal aggression while retaining the potential for aggression both in internal social control and, especially, in external competitive relations with other groups ... Politeness, like formal diplomatic protocol (for which it must surely be the model), presupposes that potential for aggression as it seeks to disarm it, and makes possible communication between potentially aggressive parties."[18] Politeness, in this view, becomes identified with mitigation and indirection; impoliteness, with directness.

In this chapter I too have been much concerned with questions of mitigation and indirection, in ways that are often compatible with Brown and Levinson's impressive study.[19] Still, a focus on verbal abuse suggests, I believe, that there can be more to impoliteness than just the absence of mitigation. The social theory cited above could be questioned (or at least amended) on its own terms; for present purposes, one might just note that it may have difficulty providing a satisfactory account of elaborations of deprecative talk. Some types of deprecation depend on creativity and novelty for their impact. To think of insult merely as the absence of politeness, or as rule "violation," or as special genres and marginalia, will fail to capture the principles on which that creativity depends, and the wide range of linguistic forms and social occasions in which it may be found.

With all the attention to politeness and honorifics, then, we have only half a dialectic. An adequate model of appropriateness must include successful insult as well as successful compliment, and insolence as well as politeness. It must also be able to show the relationship between special genres, where these exist, and the honorific, pejorative, and otherwise evaluative dimensions of ordinary talk. The study of insult thus points the way, paradoxically, to a reconsideration of politeness phenomena within a larger conception of appropriateness and socially evaluative discourse. We might further infer, too, that socially evaluative discourse of either kind, positive or negative, fundamentally concerns conceptions of responsible agency and the allocation of responsibility in talk.

NOTES

The fieldwork on which this chapter is based took place in a village in the Préfecture de Tivaouane, Senegal, in 1970–1, 1975, and 1977. Financial support was provided by the National Institute of Mental Health, the National Science Foundation, and Brandeis University. I would also like to thank the Institute Fondamental d'Afrique Noire and the Centre de Linguistique Appliquée de Dakar for institutional support, and the inhabitants of the above-mentioned village for their hospitality.

Previous versions of this chapter were presented as papers at the 1981 meeting of the Australian Anthropological Association, at the Anthropology Departments of Yale University and the University of North Carolina, and at the Center for Psychosocial Studies, Chicago. For helpful comments I am indebted to the audiences at those meetings, to Dell Hymes, and to George Joseph.

The Wolof orthography used in this paper is based on the system developed by the C.L.A.D. and officially adopted by the Republic of Senegal in 1971 (a description appears in the *Journal Officiel de la République du Sénégal*, No. 4141, 28 June 1971).

1 Evans-Pritchard writes ([1956] 1962:354): "All their social relationships have this authoritarian pattern, and it seems to me that this, as well as their belief in witchcraft, tends to produce a tortuous mind which prefers concealment and, when it expresses itself, circumlocution."

2 I certainly do not believe, however, that Wolof are specially malicious or afflicted with "tortuous minds," or that they indulge in abusive talk more than other peoples do. Much of Wolof talk is of quite the opposite character – honorific, complimentary, and even eulogistic.

3 See Brenneis (1987) for a study also arguing, though for an egalitarian social context, that "indirectness" may be accomplished in several quite different ways.
4 Potting is done by women of the *tëgg* (Smith) and *wudé* (Leatherworker) castes, especially the latter. Wolof villagers conceive of potting, smithing, and leatherworking as related occupations, and so *tëgg* and *wudé* are related castes. They are also subject to internal differentiation, however. Local *wudé* families are ranked and divided by male occupations into those who make animal harness and those who make amulet coverings; by female occupations, they are divided according to the type of pottery vessel produced.
5 What I call "construction of an equation" is similar to what Peter Seitel (1969:149) calls a "correlation": "By correlation I mean the manner in which the speaker 'matches up' the terms in the proverb with the people in the social situation and possibly in the social context."
6 Hymes (1974b:182–3) makes a similar point with regard to whether a sentence counts as threat or promise.
7 See Irvine, 1973, 1978, 1990.
8 There is a relationship with gender here: the specialists in praise-singing are usually griot men, while the specialists in insult poetry are usually griot women. The relationship is by no means absolute, however. For instance, there are some famous women praise-singers, and griot women participate in the praise-singing chorus accompanying a male soloist.
9 Exceptionally, the session may be held at night, in which case there are fewer visitors and – if there is little real scandal attaching to the family, so that the insults' content is merely conventional – some of the sponsoring women may also perform.
10 The other person mentioned in the poem, B- D-, is M- G-'s sister, a divorcee living in his household.
11 A note on the transcription of *xaxaar* texts: in examples (6) and (7), a metrical notation above each line indicates the rhythm of the spoken Wolof text, whose performance is accompanied by drums and other percussion instruments. The rhythm of the percussion accompaniment is not given, but it establishes the twelve-beat framework in which the text in (6) is uttered (in (7), an eight-beat framework). Although the durational values of the performance are precise, pitch values are not. They resemble the contours of ordinary speech, merely shifted to a high register. In this transcription, repetitions of lines are not included.
12 For some similar cases involving the boundary between "ritual" insults and "real" insults, and the possible painfulness of insults uttered in (and protected by) the ritual frame, see Labov, 1972b and Kochman, 1983.
13 The village described in this chapter has a relatively strong and active set of women's political associations, organized by neighborhood and caste. Though the traditional titles of officials in these associations recall the titles held by female officials in the old Wolof kingdoms (*lingéér* "queen," etc.), the village associations have merged with a modern political party organization. The central, co-ordinating association for the village as a whole has doubled as the women's wing of the Union Progressiste Sénégalaise, Senegal's dominant (and

at one time its only) political party. Its *lingéér* ("queen") was re-named the *Présidente des Femmes de l'U.P.S.* (She is also sometimes called *mère centrale.*) The present incumbent happens to be the chief's senior wife, but she does not owe her position to him.

Not all Wolof villages have such active women's associations, and not all villages perform *xaxaar.* I do not know how strong the connection is. Certainly the women's associations have defended the performance of *xaxaar*, and the *xaxaar* in turn plays some important role in gender politics. Although women are attacked in the poems as much as or more than men, the *xaxaar* session does represent an important avenue for female exercise of social control.

14 This conversation was recorded by Dorothy D. Wills, who visited the village in 1975. I am grateful for her help.
15 S-'s first wife, who died in the late 1960s, was M-'s sister.
16 The unusual type of "performance" of a folktale here recalls Hymes' 1981 discussion of the concept of performance and his distinction between "assumption of responsibility for knowledge of tradition and assumption of responsibility for performance" (1981:132). It is the latter that S- refuses to assume here.
17 See Irvine (1980) for a fuller discussion of Wolof requests.
18 In context, Brown and Levinson's statement is part of an argument for the sociological importance of politeness phenomena, a claim I fully support.
19 See, e.g., their call for a greater emphasis on systems of social interaction in the study of politeness phenomena (1987:47–50).

6

"GET OUTA MY FACE": ENTITLEMENT AND AUTHORITATIVE DISCOURSE

AMY SHUMAN

Introduction

The metaphor of voice, especially disparate voices, silenced voices, minority and marginalized voices, has become a familiar part of political discussions. The too easy solution, to let all voices speak, ignores the ever-present condition of interested voices with competing concerns. This chapter explores one aspect of the use of voices to protect interests: how authoritative voices are manipulated in reported speech. Throughout my discussion, I shall insist that while people challenge one another on the accuracy of their reports, the issue at stake is not accuracy but the appropriation of authority.

In exploring the interaction of competing voices, the concept of entitlement is as fundamental as that of turn-taking. Indeed, the conventions of turn-taking depend upon conventions for defending or determining the right to speak at all. If "a speaker's right to be sole talker is a claim to a turn of talk" (Moerman, 1988:19), entitlement concerns the right to make that claim. Challenges to entitlement raise questions about the ownership of talk as well as, by implication, the ownership of experience. Any claim to the authority to report on experience, to disclose, withhold, or conceal information, to be an author of events, and to repeat another's remarks is an entitlement claim.

Entitlement is more often challenged than explicitly claimed. It is not a speech act but rather belongs to culturally specific conventions of meta-communication. As part of a discourse on rights, extending from political discussions about who can speak on behalf of whom[1] to the adolescent fight stories discussed here, entitlement concerns the distribution of knowledge. More precisely, entitlement challenges are one way of shifting attention from issues of knowledge and accuracy of information to issues of distribution and relationships between people.

Whereas studies of turn-taking rely upon a concept of shared under-standings, or "what everyone knows," discussions of entitlement concern differential knowledge.[2] Probably the most familiar example of how conversation works to distribute knowledge and power in a community is research on gossip and rumor (Haviland, 1977; M. Goodwin, 1982), and the data presented here are similarly concerned with second-hand reports in which "the principal character in the story is a party who is not present," as Marjorie Goodwin characterizes similar exchanges (1982:804).

The concept of entitlement applies not only to gossip but to ownership of experience and information generally (or some might want to claim that gossip has larger implications also.)[3] To assert or deny one's entitlement is to assert or deny one's identity or one's responsibility. To claim entitlement in the name of one's position is to appropriate power. Entitlement claims involve a contest about contexts, whether the "I was there," context of personal experience or the proprietory context of "it takes one to know one." In appropriating the floor one also appropriates the context, and contexts can be multiple and intersecting. The entitlement disputes discussed here involve problematic boundaries between the context of talk and the context of the events discussed.

The boundaries between challenges to authority and challenges to accuracy are never distinct; rather there are interests at stake in resorting to one or the other in particular situations. Uses of reported speech call attention to some of the gray areas in challenges to accuracy and authority. Some of those explored here are the separation of talk about experience and experience as distinct categories, threats as a particularly interesting example of that separation, the role of the witness as a reporter of what can be claimed are someone else's experiences, the companion category of firsthand experience, varieties of referentiality (including misquoting), other means for concealing or revealing information, and, finally, the problems of appropriate context and point of view. This discussion concerns the entitlement to appropriate another's voice as a means for borrowing authority, whether in an act of complicity or resistance to that authority.

All of the following narratives, excerpted from lunch-time conversations in an inner-city junior high school, concern challenges to entitlement. While entitlement is a basic part of turn-taking in conversation, it is rarely as foregrounded as it is in these adolescent disputes where entitlement is without a doubt the most frequent kind of challenge. The narratives provide a negative example of entitlement in which entitlement challenges are always a potential threat rather than an opportunity to appropriate power.

Challenges to entitlement as part of ongoing disputes present particular problems in the relationship between responsibility and evidence. Since the disputes are ongoing, the narratives themselves shape the course of events, and what counts as evidence is constantly changing and renegotiated. Most significantly, in the adolescent disputes the accuracy of the evidence reported is far less important than the propriety of who reports it to whom.

Individual speakers rarely take responsibility for their own reports but rather, using reported speech, assign authority to some prior speaker.

In the adolescent conversations, entitlement was negotiated at two levels: at the level of face-saving, or reputation, and at the level of narrative presentation, or the use of reported speech and first-person accounts. In constant switching between these levels, participants readjusted affiliations and reframed the topics of dispute. Entitlement was not based on a set of shared rules such as the novelty of the information, the accuracy of the information, or the status of the speaker; rather, calling attention to entitlement was a means of shifting the topic and parties of the dispute. The central components of this shift in the relationship between the responsibility for speaking and topic of discussion can be discussed separately as (1) the problem of the relationship between narrative and experience in the recounting of ongoing events, (2) the distinction between spreading and containing the flow of information in a community, (3) the uses of reported speech and the status of the narrator, and (4) the consequences of either erasing, or calling attention to, any of the above relationships involving the status of speakers in relation to one another, to their experiences, to the accuracy of their accounts, or to the original speakers quoted in reported speech.

Narrating an ongoing event

The narratives discussed here were told by a group of African–American, white (Polish–American and Irish–American), and Puerto Rican inner-city junior high school students between 1979 and 1981. The texts were not elicited but were told in conversations and tape-recorded as a part of a larger study of the adolescents' use of writing and speaking (Shuman, 1986). If classified by topic, the narratives could be called "fight stories," but, as will become clear, the stories were not always about past fights, rather the story-telling situation was itself always potentially part of what was an ongoing dispute. In the world of junior high lunch-time discussions, fights did not matter unless they were recounted.[4]

These stories are useful for exploring the shaky relationship between accounts and experience that is central to discussions of responsibility and evidence. In any discussion of accounts, but particularly in accounts about purportedly actual events where the account can be part of the ongoing experience, it is important to recognize that accounts do not duplicate experiences and that experiences are only constituted as events through some representation of them.

The relationship between fights and fight stories in the adolescent community implicated a whole system of shared and exclusive information. While challenges to fight began over insults or efforts to save face, actual fights were more often battles over control of information. Far more fight stories were told than fights fought, and a fight need not have occurred for a fight story to have been told. Thus the relationship between fight and fight story, event and narrative, is not a direct mapping. Narrative and social conventions for appropriate communication together inform and constrain the relationship between event and narrative.

The conventions for entitlement – the right to tell or hear a story – require respect for the privacy of information and depend upon narrative conventions for controlling the form of appropriate disclosures. In particular, in telling fight narratives adolescents manipulated the sequential ordering of events, the use of reported speech, and claims of authorship in order to ascribe unentitled information to other speakers, or to leave information to inference.

The key to understanding the uses of entitlement in adolescent fight narratives is the relationship between talk and experience. First, fights were talked about in a different way from that in which they were experienced. Second, talking about fighting was a part of ongoing experience; talking was part of fighting, not just a report of it.

The adolescents assumed that fights followed a pattern. Since they knew how fights proceeded, they did not need to articulate each action in stories about particular fights. A narrator who told a story without outlining each sequential step could appear to know both more and less than was being told.

The adolescents' narratives were inextricably connected to the situations in which they were told: to the immediate story-telling occasion, and to the larger situation of ongoing relationships between the people involved in an incident.[5] The story-telling occasion often became a part of the ongoing dispute. Participation, either in listening or telling, implied involvement, and entitlement to involvement could always be challenged.

The stories represent a modification of Erving Goffman's concept of "replaying"; they were "couched from the personal perspective of an actual or potential participant who is located so that some temporal, dramatic development of the reported event proceeds from that starting-point" (1974:504–6). The stories could consist of threats of future hostilities as well as accounts of past minor hostilities.

The following narrative recounts a threat.[6] The telling was itself the means for communicating the threat to someone who would, perhaps, retell it to the antagonist. In the adolescent community, threats were not made directly to one's antagonist, but rather belonged to a chain of exchanges that could be interrupted, as it was in the following case, if the listeners did not do their part to retell the threat. Especially significant for the problem of entitlement, in each step of the chain, the teller's responsibility for the accuracy of the evidence shifted:

Richard:	Me and her boyfriend gonna fight?
2	Cause I was sittin' over on the table?
3	Eatin' my potato chips?
Irene:	I don't go wi' him
Richard:	And he asked for some, right?
6	I'm givin' him some
7	I took 'em outa' the bag
8	And he walked past and smacked 'em outa my hand
9	And I told him if he do it again
10	I'm gonna punch him in the face
Ellen:	And that's how it happened?
Richard:	And then he say
13	If I punch him in his face
14	He was gonna stab me, right?
15	And I told him if he do that
16	He better never come to school
17	Then he just walked away.

Three people spoke in this exchange (though a larger group, including myself, was present and, to a certain extent, paying attention). Richard narrated the event; he addressed his remarks to Ellen, and he referred to Irene, who was also present and to someone he identified as Irene's boyfriend, who was not present. As was typical of such threat narratives or previews to possible physical fights, the narrator addressed an audience that spread the news of the impending fight to both the antagonist and others. Whether or not a fight actually occurred, Richard established his reputation as someone willing to stand up for himself. His choice of Ellen as the explicit audience, and Irene as what Goffman calls an "unaddressed recipient" (1971:565) was important for managing the flow of information. Richard was threatening a fight with a boy whom he identified as "Irene's boyfriend." Irene protested, "I don't go wi' him." By her disclaimer, Irene was effectively refusing to become involved in the dispute and to carry the news of the challenge to the antagonist. Ellen was merely a vehicle for indirect communication with Irene.

Most of the adolescent stories could be categorized as fight previews rather than retrospective accounts of past fights. Fight previews reported a presumed offense, but unless the challenged person responded or the challenger persisted, the matter was usually dropped. The fight preview raised problems for its listeners in terms of entitlement. Often, as in Richard's story, the listeners were affiliated with the antagonist and felt obliged to communicate the challenge. Of course, this message would have to be reported as someone else's story, and as such would be a potential breach of entitlement. It carries the additional problem of being the bearer of someone else's bad news. In this case, the difficulty was compounded since the challenger could disavow all statements or challenge the message-bearer for not getting the facts straight. In many cases, the message-bearer was held responsible for instigating the conflict, and the antagonisms shifted from the original offense to a challenge against the person who was not entitled to talk about someone else's offense.

Threats can be categorized in Searle's classification of illocutionary acts as commissives (1976:1–23); they commit the speaker to some future course of action, in this case, a fight. However, the intention of the threat – what Searle identifies as a sincerity condition – was always questionable in the adolescent stories. The point of the story-telling may be simply to assert one's reputation as someone who fights, or to complain about the offense. One way to understand the problem the story-telling creates for the listener or witness is to see it as a transfer from a commissive into a declaration. A commissive has what Searle calls a "world to word" fit in which one wants to make actions fit the words. A declaration works in both directions – world to word and word to world – and has no sincerity condition. The transfer of the story from the person making the supposed threat to the person telling the story of the threat changes the point of view. The first can be challenged in terms of its sincerity; the second can be challenged in terms of either the entitlement to tell it or the accuracy of the information.

Spreading and containing the flow of information

Harvey Sacks discusses entitlement in terms both of rights to tell a story and of the related rights to have a certain kind of experience. An obvious aspect of entitlement concerns who has the right to talk about what. Sacks extends this concern to include entitlement to experiences. Further, story-telling occasions are themselves experiences which can be replayed; hearing a story is itself a way of having an experience which one may or may not have the right to tell. Others have approached the topic in terms of gossip and rumor (Abrahams, 1970:292; M. Goodwin, 1982).

Sacks says, "It's a fact that entitlement to experiences is differentially available." The witness to a wreck scene (Sacks' example) can claim to have suffered through the resulting traffic jam; she is entitled to an experience. But, he asks, "Do stories like this become the property of the recipient as they are the property of the teller? That is, the teller owns rights to tell this story, and they give their credentials for their rights to tell the story by offering such things as that they saw it, and that they suffered by it." He answers that a recipient of a story, who merely hears it, does not come to own it in the same way. Adolescent fight narratives demonstrate that the claim of firsthand experience is also negotiable (and not only in cases in which one can claim to have suffered through hearing a story so many times that it may be appropriated for telling). The negotiation of entitlement involves a combination of social and literary conventions: social conventions for what counts as a witness, and for what topics are tellable on what occasions, and literary conventions for how to insert one's self into a story.

For the adolescents, story-telling was not a means for gaining unlimited information about others. When false accusations were made, the accusations were simply denied, and little, if any, attention was given to substantiating the details reported in a narrative. The limits of entitlement to talk were stretched to include entitlement to observe or to know, and adolescents accepted fight challenges as the expected consequence for having trespassed the boundaries of acceptable transmission of information. Challenges were directed at the offense of speaking behind someone's back or about someone else's business rather than at communicating inaccurate information.

Certain categories of information were considered private; thus little was known about them and what was known was guarded in terms of rights to tell. Pregnancy was one such category; to say that someone was pregnant was slanderous whether or not it was true.

For example, one Puerto Rican eighth-grade girl was absent from school for a long time. Her close friends talked about her having cut school without permission. None of them had seen her either in the neighborhood or around the school, and they assumed she was going to her older sister's house every day without her parents' knowledge. One day when I was walking through the neighborhood with some of the girl's Puerto Rican friends, we met the absent girl on the street. Her friends asked her where she had been and said, "Oh you're gonna be in trouble when your mother finds out you haven't been in school. Mr. A (the teacher) was askin' about you." The girl told us that she had married her boyfriend and that she was going to have a baby. She said that the husband was 19 years old and that he had a job, so he made her stay home all day. He wouldn't let her go to school anymore because, she said, "He don't want to hear about me messin' around." A few days later, when some of the same girls from the classroom and two other girls were sitting in the school lunchroom, one of them, Leona, mentioned that Luisa, the married girl, was lucky to be home having a baby. The next day, a rumor spread that an old friend of Luisa's was going to fight Leona, the girl who had "talked" about Luisa. Leona was not entitled to report about Luisa's pregnancy.

The determination of a category as off-limits or as potentially volatile and subject to challenges of entitlement was in part a matter of the relationship between the tellers, the listeners, and the characters in the story. When the listeners were totally unfamiliar with the characters, and when the tellers could safely believe that tellers and characters would never meet, the field was potentially open for communication of details about family life. But even then, although the stories about family life were not challenged, they should be understood as unentitled tellings in which entitlement was not challenged.

Depending on the context, almost any story can be challenged as transgressing entitlement. Similarly, almost any experience can be claimed as one's own. One can claim the right to tell a story one has heard, since story-telling or story-hearing is itself an experience. However, it is one thing to claim entitlement to an experience as a witness and another to claim entitlement to a story as a hearer. Ownership of a story can imply ownership of experience.

The position of the narrator in relation to the events recounted is not a simple distinction between participant and witness to a fight. Since the fight stories were part of the ongoing quarrel, the narrator who began as a witness could develop into a disputant. Fights about a minor offense often became fights about entitlement to talk about the supposed offense. And, as in the example of Leona's report of Luisa's pregnancy, breaches of entitlement were an offense.

One incident at the junior high school dramatically illustrates the complexity of maintaining the boundaries of experience ownership and of containing the transmission of information.

In one of the few serious incidents of physical violence at the school, one girl stabbed another. The stabbing was reported in the local newspapers, some of which portrayed the event as a racial conflict, even though both of the combatants were African-American. The students objected to the news accounts, and some wrote letters to the local congressional representatives and the newspaper editors.

Letter 1:

Dear Mr. _____
I am very disapointed because of what the news and the newspaper about my school which is Paul Revere. On March 8, 1979 there was a fight on the 4th floor. One girl was persuing another girl. One of the girls was stabed and she fell backwards. As teachers and students tryed to take the knife off the girl. Other people helped the stabed girl. to get to the point on March 9, 1979 The News had in bold type BLOODY WAR. That makes it look like there was a war at my school and in my three years in Paul Revere I have never seen or heard about Anyone beeing stab. In my Three years I have had made lots of friends like Steven who is Black, Pedro who

is Spanish, and John who is white. I was hoping you would help us by calling Channel six News. It would help us a lot.

> From
> Chip
> and
> Thomas

Letter 2:

Her how it happen two girl was figthing in the room one name is Cindy and the other girl name was Sharon the one try to get the knife from Cindy so Sharon try to get it with the trash can so the trash can roll over and so she ran down the hallway so Cindy ran up to Sharon and stave her on the backside our some way elese and Sharon went to the nurse and then the nurse told the principle about it. then they to called the Policeman came and lock here up and took Sharon to the hospitol and she was crying was bad she could not breathe got and then it was time to go home the First bell Ring veryone went home and told theire mothe about it so thier mother say this is a Bad Schoal so you will be get aut their be fore April because it is so bad. School but it is not a bad shool it is nies it because the fight to much mot their this the first time some one got stave went I was thiere some Paul Revere sould not be calorized for that every one like Paul Revere. Some white people like Black people and Spanish people and black like but the dont now how it is some people like people color matter what color are you Black White or Spanish and some dont like I I like any color long I got Frient with me to play Color dont matter what color are you. Because dont got the same color dont go the same color But the inside is the sam we are sister and Brother to the leader . . .

Letter 3:

Dear Mr. _____

There was an article written in the paper March 9, 1979 about our school Paul Revere Junior High. The article was about two fourteen year old girls who were in a fight and one of the girls got stabbed.

We the kids of Paul Revere feel as though you have stretched the truth about the fight and our school. You have not only given our school a bad name but, other kids are no longer allowed to come here anymore because their parents feels that Paul Revere is a violent and dangerous place to go. You have taken away all the pride we had. We are very disappointed.

> Sincerely
> Paul Revere
> Bloody war
> Paul Revere
> Good School!

In their letters, the students charged that the newspaper accounts "stretched the truth about the fight," but more importantly, the students charged that the newspaper accounts misrepresented the school as a place of racial animosities. The author of the second letter presented what she claimed to be a more accurate version of what happened. The first and third letters charge that the newspaper accounts "stretched the truth," and that, more importantly, they tarnished the reputation of the school. Other letters and comments about the event criticized the newspapers' reliance on third-person accounts since the student interviewed by one of the newspapers was not a witness to the stabbing.

In effect, the news accounts claimed entitlement to the experience as a community event worthy of reporting, and they claimed this entitlement through what they heard rather than what they saw. The students objected that it was not a community event, and further, to portray it as a racial incident suggested that such incidents were typical at the school. The students' primary objection was that the newspaper accounts did not mention that this was the first stabbing to occur in recent memory. The failure to include this information suggested to the students that the newspaper had not presented the whole story. In other words, a second-hand report was partial, lacking both the status of an eye-witness and the knowledge of what aspects of the event should be included in the account.

All of the letters concerned ownership of experience. The first and second letters were an attempt to set the story right and were oriented toward accuracy. They both began with an account of what happened and ended with a statement about racial harmony. Their point was that the newspaper misrepresented the story both by failing to mention that such violence was rare at the school, and by not understanding that students made friends across racial groups. The third letter, written by a much better student than the first two, directly challenged the newspaper for hurting the reputation of the school.

If taken in the context of reports about fights, the letters to the editor can be seen as efforts to save face in response to challenges to one's reputation. The first two letters, in this context, were not just reports of facts oriented toward accuracy; rather, accuracy was at the service of reputation. The issue at hand in disputes about accuracy, in the context of adolescent reports about fights, was: who has the right to speak about an event? According to the students, since the newspaper reporters had gathered information from a girl who had not seen the incident, the facts were not correct and, more importantly, the story was not hers to tell. In Sacks' terms, the newspaper reporters could claim to be representatives of a community that, while not directly experiencing the events, has "suffered by it," and this is the basis of a reporter's right (newspaper reporters often insist upon the stronger word, "duty") to report it. Alternatively, the students challenged that not only were the reporters unentitled listeners, but, further, they had listened to unentitled tellers.

My concern here is not the question of the rights of newspapers to report on events, nor the boundaries between private and community experience. Obviously, the community can claim an interest in violence in schools; rather, I am concerned with the confusion between getting the facts straight and ownership of experience, and as awkward as the students' letters are in presenting their case, they provide an example of a subtle shift from the accuracy of evidence to the responsibility and ownership of evidence. In the simplest sense, the students claim that, without accurate information, the newspapers cannot make the claims that they do about the school. In a more complex sense, the connection between information and reputation depends not only upon relative points of view, but on a pre-established hierarchy of vantage points based on ownership of experience. The hierarchy in the case of the adolescents begins with the proximity of the person to the event but also includes the question of who has suffered by the event. By reporting the event in the newspaper, the focus shifted from the fight between the girls to the reputation of the school. Such shifts were familiar to the students whose fights were always ultimately about reputation rather than about whatever precipitated the fight. It was this shift that the students protested, and it is not surprising that they based their protest on the matter of the questionable distance of the reporter from the event. What looks like a challenge to accuracy is, in the context of the adolescent fight stories, a challenge of "says who?"

Reported speech

Quotation is a way of reclassifying a message. As Gregory Bateson writes, "an effect of the metamessage is in fact to *classify* the messages that occur within its context" (1979:116). He refers to the classical paradox, "Epimenides was a Cretan who said, 'Cretans always lie,'" as a quotation within a quotation. "The larger quotation becomes a classifier for the smaller, until the smaller quotation takes over and reclassifies the larger, to create contradiction" (Bateson, 1979:117). Reported speech, as a particular kind of metacommunication, raises questions of authority, referentiality, and entitlement.

The following story reports several layers of offense in which the antagonisms between the original disputants (Ginger and Rose) shifted to a fight between Rose and Mary, who had supposedly started a rumor that she wanted to fight Rose. After the fight, Rose told the story to a group of classmates standing in the hall outside the classroom. Rose had just returned from an absence following the fight, and this was the first time some of the listeners had heard Rose's version of what happened. Her account refers to the rumors that preceded the fight (quotation marks indicate reported speech):

Rose: Ginger and Allen were talking
2   and Ginger said, "I better not be around you
3   or Rose will get in my face"
4   Mary said, "If Rose is bothering you
5   I'll kick her ass"
6   So people started saying that Mary wanted to fight me.
7   So I went up to her
8   and said,
9   "I hear you want to fight me."
10   And she said she didn't say that
11   and that if she wanted to fight me she'd she'd tell me personally
12   That's when she slugged me.

In order to portray herself as the victim, Rose had to condense several events into one scenario. First, the account refers to the report of "talk" between Ginger and Allen in which Ginger suggested to Allen that Rose might be offended and retaliate ("get in her face") for talking with him. (Among the adolescents, "talking" between the sexes could imply a romantic interest. A common retort to someone making a threat was "get outa' my face.") Second, the account refers to a separate conversation in which Mary threatened to retaliate against Rose for Rose's presumed threat against Ginger. (How this threat was communicated is unexplained.) Third, Rose heard about the threat against her. Fourth, Rose confronted Mary; Mary denied the threat and then slugged Rose.

The entire account was based upon things that may or may not have happened and that, in any case, involved talking or reports of talking. Talking itself was a potential offense among the adolescents, and this case involved two of the most often contested offenses: talking with a potential romantic partner and talking about others in their absence "behind their back." The account assumed shared knowledge, an "information state" of some facts, for example, that Rose considered Allen to be her boyfriend, but omitted crucial conversational links. One of the crucial missing pieces here was how Mary learned that Ginger was concerned about complaints from Rose since, supposedly, Ginger addressed her remarks to Allen privately.

All of the reported speech used direct discourse except (6) "People started saying," and (10)–(11) Mary's comments to Rose. If we can exclude "People started saying" as a separate case since it does not identify a particular speaker, we can note that Rose used direct discourse for her own speech and for speech between others, but not for discussion between herself and another person. Rose quoted Ginger's prediction of a future antagonistic conversation with her, what Sternberg calls "prospective discourse" (1982:138).

If told out of context, the final line, "That's when she slugged me," acts as a (literal) punch-line in which Mary's actions contradict her words.[7] In the context of the story-telling occasion, the contradiction, reinforced by the use of reported speech, allowed Rose to present herself as the only person in a long chain of hearsay who was willing to confront someone face-to-face. Therefore, while Rose initiated the confrontation, it can be seen as a positive act, as speaking directly to an antagonist rather than speaking "behind her back." Rose reinforced her position by claiming that she did not initiate the physical fight; she further minimized the physical fight's significance by excluding a blow-by-blow account of it from her story.

Rose's story involved a typically convoluted set of minor offenses in which all messages were communicated indirectly (and reported as direct discourse in the narrative) until the final face-to-face confrontation, which was represented with indirect discourse. The supposed initial offense was Ginger talking to Allen, and Ginger, not Allen, was the offender. Rose let the encounter between Ginger and Allen stand as a fact, complete with a quotation of what Ginger said, but did not substantiate the possibility that she (Rose) might have been offended. She let Ginger's remarks stand as prospective (indirect) discourse and left herself out of the course of events except by reference. By beginning the story with an initial offense against herself, Rose offered an alternative to the possibility that she started the fight with her (also unsubstantiated) challenge. Rose's account presented the fight scenario as a shift from an antagonism between Rose and Ginger to one between Rose and Mary. The first offense was talking to someone else's boyfriend. The new offense was the accusation that Mary threatened Rose indirectly rather than face-to-face. Rose, in her own account, was a twice-offended victim who had never threatened anyone.

Rose reported speech from situations in which she was not present. Her story was about talking behind people's backs, or what Marjorie Goodwin calls, "he-said-she-said stories" (1990):

The speaker, as author of her own actions, has a right to monitor descriptions others make of her. The accusation is a challenge to the hearer about whether the hearer in fact made such a statement about the speaker. The structure of the utterance further locates the statement about the speaker as having been made in the speaker's absence. The act of the hearer at issue thus constitutes what the participants describe as "talking behind my back" and this act is considered an offense.

(1978:435)

In Rose's story, everyone (Ginger and Allen, Ginger and Mary, and other people) is talking behind her back. The listener is left to interpret the apparent contradiction between Mary's disclaimer:

10   And she said she didn't say that

and her slug, but in either case (talking behind someone's back or giving the first punch), Rose is the victim. The adolescent girls always presented themselves as victims who fought only because they had been pushed too far (Shuman, 1986:128). The story is a "he-said-she-said" story, a story about who said what to whom. Rose's story, her turn at talk in the conversation, ended at the point at which her retaliation would be justified. By recounting a series of conversational excerpts of reported speech, she successfully presented Mary's slug as an unreasonable instigation.

The offense of using reported speech can focus on a lack of correspondence between original and reported remarks (a problem of accuracy), or on an unauthorized use of those remarks (a problem of entitlement). In Goodwin's discussion, reported speech is one kind of "talking behind someone's back." The potential offense is less a matter of accuracy than of entitlement. In John Hewitt and Randall Stokes' terms, "Issues of substance have been transformed into issues of participants' identities" (1975:9).

The offense of "talking behind someone's back" is very often not an error of inaccuracy but an infringement on the rights of entitlement. In his essay on mimesis and reported speech, Sternberg suggests that constraints of mimesis, of accurate reporting, of "whatever discrepancies there may be between original and quote" (1982:153) are central to the social contracts of reporting – that is, the greatest challenge would be that one had been misquoted. He allows that a quotation might reproduce the actual words but still manipulate the "original meaning," but this point, too, insists upon misquotation as the primary concern. The adolescents, and, I would suspect, other groups as well, were concerned with entitlement, not only with the faithfulness of a copy in relation to an original, but with the right to use someone else's speech at all.

The significant difference between questions of accurate retelling and questions of entitlement to retell is in the ways in which they manipulate the relation between the retelling and the supposed original. The larger question of concern here, and one addressed by Sternberg as well, is that of frames of referentiality. Reported speech has several possible referents, including the situation in which the quoted speech was first uttered, and other contexts in which it has been, or could be, used. The referentiality of reported speech is further complicated by the fact that retellings are used both to reveal and to conceal information. In other words, reported speech involves not only questions of accuracy, but questions of control of the flow of information, that is, questions of entitlement.

The relationship between the story-telling situation and the events described is especially complicated in the narratives of everyday life since the story-telling can be part of the ongoing experience. Here it is important to point out that the stories about everyday experiences do not replicate experiences, they construct them. The clarity of an account, the accuracy of the portrayals, and the presentation of events in chronological order, are conventions for concealing as well as for revealing information.

The girls talked about fights more than they fought, and talking was a way of avoiding fighting. If a girl could shift the focus, as Rose did, from an initial offense, to some other offense, usually talking behind someone's back, she could successfully divert antagonisms away from herself.

The easiest way to shift antagonisms is to insert a predominant claim (one that supersedes other claims) such as entitlement. Reported speech refers both to something someone else said, and to the present context in which it is repeated. In a discussion of how tellers "smooth the way, as it were, from the conversation," Livia Polanyi refers to the problem of "demonstrating the relevance of what has gone on in the storyworld to concerns outside of the storyworld" (1985:164). The difference is that, rather than smooth the way, adolescent tellers, hoping to divert antagonisms, called attention to story-telling. Boundaries between the story-realm, "the recounting of events and acts in narrative discourse" and tale-world, "a realm of unfolding events and enacting characters" (Young, 1987:24), are always complicated by reported speech, but are especially complicated by relations between fights and fight stories.

Reported speech in the adolescents' stories served more than a descriptive purpose for telling what happened. The "he-said-she-said" sequence was a resource for retrospectively inferring a causal sequence. Rose may not have known exactly what Ginger said to Allen (and it is unlikely that she did), but she knew how to present their supposed conversation as reported speech. Statements such as "Rose will get in my face," and "If Rose is bothering you, I'll kick her ass," were so common in the everyday speech of the adolescents that they could be easily claimed as anyone's exact words.

The relationship between experiences and reports of experience, in this case, fights and fight stories, can be understood in terms of what H. G. Gadamer has called "temporal distance" (1975:124). Gadamer states that understanding requires temporal distance, the "filtering process" which allows one to stand back from experience. Reported accounts imply temporal distance, but this distance is not an "objective" stance which allows one somehow to perceive a situation more accurately; rather,

Gadamer states, "We define the concept of 'situation' by saying that it represents a standpoint that limits the possibility of vision" (1975:128). The limited vision belongs not only to the listener, who hears a story without the opportunity of firsthand experience, but also includes the firsthand experience as a limited perspective.

"Firsthand experience" is a negotiated category of reported experience rather than an observable "fact."[8] Among the adolescents, the claim to firsthand experience was often disputed as only partial knowledge, and people often claimed hearsay as a firsthand experience. These contradictory claims contributed to a climate in which disputes could escalate far out of proportion to the incidents which prompted them.

Use of the category of "firsthand" makes a claim based on the presence of a person in a situation. The fact of presence is often used to assume firsthand knowledge as though presence were responsible for the knowledge. In the case of adolescents' narratives about prior conversations, a speaker asserted as firsthand experience statements made by another person.

Reported speech is part of the larger category of transmitted words, or any discourse which refers to another source (including written sources, supposed sources such as "it is said," and authorized statements). Transmitted speech, whether described or reported, places the author in the position of recontextualizing others' words.[9] This is one of the primary means for establishing distance between author, teller, narrator, and reader or listener. In reported contemporary speech, a recognized part of the speech of the teller and listeners, the source and the narrator and/or listener belong to the same speech community. Greatest proximity exists when all three share speech. Distance begins when the teller asserts shared speech with the source and excludes the listener, or the teller excuses himself/herself from an association suggested between the source and the listener. One means for creating distance between text and listener or reader is what M. M. Bakhtin calls "authoritative discourse":

> The authoritative word is located in a distanced zone, organically connected with a past that is felt to be hierarchically higher ... The degree to which a word is recognized by us or not – is what determines its specific demarcation and individuation in discourse; it requires a *distance* vis-a-vis itself (this distance may be valorized as positive or as negative, just as our attitude toward it may be sympathetic or hostile).
>
> ([1934] 1981, 342–3)

Authoritative discourse is not necessarily lodged in persons as speakers and could include sacred words, beliefs, or other fixed texts. Bakhtin contrasts authoritative discourse, which "permits no play with its framing context" with internally "persuasive discourse," contemporary shared speech, which includes "retelling a text in one's own words, with one's own accents, gestures, modifications" (Bakhtin, [1934] 1981:342). In the adolescent world, the school, the church, and family adults represented "authorities": their discourse ranged from the contemporary and shared, to the authoritative. The "he-said-she-said" stories rarely reported the exact words of these authorities; rather, they described them. Reported speech conveyed not only the words but a sense of their performance; described speech did not insist that the words were repeated exactly as heard.

Reported speech was one of the main means available to an author for manipulating the distance in time between author, narrator, and listener or reader. Reported speech afforded the possibility of multiple voices traceable to distinct time frames. In addition, reported speech could rely upon shared understandings of the way something would be said in order to imply what someone had said. The pregnant girl – Luisa's – use of the phrase,"He don't want to hear about me messin' around," implied that her husband had said, "I don't want to hear about your messin' around." Just as proverbial sayings ascribe statements to an authoritative potential speaker, the adolescent familiar jargon provided quotable phrases, convincingly ascribed to other speakers.

The report of a past conversation located an event in time, and the narrator, as a mediator between the past conversation and the present story-telling, had the option of further distancing the narration by not accounting for his/her own position in the events. In the adolescents' oral narratives, the narrator almost always placed herself within the events as a first-person witness or antagonist. Only in reports of television soap operas and a few accounts of the non-adolescent world did narrators omit their positions as witnesses. In fight previews and stories told during an ongoing dispute, the "fight" consisted entirely of words, reports of what people said to one another, and reported speech consisted primarily of description of offenses, accusations, and threats.

Reported speech is one device for recontextualizing. The teller not only claims entitlement to use words from another source but also entitlement to recontextualize or reframe the words as part of a particular perspective, point of view, or stance.

The consequences of entitlement

Entitlement can be approached from many angles: as an author's right to produce or perform a text, as an addressee's privilege to repeat what has been told, or as a way in which texts can be embedded, self-referenced, cross-referenced, and otherwise legitimated. In any case, a discussion of entitlement in narrative exposes cultural conceptions of the categories of author, text, and reports of experience. Framing a discussion of reported speech within the larger concern of entitlement calls attention to reported speech not only as a literary device, but more importantly as a cultural convention subject to cultural negotiations for its appropriate use.

Challenges to entitlement are a means of bringing about a shift of focus from the accuracy of the evidence to the responsibilities of the speaker. One way of understanding this shift is in terms of the "double-directed" speech created by reported speech. Reported speech is a way of maintaining two voices and of manipulating the distance between them. In some models, for example that proposed by V. N. Voloshinov and Bakhtin in their discussions of reported speech, the question of whether the voices are in solidarity or in conflict is crucial. Voloshinov differentiates reported speech on the grounds of whether it adopts the dogmatism of the authority quoted, or confronts and attempts to challenge that authority ([1929–30]1973:120,138).

The adolescents' fight narratives present a different problem. The person quoted in the fight narratives was not an authority in Bakhtin's sense, and the adolescent speakers were not concerned with confirming or denying the status or authority of the prior speaker; rather, reported speech was used to deflect responsibility. In Voloshinov's terms, the speaker was a narrator rather than a character in the events recounted. While Voloshinov does not discuss the problem of the entitlement to report another's speech, the issue is not irrelevant to his argument. As an extension of Bakhtin's concept of authoritative discourse we can consider the possibility of both non-authoritative sources and alternative ways of creating conflict between sources and reporters.

Any use of reported speech indicates a distance between the quoted source, the current narrator, and the listener–audience. The significance of the distance is not a matter of only the formal configurations between participants in a speech event but rather is determined by cultural categories involving, for example, the authority to present a point of view and the ways in which events are represented. Bakhtin's model places all of the burden of distinction between uses of reported speech on the creation of distance between the source and the reporter. However, in the case of the adolescent fight narratives, distance did not have the consequence of undermining authority.

The adolescent fight narratives were characterized by the changing perspectives and positions of the participants in the ongoing events, by a precarious relationship between loyalty and responsibility in establishing a speaker's credibility, and by categories of offenses, such as spreading information considered private. Each of these characteristics corresponds to issues addressed by Bakhtin. Although conflated in Bakhtin's model, the first characteristic corresponds to the problem of competing points of view; the second corresponds to the choice of solidarity with, or resistance to, an authoritative source; the third problem, concerned more directly with the entitlement to knowledge, corresponds with Bakhtin's general category of authority. Since Bakhtin's discussion focuses on the novel, he quite understandably limits his concern to the relationship between the quoted sources and the narrator. The entire concept of authority changes when considered in terms of ongoing communication in everyday life in which, for example, a witness can compete with a prior speaker for authoritative status. An examination of the differences between Bakhtin's examples from modern novels, and the uses of reported speech by the adolescents, is helpful for understanding what is at stake in Bakhtin's claims for reported speech as a way of undermining authority. Bakhtin's central issue, solidarity with, or resistance against, the authoritative source, can be broken down into components more relevant to the adolescent fight narratives, and each of these components represents a different kind of claim, a different kind of responsibility, that a speaker can claim or deny in relation to the experiences reported.

The problem with phrasing the issue in terms of competing points of view is that it focuses on the perspective of the participants, as if the experience remains a static thing represented differently only because it is seen differently. Telling a story always involves conventions for asserting a point of view, and one aspect of the entitlement to tell a story is the question of entitlement to a certain point of view. However, the phrase "everyone is entitled to his/her point of view" (though it is said as if quoted from authority), is not entirely accurate, especially if it implies that everyone is entitled to *express* that point of view without taking responsibility for the consequences. As soon as one takes a stance, one is a participant and not an observer and must take the consequences of involvement.

Point of view is one convention for manipulating expectations and for persuading the listener to adopt certain ideas and attitudes. In an issue of *New Literary History* devoted to the topic, Margaret Gilbert describes convention as a co-ordination problem in which common-interested parties perceive at least two possible solutions to a single problem (1983:225–51). In the case of the adolescent narratives, the co-ordination problem occurs when a person relates a story about a conflict or a potential conflict with an absent person. The listeners must decide whether they are entitled to report what they have heard or whether they will be accused of talking behind someone's back if they repeat the story. E. D. Hirsch has argued, "convincing discussion of convention and context has always implicitly recognized that the real function of context is to supply probabilities of intent, nothing more" (1983:392). And indeed, I did find that the shifting status of the adolescent fight stories, both as reports of events and as part of ongoing fights, could be understood as a problem of point of view, or a kind of switch in intent between the status of the disputant, the offended person, the challenger, the witness, and the conveyor of news. However, whereas Hirsch's purpose in making this statement is to discredit interest in context and particularly social conventions for reading, I see his equation of intentionality and convention as argument for the inextricable relatedness of point of view and entitlement, authorship and authority.

In literary studies, problems of intent are often connected to problems of allusion (Wimsatt and Beardsley, 1987:112–13). The attempt, in literary studies, to recover an author's intent by tracing the allusions in the author's text raises the same questions of authority and authenticity that are raised in any use of reported speech, only the process and roles are reversed. The author who does the alluding becomes the authority, and instead of questioning the speaker's right to quote, critics use the "original" reported texts to bolster or challenge their own and one another's authority as interpreters. In both cases, reported speech involves explicit challenges or claims to truth regarding the integrity of some original and often covert claim to entitlement.

Recounting an experience in narrative form fictionalizes the experience and personalizes it. In each telling, the teller or author authorizes a particular version of the experience. Any question of the authorization to take a particular stance challenges entitlement. The question is: does the experience belong to the author? It is not a question of accuracy, but of authority and agency (Smith, 1988).

Harvey Sacks was correct to approach the matter of entitlement in terms not of privacy of the topic of a story but of ownership of the experience. What looks like privacy is actually a way of controlling information, of protecting the authority to assert a particular point of view.

If narrative genres could be identified by the way in which knowledge was organized in a story, then adolescent fight stories could be identified by their embedded patterns of concealment and their narrator's shifting point of view. An epistemological approach to conversational narrative would demand attention not only to the text itself but also to the distribution of knowledge in the adolescent community. What might appear, to the outsider and the adult, to be ill-formed narratives which fail to decontextualize, to provide listeners with the contextual information necessary for understanding a story, could then be better understood as appropriate concealments. By appropriately withholding some information and by using reported speech to ascribe evidence to other speakers, the tellers of "he-said-she-said" fight stories could hope to escape entitlement challenges.

All of the examples discussed here concern ways in which texts become permeable to social worlds: the fight preview shows how quoted speakers can be constituted as allies, or ridiculed others; the pregnancy story raises the issue of restrictions on knowledge about others; the letters to the newspaper editor raise the issue of unentitled accounts; Rose's fight story demonstrates how focus is diverted from an initial antagonism to an antagonism about speaking. In part, these texts are permeable through what appear to be the shifting positions of their narrators as firsthand witnesses or third-hand retellers, as characters in their own stories or as ancillary persons, and, more generally, as implicated or not in the consequences of the events. The appearance of shifting points of view can, and often does, disguise another set of relationships. Point of view in the sense of proximity to an event is sometimes used as an index to the accuracy of a narrator's account (a witness would be deemed more credible than someone who learned of the event second-hand, although see Philips (this volume) on the cultural specificity of such indexes). However, the issue of accuracy based on proximity also can be used to conceal the interests of speakers. In this sense, the issue of accuracy conceals the problem of agency, or who gains from distributing or withholding information and knowledge. As long as some authority could be evoked as a source of accurate information, as long as a speaker could appeal to the fact that something had been said by someone else, the focus could shift to the accuracy of reporting and could hide the complicit relationship between speaker and source.

Challenging entitlement and using reported speech together provided a complex way of shifting the relationship between speakers and the information recounted by the adolescents. They challenged a narrator's proximity to an event as a question of entitlement rather than of accuracy, and they used this challenge to deflect attention away from the topic of the account itself. Narrating an event involved attention to both face-saving (an entitlement problem) and reported speech (a way of appropriating someone else's proximity to an event).[10] They conflated these two strategies, combining the social problem of reputation with the narrative problem of reported speech.

While the adolescents were masters of shifting the focus of accusations from an antagonist to the bearer of messages about the antagonism, they became trapped in their own metacommunicative moves. They engaged in metacommunicative shifts in discourse for their own sake, or for the sake of shifting from the topic of conversation to conversation as a topic, rather than toward the purpose of understanding disputes as a category of behavior; that is, they did not, as a result of mastering "he-said-she-said" routines, become reflective about the assumed sequence of fights; they considered fights to be the inevitable result of people talking about one another and other daily offenses. Or, even when they were reflective about fight routines, and there is some evidence that they were, "he-said-she-said" routines did not necessarily lead to diplomacy but more often became incorporated into the fight sequence.

The alternatives of resisting or complying with authoritative discourse are only two of many possibilities for the appropriation of reported speech. At the very least, another appears in the possibility that the reported speech may not be constituted as authoritative. Rajeswari Sunder Rajan and Zakia Pathak offer a dramatic example in their discussion of the case of Shahbano, a divorced Muslim woman who appealed to the (Hindu-dominated) Indian courts for a larger divorce settlement and found herself in a situation in which she was asking for protection from Hindu men against Muslim men. As the authors point out:

"Protection" can confer upon the protector the right to interfere in areas hitherto out of bounds or the authority to speak for the silent victim; or it can serve as a camouflage for power politics. An alliance is formed between protector and protected against a common opponent from whom danger is perceived and protection offered or sought, and this alliance tends to efface the will to power exercised by the protector. Thus the term conceals the opposition between protector and protested, a hierarchical opposition that assigns higher value to the first term; strong/weak, man/woman, majority/minority, state/individual.

(1989:566)

I have suggested that the concept of entitlement concerns the ways in which texts are permeable to social worlds. But much more is at stake here than the use of frames or what Gilbert (1983) calls a "co-ordination problem." At the very least, entitlement claims and challenges are one of the ways in which texts are constituted by contexts. Rather than identify points of view as orientations within texts, or within readers or social communities, and rather than set up an opposition between authorities and those who are dominated, we can consider the problems in terms of claims of ownership and appropriation, and can understand discourses as framing particular kinds of subjectivity. If conventions are, as Gilbert suggests, a co-ordination problem, then the problem is not to co-ordinate realities but to comply with, or resist, the particular co-ordinated conventional discourse.

Entitlement is not just another name for either mismatches or fits between texts and contexts; rather, entitlement is one kind of metacommunication concerned very specifically with situations that call attention to the relationship between text and context. Unlike the concept of perspective, which places the burden of mismatch or fit on the spectators and leaves the object in view intact, and unlike the concept of double-directed voices, which calls attention to an opposition between authorities and those who would be dominated, the concept of entitlement does not depend upon the possibility and/or problems of fits and mismatches. Quite simply, entitlement concerns ownership of experiences and the right to represent those experiences. For some groups, such as the adolescents discussed here, entitlement became an explicitly addressed issue, but this is not to suggest either that entitlement is only a factor when it becomes explicitly discussed, or that entitlement is ever-present in all communication; rather, it is a part of those communications involved in disputing the rights of speakers to represent others.

Both discussions of competing points of view and discussions of authoritative discourse involve entitlement. In discussions of competing points of view, the problem is phrased as one of potential misunderstandings between people with different perspectives. The distance between their points of reference or horizons of understanding is said to account for their lack of shared knowledge. The argument is that people take a stand based on their biases, their point of view, and thus they cannot be objective about the knowledge at hand.[11] The concept of entitlement enters into such arguments only as a problem of taking a stand.

In discussions of authoritative discourse, the distance is configured differently, and rather than a problem of the impossibility of objectivity, it is one of the displacement of original meaning, appropriated by new speakers. The entitlement question is: who appropriates whom in whose name for whose benefit?

The concept of entitlement helps to do away with frameworks that leave original knowledge intact and instead calls attention to particular agents' interests in controlling knowledge. However, identifying these interests does not in itself resolve any problems. The concept of multiple perspectives and that of authoritative discourse are both emancipatory concepts that provide their own sorts of resolutions to misunderstandings. Bakhtin's proposal, in which multiple perspectives are maintained in a dialogue that undermines any monolithic authoritative discourse, is an example.

The concept of authoritative discourse implies both the possibility of non-authoritative discourse and the probability of conflict between discourses. In Bakhtin and Voloshinov's description of varieties of combined discourses in the novel, one kind of conflict is preferred, that in which a plurality of voices maintain their identities in a dialogue. Bakhtin praises this plurality of voices as a means for undermining authoritative discourse.

Another way to describe the appropriation of authoritative discourse is the concept of displacement, the idea that an original discourse has been borrowed by a different discourse which bears traces of its source.[12] Bakhtin's concern is the way the original discourse is represented, whether by adhering to its original integrity (in solidarity with authority), or by parodying its authority. The crucial question in borrowing, displacing, or appropriating discourse is whether the distance (Bakhtin's term) or difference (Derrida's term) between the presumed original and current appropriation has been effaced. Bakhtin phrases this effacement in terms of monologic discourse in which these is no apparent distance between an original and a quotation, and Bakhtin's project is the description of the tracks left by various forms of appropriation, specifically in reported speech. The preferred representation is one in which the tracks of appropriation are still visible, where both the voice of the authority and the voice of the person quoting are maintained.

Derrida questions the whole concept of disjunctures and displacements as a concept in which representations are always supplements to "nature" (1976:144,163) and in which the act of appropriation, the supplement, potentially transgresses some prohibition. (For Bakhtin, however, this transgression is what enables a narrator to undermine authority.) According to Derrida, speech is always already supplementary, always already imitations and substitutions (1973:224). The sign and the signified are always already displaced rather than traceable.

Derrida's position has two implications for the appropriation of reported speech. First, in keeping with Bakhtin's model, the conflict between the original and the appropriated discourse does not concern the validity of some original signified truth but concerns rather the path or trace posited as a relationship between them. Second, in contrast to Bakhtin's model, Derrida's position erases the difference between monologic conformity to authority and dialogic resistance to authority. The larger problem is appropriation and the role of the agent who represents someone else's words. In Bakhtin's model, monologic discourse, in effacing the distance between the authority and the narrator, effaces the agent, the narrator. Uses of reported speech become a game of presence and absence in which, by acknowledging the presence of authority, the speaker can make herself absent. An absent speaker takes no responsibility for the words said.

However, is it really the case that keeping both voices present, creating dialogue, is a special sort of accomplishment? Why not acknowledge the alternative strategy of making a present voice appear absent as equally dialogic? An absent voice isn't after all an emptiness, but is rather a place-holder for a missing voice. In many systems, only those missing voices that acknowledge their own absence count. But what happens when an absent voice is acknowledged in retrospect?

The adolescent uses of reported speech can be seen as an example of speakers who manipulate their own absence and presence in order to manipulate taking and denying responsibility for their words. According to Bakhtin's model, the fight stories might be considered monologic in the sense that they do not disrupt the authority of the quoted speaker. However, this isn't sufficient to explain cases like this in which a speaker has invented the original quote in order to absolve herself of responsibility. The distance in this case lies not in a lack of conformity to an authority but in leaving the marks of the trace. The speaker effaces herself from time to time, but rather than efface the traces between hers and another discourse, she makes them more apparent. It is this relationship, between apparent and effaced tracks, and not the one between present and absent speakers, that is crucial in shifting attention away from the question of the accuracy of the account, away from the knowable or unknowable signified, and instead, toward the tracks themselves.

The study of entitlement is a study of a particular kind of appropriation. Any claim to knowledge invokes claims for a relationship whether between knowers and known, knowers and deceived, or knowers and those who do not know. The concept of entitlement provides one way of investigating how appeals for accurate accounts of reality couch and conceal the question of whose reality is recounted.

NOTES

I am grateful to Katharine Young, Susan Ritchie, Judith T. Irvine, and Jane H. Hill for critical comments on this chapter.
  1 See, for example, Edward Said's discussion of colonialists' claims to speak for their subjects (1978:34–5). In a typical entitlement challenge in a film review, Laurence Jarvik and Nancy Strickland ask, "Did Louis Malle have a right to make *Au Revoir Les Enfants?*" They discuss "the propriety of a French Catholic person filming what is perceived to be a Jewish subject" (1988:72).
  2 See Aaron V. Cicourel's discussion of conversation studies and shared knowledge (1974:42–73).
  3 See, for example, a book-length discourse on the appropriate and inappropriate uses of information about other people in orthodox Jewish society (Pliskin, 1975).
  4 Rather than follow conventions for describing an ethnographic present, I use the past tense to indicate observations about the adolescent community during the period 1979–81, and the present tense for this discussion. See Wolfson, 1978.
  5 For a discussion of story-telling situations, see Katharine Young (1987), chap. 1.
  6 All personal names as well as the name of the school and newspaper are pseudonyms. The following transcription signs are used:
      ? indicates raise in intonation
      New numbered line indicates a pause.
  7 Richard Bauman finds that verbal punch-lines that use direct discourse in contrast to preceding lines using indirect discourse work

      by rekeying a situation, overturning the apparent direction of the interaction and the moral alignments and attitudes that have seemed

> to control it and establishing an ironic alternative, not as a substitute but as a coexistent perspective. The effect of the punch-line is to that extent subversive, a breakthrough both on the part of the one who is reported to have spoken it and on the part of the narrator into a kind of skepticism and relativism that takes pleasure in refusing to take ideal, normative moral expectations too seriously – a "comic corrective."
>
> (1986:75)

8 Michel Butor suggests that the use of first- or third-person narration is a literary convention:

> It is easy to show that, in the novel, the simplest, most basic narrative form is the third person, and that each time an author uses another, he does so in a sense figuratively – inviting us not to take it literally but to superimpose it on the basic form which is always implied.
>
> (1965:60)

9 For a discussion of reported and described speech, see Ryan (1981:127–55).
10 See, for example, Jacques Derrida's discussion of face, and thus orality, as unmediated proximity, "The face does not *signify*" (1978:100).
11 This position is taken, for example, by Benjamin R. Barber, "The Most Sublime Event," *The Nation*, 12 March 1990, p. 351.
12 See Jacques Derrida, *Speech Phenomena and Other Essays*, p. 156.

7
REPORTED SPEECH AND AFFECT ON NUKULAELAE ATOLL

NIKO BESNIER

Introduction

Reported speech is both the representation of linguistic actions and commentaries about these actions. This chapter investigates how the "representation" and the "commentary" may interact with each other in the structure and use of reported speech on Nukulaelae Atoll, a Polynesian community. In this study, I address the following questions: (a) What are the different ways of expressing reported speech? (b) What are the preferred strategies for reporting speech? (c) How is affect communicated through reported speech? (d) How do the quoted speaker and the quoting speaker share responsibility for the information communicated in reported speech? (e) How do all the above factors reflect the speech community's attitudes towards the speaker's responsibility in talk? I shall show that, on Nukulaelae, a tension exists between the (perhaps universal) need to communicate some affect in everyday communication and the local norms against communicating affect overtly. This tension is resolved through the simultaneous use, in reporting activities, of overt keys that are affectively neutral, and covert keys that are high in affective content. The strategic choice of keys in turn correlates with relative degrees of evidentiality: affect is communicated through keys which allow speakers to present themselves as minimally accountable for the content of their talk.

Reported speech

Reported speech has been studied by researchers from a variety of perspectives. Literary critics have looked at the significance of reported speech for questions of authorship and narratorship. Linguists and philosophers of language have concentrated on technical structural questions. Until recently, anthropologists and ethnographers of speaking had paid little attention to reported speech as a social tool, despite the importance of reporting activities and other types of "replayings" (Goffman, 1974:530) in ethnography.

Early in this century, Bakhtin ([1934] 1981) and his collaborators, Voloshinov ([1929] 1978), and Medvedev ([1928] 1985),[1] in the process of laying the foundation of a Marxist theory of literary semiotics, addressed the literary problem of the relationship between narrator and text. Bakhtin was concerned with the ways in which the narrating voice and the narrated voice influence each other in literary discourse. He established correlations between various reported speech strategies and their semiotic functions. Consider, for example, the following contrast between directly quoted discourse (sentence (1)a) and indirectly quoted discourse (sentence (1)b):

(1) a.   She stopped and asked, "Is that the car I saw here yesterday?"

    b.   She stopped and asked if that was the car she had seen there the day before.

(adapted from Pascal, 1977:8)

According to Bakhtin and his followers, the use of direct quotes reflects a concern for the integrity and authenticity of the quoted message (Voloshinov, 1929[1978]). Direct quotation is characteristic of a *linear style*, in which the author of the quote and its reporter are kept maximally distinct from each other. Indirect quotes, in contrast, are characteristic of a *pictorial style*. The indirect quote merges with the ongoing discourse, thus allowing for greater manipulation of the meaning and interpretation of the quote. The interplay of voices in reported speech is an instance of the "heteroglossia" that Bakhtin and his followers claim permeates all social discourse.[2]

Bakhtin shows how the quoting styles that novelists give to their characters are semiotically significant. The choice of a quoting strategy indexes how reporters wish their audiences to feel about the meaning and significance of the quote. Furthermore, Bakhtin claims, the range of grammaticalized reported speech strategies, which differs widely from language to language, reflects speech communities' ideologies of communication, knowledge, and interaction.

To date, few linguists and anthropologists have taken up the challenge of testing Bakhtin's hypothesis. While Bakhtin's theoretical agenda has informed the foundation of the "reflexive" or "critical" school of anthropology (e.g. Clifford, 1988), it has yet to influence the more microscopic concerns of the field, even though the notions of "voice" and "heteroglossia" are useful tools in the analysis of ethnographic data (Trawick, 1988). Linguistic approaches to reported-speech phenomena have largely been confined to the study of finer structural questions: whether indirect quotes can be derived from direct quotes (Banfield, 1973, 1982; Kuroda, 1973; Wierzbicka, 1974); the extent to which quotes are structurally and semantically integrated into the framing discourse structurally or semantically (Davidson, 1984; Partee, 1973); whether a quote functions grammatically as the direct object of the quotation verb (Munro, 1982); whether lexico-semantic universals of speech-act verbs can be established (Verschueren, 1984); and when and why tense and deixis shift in indirect quotation (Comrie, 1986). With a few exceptions (e.g. Silverstein, 1985; Tannen, 1986, 1988; various contributions to this volume), linguists have focused their attention primarily on the grammatical structure of reported speech construction, rather than on the meaning of reported speech in linguistic performance.

Affect and evidence

The grammatical bias which characterizes this literature is a symptom of the neglect by linguists of the affective component of language. That affect plays a leading role in language rests on the recognition that, in addition to its referential and social communicative functions, language communicates feelings, moods, dispositions, and attitudes toward the propositional content of the message, the situation, and the social context of the interaction (Irvine, 1982a; Ochs, 1982, 1986).[3] Affective meaning is thus a "metacommunicative commentary on a referential proposition" (Irvine, 1982a:32). Affect may be lexicalized (i.e. communicated through lexical devices whose sole purpose is to communicate affect); but it may also be communicated, less overtly, in the prosodic structure of an utterance (through intonation or stress, for instance), or in its syntactic structure (through the marking of pragmatic salience, for example). The communication of affect is thus a multi-channel phenomenon (Irvine, 1982a:38–9), which is intertwined in a complex manner with referential and social meanings.

The channels through which affect may be communicated have different characteristics. An affective interjection (e.g. "alas!" "hurray!") communicates affect more *transparently* (Silverstein, 1981) than syntactic or prosodic devices with equivalent meanings, in the sense that an interjection is typically recognized, in many folk linguistic ideologies, as the primary locus of affect in language. Thus an interjection of excitement or sorrow will place the speaker's excitement or sorrow on record, while an excited tone of voice is likely to be less readily identifiable as the vehicle through which these emotional states are communicated. Furthermore, there is a correlation between relative transparency and communicative efficiency. The less transparent an affect-communicating strategy is, the more efficiently the affect will be communicated. For example, the primary function of the syntactic structure of a sentence is to communicate referential meaning (which noun-phrase is the agent, which is the patient, etc.). If an affective component is superposed on this referential function, it will be processed by the recipient at the same time as the referential component; affect, thus, will come "for free." In contrast, an affective interjection does not have a significant referential function and thus will be perceived solely as an affect-communicating device. In the first instance, the affective component is processed less consciously than in the second instance, and often lies outside the limits of awareness (Silverstein, 1981) of both encoder and decoder. Thus the choice of "keys" (Goffman, 1974) that speakers of a language make in communicating affective meaning is a loaded factor in and of itself.

To the dimension of transparency we can add a further dimension, that of evidentiality. Evidentiality, which may be defined, for the purpose of this discussion, as the expression of "the kinds of evidence a person has for making factual claims" (Anderson, 1986:273), is recognized as an important component of speech reporting by such scholars as Goffman:

> When a speaker employs conventional brackets to warn us that what he is saying is meant to be taken [. . .] as mere repeating of words said by someone else, then it is clear that he means to stand in a relation of reduced personal responsibility for what he is saying.
>
> [1974:512]

It is important to distinguish the different components of "what a speaker is saying" and to understand patterns of preferred usages in the context of the speech community's norms of responsibility and accountability.

In this chapter, I shall attempt to establish explanatory links between the structure and the cultural meaning of reported speech. I shall show that the choice of channels for the communication of affect in reported speech is a reflection of local theories of information, authorship, and meaning.

Reports and authorship on Nukulaelae

This section presents the ethnographic background of this study. I stress the cultural salience of speech-reporting activities on Nukulaelae, and then present the main feature of Nukulaelae ideologies regarding the nature of information, of authorship, and of epistemic authority. These remarks are based both on ethnographic observations and on inferences from discourse data. I shall show that reported speech is a culturally salient speech device on Nukulaelae. It is acquired early and is used in a wide variety of contexts. I shall show also that Nukulaelae islanders avoid issuing interpretations and inferences from other people's behavior and speech. Furthermore, knowledge on Nukulaelae is owned communally, and the individual has little power to modify that knowledge. Finally, I shall point out that the boundary between linguistic action and social action is not clearly defined on Nukulaelae.

My data were collected on Nukulaelae, a small and isolated atoll of the

Tuvalu group (formerly the Ellice Islands). Its population of 310 is predominantly Polynesian in origin, culture, and social organization. Nukulaelae social structure is one of the most egalitarian and least stratified in Polynesia.

Cultural salience of reported speech

Speech reporting plays an important role in everyday interactions on Nukulaelae. It plays a crucial role in gossip and story-telling, two highly salient speech events. Typically, Nukulaelae conversationalists construct their stories almost entirely as a string of reported turns:[4]

(2) *Koo fakafetaui ifo Samasone au. 'sss!*
     Samasone came down to meet me. (He said,) 'Hey!
     Au e ssili atu hua kia koe i te:: fekau nei a: Luisa
     I just want to ask you about Luisa's request
     ne hai mai kee taaofi koe i te:: te faamanatuga.' 'Io?
     that you should be prevented from (taking) communion." (I said,) 'Oh?
     I te aa?' Me i te tala teelaa ne hai i: i: i
     And why?' (He said that) it was about the story to the effect
     futi kolaa o: laatou ne taa nee au.
     tha:t tha:t I chopped down some banana trees of theirs.
     Aku muna 'ttaa, a ko au nei e- e(i) he tino fakavalevale?'
     I said, 'Come on, am I crazy or what?'

Reported speech is used as a story-telling strategy even when verbal actions play a secondary role compared to nonverbal events in the report. Furthermore, reported speech can be used even when the reported events were not witnessed by the reporter. Reported speech is thus the most important action-reporting device in Nukulaelae discourse.

Reported speech skills are acquired early. From a very early age, Nukulaelae children are sent on errands (*fekau*) from one household to another; they are expected to convey complex verbal messages, repeated exactly as uttered by the sender. If children modify the content of the message in any way, they may be punished. Thus, very early on, children learn to repeat another person's speech exactly as originally uttered and to follow metalinguistic directives.

Instructions for errands are not the only context in which children are exposed to directives to repeat speech strings. Teasing often consists of one person "feeding" lines to another, who then repeats the utterance exactly as uttered by the prompter. Children and adults take part in these events, both as teasers and victims:

(3) [Tuufue and Sina, two female caretakers, are teasing 3-year-old Vave
     about not knowing who his blood parents are. T first prompts S,
     who then prompts the author to ask Vave who his parents are.]
→   T: ((prompting Sina)) *Ssili laa: mo ko(o)i tena tamana*
                Ask (him) who his father
        mo tena maa:tua.
        and his mother (are).
     S: ((to V)) *Kooi tou tamana mo tou maatua?*
                Who (are) your father and your mother?
     V: (   )
     T: ((to Vave)) *KOOI TOU TAMANA!*
                Who is your father?
     [...]
→   S: ((prompting Niko)) *Ia, hai! hai te fesili EE Niko!*
                Now, ask, ask the question, Niko!
     N: ((to Vave)) *KOOI!*
                Who (are they)?

Knowledge and inference on Nukulaelae

Nukulaelae islanders are remarkably wary of voicing conjectures, interpretations, and inferences from observable facts. Interpreting and conjec-
turing are behaviors that children, adolescents, and irresponsible gos-
sipers engage in; they are two components of *fakavalevale* ("irresponsible,
demented, asocial") behavior. Similar restrictions exist against interpreting the verbal and nonverbal behavior of others. As in Samoa (Ochs,
1982), meaning is rarely assigned to the babbling of infants, other than as
being responses to physiological stimuli like hunger. While "conversations" between preverbal infants and adults do occur, turn-taking is
manipulated so that the child's turns appear to be repetitions of the
adult's turns, rather than original contributions to the "conversation."
While individuals are occasionally recognized as having intentions
guiding their verbal and nonverbal behavior, the nature of these intentions is not commonly speculated upon. Intentionality is infrequently
considered in the evaluation of behavior (see Duranti, 1983b, for similar
remarks about Samoa).

   One consequence of avoiding inferences about the behavior and speech
of others is that thoughts are almost exclusively self-reported. The
thoughts of others are generally not reported. Furthermore, when
thoughts are self-reported, they are constructed like reported speech; the
boundary between reported thought and reported speech is marked
neither lexically nor grammatically.

Knowledge, including inferential knowledge, is owned communally on Nukulaelae. It is not up to single individuals, whatever their status, to assign meaning to an event. Individuals inherit knowledge from the group. As a single member of the group, one does not have the power to modify or add to that pre-determined knowledge. Only socially-recognized knowledge and inference are acceptable. For example, in narrating traditional history, Nukulaelae islanders are always careful to frame[5] their narratives as reports of what others have told them; they stress that they are conveying public knowledge and not their own interpretation of the story:[6]

(4) [Beginning a historical narrative]
     A te tala ne lagona nee au mai i toeaina i ttaimi teelaa
     [This is] the story that I heard from old men about
     maafai koo oko ki te aso fakamanatu o Niuooku.
     the period of commemoration of the Níuooku [affair].
     Teenaa laa e maasani saale toeaina o ttuu i loto o te
     Now, old men usually get up in the
     maneapa o fakamatala nee laatou a te tala teenaa [. . .]
     maneaba and they re-tell this story [. . .]

By using such frames, the speaker signals that the legitimacy of the discourse stands on collective, rather than personal, authority. As will be seen below, reported verbal interactions must similarly be presented as faithful, integral, and authentic renditions.

Finally, linguistic action and social action are seen as one and the same on Nukulaelae. The islanders are concerned with the contextual appropriateness of speech, and with its consequences, as much as with its descriptive uses. Social performativity (in status negotiation, in the management of identity, etc.) is as important a component of speech as its indexicality.[7] In the context of this fact, the productive use in everyday talk of reported speech, as the linguistic representation of both linguistic and social actions, can be seen as a reflection of the intimate relationship of linguistic and social action in Nukulaelae culture. The identification of linguistic action with social action also implies that both are on a par with respect to evidentiality and responsibility: individuals are as responsible for their speech (even when they are merely reporting someone else's) as they are accountable for their social deeds.

I have described how reported speech activities play an important role in Nukulaelae verbal interactions, and have made a number of ethnographic observations as background to the linguistic analysis to follow: Nukulaelae islanders avoid interpreting one another's linguistic and nonlinguistic behavior; knowledge on Nukulaelae is owned communally; and no clear boundary exists on Nukulaelae between linguistic action and social action.

The structure of Nukulaelae reported speech

I shall now describe the strategies used in framing reported speech and the ways in which affective meaning is communicated in reporting speech. The goal of this discussion is to analyze how the ideologies described in the previous section are reflected in the linguistic organization of reported speech.

Reported-speech frames

Nukulaelae Tuvaluan has grammatical strategies to express both direct and indirect quotation. As in English, indirect quotation is syntactically more "fused" (Givón, 1980) or "bound" (Haiman and Thompson, 1984) to the non-quoted environment than direct quotation: an indirect quote is generally subordinated to the framing clause; and it depends on the non-quoted discourse for intonation, pronominal reference, and time-and-place expressions (but not tense, as will be seen later):

(5) [Elicited examples]
   a. *Muna mai a Ioane 'au kaa fano maataeao'.*
       word Dxs of Ioane I Irr go tomorrow
       "Ioane said to me, 'I am leaving tomorrow'."

   b. *Muna mai a Ioane iaa ia kaa fano i   te suaa aso.*
       word Dxs of Ioane that he Irr go on the other day
       "Ioane said to me that he was leaving the following day."

In Nukulaelae discourse, there is a clear preference for direct quotation over indirect quotation. Indirect quotation is most often utilized to embed a quotation in another quotation. It is sometimes used to quote a communicative act which the reporter did not witness. Indirect quotation, furthermore, is restricted to one-sentence, one-turn quotations; for quoted discourse that consists of more than one sentence or turn, direct quotation must be used. Thus Nukulaelae speakers prefer a linear style (Voloshinov, 1929[1978]), which allows them to maintain a clear distinction between authorial voice and reported voice. This reflects the Nukulaelae concern for the *presentation of reported speech as an authentic reflection of the original utterance.* This concern, however, only dictates that the *wording* of the quote be an accurate (or at least plausibly accurate) rendition of the original utterance,[8] thus leaving other aspects of discourse structure open for manipulation.

Speech-act expressions

The same concern is reflected by the form of speech-act expressions which frame reported speech. Quoted discourse, whether direct or indirect, is typically introduced by an expression which identifies the quoted voice and marks the boundary between the quote and the rest of the discourse. The most common such expression is a noun phrase, consisting of the noun *pati* or *muna* "word" in the plural, modified by a possessive noun-phrase or pronoun referring to the quoted voice. The speech-act expression and the quoted string form an equational structure (equivalent to copular uses of *be* in English):

(6) *Muna a Tito 'Ia, naa ttoki laa ttuaakoi!'*
      words of Tito OK do plant then the + boundary
      "Tito said, 'OK, get that boundary planted, then!'"

Hence a reported-speech string is typically presented as being *equal to the wording* of the original utterance. Reported-speech strings may also be introduced by the polysemic verb *fai* (in free distribution, in the Nukulaelae dialect, with the form *hai*) "to say, to tell, to do, to make, etc."

Occasionally, when the identity of the participants in the reported conversation has been clearly established in the previous reported turns, the speech-act expression is omitted between two turns of a directly reported conversation. In such cases, the change of turn is marked by changes in pitch and volume from one turn to the next:

(7) [Reporting an interaction that had taken place in Funafuti, Tuvalu's capital]
      Ana muna ((whispered)) '*sss!*
      my speech   Exc
      ((creaky voice, mid-high pitch)) *taaua   kaa alo!'*
                                        we-2-i Irr go
      ((normal voice and pitch)) *Muna a Moose*
                                  speech of Moose
      ((mid-high pitch, rising)) '*Ki fea?*'
                                  to where?
→   ((creaky voice)) '*Taa   alo ki te malae.*
                         we-2-i go to the green
      ((loud, addressing a third party)) *Tautai!*
                                          Tautai
      MAAUa nei kaati   kaa ttipa   aka   peelaa,'
      we-2-e here perhaps Irr stroll please thus
→   ((loud, asking for clarification)) '*E   AA?*'
                                          Nps what?

→   ((slightly creaky)) *'Maaua nei   kaa ttipa aka*
                        we-2   here Fut stroll please
    peelaa ki te   airport i   koo'
    thus to the airport at there
→   ((high pitch, low voice)) *'Io!'*
                              yes

"He said, 'Hey! Let's go!' Moose then said, 'Where to?' (He
answered,) 'Let's go to the village green. [Addressing a third party]
Tautai! We are going off to stroll this way.' (Tautai asked,) 'What
(did you say)?' (He answered,) 'We are going off to stroll this way to
the airstrip.' (Tautai then said,) 'All right.' "

In any other circumstances, when the framing verb is omitted, a
self-repair is commonly triggered:

(8) *'Heki TAA:Itai-'*   *MUNA a:* Tito *me   heki taaitai*
     Neg anywhere-near word   of Tiki Cmp Neg anywhere-near
     eiloa   ki loto.
     indeed to center

" '[The fish] was nowhere near-' Tito said that [it] was nowhere near the
center [of the fishing net, and they were already folding the net up]."

An important characteristic of the speech-act expressions used in framing
reported speech is that most are straightforwardly descriptive. Both *muna*
and *fai*, for example, can introduce statements, questions, commands, and
interjections. Unlike speakers of many other languages, Nukulaelae Tuvaluan speakers rarely make use of "graphic introducers," i.e. speech-act
verbs which describe the manner in which the quoted string was originally
uttered (Tannen, 1986, 1988).[9] The most commonly used speech-act
expressions convey little information about the manner in which the quote
was originally uttered and are devoid of overt affective meaning. When
reporters wish to describe lexically the manner in which the quote was
originally uttered, they usually do so before the speech-act verb:

(9) [Narrating a net-fishing expedition.]
     Au e   mmiti   atu ki ei, ((whisper, high pitch)) *aku mu(na)-*
     I Nps whisper atu to Anp   my word
     'sss-! Te kogaa   kanase!'
     Exc the school-of trevally

"I whispered to them, and here were my words, 'Psst! A school of
trevallies!' "

The primary role of speech-act verbs is to mark the boundary between the
quote and the rest of the discourse.

Quoted discourse is thus most frequently framed by a speech-act expression. The canonical expression used for this purpose is a nominal expression, which is apposed to the quoted string in an equational structure. A number of other framing strategies exist, some of which are more specific in meaning. Speech-act expressions are neutral in affective meaning; their role is limited to marking the boundary between non-reported and reported speech (or between two quoted turns), and between the reported voice and the authorial voice.

Tense

I shall turn now to non-lexical framing strategies and show that, while tense frames reported speech in a transparent but affectively neutral manner, deixis, intonation, and discourse organization are highly sensitive to the affective design of the reporter.

The tense of quoted speech, whether reported directly or indirectly, is always in reference to the situation in which the discourse was originally uttered. Nukulaelae Tuvaluan has no temporal concord system (see Comrie, 1986) regulating the tense of indirect quotations:

(10) *Ne hai mai mo   ko te kau   kolaa e   olo o   pei   tili.*
      Pst say Dxs Cmp Foc the group those Nps go   Cmp throw fishing-net
      "He told me that it was those guys that were going [lit. are going] net-fishing."

Tense thus functions as a marker of the change in temporal perspective that accompanies changes from non-reported to reported discourse. At the affective level, however, tense does not fulfill any discernible function. In particular, the absence of a tense-concord system does not allow the tense–aspect–mood variations which can be manipulated for affective purposes in many other languages.

Adverbial Deixis

In contrast to the two framing devices seen so far, adverbial deixis has both referential and affective functions. In Nukulaelae Tuvaluan, there are two major deictic adverbs: *mai*, whose unmarked meaning is "towards the current speaker" and *atu* "toward the interlocutor, away from the current speaker." Examples (5), (9), and (10) include occurrences of these adverbs which illustrate their primary use.

Mai and *atu* are also used in many contexts in which neither the speaker nor the interlocutor is involved as a participant in the discourse. Their meaning is thus broader than their directional meaning (see Hohepa, [1981], for similar remarks on the Maori cognates of these two adverbs). The following illustrates such a context:

(11) *Kaa ttogi   atu   nee laatou, kaa ttogi   mai*
      Irr   barter thither Erg they-3 Irr   barter hither
      te   lua sefulu seeleni teelaa ki laatou, kaa talia   eiloa
      the twenty   shilling that   to them-3 Irr allow indeed
      laatou o   olo ki olotou manafa.
      they-3 Cmp go to their   land

      "If they exchanged [their land] away (*atu*), and they exchanged [got
      in exchange] (*mai*) the twenty shillings, they'd surely be able to go
      to their land."

This example is taken from a narrative of an early episode of contacts
with Europeans in the nineteenth century (described further in Munro
and Besnier, 1986), in which neither speaker nor interlocutor was
involved. *Mai* and *atu* in such contexts denote, respectively, direction
toward and away from the point of highest empathy (Kuno, 1976) from
the speaker's point of view. In the above example, *mai* is used when the
action if directed towards Nukulaelae people (with whom the narrator
empathizes most), while *atu* is used when the action is oriented away from
them or towards the Europeans.

Deictic adverbs often modify speech-act expressions in reporting
speech, where their affective use is commonly exploited, as illustrated in
the following example:

(12) *Fakalogo au nei* ((chuckling)) *ki te   mea a Mele*
      overhear I   this   to the thing of Mele
      e   fai mai   kiaa Saavave, [...]
      Nps say hither to   Saavave

      "I [then] overheard what Mele told hither (*mai*) to Saavave [...]"

Adverbial deixis, which is common in reported-speech contexts, is a
device that has the dual role of marking directionality (its referential
function) and focus of empathy (its affective function). Note, however,
that to arrive at the affective meaning of deictic adverbs requires inferencing. It is thus covert and indirect, and places the speaker in a position of
diminished responsibility for meaning.

Prosodics

As Bolinger (1982) points out, intonation, and prosody in general, is
"fundamentally emotive" (1982:530). Not surprisingly, in many speech
communities, prosodics is privileged in the communication of affective
meaning. On Nukulaelae, it is readily exploited as an affect-communicating channel in reported discourse.

As discussed earlier, Nukulaelae islanders overtly prescribe that another person's speech must be presented as the faithful rendition of the original utterance. Nukulaelae reported speech is seen as a change of voices where the voice of the quoted party takes the floor, thus backgrounding the voice of the reporter. This norm appears to have a direct effect on the prosodic structure of reported-speech constructions: transitions from non-reported to reported speech (and vice versa) are accompanied by sharp prosodic changes, as the reporter strives to present a quote as originally uttered. In the following excerpt, the quoted discourse is strikingly divergent from the rest of the discourse in its intonational contour and pitch:

(13) [Narrating a land-boundary dispute.]
((slowly falling pitch)) *Muna a   Tito,* ((high pitch, rising)) '*Ia!*
               word of Tito   well
((high pitch, falling)) *naa ttoki laa   ttuaakoi.'*
               do erect then the + boundary
((mid-low pitch)) *Tafuke aka a   Tautai, puke te lau paepae,*
               move then Cnt Tautai grab the boundary + stone
palele   ne ttoki.
finished Pst erect

"Tito say, 'OK, get that boundary marked!' Tautai then moved forward, grabbed the boundary stone, and (before you know it) he had (the boundary stone) erected."

Prosodics thus serves as a framing device for reported speech.

But the affective content of prosodic structure also plays an important, off-record, and covert role in Nukulaelae reported speech. Like members of many other speech communities (Davitz, 1964), Nukulaelae islanders associate subjectively active feelings with high pitch, flaring timbre, and a fast rate of speech, while passive feelings are associated with low pitch, soft voice, and a slow rate of speech. As discussed elsewhere (Besnier, 1990b), the overt display of subjectively active feelings of any kind is given a negative evaluation on Nukulaelae. Responsible adults do not let their emotions and internal states interfere with their social relationships and affect others. A responsible person is calm and unemotional.

Nukulaelae speakers exploit these norms in reporting one another's speech. In reporting the speech of a person whom they wish to present in a negative light (as often happens in gossip), Nukulaelae speakers attribute to the quoted speech the prosodic structure of a less than rational individual. Observe the pitch, tempo, and voice quality of the reported string in the following example:

(14) [Narrating a first acquaintance with a flush toilet.]

((normal pitch, normal tempo)) *Muna mai*
                                    speech Dxs
((high pitch, animated tempo)) '*PPAKI-! PPAKI-!*
                                      pluck   pluck
((whisper)) *Taapaa ee!*
                    Exc
((very high pitch)) *A   te   mea   laa   maa ppuna mai kia AKU!'*
                    Cnt the thing then Prc jump Dxs to me

"(She) tells (her), 'Flush! flush! Hey! But the (water) is going to jump at me!'"

Prosodic structure is indeed one of the primary means through which Nukulaelae speakers communicate affect in reported discourse. Crucially, it is also one of the levels of linguistic structure that are most elusive to conscious metapragmatic awareness (Silverstein, 1981) and, in consequence, one for which speaker responsibility is least imputable. Prosodics is a level of linguistic structure at which the voice of the reporter is allowed to infiltrate the reported discourse.

Pragmatic organization of quoted discourse

Similarly, the pragmatic organization of quotes (length, degree of planning, rhetorical style) carries affective meaning in Nukulaelae discourse. Contrast the two following quoted turns, taken from the report of a confrontation between the reporter and a third party (the transition between the turns is indicated by the arrow in the left margin):

(15)   *Aku muna   'Luisa, lle:i,* (0.3) *i   au ne m- manako*
      my   speech Luisa good   because I Pst   want
      kee:fetaui taaua   i   Fagaua kae:- mea aka laa   koe
      Sbj meet we-2-i at Fagaua but thing then then you
      koo tele mai ki Olataga. (1.2) *Ko au fua e: faipati atu*
      Inc run Dxs to Olataga   Foc I just Nps speak Dxs
      kiaa koe ki luga i te: (0.3) *peelaa mo tau: fekau*
      to   you about the   like   your message
      ne avatu   nee Samasone.'
      Pst transmit Erg Samasone
→   (2.2) ((high pitch)) *Muna mai '*io-, ((fast)) *io- io-!'*
                          say   Dxs yes   yes yes
      ((laughter)) *(Muna) hh a   tou   fafi(ne)!*
                    say   Cnt your woman

"I said, 'Luisa, good [I am glad we are running into each other], because I very much wanted to meet you on Fagaua but – the thing is that you had come over here to Olataga. I just wanted to talk to you about, like, your complaint [that I heard about] through Samasone.' She says, 'Yes, oh, yes – yes –!' That's what she said, the woman!"

The speaker's self-quoted discourse has many features characteristic of planned discourse (Ochs, 1979): the turn is long, the sentences complex, and repetition of words and repairs is kept to a minimum. The turn also has the prolix quality characteristic of rhetorical speaking on Nuku-laelae.

In contrast, the other quoted turn is highly unplanned: it is short, erratic in tempo (which speeds up half-way through the turn), and full of repetition. The following are two further examples of the same speaker as in example (15) reporting the utterances of two other speakers to whom he strives to attribute, as in (15) above, emotional, unpredictable, and generally negative character traits:

(16) *Muna mai. 'Koo hee:ai- HEE:ai he: mea*
      say   Dxs Inc Neg   Neg   a   thing
      e: (0.7) onosai   e:i-'
      Nps   suppress-feeling Anp

      "[She] says to me, 'there is nothing – no harbored feelings between us any more.'"

(17) ((high pitch)) *Muna mai 'heeai laa   hoku ssee   i   ei,* (0.5)
                      say   Dxs Neg   then my wrong in Anp
      ((mid-high pitch)) *e   ssee   eiloa   ko: ko laatou'*
                         Nps wrong indeed Foc Foc they-3

      "She says, 'I did nothing wrong, they were the ones that did something wrong.'"

The rhetorical style of a quote is a tool exploited by the reporter to communicate affect. The work of Sapir (1927) and of Friedrich and Redfield (1978) has shown how rhetorical style is an important communicative index of personality. By attributing the rhetorical features of the styles of presentation that are evaluated either positively or negatively by members of a speech community, the reporter attributes certain personal characteristics to the quoted individual. The rhetorical style of quotes allows the reporter's voice to "leak" onto the quote, and yields what Bakhtin ([1934] 1981:364) calls a *parodic stylization* of the quoted voice. This parodic stylization enables the reporter to manipulate the audience's perception of the quoted individual.

Table 7.1 *Structure and function in Nukulaelae reported speech*

Framing device	Example	Referential function	Affective function
quoting strategy	direct, indirect	neutral	socially acceptable reporting
speech-act expression	*muna* 'word', *fai* 'say'	boundary marking	neutral
tense and mood	*e* "present", *kaa* "irrealis"	shift in point of reference	neutral
deictic adverb	*mai* 'hither', *atu* 'thither'	direction of action	focus of empathy
prosodics	intonation, pitch	boundary marking	presentation of quoted speaker
reporting style	lengthy/planned, brief/unplanned	description of quoted turn	presentation of quoted speaker

Reported speech: overt and covert meaning

In the previous section, I presented various features of the structure of Nukulaelae reported speech. I illustrated how each functioned as a key that can communicate referential meaning, affective meaning, or both. Table 1 summarizes the main points that were made in the discussion of these features.

What transpires from the overview of these features is that they do not communicate referential and affective meaning to the same degree. As Du Bois (1986) shows, quoting involves a transfer of control (and of the focus of scrutiny) over some (but not all) levels, the affective level being, in the case study I have presented here, the one level over which control is not transferred to the quoted voice. While some linguistic strategies clearly function as keying devices that signal whether a particular string is reported or not, others do not have such a function; while some keys are affectively neutral, others are deliberately used by speakers to communicate affect. Contrast, for example, the quotative verb or expression (shown to function in most circumstances as a reported-speech key devoid of affective meaning) with prosodics, whose primary function is to communicate affect. Reported-speech keys thus vary in the extent to which they allow leakage of the quoting voice onto the quoted voice.

Of the various keys which communicate affect, one generalization can be made: they do so in a covert and non-transparent fashion. Instead of communicating affect in reported speech through lexical means or through indirectly reported speech (cf. Bakhtin's pictorial style), Nukulaelae speakers communicate affect in prosody, deictic adverbs, and the rhetorical style of the quote, while maintaining every appearance, at more overt and transparent levels, of presenting an exact rendition of the quoted voice. While adhering to the cultural norm dictating that speech be reported faithfully, Nukulaelae islanders can also superpose affect in a covert off-record manner, in a manner that is also most likely to escape scrutiny. Thus Nukulaelae speakers betray an intense awareness (whether conscious or unconscious) of the relative evidential load of various keys in reporting discourse.

Conclusion

In this chapter, I have attempted to exploit insights from Bakhtinian literary theory on reported speech in an analysis of the use of reported speech in Nukulaelae everyday discourse. I have shown how, like the Western novelists upon whom Bakhtin focuses, Nukulaelae speakers exploit the inherent polysemy of linguistic signs: not only does language carry informational value, but it is also used to pass judgments, to present personalities, and to negotiate the degree to which one is accountable for these. Many, if not most, units of linguistic structure can be used for far more than one communicative purpose at the same time, and successful communicators in particular speech communities constantly exploit this polysemy. How different linguistic signs may be exploited for each of these purposes appears to be culture-dependent, and merits further investigation.

My analysis of fragments of Nukulaelae discourse has highlighted the relationship between the quoting voice, the quoted voice, and selected formal features of the discourse, particularly those that are foregrounded in the communication of affective meaning. I identified several pivotal aspects of the structure of Nukulaelae reported speech, some of which "overlap" with one another in real time, others of which occur in close proximity to one another. These formal features, which can be isolated through a close, grammatically informed microanalysis of natural discourse, provide a certain polysemic "density" to moments in the interactional space where reported speech becomes salient, in that the meaning of what is said becomes complex and multiple when speakers use reported speech.

Furthermore, formal features of discourse are tied in a complex manner of the polyphony of voices that pervades all discourse (as Bakhtin tells us). This polyphony is particularly complex in reported speech. What I have shown here is that the relationships that are thus established between voices and formal features place the former in different positions of responsibility *vis-à-vis* meaning. In everyday talk on Nukulaelae Atoll, the more affectively charged features are also the least transparent, and thus the least likely to become the target of interlocutors' scrutiny. Features which remain in the foreground, which are left open to scrutiny, typically are affectively neutral. They are also, in some sense, the least "interesting" aspects of the discourse from both the native interlocutor's and the analyst's points of view. Thus, in the same discourse "move" (e.g. the act of reporting what someone else said), speakers can negotiate the degree to which they take responsibility for different aspects of meaning (Hill and Irvine, this volume), and the way in which they do so will be highly constrained by societal norms: how and when one should communicate affectivity, the extent to which interactions in particular contexts are viewed as "on record," and so on.

I am not of course suggesting that Nukulaelae islanders are unique in the ways in which they negotiate responsibility for the affective components of reported speech. In fact, the patterns described in this chapter may be found to various degrees in many cultures. I have attempted to describe reported speech and affect in one cultural setting as a plea for further research in other cultural settings. Much research remains to be done before a typology of reported-speech framing strategies and of "affect-leaking" strategies can be established, and before general correlative patterns can be sought that link cultural ethos and symbolic form. This research will need to address also how such categories as gender and age are interwoven with issues of language ideology and language structure in particular speech communities, questions which I have ignored in this preliminary effort.

Further work needs to focus on the relationship between language structure, language use, and sociocultural ideologies of discourse in other contexts which centralize "replaying" and the communicative "embeddings" that characterize replays, of which speech reporting is but one instance (Goffman, 1974:530–1). Indeed, replaying activities are central to the ethnographic experience, which typically relies heavily on informants' descriptions and interpretations of everyday events, cultural concepts, and ideologies, and the representation of social action by native actors (Briggs, 1986). How responsibility, affect, and language structure are intertwined in these replays deserves the sort of scrutiny I have given to Nukulaelae reported speech in this chapter.

APPENDIX: ABBREVIATIONS

Transcription conventions

(1.2)	length of significant pause in seconds
word-	abrupt cut-off
word	forte volume
WORD	fortissimo volume
hhh	exhalation
.hhh	inhalation
wo::rd	non-phonemic segment gemination
?	rising pitch (not necessarily in a question)
,	slightly rising pitch
.	falling pitch (not always at the end of a sentence)
!	animated tempo
=	turn latching
//	beginning and end of turn overlap
((*text*))	information for which a symbol is not available
((high))	dominant pitch level of utterance string
((creaky))	voice quality
( )	incoherent string
(word)	conjectured string
→	position of illustrative element

Interlinear morphological glosses

Anp	anaphoric pronoun	Nps	non-past
Cmp	complementizer	Prc	precautionary
Cnt	contrastive marker	Pst	past
Dxs	deictic adverb	Sbj	subjunctive conjunction
Erg	ergative case	2	dual
Exc	exclamation	3	plural
Foc	focus marker	i	first-person inclusive pronoun
Inc	inchoative	e	first-person exclusive pronoun
Irr	irrealis	+	morpheme boundary
Neg	negative (ad)verb		

NOTES

Acknowledgments. The research on which this chapter is based was conducted on Nukulaelae in 1980–2 and 1985, and was partially funded by the National Science Foundation (grant no. 8503061) and the Fondation de la Vocation (Paris). Thanks are due to the Government of Tuvalu and to the people of Nukulaelae for permission to reside on the atoll and conduct research. The original version of this chapter was presented as a paper at the 82nd Annual Meeting of the American Anthropological Association in 1983. Also subsequent reincarnations were given in colloquia at Hamilton College, the University of New Mexico, New York University, and Yale University; this version reflects primarily the analytic stance I adopted in 1983. I am grateful to the late Faiva Tafia, to Kelese Simona, and to Mele Alefaio for sharing their insiders' view of the questions addressed here, and to Ed Finegan, Mike Goldsmith, Jane Hill, Judy Irvine, Francesca Merlan, Elinor Ochs, Alan Rumsey, Deborah Tannen, and two anonymous reviewers for their comments on earlier versions. The usual disclaimers apply.

1 Many questions remain unanswered regarding the extent to which Bakhtin was himself the author of volumes published under Voloshinov's and Medvedev's names. The controversy is summarized in Clark and Holquist (1984).

2 A third major reporting style is free indirect quotation ("She stopped; was that the car she had seen yesterday?"), the nature of which has been the topic of much debate in literary circles (e.g. Cerquiglini, 1984). In free indirect quotation, the two voices are maximally blurred, thus allowing for even greater manipulation of the quoted message. Although there are instances in my corpus of Nukulaelae texts of constructions which resemble free indirect discourse, I shall not discuss them here for lack of space.

3 While some writers (e.g. Burke, 1935) merge the social and the affective components, Irvine (1982a) presents convincing arguments for treating them as distinct categories.

4 The examples cited in this paper are taken from a corpus of texts from various Nukulaelae spoken and written genres, amounting to approximately 500,000 words of text. Most example used here are from unelicited conversations and elicited oral narratives. A key to abbreviations and transcription conventions is provided in the appendix. Most of the personal names that appear in the examples have been changed.

5 "Frame" refers to the communicative signals indicating how an utterance or action must be interpreted (Bateson, 1972; Goffman, 1974).

6 Occasionally, narrators or conversationalists will express their own opinions about a particular event in overt ways. These will be carefully marked as distinct from the event narration and will occur only in private off-record contexts.

7 This is reported to be also true of other Pacific cultures like Samoa (Duranti, 1983b), and the Ilongots (Rosaldo, 1982).

8 It is significant that, when Nukulaelae islanders speak about language or utterances, they speak of it as a set or string of words (*pati* or *muna*).

9 Graphic introducers do exist in Tuvaluan (see Verschueren, [1984] for a partial list). However, they differ from their English counterparts in at least two ways. Firstly, they do not have the evaluative function which English graphic introducers have (Tannen, 1986, 1988). Secondly, their number is more restricted; witness the phenomenally large inventory of English graphic introducers described by Wierzbicka (1987).

8

DISCLAIMERS OF PERFORMANCE

RICHARD BAUMAN

I first became interested in the concept of performance as part of a general reorientation that has been taking place among students of folklore over the past twenty years or so from a conception of oral literature as things – texts, items, mentifacts – to verbal art as a mode of action, specifically as communication. Performance was an early focus of this reorientation, in part because it conveyed a dual sense of artistic action and artistic event (Bauman, 1977a; Ben-Amos and Goldstein, 1975; Paredes and Bauman, 1972); the ethnography of speaking, from which emerging performance-centered approaches drew much of their impetus, was organized in large part around the analysis of speech acts and events (Bauman, 1987a).

At first, performance was employed as a general cover term for verbal art as action, the situated doing of the artistic oral forms in which we had always been interested. This usage was – and remains – useful in its conception of oral literature as practice, a reuniting of text and context in action. By context here I mean situational context, not simply the general cultural or institutional setting in which a given item of oral literature is grounded, but the communicative event as a social accomplishment (Bauman, 1983). But it soon became apparent that to consider performance simply as the doing of whatever we had considered verbal art in traditional genre- and text-centered terms did not serve very well to advance our understanding of verbal art as a distinctive way of speaking. What was called for, clearly, was a conception of performance as a special mode of communication in its own right. Toward this end, I have myself been engaged for some years in the formulation and exploration of a performance-centered approach to verbal art (Bauman, 1977b, 1986; Stoeltje and Bauman, 1988).

Briefly stated, I understand performance as a metacommunicative frame, the essence of which resides in the assumption of responsibility to an audience for a display of communicative competence (the knowledge and ability to speak in socially appropriate and interpretable ways [Hymes, 1971: 58]), highlighting the way in which verbal communication is carried out, above and beyond its referential content. In this sense of performance, then, the act of speaking is itself framed as display, objectified, lifted out to a degree from its contextual surroundings, and opened up to scrutiny by an audience. From the point of view of the audience, the act of expression on the part of the performer is thus laid open to evaluation for the way it is done, for the relative skill and effectiveness of the performer's display. Performance thus calls forth special attention to, and heightened awareness of, both the act of expression and the performer. Integral to the conception of performance as a frame that puts on display the intrinsic qualities of the act of communication itself is the way in which this framing is accomplished, or, in Goffman's terms (1974), how performance is keyed. Each community will conventionally make use of a structured set of distinctive communicative means from among its resources to key the performance frame, such that communication taking place within that frame is to be understood as performance within that community. These keys may include special formulae ("Once upon a time ..."), stylizations of speech (e.g. rhyme, parallelism, figurative language), appeals to tradition as the standard of reference for the performer's accountability ("The old people say ..."), special codes (e.g. archaic language), and so on. The culture-specific constellations of communicative means that serve to key performance in particular communities are to be discovered empirically; they may be expected to vary cross-culturally.

Viewed in the terms I have just outlined, performance may be understood as the enactment of the poetic function, the essence of spoken artistry. But the poetic function is but one of a simultaneous multiplicity of speech functions, all of which are always co-present though in variable and shifting hierarchies of dominance (Jakobson, 1971). Accordingly, in any act of speaking, performance may be dominant in the hierarchy of multiple functions served by speech or it may be subordinate to other functions – referential, rhetorical, phatic, metalingual, or any other. Thus, for example, the Kuna *nia ikar*, used primarily to cure mentally deranged persons, may secondarily be appreciated by the hearers for the skill of the curing specialist's speaking; on the other hand, performance becomes primary when the specialist chants the same *ikar* at a puberty rite (Sherzer, 1983:148–9). The relative dominance of performance, then, will depend upon the degree to which the performer assumes responsibility to an audience for a display of communicative skill and effectiveness as against other communicative functions. It may range along a continuum from sustained, full performance (Hymes, 1974a:443), as when a Turkish *aşik* tells his tales at a coffeehouse (Başgöz, 1975), to a fleeting breakthrough into performance, as when a child employs a new and esoteric word in conversation with her peers as a gesture of linguistic virtuosity. Lying somewhere between the two poles might be hedged or negotiated performance, as when a salesman presents an off-color joke as having been picked up from someone else in case it is not well-received by his client, but tells it as well as he can in the hope that the skill and effectiveness of his presentation may be positively evaluated.

Understandably, our analyses of oral literature have tended to center on forms and instances of apparent – or assumed – full performance. We tend to seek out and record the star performers and favor the most fully artful texts. But we lose something by this privileging of full performance just as we do by taking any doing of an oral literary form as performance. In order to understand the dynamics of performance in all its complexity, we must extend our investigations to performances that are hedged, ambiguous, negotiated, shifting, or partial – instances where speakers may not wish to take full responsibility to their audiences for a display of communicative competence. That is my concern in this paper.

One may find in the literature a very few studies that confront the problematics of performance along the lines I have suggested. The best of these is Dell Hymes' "Breakthrough into Performance" (1975), in which close textual and contextual exegesis of the renderings of three traditional Chinookan oral forms reveals in formal and functional terms the interplay of performance and other communicative frames (report, translation), as well as the key importance of the ethnographer's role in the interaction with regard to the framing of the oral presentation. I might also mention Harvey Sacks' "An Analysis of the Course of a Dirty Joke's Telling in Conversation" (1974), in which Sacks shows how performance can be hedged in such a way that, if audience evaluation of a joke's telling is negative, an intention to perform can be disclaimed and alternative framing of the presentation, already provided for, can be fallen back upon. What I propose to do in this paper is suggest some further extensions of these lines of inquiry into shifting, less than full performance.

The materials I shall treat are all drawn from a single afternoon's work (27 July 1970) with one individual during my fieldwork in the La Have Islands, which lie off the shore of Lunenburg County at the mouth of the La Have River on the south-west coast of Nova Scotia. The group includes about twenty named islands, fourteen of which have been inhabited at one time or another since the late 1840s by the largely Irish and German forebears of the present inhabitants. The islands vary considerably in size, from little more than exposed rocks to several square miles, with the houses ranged around the shore in settlements of from one to more than thirty households per island. Local communities are not confined to single islands, for segments of some adjacent islands are connected, rather than separated, by the channels that flow between them, while various parts of other islands belong to different communities. The region has always been one where people are oriented as much to the water as they are to the land.

The settlement and growth of the La Have Islands were fostered by the development of the Lunenburg County fishing industry. With the depletion of the inshore fishery and the mechanization of offshore fishing, the area has undergone a steady decline. Lobstering is the mainstay of the present economy, supplemented by some inshore fishing, but economic opportunity is severely limited in the area and most of the young people are leaving. At the height of island prosperity, between 1890 and 1925, there were approximately 100 households on the Islands; at the time of my fieldwork, a number of formerly inhabited islands were deserted and the permanent population numbered about 150 people.

A central concern of my fieldwork in the La Have Islands was to explore the locally defined esthetic of spoken language, which led me to a focus on the principal marked occasion for speaking in traditional Island culture, namely, evening sessions of male sociability at the general store (Bauman, 1972). As a people who depended upon fishing for their live-lihood, the La Have islanders traditionally had little leisure time during the spring, summer, and early fall months when the weather allowed them to be on the water. It was only during the fall and winter months, when the days were too short and the weather too cold for fishing, that they could enjoy the luxury of leisurely evenings, and it was on these fall and winter evenings that the men congregated at the general store. Every night in this season, from early evening until 11 or 12 o'clock, the store at the north end of Bell's Island was filled with men who gathered to enjoy one another's company in cardplaying and conversation.

One of the major genres that figured in those encounters was the *yarn*. In La Have Island usage, a yarn was a narrative, told and accepted as essentially true, though with some license for creative exaggeration, about something that transcended common knowledge, experience, or expecta-tion. Yarns dealt for the most part with unusual work experiences, travels to distant places, encounters with the supernatural, and memorable local occurrences. An important feature of the yarn was that it should report personal experience or the experience of others with whom the narrator was linked by a chain of transmission, and to whom it could be attributed. Although yarns were told and accepted as essentially true accounts of actual events, it is clear that some at least of the tales of encounters with the supernatural were traditional legends, also found elsewhere but localized by the islanders.

Now, at the time of my fieldwork in 1970, the last general store had been gone for thirty-odd years, and the heyday of the evening sessions had waned even earlier, so, like many ethnographers, I was studying memory culture and my sources were of middle age or older. On the particular afternoon in question, I was working with one of the best of them, a man named Howard Bush, of Bush Island, then eighty-seven years old. My

goal was to record examples of the kinds of yarns that figured so promi-
nently in sessions at the store. While Mr. Bush had been present at many
of those sessions, he had never been prominent among the active participants in the story-telling there, partly because pride of place was given to
older men and he had still been comparatively young when the period of
active story-telling entered its decline. He remembered a fair number of
stories from the tellings of others – on that afternoon I recorded fifteen
narratives from him – but a number of factors bore heavily on his
recounting of them to me, relating to his willingness to assume responsibility for a display of competence in telling them.

First of all, while yarns were understood to be narratives recounting
personal experience, my interest in the stories told at the general store
constrained Mr. Bush to dredge up and retell what were not for the most
part his own stories, but rather ones that had originally been the personal
narratives of others. Furthermore, as I have mentioned, one of the basic
conventions of yarns was that they be told and accepted as essentially
true, with corroborating detail and other devices of verisimilitude, such as
direct claims of veracity, appeals to eye-witness knowledge, and so on.
Mr. Bush was at an obvious disadvantage here, telling the stories of
others called up from distant memory at a remove of up to seventy years
or more. Not surprisingly then – I say this with hindsight and hindsight is
rarely surprising – our recording session became an extended negotiation
about performance (see Briggs, 1986). I propose to look here at four of the
yarns I recorded to illustrate some of the dimensions and products of that
negotiation.

The first text I shall examine is also the first narrative that Mr. Bush
told me during our afternoon session. In arranging my visit with him, I
had indicated that I was interested in yarns of the kind told at the general
store and when we began our conversation he told me that he had recalled
one that he had heard his uncles – participants in the narrated event – tell
"dozens of times."

Text 1
There was an old fella, years ago, he lived in La Have River and he kept a shop, a
small shop, and he had a small vessel. And every . . . about every week he'd come
down here trading, uh, goods out of his shop for fish. And he had a monkey. [RB:
A pet monkey.] He had a pet monkey. And he'd always bring that with him.

Well, uh, I get kinda worked up, and I can't think about what I want to say.
[eleven second pause].

The people would salt their fish in butts, you know, puncheons we call them.
And when the fish was forked out it would leave the . . . it would leave the pickle
about half, half in the butt.

And, uh, the people used to bring cod oil and bring, uh, fish and trade it for
these shop goods, you know. And he was always three parts drunk himself. He
sold . . . he sold some and he was always about three parts, and he'd be in the
cuddy and when the people would bring this oil – they'd tell him they was here

with some oil – well, uh, he'd say, "You go measure it." Well they'd measure one gallon of oil and two of water. They sold him more, uh, more water than what they did oil. But he didn't know it at the time.

And the boys – my father then was one of them at that time, but he must've only been a small boy, and his brothers – they was anxious to try to dump this monkey into the puncheon, into the puncheon of pickle (laughs).

So they rigged up a scheme. They took a board and they put it, uh, just on it ... on a ... so it wouldn't take much to tip it, you know. But this monkey's jumping around everywhere, like some dogs is. So when he jumps on this board it'll tip him into the pickle.

Anyway, it did. That's 'cause it ... it dumped him in the puncheon of pickle one day. This old man was three parts drunk. He heard the monkey hollering and, uh, he couldn't find it right away, where it was.

And at last he did find it.

And I don't know how he got it out. That I can't tell you. He mighta maybe put the board down with a slant, and maybe he crawled out. I imagine that's the only way he would get it out.

And, uh ... I don't know if I can tell you very much more about that or not. I don't think there's very much more to it.

This is a story about a practical joke, of a kind widely told in rural North America; practical jokes and narratives about them are, in fact, part of a unified expressive tradition (Bauman, 1986:33–53). Notwithstanding his having heard the story of the monkey in the pickle dozens of times and having planned to tell it to me in advance of our session, Mr. Bush expresses his difficulty in actually recounting it at two points in the text, once near the beginning, and once at the end. In the first instance, after a reasonably adequate orientation to the story by island standards, introducing the dramatis personae, locating the action in terms of place, and presenting the potentiating conditions for the narrated event, the narration breaks down quite decisively, signaled by Mr. Bush's statement, "Well, uh, I get kinda worked up, and I can't think about what I want to say," followed by an eleven second pause before he resumes the story. Then, at the end of the narrative, he encounters further problems in producing a satisfactory ending. After indicating that the old trader finally did locate his distressed monkey, he runs out of information concerning the narrated event and shifts into a confession of his difficulty in bringing the story to effective closure:

And I don't know how he got it out. That I can't tell you. He mighta maybe put the board down with a slant, and maybe he crawled out. I imagine that's the only way he would get it out.

And, uh ... I don't know if I can tell you very much more about that or not. I don't think there's very much more to it.

These two trouble spots and Mr. Bush's metanarrational comments concerning them invoke both aspects of communicative competence. The earlier one indicates a breakdown in his *ability* to sustain the narrative line and the flow of narration, while the second implicates his lack of *knowledge* concerning the outcome of the narrated event and thus of the conclusion of the narrative. Mr. Bush's confession of nervousness and inability to think of what to say after the opening orientation section constitutes a disclaimer of performance on the grounds of an incapacity to continue the very act of narration, though the story was familiar to him from repeated hearings. The problem, apparently, lay in constructing an adequate narration for me, as an outsider. I base this interpretation on the information presented as Mr. Bush resumed the narration after his disclaimer and the lengthy pause that followed, namely, the explanation of the practice of salting fish in barrels. Every adult islander would be expected to know all this, but Mr. Bush appears to have realized that I might not. Because the nature of the pickle is so central to the point of the story, he felt the need to provide the relevant information as his uncles never had to do, and I believe this realization was sufficient to undermine his narration, never strongly confident to begin with.

The difficulty that Mr. Bush encounters at the end of his yarn is of a different nature. Whereas the early breakdown stems from a lapse in his ability to sustain the narration, the problem at the end implicates the other aspect of communicative competence, that is, his lack of knowledge concerning the features of the story that he feels are necessary to an appropriate telling. The problem, as noted, has to do with bringing the narrative to effective closure. Mr. Bush apparently senses that the eventual finding of the monkey in the barrel of pickle, the last thing he recounts with assurance, is not an effective point on which to end the story. A comment on the appearance of the pickled monkey or the reaction of the drunken old trader would have been effective here, exploiting the potential for burlesque provided by the monkey's immersion in the strong brine or the trader's inebriated state, but we cannot know how Mr. Bush's uncles ended the story, or whether he had forgotten what they said. We can observe, though, that Mr. Bush fulfills the need he feels for more detail by speculating, rather anticlimactically, on how the monkey was extricated from the barrel, concerning which he has no definite knowledge. Having suggested what might plausibly have happened, he still feels a lack of closure, and so confesses to a lack of anything else to tell. This, then, is a disclaimer of performance on the grounds of insufficient knowledge. In both instances, whether on the basis of a lack of ability or knowledge, he excuses himself from full competence and thus from full responsibility in recounting the story. The first yarn, however, is the only one in which Mr. Bush's disclaimers of performance invoked his ability to narrate; all subsequent disclaimers appealed to insufficient knowledge, as his nervousness in the encounter diminished.

In the second example (Text 2, below), I had asked Mr. Bush if he had heard a story told to me by another man, the father of his son's wife. This is, in fact, a localized version of a widely told traditional treasure legend (Granger, 1977:168; Thompson, 1955–8, motifs C401.2, N553.2), of special sociolinguistic interest because of the core motif in which successful recovery of a buried treasure, associated with the devil or other forces of evil, can be achieved only by the strict maintenance of silence; when one of the diggers speaks, an expression of his humanity or a reaffirmation of his human social ties, the treasure is lost, reclaimed by the devil:

Text 2
RB: Did you hear ... [the story about the treasure]?
HB: I don't ... I can't tell any story about it. But, uh,
I know ... I know I heard the story about where they went to
dig this chest of money, and, uh, they was down to the chest
of money, far enough for to see the handle on it. And they
hadn't, uh, they wasn't to speak. There wasn't a word to be
spoke. And they had the rope through the handle ...
RB: Mn hmm.
HB: ... for to snake it up out of the ground. And one fellow
spoke, and tore the handle right off the chest. They had the
handle. They had the handle on the rope.
Now I ... now that's the story I heard, now.
RB: Yeah. That's ... who ... who was it told that story?
HB: I don't know. I don't know. I can't say.
RB: Do you recall how they found that money? Was it in a dream?
HB: No, I don't think ... I don't think so.
They lost the money. The money went down. The Old
Fellow to ... took it back again.

Mr. Bush's opening response to my request for this yarn is a disclaimer of his ability to "tell any story about it." But then he proceeds to recount precisely the narrative I was asking about, but framed at both the beginning and the end as a *report* of his having *heard* the story: "I know I heard the story," and "Now that's the story I heard, now." The narrative itself is very lean, containing none of the locational, motivational, or personal orientational information that conventionally opens a yarn: where it happened, what motivated the action, who was involved. Thus, Mr. Bush's opening disclaimer is not a denial that he knew the story, at least in its outlines, nor a breakdown in his capacity to narrate, but a statement of his lack of competence to tell it as a yarn should properly be told. He is unwilling to assume responsibility for an adequate narration, an appropriate telling in island terms. He does produce a narrative, but won't undertake to perform it because he does not know it well enough.

Moreover, the narrative he does present is not even a full outline of the story as he recalls it. He ends his account initially with the tearing of the handle from the treasure-chest. It is only in response to my further questioning – though not in direct answer to my question – that he provides the additional information that the money was lost, reclaimed by the devil. Thus, consistent with his professed unwillingness to perform the story, resorting rather to a report of having heard it, Mr. Bush's initial report is restricted to what is in effect a metonym of the full story, sufficient to identify it but short of a complete account.

In examining the formal features of the narrative, we may observe that the text is marked by a number of parallel syntactic constructions which become more apparent when it is set out in lines determined by breath pauses (see Tedlock, 1972). I have connected the parallel lines in brackets:

> I know I heard the story about where they went to dig this chest
>   of money,
> and uh,
> they was down to the chest of money far enough
> for to see the handle on it.
> And they hadn't, uh,
> ⌈they wasn't to speak.
> ⌊There wasn't a word to be spoke.
>   ⌈And they had the rope
> ⌈⌊through the handle
> │for to snake it up off the ground.
> │⌊And one fellow spoke
> │ and tore the handle right off the chest.
> ⌊ ⌈They had the handle.
>   ⌊They had the handle on the rope.

I draw attention to the parallelism in the text because this device is frequently employed in oral literature as a key to performance. The question must arise, then, of why parallelism should be so prominent in this text when Mr. Bush has so clearly disclaimed responsibility to perform it. The answer, I believe, is that parallelism is not here as a market of artfulness, but is rather an artifact of the narrator's insecure command of the story line, a means of nailing down successive bits of the story as he recalls them, and as he tries to call up what happens next. The parallel constructions represent a reuse of already proven constructions in lieu of providing new information of which Mr. Bush has relatively little at hand. Parallelism is, after all, a basic device of cohesion in a discourse which can serve, as here, to maintain discursive continuity in the absence of other means to do so. This is an instance of what Silverstein (1984) aptly calls "the pragmatic 'poetry' of prose," the quotation marks around "poetry" indexing the absence of purposeful artfulness. Parallelism is thus not here a key to performance, but an index of its absence.

The third narrative (Text 3, below) has certain features in common with the preceding two but contrasts significantly with them in regard to performance. This is a story that Mr. Bush had from his uncle, from whom he heard it on a number of occasions. Like the account of the lost treasure, this is a localized version of a widely told legend in which the devil, sitting in on a card game (here because the blasphemous participants had in effect called him into their presence by their swearing) is given away by his monstrous feet (Thompson, 1955–8, motif G303.4.5.3.1):

Text 3
RB: I wanted to ask you also about that Solly Richards story, about the ...
HB: Oh, about the devil (laughs).
RB: Yeah.

[I]
HB: Well, when they was in this old shop playing cards, they played every night, or near about every night outside of Sunday night. It was in Elmer Cane's shop, was called Elmer Cane's shop, well it was Elmer Cane. And they carried on the devil, they swore, you know how it went on, maybe I suppose half tight. And one of them was my uncle, was ... was my wife's [sic: mother's] brother.

[II]
And one night they was playing and a man come to the door. I don't know if he knocked or not. There's no doubt maybe he did, for he was a stranger.
Anyway he went in, and he asked them if he could have a game of cards with them and they said "yeah." And he sat down to the table.
And after a little while one fellow looked under the ... lost a card and he looked down under the table to get to it and he saw this funny looking foot (laughs). Looked like a horse's foot.
They knocked off playing. And he left. The man left.
But I don't remember ... I don't know what to tell you, what he done when he left, but I think he done something to the shop. I think he took a chunk with him. I think he took a piece of the shop with him or tore it to pieces or something.
It was the devil.
RB: Yeah.

[III]
HB: And my uncle told me ... well, he didn't tell me, he told us within the house, all hands. He went home, he went to bed, and he had no rest the whole night. He couldn't get asleep, he said. He was playing cards with the devil all night. He had no rest at all, he said. He was ... like it seemed he was in a blaze of fire. "That settled the card playing there," he said. It settled him and it settled it there.

The text may be seen to fall into three parts, indicated by Roman numerals. The first part (I), the orientation, is fully adequate by traditional standards, setting the scene for the narrated event by place (the shop), participants (including Mr. Bush's uncle), and potentiating action (playing cards, drinking, and especially blasphemy).

The middle section (II) does not display the confidence of the orientation. Here Mr. Bush makes two admissions of ignorance, once with regard to whether or not the devil knocked at the door of the shop, and later with regard to damage caused by the devil on his hasty departure from the premises. In the former, he is able to make some effort toward supplying circumstantial detail of the kind called for by the genre by drawing on his cultural knowledge concerning island etiquette: strangers are required to knock before entering. Nevertheless, he hedges his guess by saying, "There's no doubt maybe he did," the "maybe" undoing the apparent certainty of "There's no doubt." Concerning the damage to the shop, his memory fails him again, but here he has no cultural knowledge to furnish narratively relevant information. Accordingly, he confesses, "I don't know what to tell you," that is, in effect, "I don't have sufficient information to sustain an appropriate narrative performance at this point." Here again, the apparent syntactic parallelism of "I think he done something to the shop"/"I think he took a chunk with him"/"I think he took a piece of the shop with him," are not keys to performance but indices of insecurity, the repetition of the same syntactic frame while trying to dredge up additional forgotten elements of the story.

In the concluding part of the narrative, however, Mr. Bush is on his firmest ground yet. Note that here the narrated event has shifted; he is no longer recounting the encounter with the devil in Elmer Cane's shop but his uncle's later account to himself and others concerning the effects of the diabolical experience. Here Mr. Bush was himself a participant and can supply a full personal account. At this point, his mode of presentation shifts markedly. I have set out this concluding passage in lines to make its artfulness more clearly apparent:

He went home, he went to bed,
and he had no rest the whole night.
He couldn't get asleep, he said.
He was playing cards with the devil all night.
He had no rest at all, he said.
He was . . . like it seemed he was in a blaze of fire.
"That settled the card playing there," he said.
It settled him and it settled it there.

The passage is marked, first of all, by parallel syntactic constructions in the first six lines and the last two lines of the above excerpt, making for two parallel sets. This is not the hesitant, repetitive, insecure parallelism of the earlier examples; beginning with "He went home," Mr. Bush's voice becomes louder, more forceful, and higher in pitch, and in the seventh line the quoted speech of the uncle's statement takes on a shift in voice, re-enacting his emphatic delivery. Moreover, the lines display perceptible patterns of rhythmic stress, with two beats in the first line and four in each of the remaining lines (the sixth line is garbled):

He went hóme, he went to béd,
and he had nó rést the whóle níght.
He coúldn't gét asleép, he sáid.
He was pláying cárds with the dévil all níght.
He had nó rést at áll, he sáid.
He was ... liĸe it seemed he was in a bláze of fíre.
"That séttled the cárd playing thére," he sáid.
It séttled hím and it séttled it thére.

This is a breakthrough into performance, signaled, or keyed, by this confidently rendered, mutually reinforcing set of formal devices: syntactic, prosodic, and paralinguistic.

The final narrative we shall consider is a local character anecdote, recounting an event at which Mr. Bush himself was present. As it happens, the event took place at the general store itself, in a milieu of male sociability within which such stories were characteristically told:

Text 4
RB: One story I know you know about was Frank Bell and the eggs.
HB: Right. Yes, that I know is true. That I seen him do. I sat right, right in the shop and seen him, seen him do that.
He always used to torment Aubrey Sperry, that was the boss of the shop, 'bout he could ... he could suck three dozen eggs and eat the shell of the last one. Well, every time he came to the shop he'd be tormenting Aubrey. At last, Aubrey got kinda tired of it.
One day he come up starting in, he says, "I could suck three dozen eggs and eat the shell of the last one, and I want a bet for five dollars." Aubrey goes to the till and he lays down a five-dollar bill and he counts out three dozen eggs.
And ... oh, there was – I don't know – maybe seven or eight young fellows, lot though, not my age, but young, young fellows, sitting around. All hands begin to laugh. He didn't go right away, you see, and they begin to laugh. Well, he thought they was laughing at him while he didn't take right ahold of the eggs. He was going to take back water [i.e. back off], and it looked like if he was going to take back water. But we laughed at him, and then that give him ... he went to work at it.
Now I don't know how many he sucked – he punched the holes in the ends and he ... I guess he must have sucked pretty near a dozen the first time. Then he lit his old pipe. He had a little smoke, not very long. He took a couple more, half a dozen or so. And that's the way, till he had them all down. He'd suck so many and then he'd have a little smoke. And he talked a very, very short time, and he left. "I guess I'll go home."
He went down the road, not very far down the road, there was a man coming up while he was going down – they passed when they was coming up – and they seen where he stood right over there and vomit them up. He put his finger down, you see, and he vomit them up, so that they wouldn't make him sick (laughs).

In this story, by contrast with others, Mr. Bush is fully secure in his performance from beginning to end. The key factor, obviously, is that this yarn allows him to speak from his own personal experience as a marginal participant, as he is clear to establish at the outset: "Yes, that I know is true. That I seen him do. I sat right, right in the shop and seen him, seen him do that." Not only can he testify directly to the veracity of the story, but he can supply abundant circumstantial detail, a hallmark of good yarn narration. The two fleeting departures from the assured and fluent narration that characterizes his telling of this story occur in his hedging about exactly how many men were in the shop and exactly how many eggs Frank Bell sucked before taking up his pipe for the first time, small lapses quickly redressed by settling on the figure of seven or eight young fellows and a dozen eggs. This is, on the whole, a confident narration. With this yarn, then, Mr. Bush is ready to take full responsibility for correct, authoritative performance, keyed by his opening appeals to firsthand knowledge and the resultant truthfulness and reliability of his account.

The four narratives we have examined are, as I have indicated, selected from a total of fifteen told to me by Howard Bush in the course of one afternoon. Nevertheless, I believe they serve well to illustrate the negotiated and shifting dynamics of his narration *vis-à-vis* performance. The first of his yarns, about the monkey in the pickle, highlights clearly the two dimensions of communicative competence on which performance rests, namely, the knowledge and ability to communicate in socially appropriate and interpretable ways. In Mr. Bush's attempt to recount this narrative, each in its turn serves as a basis for a disclaimer of performance, that is, a statement of unwillingness to assume responsibility to his audience for a display of skill and effectiveness in story-telling. Early in the story, Mr. Bush confesses an inability to proceed with the act of narration itself because he can't think of what to say, and his speech is broken off for a time until he can gather his thoughts sufficiently to resume. Then, toward the end of the story, he excuses himself from responsibility on the basis of insufficient knowledge to render the story effectively by local standards. Thus, first a lack of ability, then a lack of knowledge constitute the basis for his incapacity to perform the narrative.

In the next text, about the lost treasure, performance is again disclaimed on the basis of inadequate knowledge of the story. Here Mr. Bush undertakes only to report the yarn, which he does by presenting just the core motif as a metonym of the complete narrative.

In the story of the devil as cardplayer, by contrast, we find a more complex dynamic at work. Mr. Bush's presentation reveals a shifting hierarchy of dominance in this text, in which he is willing to assume responsibility for the correct doing of the orientation section, disclaims performance in the course of recounting the central narrated event – the recognition of the devil by his fellow cardplayers and his departure through the wall of the shop – and breaks through into full artistic performance at the end, where the narrated event has shifted to one in which he himself was present, namely, his uncle's account of the terrible aftermath of his diabolical encounter.

In the final example, the anecdote about Frank Bell and the eggs, the narration is framed fully as performance. Here, Mr. Bush is able to assume responsibility for a display of narrative competence throughout, sustained by his own eye-witness participation in the actual event.

What implications can we draw from this sampling of four narratives and the presentational dynamics that give them shape? First, I would like to argue, on the basis of this exploration, for the productiveness of considering performance not as any doing of an oral literary form, but as one of the range of interactionally defined presentational modes, or frames, which may be more or less functionally dominant in any act of spoken communication or at any given point during its course. This perspective allows us to chart more closely the culturally shaped, socially constituted, and situationally emergent individuation of spoken art. Investigations along these lines, must, of course be founded on the ethnographically determined understanding of the standards of communicative competence that are placed on display in performance, and how the speaker signals or disclaims the accountability to an audience for a display of competence. All of these factors are to be discovered in community specific contexts; what may be accomplished by code switching in the breakthrough into performance by Philip Kahclamet, as reported by Hymes (1975), may be signaled by certain formal patterns or claims to eye-witness knowledge by Howard Bush. Likewise, a disclaimer of performance may itself be a key to full performance, as in the Iroquois oratory described by Michael Foster (1974b:84), or, as in the case of Mr. Bush's narration, it may signal a genuine unwillingness to be accountable for performance. Moreover, while there are a number of devices and patterning principles that have been widely documented as features of verbal art, the discovery of keys to performance cannot rely on a priori formal assumptions about what constitutes artful language. Our analysis has suggested, for example, that parallelism, identified by Jakobson as constitutive in the poetic function (1960), may be an artifact of an incapacity to perform, a signal, indeed, of the absence of performance. On the other hand, a fully crafted use of parallelism, reinforced and intensified by other formal features and evidences of presentational confidence, may in fact key a display of communicative competence in the performance of the same individual. Only by close ethnographic analysis of form–function interrelationships in situated contexts of use can such nuances be discovered.

Finally, I would underscore the importance of a sensitivity to the influence of the ethnographer on the dynamics of performance. The situation and the audience may have a determinative effect on a speaker's willingness to assume responsibility for a display of communicative competence and this is no less true when the audience is an ethnographer than under conditions of so-called "natural" native performance – another problematic concept. It is evident that the texts produced by Howard Bush are, to a substantial degree, the emergent products of my casting him in the role of oral narrative performer, and of his own ambivalence about assuming that responsibility because of a sense of the limits of his competence to do so. This can hardly be a unique situation; I have observed a similar dynamic in other fieldwork encounters not my own. But just as presenters of oral literature may subtly reject the mantle of performer that we wish to impose upon them, so too many individuals from whom we seek straightforward ethnographic information perform to us without our being aware of it (Paredes, 1977). Ethnographers, like linguists, have a strong bias toward the referential function of language – we tend to believe what we are told and expect straight answers to our questions – but we are all susceptible to being performed to, and we must be able to understand when the forces of performance take precedence over straightforward referentiality. A sensitivity to performance is thus a necessary part of critical, reflexive ethnography, not only in the study of oral literature but in fact in all instances of data gathering through verbal interaction with native sources. Thus, I submit, the more we can learn about performance, the better will be not only our understanding of oral literature but our general practice of ethnography as well.

9

MRS. PATRICIO'S TROUBLE: THE DISTRIBUTION OF RESPONSIBILITY IN AN ACCOUNT OF PERSONAL EXPERIENCE

JANE H. HILL and OFELIA ZEPEDA

Introduction

In accounts of personal experience speakers attempt to construct a favorable presentation of self, and to mitigate representations of experiences that might tend to damage this construction. In so doing, they reveal everyday cultural frames through which agency and responsibility are understood. We analyze an account by a middle-aged Tohono O'odham woman, Molly Patricio,[1] who lives in a reservation community near the city of Tucson, Arizona. Mrs. Patricio uses a variety of rhetorical devices to reduce the likelihood that she will be held "personally responsible" for the "trouble" she addresses, a nineteen-year-old son who has yet to graduate from high school. The effect of these devices is a representation of responsibility as "distributed" in a complex social field, rather than concentrated in a single agent. Mrs. Patricio's account is a complex discourse which can be analyzed as consisting of a series of argumentative moves. Within the series, distribution is accomplished across two social fields. The first is that of the dramatis personae represented in the narratives embedded in Mrs. Patricio's arguments, a social field in what Chafe (1980) calls the "story world." The second is distribution of responsibility within the argument's local interactional context, Chafe's "interactional world," through achieving complicity with the interlocutor. The most important rhetorical device used for this distribution is reported speech or "constructed dialogue" (Tannen, 1988) in the "voice system" of Mrs. Patricio's account.[2]

The rhetorical devices that create "distribution" diffuse responsibility, and permit Mrs. Patricio to be explicit in her account of her trouble. This "distribution" within a micro-interactional context creates metaphorically the effect of multiple participation in a speech event, even where only one person is speaking. The effect of such framing on "responsibility" is pointed out by Irvine (this volume). Irvine suggests that speech events involving insults will exhibit a reciprocal relationship between the explicitness of an insult and the number of participants involved in the event. In the Wolof *xaxaar*, shocking insults about a new bride and her family are uttered in their presence. Yet the complex participant structure of the *xaxaar* permits speakers to bring these off very explicitly without violence or immediate reply. Should the same insult emanate from a clearly localizable single voice, the result would be catastrophic. We extend this insight about "insult" to other types of speech for which "responsibility" is at issue, such as an account of troubles. The rhetorical achievement of "distribution" in such accounts is, we believe, metaphorically equivalent to increasing the complexity of participant structures, and thus it also diffuses responsibility.

Mrs. Patricio faces problems in the management of a complex identity, and is vulnerable to accusations that she has not been "responsible" in an important task, ensuring that her children are successful in school. In narratives embedded within her account of why such accusations would be wrong, the constructed dialogue of several figures functions as a metaphor (Tannen, 1988) for a small society of people involved in the events she recounts. The representation of this story-world society makes these events sociocentric, rather than egocentrically focused in Mrs. Patricio's "own" experience. Constructed dialogue does not, however, have only the semiotic effect of metaphorical creation of the story-world society. It also functions in the interactional world in which the narrative takes place to "distribute" the question of responsibility away from the moral presence of Mrs. Patricio, who, as she constructs the reports, can be seen as no more than an "animator," the puppeteer with minimal moral exposure suggested by Goffman (1974, 1981). We argue that part of the semiotic foundation for this "lamination" or split in the speaker into a variety of presences is that propositions embedded in the story world, and embedded in turn in constructed dialogue, are relatively inaccessible to challenge by the interlocutor. We develop this argument based on the structural analysis of anaphoric accessibility in discourse elaborated by Polanyi and her co-workers (Polanyi, 1985, Scha and Polanyi, 1988, Polanyi and Martin, 1989). We note also the relevance of theoretical contributions by Chafe (1980) and Langacker (1985) to an understanding of the semiotic functions of narrative in the distribution of responsibility.

Besides constructed dialogue, Mrs. Patricio uses a variety of other devices to distribute responsibility. Rather than making direct statements, she invites her interlocutor to draw conclusions. She uses impersonal reference, and she represents herself as being unable to influence directly the course of events, both because she is legally unable to do so and because she lacks the necessary knowledge at crucial junctures.

Mrs. Patricio's argument

The entire argument is given below, so that the reader can examine it
before reading our analysis:[3]

1.   ... We've been,
2.   *gḍhu haha 'i ha'ap ki:*
      JUST LIVING RIGHT OVER THERE
3.   in town all this time
4.   until two years ago [mhm]
5.   (when I finally) moved out here [mhm].
6.   That's why *mo g ñ-*,
      WHY MY,
7.   *ñ-ma:mad pi ho:hoid 'i:ya'a [ooh]*
      MY CHILDREN DON'T LIKE IT HERE ...
8.   They come,
9.   but they wanna go back into town cause[
      Interviewer: [*Mhm, hemakc hab ñ-a:g hegam mañ, mañ wenog man
                     am si we:pege*
                  ONE OF THEM TOLD ME THAT, THAT
                  WHEN I MET HER THE VERY FIRST TIME
                  am, m – mai 'i:da [] Lily [] kaij 'atpi s-ma:c hegam
                  [MP: mhm]   [MP: mhm]
                  THIS LILY SAID THAT APPARENTLY
                  THEY KNEW HER,
                  ha'i hegam mo ha'ap ḍ 'amjeḍkam c hab kaij,
                  SOME OF THEM WHO WERE FROM THERE
                  (RESERVATION) AND THEY SAID
                  "Ooh, she's a ... a town O'odham all right[   ] in
                  town
                                          [MP: Yeah, they
                                          used to tease]
                  and she's, she's she's from in town, and I didn't
                  know what
                  they meant [ ], *kia hia 'ep*, that's what they
                             [MP: Uhhuh] YET
                  meant,
10.   [Yeah, they,] uhhuh, they used to tease them [mhm]
      [one of those .....]
11.   *C 'ep n* you know,
      AND ALSO
12.   like a lo:t of .. O'odham
13.   that went to

14. Garcia school,
15. Or wherever school they went to,
16. They had a hard time [mhm]
17. *Mat o 'i uh, ... uh wd ...*
    WHEN THEY WOULD
18. can't get used to
19. m the *milgan*? [mhm]
    WHITE PEOPLE
20. And here they,
21. they didn't have no trouble *'idam* [mhm]
    THESE (HER CHILDREN)
22. *K 'am 'apş 'i ...*
    AND THEY JUST
23. *m aş 'i hihi* most of them,
    THEY JUST CONTINUED ON
24. But my oldest son { modifying material deleted for confidentiality}
25. *mat cem 'e-maşcam c-eḑ ...*
    WHEN HE ATTEMPTED TO GO TO SCHOOL
26. and some friend of mine *hab kaij,*
    SAYS
27. "*K hebai 'e-maşcam* g your son
    WHERE IS YOUR SON GOING TO SCHOOL
28. *c hab gmhu 'ab ge 'aigo himad.*"
    SINCE HE WAS UNEXPECTEDLY GOING AROUND OVER ON THE OTHER SIDE OF TOWN.
29. And yet he was supposed to be at Central. [hhhhhhhhhhhhh]
30. So, I, I found out
31. he was ditching school
32. *K 'eḑa 'an hema ki: g* her, his friend and ...
    AND YET ONE OF HIS GIRLFRIENDS LIVED HERE
33. one lived right near us,
34. And *tp heg 'ab 'i wehemat*
    APPARENTLY THAT KID WAS OVER THERE WITH HER
35. *c 'ab hihim* [mhm]
    AND WAS COMING HERE
36. *c 'i hu ha'ap daḑhiwap* [oh]
    AND THEY'D STAY OVER HERE
37. until it was time
38. for school to be out, [mm]
39. they they'd ...
40. *cem s-ke:id*
    IT DIDN'T HELP TO SCOLD

41. And I send him off to ..
42. St. John's? [mhm]
43. *T 'oya s s-ho:ho'i [] e:p g*
    HE REALLY LIKED IT [hnhnhn] EVEN THE
44. *pa, papal 'amai'i* [hnhnhn]
    EVEN THE PRIESTS THERE
45. And he was in charge of . . .
46. dance group
47. *c uḍ 'ep ha*-chauffeur, you know, [oh]
    AND HE WAS ALSO THEIR CHAUFFEUR
48. *mat g* Indian Dancers? [mhm]
    THE ONES WHO WERE THE
49. *mo an o'oyopo* . . .
    WHEN THEY'D GO ALL OVER
50. I had two of the boys there. [mhm]
51. *Idam u:h*
    THESE
52. Lina went to th– mm
53. *All* of them went from Garcia to . . .
54. Lincoln in uh . . .
55. Central High ..
56. Except for the/
57. t–, n–,
    OUR–, MY–,
58. my oldest daughter went to Pima
59. I mean to the University for one year.
60. *K 'am hab aṣ 'i 'ep ha'asa.*
    AND THEN SHE JUST STOPPED
61. *K hegam hi*
    AND THEY DID
62. *gmhu* graduate in *ḍ* St. John's
    OVER THERE
63. *Hegam* the two boys [mmm]
    THOSE
64. Lina in uh
65. in uh Phoenix Indian? [Mhm, mhm]
66. Brenda *'abai 'i:ya* at Central High and
       RIGHT HERE
67. She was there at U–
68. at the University *ba 'e:p.*
       THERE ALSO
69. But the last one
    (Breathy, fortis)
70. I'm having trouble with him

71. cause he won't stay-hay (laughing) in school
    [h-h-h-h-h-h]
72. Well he, he, he says he's in school but . . .
73. 'N he was at Mountain View and
74. All students
75. were gonna be transferred
76. to Hanging Rock
77. And he didn't like that
78. *K 'ab 'u:pam*
    AND HE BACK
79. *'i 'ep 'e-*transfer *hejel* [mhm]
    AGAIN TRANSFERRED BY HIMSELF
80. *Pi ma:c*
    I DIDN'T KNOW
81. and then uh
82. this year . .
83. *hemu 'am 'ep cem hi: 'e:p*
    NOW HE'S TRYING TO GO AGAIN
84. He, all three years in a row he dropped out
85. *Hemu 'am 'ep hi:* to Mountain View and then
    NOW HE (WAS?) GOING AGAIN
86. *pi ha'icu ma:c* until
    I DIDN'T KNOW ANYTHING
87. about uh two weeks ago *mo g* one of my . . .
    WHEN
88. well one of my son's girlfriend
89. *Hab kaij maṣ haba*
    SHE SAYS THAT SHE
90. *'an hebai ce:g*
    FOUND OUT
91. *k aṣ hab kaij heg* that uh . .
    AND SHE SAID THAT HE
92. that he transferred himself back to Central High, so
93. Next thing I know he'll probably be in Skyline h-h-h-h-h-h
    [h-h-h-h-h]
94. Mhm, so
    I: What grade is he in?
95. He's he would have been in the
96. the senior year now [Ooh]
97. but like I said he dropped
98. He would have graduated two, three years ago [h-h-h]
    (shift to high-pitch register)
99. *K* he was one of those that
    AND

100. *Mat 'imhu a 'i-wui o* grad̲uate [mhm, mhm]
     THAT WAS GOING TO GRADUATE AHEAD OF
     SCHEDULE
101. And he was
102. But he d̲i̲d̲ that
103. so it k̲e̲p̲t̲ [mhm]
104. I tell him,
105. "Y̲o̲u̲'̲r̲e̲ gonna grad̲uate with the grand̲children" h-h-h-h-h-h-h
     [h-h-h-h-h-h]
106. Ahh, yes, and then they tell me
     [hnhn]
107. "How old is . . .
     (shift to high pitch)
108. They ask me,
109. "How old is he?"
     (shift to high pitch)
110. "Nineteen." [Oh!]
111. "O:h, then, . .
112. you can't do n̲o̲t̲hing about it."
113. And I said,
114. "I kno:w" [hmhm]
115. I, I didn't,
116. We had a workshop at uh
117. Pima College and uh
118. that's when *mo hab kaij g* u:h
     WHEN SHE SAID,
119. Hulia Moore that anybody [ ] nineteen
     [mhm]
120. you can't do nothing about it. [h-h-h]
121. And he had gone to the restroom
     (shift to high pitch)
122. and *heg*　he just w̲a̲l̲k̲e̲d̲ in
     THAT ONE
123. when she was saying that [Oh!　h-h-h-h]
124. so he heard that, y'know. [H-h-h, mhm, mhm]

The context of the account: O'odham identities

Mrs. Patricio's narrative was collected during a study of regional variation in the Tohono O'odham language.[4] It is part of a long answer to an interview question about where Mrs. Patricio and her family have lived. Zepeda, the interviewer, found this story both witty and memorable. Hill was not present during the interview, but Zepeda thought that the story was so interesting that she told it to Hill a few days later. Hill remembers Zepeda's version of the story as a very sympathetic one, which characterized the son as a bright and imaginative, but problematic child.

In discussing her residential history, Mrs. Patricio says that, while she was born on the reservation, she lived off-reservation for most of her adult life, and her children were all raised in the city of Tucson. She has recently moved back to the reservation. This life course (which is very common) means that Mrs. Patricio and her children have problematic – even stigmatized – identities, which she must manage in her discussion.[5]

Mrs. Patricio's own identity is problematic because she does not consider herself a full speaker of O'odham. Since English is Mrs. Patricio's dominant (although it is her second) language, she is somewhat unusual among people of her age living on the reservation. She was reluctant to be a subject for the dialect interview, and during the interview she stated that she often asks an elderly neighbor about the proper way to say things.[6] Mrs. Patricio evidently feels that her "best" identity is the one she conveys in English, and the code-switching in the narrative may derive partly from a conflict between her desire to project this identity and her role as a consultant in the dialect study. Zepeda believes that some of the code-switching in the narrative occurs because Mrs. Patricio cannot find the proper O'odham expression. Mrs. Patricio's code-switching is, however, very fluent, suggestive of the sort of community norms for bilinguals described by Gumperz (1982).[7]

Even more problematic than Mrs. Patricio's own identity is that of her children: at lines 6–9 she observes that her children "don't like it here" (on the reservation), and don't like to stay long when they visit. This problem becomes the object of a negotiation between Mrs. Patricio and Zepeda, who labels this identity problem in a brief but intricately laminated set of voices represented in both English and O'odham, in speech indented between lines (9) and (10). Zepeda observes that a Patricio daughter told her that people on the reservation tease the daughter about being a "town O'odham."

The term introduced by Zepeda, "town O'odham," is one of several types of identities recognized by O'odham people (*O'odham* means "person, people" but has come to mean specifically a Piman-speaking Indian). People living off the reservation will refer to people who live there as *tohono c-ed o'odham* "people out in the desert." The designation of people as "from the desert" has yet another meaning. People living on the reservation refer to people living in more remote regions as *tohono 'amjed* "from the desert" or *gdhu si tohono 'amjed* "from the middle of the desert," usually meaning that they have little contact with outsiders.

People living at the San Xavier Reservation (a small part of the

O'odham reservation separated from the main reservation and located close to Tucson) claim a special identity. San Xavier is noted for its surface water and abundant springs and thereby is named *Wa:k* "Water Place" (the springs no longer flow, though, due to the drop in the local water table in the last fifty years). People living at Wa:k call themselves *Wa:k t-ab o'odham* "People of Wa:k." That this is an important distinction became clear when the then Papago Tribe requested the entire population to change the tribal name to the new "official" name, Tohono O'odham "Desert People." Wa:k people were of the opinion that they are not Tohono O'odham, but *Wa:k t-ab o'odham*, people from wetter regions.[8]

While the Tohono O'odham Reservation lies entirely in the United States, Piman speakers live on both sides of the border. The designations *ganhu 'aigo 'amjeḍ* or, more simply, *gnhu 'aigojeḍ* "from the other side" include people who currently live (or who originally came from) Mexican communities, including Sonoita, Hermosilla, Caborca, Quito Vak, San Francisquito, and several smaller villages.[9]

People living off-reservation in rural communities, particularly those noted for cotton farming, are referred to by some as *toki 'oidag 'amjeḍ* "from the cotton field" or *oidag 'amjeḍ* "from the fields." People living in rural farming communities may never for one reason or another have maintained residence on the reservation; this practice is common among people who came "from the other side," who moved into Arizona along with other Mexican migrant workers and took up residence in the many rural communities that surround the northern and eastern periphery of the Tohono O'odham reservation.

The term Zepeda quotes to Mrs. Patricio, "Town O'odham," has a number of synonyms: *wi:piñdam* "toothpick suckers," *go:k da:sa i'idam* "drinkers of two cups of coffee." These designations emphasize a reservation view of town Indians as people who live a soft, luxurious life, sitting around in restaurants. "Town O'odham" are typically those who maintain a permanent residence in town, usually Tucson. People who were born and reared in urban settings may claim a particular part of town as "home," whether it be South Tucson or a particular South Tucson *barrio*. These "Town O'odham" are distinguished from those who merely maintain a temporary residence. Such temporary O'odham residents in urban settings are said to be *'ab aṣ daha*, literally, "just sitting there" (better translated as "visiting," "staying in a place for a short duration"). Zepeda has known cases of *'ab aṣ daha* that lasted fifteen to twenty-five years. These people always have plans to return to the reservation, but "Town O'odham" have no such specific plans.

These different kinds of identities are not ranked; O'odham agree that, while there are different kinds of O'odham people, they are all equal (local pride aside). But these unranked distinctions are not trivial, and they emerge as particularly salient when people end up in the "wrong place," as outsiders in a community. Such distinctions are often cited in local-level negotiations for such resources as acceptance in a family for in-marrying spouses, and a pattern of hazing and teasing "outsiders" is well-documented among O'odham people.

Mrs. Patricio's reaction to Zepeda's suggestions reflects this perspective. While she agrees that reservation people tease her children, she is not anxious to develop this theme. Her rhetorical strategy is to return her children as fast as possible to their correct "place," in the town, so that the awkward insider–outsider juxtaposition will no longer be relevant. In order to do this, she develops an argument that represents her children's "town" identities in a very positive light. In contrast to her own non-prototypical identity in the reservation community, her children are very successful in the town. Unlike many O'odham youngsters who didn't succeed in school because they "can't get used to the *milgan*" ("white people, Anglos", from Spanish *americano*), Mrs. Patricio's children "didn't have no trouble" (lines 20, 21). As she enlarges upon this theme, though, she reveals that educational success still evades her youngest son. This child's failure to graduate is a tricky area to negotiate rhetorically, since Mrs. Patricio risks suggesting not only that her children have not been completely successful, but that she herself has somehow failed in her responsibility. The telling of the story risks her own positive face (Brown and Levinson, 1978), and perhaps also the positive face of Zepeda as another O'odham person.[10] Thus she must defend rhetorically against such a risk, and she uses a wide variety of devices to do so.

Preliminary analysis of the argument

Mrs. Patricio's account takes the form of a series of argumentative moves, beginning at line 11. The large structure of the argument, its organization into a series of two major moves and a series of sub-moves, is shown in Figure 9.1, based on Polanyi's Linguistic Discourse Model. We shall discuss this model below. Within each major move, sub-moves with embedded narratives tell of a Patricio son's truancy. Lines 11–23 begin the first major move, asserting that, unlike many O'odham, the Patricio children "didn't have no trouble" in school. The first sub-move, lines 24–50, recounts a successful intervention that warded off possible "trouble." When Mrs. Patricio learned that her oldest boy was ditching school in Tucson, she sent him off to a parochial school, where he did well and graduated. Lines 51–68 elaborate the account of educational success by other Patricio children.

The second major move begins at line 69. In this section, Mrs. Patricio

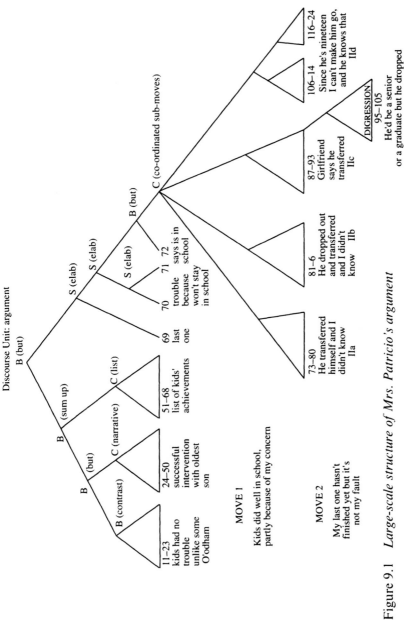

Figure 9.1 *Large-scale structure of Mrs. Patricio's argument*

tells of an apparent failure. When Mrs. Patricio learns that her son is not making progress towards graduation, she cannot intervene, since by the time she discovers this he is no longer a minor. But she tells this trouble in such a way that, instead of being blamed, she achieves chuckling complicity with Zepeda, a complicity and involvement sufficiently compelling that Zepeda still felt rather good about it several days later. Our analysis concentrates on the narratives and quasi-narratives embedded in this second move, and the way they work to "distribute" responsibility for an undesirable situation.

The tale of Mrs. Patricio's youngest son opens with an orientation section, at lines 69–71. The boy "won't stay in school;" this turn of events is a "trouble," with strong emphasis on this word (represented by the underline in line 70). Mrs. Patricio argues that this "trouble" is not something that she can be held fully responsible for. First, she asserts that she did not possess the knowledge she needed in order to intervene. Mrs. Patricio has argued that such knowledge is important in the sub-narrative about her oldest son's truancy and eventual educational success in the first major move. When Mrs. Patricio learned from a friend that her oldest son had been seen wandering around town during school hours (lines 26–39), she sent him off to a strict parochial boarding school, St. John's Indian School at Laveen, Arizona. But in the second subnarrative the necessary knowledge does not arrive in time, so Mrs. Patricio cannot act appropriately. Her son doesn't tell her what he's doing; on the contrary, he misleads her. "He says he's in school" (line 72), but in fact he is dropping out and changing schools without letting her know. Twice she asserts *Pi ma:c ... pi ha'icu ma:c* "(I) didn't know ... (I) didn't know anything" (at lines 80 and 86).

In lines 87–92 Mrs. Patricio shows how she acquired belated knowledge through a third party, her son's girlfriend. Not only is this knowledge late in coming ("about two weeks ago" (line 87)), the third-party origin of this knowledge is emphasized by its representation in O'odham, which requires the use of the "reportative" modal -*ṣ*, seen in line 89 on *m-a-ṣ* "complementizer-3rd person auxiliary–reportative modal" ("that she reportedly"). The use of the O'odham reportative emphasizes that evidence for her son's status comes from the son's girlfriend's report, not from Mrs. Patricio's direct knowledge.

At the local interactional level Mrs. Patricio uses an interesting rhetorical device to distribute responsibility to the interlocutor. She does not directly assert that she is out of control of the situation, but instead invites Zepeda to draw this conclusion. At line 93, in a voice that seems about to break into chuckling, she says, "Next thing I know he'll probably be in Skyline." A local person like Zepeda knows that "Skyline" is an upscale high school on the far side of the city from the urban Indian community;

for an O'odham student to turn up there would be very unexpected, and Zepeda finds this funny, joining Mrs. Patricio in the laughter that ends line 93.

At line 94 Zepeda asks what grade the boy is in. This question apparently interrupts the beginning of a new section of the account (we don't know what Mrs. Patricio might have said after line 94 had Zepeda not broken in), but permits Mrs. Patricio to assert that the boy is a good student; if he hadn't been dropping out and changing schools, he would have graduated ahead of time. This assertion supports Mrs. Patricio's general contention that Patricio children are bright and competent urban people.

In the climax of this assertion, at lines 105–6, Mrs. Patricio again accomplishes a "distribution" at the level of the local interaction by constituting herself as a figure in constructed dialogue: "I tell him, "You're gonna graduate with the grandchildren." She and Zepeda both laugh at this rhythmic and alliterative speech. This representation is interesting for several reasons. By appearing in the voice of a "figure," it is distributed away from direct access to challenge by Zepeda, as will be suggested below. It also shows that Mrs. Patricio is a very education-oriented parent. Such speech is an unusually direct sanction, since O'odham parents rarely reprimand children by referring to the child's own behavior. They prefer to nudge children toward proper conduct by talking about other young people who do well by behaving correctly. The statement also contradicts a conservative O'odham opinion that the sort of age disparity that develops when a child falls too far behind in school is so undesirable that it is best simply to drop out. Mrs. Patricio shows here that, unlike more conservative O'odham parents, she is not disturbed by this age disparity. She expects her son to graduate, even if he is still in school with his own nieces and nephews. Mrs. Patricio thus represents her views about education as typical of an English-language, urban-oriented Indian identity.

In her final argumentative move, beginning at line 106, Mrs. Patricio again distributes responsibility for her "trouble" across several voices, thus metaphorically placing events in a social field, rather than locating them in the agency of individuals. The move begins with an introductory sub-narrative (actually a sort of quasi-narrative, since its present-tense verbs and the use of "they" suggest that it summarizes several conversations). During this quasi-narrative Mrs. Patricio shifts from locutionary verbs like "tell" (line 106) and "ask" (line 108) to "dramatic" dialogue without locutionary verbs at lines 110–12:

110. "Nineteen" [Oh!]
111. "O:h, then, . . .
112. you can't do nothing about it."

The absence of locutionary verbs is a rhetorical device that places "they" and Mrs. Patricio (represented through the voice of her "figure") entirely in the "story world," removed from the interactional world. Longacre (1976) has pointed out that such "dramatic" dialogue is characteristic of narrative peak, the moment of maximum plot tension and maximum involvement between narrator and interlocutor. We return to this section again below to discuss the involvement signaled by Zepeda's "Oh!" in response to 110.

The second part of this sub-move develops a specific example of the type of conversation reported in lines 106–14 as the first event in a tiny narrative. Here Mrs. Patricio distributes responsibility through several techniques. She uses reported speech (in indirect discourse), but also the rhetorical technique of impersonality. A new figure enters the narrative, "Hulia Moore." Her speech is represented in indirect discourse under English "that." The use of "you" in the representation in line 120, "you can't do nothing about it," repeats the "you" of line 112, "you can't do nothing about it," in the previous quasi-narrative. But while in line 112 "you" seems to be a deictic, a direct address to Mrs. Patricio as a hearer within the story world, the "you" of line 120 is referential, an example of "impersonal you." Kitagawa and Lehrer (1990) have provided a test for this difference. In indirect discourse deictic "you" will undergo deixis shift to "I": "Hulia Moore said that if he's nineteen, I can't do nothing about it." The absence of such a shift in line 120 reveals the impersonal usage (note that a shift from "can't" to "couldn't" may not be possible in Mrs. Patricio's English). The use of "anybody" in line 119 also makes clear that the sentence is "impersonal," and implies that the "trouble" is general in a social field consisting of parents of nineteen-year-olds, and not specific to Mrs. Patricio. In addition, of course, "You can't do nothing about it" is a claim that Mrs. Patricio cannot be held responsible for her son's behavior, and gains authority by being uttered, not in her own voice ("I can't do nothing about it") but in the voice of a neutral observer from outside the family.

Finally, the episode distributes responsibility by arguing that Mrs. Patricio herself did not reveal to the boy her lack of authority over him (it is likely that the "I didn't" at 115 begins a sentence, abandoned for a richer rhetorical move, that would have gone something like: "I didn't tell him that I can't make him go to school; he found out by accident"). Instead, he acquired this knowledge by overhearing Hulia Moore talking. Zepeda clearly accepts the significance of this, as shown by her laughter after line 124; shared laughter throughout the narrative suggests that the speaker has successfully negotiated a complicity with Zepeda about the nature of the "problem" and how responsibility should be assigned.

Mrs. Patricio's argument thus successfully "distributes" responsibility.

She uses a wide range of strategies to suggest that her "trouble" with her son is not focused on herself as an "individual," a "responsible" parent, but across a broad social field in which knowledge and possibilities for action have a variable potential. She successfully involves her interlocutor as a sympathetic and amused participant in this social field. Thus she is able to avoid compromising her assertion that her children are successful urban Indians, and that she herself is an education-oriented parent who has helped make this success possible.

We can contrast the strategies that Mrs. Patricio actually uses with possible alternative strategies with exactly the same referential content. First, she might have constituted her argumentative moves as bald assertions, located in the "now" of the interview world and addressed directly to Zepeda's "you": "I really value education, as shown by my children's achievements. Just one of my children is having problems finishing school, but it's not my fault." Even after choosing to develop small narratives as part of her argumentative moves, Mrs. Patricio still had options other than the ones she used. She could have departed briefly from the story world and made direct statements to the interviewer about her own thoughts: "I think he's going to take a long time to graduate"; "I've found out that since he's nineteen I can't make him stay at school"; "He knows I can't make him stay in school since he's nineteen." Such evaluative statements in the interactional world (what Labov [1972a] has called "external evaluation") might even have been made without the use of "I" which would profile her own affective involvement (as Goffman points out, to say "I" creates a "distance." (Goffman, 1981:148)). Mrs. Patricio could have said, "He's going to take a long time to graduate," and "He knows he can make his own decisions about school as an adult of nineteen." Mrs. Patricio does not select these devices, and there is some evidence that such a selection is seldom desirable. Once narrative is selected as the genre through which an argumentative move will be elaborated, the moral point or central moral conflict of an experience is preferably asserted in the story world, not the interactional world. Labov (1972) pointed out this preference when he noted that skilled vernacular narrators make more use of "internal" evaluation – evaluation in the "story world" – than of "external evaluation" in the interactional world. Even morals asserted in codas in the interactional world will be removed at one step from the immediate I–you locus, either by being couched as an explicit performative – "It's like I always say … " – thereby "objectifying" the speaker, or by being expressed as universal wisdom – "It's like they say … " (proverbial expression fills ellipses).

The social distribution of responsibility across a variety of figures is common in conversational narrative. In Mrs. Patricio's story, the distributed responsibility is negative, but responsibility for success is also often distributed. For instance, in the story, "I knew him when," published by Schiffrin (1984), the narrator reminisces about a school friend who became a famous comedian. He argues that he recognized very early that the boy knew how to make an audience laugh. The point is made with special force by constructing a social field which includes not only the narrator and his friend, but an amused audience (at a music recital) and a teacher who "breaks up" at the friend's wit; the teacher's amusement is represented through her constructed dialogue.

The formal analysis of the argument: world structure, pragmatic accessibility, and discourse anaphora

Why do argumentative moves often include embedded narrative? And why do conversational narrators so often develop the "point" of their stories through the construction of multi-character dramas? A variety of semiotic purposes is no doubt thus served; our concern is with the management of responsibility. Chafe's (1980) discussion of the division of semantic and pragmatic "worlds" between the story and the interaction suggests one reason why devices such as conversational narrative and constructed dialogue within such narrative work to distribute responsibility. Chafe observes that when speakers shift between these worlds they often exhibit "hesitating and stumbling." This behavior suggests that "a shift of worlds is the most radical kind of reorientation one can make, involving as it does not only spatio–temporal and social differences, but a fundamental difference in expectation" (Chafe, 1980:47). If it is difficult for a speaker to make the rhetorical moves necessary to get from one world to another, this may be doubly difficult for an interlocutor. Thus to make an argumentative point within the "story world" of a sub-narrative probably makes the truth of such a point relatively inaccessible to challenge, compared to assertions in the interactional world. The fact that it is very difficult for interlocutors to access world-lines laminated away from the interactional world by speakers may be one source of the well-known preference for "self-initiated repair" (Schegloff, Jefferson, and Sacks, 1977).

Chafe's proposal about the rhetorical distance between semantic worlds is supported by the effects of world shifts on anaphoric accessibility in discourse. Clancy (1980) points out that shifts between the story world and the interactional world often involve reintroduction of definite anaphoric reference when one would not expect this in terms of measures of linear distance, such as those developed by Givón (1985). Thus story characters are often introduced anew after such a shift, or characters referred to in indefinite reference in the story world ("a boy") might be referred to as definite in the interactional world ("the boy").

While Chafe and Clancy distinguish only between the story world and the interactional world, patterns of anaphora suggest that the story world itself is internally differentiated, with constructed-dialogue direct discourse establishing a separate "world-line" embedded within the story world. Thus nominal reference in direct discourse is relatively inaccessible to anaphoric reference in narrative sentences; for Chafe and Clancy, these are part of the story world.[11] This can be seen in a modern Nahuatl story about a fight between a goat and a bull, in which the breaking of the bull's horns, introduced in a narrative sentence, is repeated in a sentence in constructed dialogue:

1. *Pos ōcxihxicohqueh in toro, ōccuacuanpapayatzqueh. Ōtlaxichoh in chivo. Pos ōcyequitoh in toro, quihtoa, quilia in huelita, "Amo, siempre yōnexihxicoh, xiquit, hasta yōnēchcuacuanpapayatzqueh."*

Well they defeated the bull, they broke his horns. The goat won. Well the bull correctly said, he said, he said to the old lady, "No, I am always defeated, look, they even broke my horns."

A reintroduction in the opposite direction, with the constructed dialogue appearing first, comes from a story of a possum who deceives a coyote by giving him hard, green sapote fruit instead of good fruit:

2. *Quihtoa, "Nitlacuatl, pero de tzapotl, in tla ticnequi ce tzapotl, nimitzye-coloti. Tiahue." Yōtlehco īpan tzapote, ōquimaca in tzapotl xoxohqui.*

He says, "I'm a possum, but of the sapote kind, so if you want a sapote, I'll offer you one. Let's go." He climbed into the sapote tree, and he gave him a green sapote.

English speakers can test their preference with a hypothetical example, an alternative telling of part of "Little Red Riding Hood."

3. Little Red Riding Hood said to the wolf, "What big teeth you have!" "The better to eat you with, my dear."
   a. ?They were white, shiny, and sharp.
   b. Those teeth were white, shiny, and sharp.

For the authors, (3b.) is preferable. The preference seems less strong if the reported speech is made direct, as in (4). Although the (4b.) sentence still makes for livelier narrative, the anaphoric reference of "they" in (4a.) seems more accessible than in the example with direct-discourse constructed dialogue.

4. Little Red Riding Hood told the wolf that he had very big teeth, and he told her that they would make it easier to eat her.
   a. They were white, shiny, and sharp.
   b. Those teeth were white, shiny, and sharp.

Patterns of repetition constitute another line of evidence about the differentiation of worlds achieved in vernacular narrative. While the rhetorical
use of repetition in English vernacular narrative is less extensive than in
the narrative traditions of many other speech communities, English
speakers can easily repeat propositions appearing in constructed dialogue
by locating these in separate represented conversations. This occurs in
Mrs. Patricio's narrative. In line 110 Mrs. Patricio is represented as saying
"Nineteen"; in lines 111 and 112 a constructed-dialogue voice says, "O:h,
then, you can't do <u>no</u>thing about it." Precisely the same content is
repeated in the indirect discourse at lines 119 and 120 where Hulia Moore
says that "anybody nineteen, you can't do nothing about it." This
repetition enhances the point of the story, but it is more than rhetorical.
In referential terms, it is the only way of picking up the critical information about the age "nineteen" which is overheard by Mrs. Patricio's
son. If lines 119 and 120 had been, "Hulia Moore told me that too," the
anaphoric element could have been only to the propositional content of
line 112, "You can't do nothing about it." The anaphoric reference
permitted is to the global propositional content of the last speech. For
instance, such is clearly the reference of the "that" in 123, "when she was
saying that," and again in 124 "so he heard that, y'know," where "that"
refers to "what Hulia Moore said" at lines 119 and 120. But unmarked
(zero or unstressed "that/it") anaphoric reference at (119–20) to the
content of all the previous conversation at (109–12) would not have been
possible.[12]

The observations by Chafe, Clancy, and others about pragmatic and
anaphoric inaccessibility of constructed dialogue, and the odd developments of repetition and anaphoric elaboration around it, provide the
beginning of the explanation we require for why Mrs. Patricio chooses to
embed narratives and constructed dialogue in her arguments. We can
explore this issue in more detail by examining Mrs. Patricio's narrative
from the perspective of the computational model of discourse, the LDM
or "Linguistic Discourse Model" proposed by Polanyi and her co-
workers (Polanyi, 1985; Scha and Polanyi, 1988; Polanyi and Martin,
1989). Polanyi bases her model on insights into the hierarchical structure
of discourse first reported by Linde (1972) for descriptions of space, and
Grosz (1977) for task-oriented dialogue. Linde and Grosz observed that
some patterns of anaphoric accessibility can be accounted for in structural terms. Polanyi models this in the following way: the structure of
discourse as a parse tree constructed from left to right. Anaphora only
succeeds within a currently active branch of the tree, and cannot access
material subordinated on a part of the tree that has been completed or
"closed." Such material is "structurally inaccessible." Access is not absolutely precluded, since, as Polanyi points out, in real-life discourse anyone

can say anything at any time. But if speakers desire to establish such access, they cannot use unmarked anaphoric elements such as zero or unstressed pronouns and demonstratives. Instead, they must use highly marked and explicit forms, often marked by elements described by conversational analysts as "repairs," such as "Oh, by the way," or "That reminds me, I forgot to mention," etc.

A tentative discourse parse tree of lines 73–124 of Mrs. Patricio's argument is given in Figures 9.2, 9.3, and 9.4. The text on the leaves is paraphrased in order to fit into the diagram.

While it is not the purpose of the present paper to argue in detail for the Linguistic Discourse Model, or to explore every aspect of this complex text within the model, a brief review of how the figures are constructed is necessary. Large structures within the Interaction (such as argumentative moves or narratives) are labelled Discourse units or DUs. Each leaf of the tree consists of a Discourse Constituent Unit or DCU; these are normally clauses. Each new DCU is related to the previous one by semantic and pragmatic computation. Only three types of relationship are permitted. Co-ordination nodes (marked "C") indicate that the new node is related to the preceding dcu (or subtree consisting of several DCUs) as part of an ongoing discourse activity. For instance, the events on a narrative event line are related to one another by co-ordination. This is seen in Figure 9.4 in the subnarrative at lines 116–24, where Hulia Moore's speech, at lines 118–20, constitutes the first event. The son's "walking in" while she was talking and overhearing her is the second event. Thus the subtree made up of lines 121–24 is related to 118–20 by a C node. Several C nodes in the present analysis relate topics and comments; thus *Pi ma:c* "I didn't know" at line 80 is a comment on the event represented in 73–9.

Subordination nodes (marked "S") indicate that the new node is related to the preceding node as an elaboration or interruption of the discourse activity. Thus, in Figure 9.4, the anecdote about Hulia Moore's remark seems to be at least in part an elaboration or example of the quasi-narrative material at lines 106–14, and can be related to these lines by a "S" node (at another level, it seems to constitute a new narrative sub-move, asserting that Mrs. Patricio did not, herself, tell her son that she is not legally empowered to make him attend school; such ambiguities offer a rich area for further study).[13] Note that some subordination nodes, labeled SC, are reversible: subordinated material, such as preposed relative clauses or durative-descriptive material in narratives, may be preposed to matrix clauses or event-line clauses, meaning that the subordinated material is to the left, not the right, of the matrix.

Finally, binary nodes, marked "B," express rhetorical and logical relationships between parts of two-part discourse activities such as repetition, cause–effect, if–then relationships, question–answer pairs and

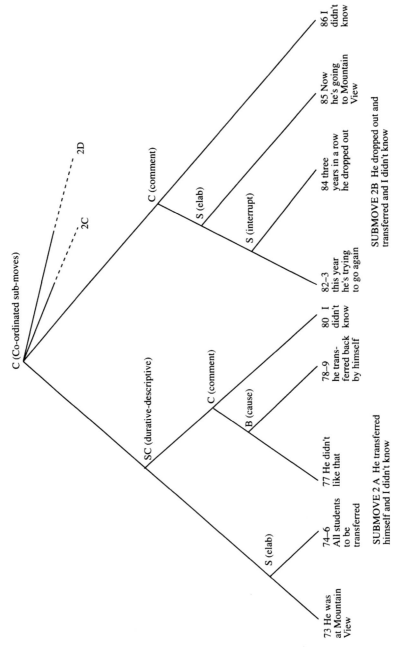

Figure 9.2   *Sub-moves 2A and 2B*

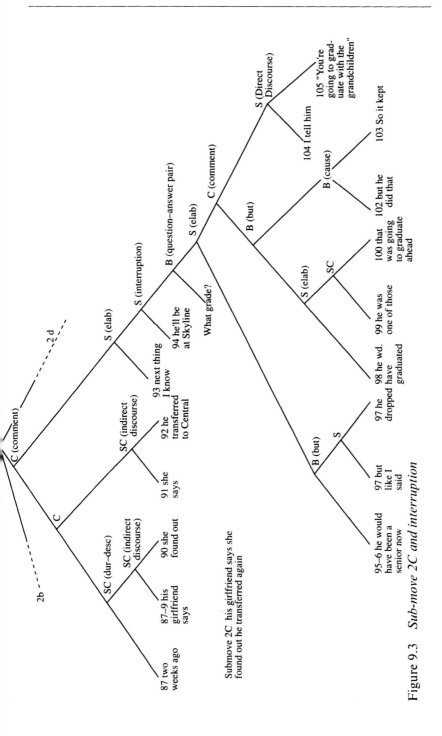

Figure 9.3 *Sub-move 2C and interruption*

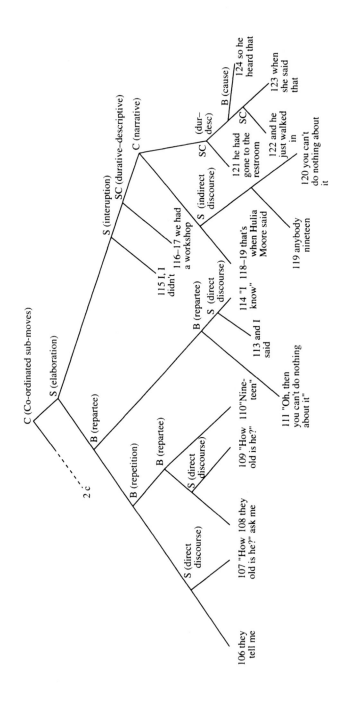

Figure 9.4   *Sub-move 2D*

other embedded repartee, and disjunction with "but." Examples of two types of binary nodes, repetition and repartee, are found in Figure 9.4 in 106–14.

Subtypes of each kind of node (C, S, and B) are labeled (such labels can be seen in the figures); one goal of research on the Linguistic Discourse Model is to determine the size of the inventory of such labels, which stand for discourse "operators" which may surface phonologically.

Polanyi and Martin (1989:28) summarize the parsing algorithm used in the Linguistic Discourse Model. Trees are constructed by determining the relationship (S, C, or B) of each incoming DCU to the tree that has already been constructed. If the new DCU elaborates the immediately preceding dcu, then it is attached to it as a right sister under a newly created subordination node. If it is not an elaboration, then the parser searches the open right edge of the discourse parse tree looking for semantic or syntactic matches. Once a match is made, the new dcu is added at the appropriate existing node (for instance, at the C node of an ongoing narrative event line), or a new node is created. If there is no match, the new DCU is considered an interruption and is added under an S node at the bottom of the parse tree. This is exemplified in Figure 9.2, where Zepeda's question and its answer constitute an interruption, although Mrs. Patricio fits the answer nicely into the overall argument as an embedded sub-move. The parser includes a buffer; an example of the necessity of such a buffer is seen at 116–17, "We had a workshop at Pima College." It turns out that this workshop was the occasion for a conversation that can be taken to elaborate through exemplification the type Mrs. Patricio reviews in 106–14, but this is not immediately obvious.

The discourse parse trees in Figures 9.2–4 model the structural situation of constructed dialogue, and provide an account of its anaphoric inaccessibility. Since the parser computes semantic matches, constructed dialogue nodes are only available for attachment of new B nodes, during ongoing repartee within some world in which that repartee takes place (and of course constructed dialogue can contain internal co-ordination and subordination). The only possible context in which a DCU not in the constructed-dialogue world can be attached to constructed-dialogue DCUs is a true interruption, as when a narrator suddenly interrupts the tale to shoo a dog or hush a baby. Thus the "structural inaccessibility" of repartee or constructed dialogue is modelled by a parsing algorithm that is independently motivated.

It is important to observe that the determination of a relationship of a new DCU to an existing parse tree is determined by semantic and pragmatic computation, not by the discourse particles that the new DCU may include (Polanyi and Martin, 1989, discuss this point in detail). Yet the distribution of discourse particles in Mrs. Patricio's argument does provide additional evidence for the structural status of repartee. Polanyi gives a special status to the discourse POP, an abstract element that marks the formation of a new front node and thus closes off the preceding topic chain.[14] POP elements are often represented at the surface. In English they may appear as discourse particles such as "Well," and "So"; they can also be represented prosodically, by postural shifts, gestures, and a variety of other devices. An example is the POP "Ahh, yes" at line 106. Mrs. Patricio has digressed in lines 95–105 in order to answer Zepeda's question, "What grade is he in?" At 106, she begins, "They tell me . . . " The immediately preceding dcu is a comment (which takes the form of Mrs. Patricio reporting her own speech to her son) on the problem of his failure to graduate, discussed in lines 98–103. The DCU at 106 is clearly not semantically matched to 105, since it seems to involve new dramatis personae (although the historical-present verb "tell" is parallel); we cannot explore this kind of poetic effect in the present paper, but it does argue that other structures besides those revealed by the LDM are in play here (as suggested by the work of Woodbury, 1987). Thus a POP particle like "Ahh, yes" is not unexpected here, and serves as an extra signal that the structure in 95–105 is now closed off.

Line 116 contains a POP represented propositionally, not through a discourse particle. Line 116 constructs a new story-world context, "the workshop at Pima College" (there is also prosodic differentiation between 114 and 116). The attention to the new time and place signals that the representation of the previous conversation, at an earlier time, is "closed." Another POP is found at line 121; this POP is signaled by the shift to high pitch and by the particle "and." The distribution of these POP types provides supporting evidence for the construction of the tree, and the structural position of constructed dialogue.

While Polanyi's Linguistic Discourse Model certainly does not solve all the conundrums posed by constructed dialogue, it does suggest structural reasons for peculiarities of anaphora around this device observed by Chafe (1980) and his students, and provides an avenue for exploring why propositions represented in constructed dialogue might be relatively "safe," inaccessible to challenges by the interlocutor, and thus a likely site for the development of possible face-threatening material for which a speaker does not want to assume sole responsibility. It also highlights a paradox: while propositional material expressed within constructed dialogue is anaphorically inaccessible to dcus located in the interactional world, its rhetorical force is one of greater affective involvement. Tannen (1988) has noted the "involving," "rapport-building" function of direct-discourse constructed dialogue. Dramatic or "mimetic" constructed dialogue may be especially involving, since by deleting locutionary verbs the speaker refers partial responsibility for reconstructing the sequence of events to the hearer. Such heightened involvement after "dramatic" speech is evident here. For instance, after the figure of Mrs. Patricio tells someone the boy's age, nineteen, at line 110, Zepeda says "Oh!", much as if she herself had been directly addressed. This "Oh!" (it might even be "Oops") is a much stronger response than her usual attentive mode. Zepeda is clearly "involved" even by constructed dialogue which is not "dramatic," as evidenced by her laughter in response to Mrs. Patricio's representations of her own speech at lines 93 and 105.

The formal framework we have been using suggests a direction in which we might work to untangle this apparent paradox, of relative inaccessibility at the propositional level combined with heightened involvement of the interlocutor. Involvement may be partly the necessary obverse of the inaccessibility to question of the constructed-dialogue propositions. The interlocutor is especially compelled to agree with these, since it is so difficult to develop the sequence of conversational moves which might be required to make them accessible to questioning. Thus responsibility is distributed not only across the figures in the narrative, but onto the listener as well, who is drawn into complicity in what is asserted by the structural properties of the device of constructed dialogue.

The structural analysis of the inaccessibility of propositions in constructed dialogue suggests one way we might understand why speakers choose narrative as the form of elaboration of argumentative moves. Langacker's (1985) analysis of the expression of subjectivity in English, motivated by theoretical concerns within his "cognitive grammar," also contributes to our understanding of this choice. He argues that there is a continuum in English between the most subjective and most objective possible points of view on a situation. In the most subjective utterances, the presence of the speaker (and listener) as "observers" is completely implicit. This is illustrated by such propositional assertions as "Tuesday is the second day of the week," or "Phoenix is 110 miles north of Tucson." In more "objective" utterances, the speaker is foregrounded and represented as an object of attention. A slightly increased objectivity appears with deictic elements that Langacker terms "epistemic predications" such as "This" or tense-aspect markers. Thus "Tuesday was awful," or "It's a long boring trip to Phoenix" relativizes this referential content to the I–you situation of speaking. Even greater objectivity is achieved when speech-act participants are brought "onstage" by using words like "I," "you," or "me," especially in explicit performatives like "I'm telling you Tuesday was awful." A particularly heightened type of "objectivity" occurs in what Langacker calls "displacement," as in "Come sit next to your mother" (uttered to someone by her mother), or "cross-world identification", when a speaker establishes herself as a figure in another world: "In my next film the CIA is trying to kill me."

The representation of self by a speaker as a "figure" within a world laminated away from the interactional world, whether through narrative or through some other device, falls close to Langacker's objective extreme. This "objectivity," by foregrounding the speaker as an objective presence (creating a sort of double presence, since the subjectivity does not disappear), heightens the degree of distribution of representation across semantic space. It creates, metaphorically, more "persons" in this space.

Langacker (1985) proposes that the greater the objectivity of an utterance, the longer it is: length is an icon for objectivity. If this proposal is correct then narrative, which is a very lengthy way to develop a point (requiring as it does at least two events), falls at the extreme of the iconic continuum. The distance between the "figures" thereby made available for observation, and the speaker and the interlocutor (who are always implicit in the interaction) is thereby maximized; the greatest possible "distribution" is achieved within the interaction. Presumably this tension also maximizes the pleasure of "involvement" (created also, we have proposed, at least partly by structural barriers at the propositional level).

Conclusion: narrative, voice, and the socialization of responsibility

Mrs. Patricio's narrative creates a complex world of social differentiation and interactional space across which her "trouble" with her son is distributed. Mrs. Patricio's presence, the locus of face, knowledge, and responsibility, is not an atomic individuality, but a diffuse and highly socialized construction. This socialization and diffusion, accomplished through the "distribution" of responsibility, may have little to do with the fact that Mrs. Patricio and her interlocutor, Ofelia Zepeda, are Tohono O'odham people. Similar rhetorical strategies can be seen in vernacular oral autobiographical narrative collected from middle-aged Philadelphia Jewish men (Schiffrin, 1984), from black teenagers (Labov, 1972a), and from Nahuatl-speaking Mexican peasants (Hill, 1989). The analysis of such narratives suggests that "individuality" in its stereotyped form is rare in vernacular conversational narrative. For many Americans, "individuality" as the locus of responsibility and agency may be largely an artifact of formal and public life as constituted through the legal system, through the practice of formal religion, and in formal political and economic discourse. It may not be salient in quotidian accounts of experience.[15]

This analysis of the distribution of responsibility through narrative and quasi-narrative in argument suggests several points. First, we find that the formal, computational investigation of discourse is highly relevant to our concerns about language in society, rather than an irrelevant or even hostile pursuit. While it is often suggested that evidence from the analysis of actual interaction will necessarily contradict formalist claims, this is not the case here. Second, our analysis suggests that perhaps language need not be seen, as Banfield suggests, as "the repository of an objectivized knowledge of subjectivity," with the latter a "silent, shifting point of consciousness which is the I's special reference" (Banfield, 1982:97). While attention to point of view at the level of the clause (as in Banfield's work) may suggest such a position, attention to larger structures in narrative discourse reveals to us a socialized, distributed universe where many points of view are closely juxtaposed. Much of linguistic structure itself may be ideologically quite neutral: we must consider the possibility that ideologies of the self are founded, not upon what is intrinsic in linguistic structure, but upon what our cultures invite us to notice in it. The analysis suggests, in fact, that the capacity for discourse to evoke metaphorically the complex sociality of experience may be critical to the social life of language. Just as explicit insult can be managed by its production through complex participant structures, life's ordinary dilemmas of accountability and responsibility can be managed through the metaphorical creation of a social drama with many actors, and by the devices of "objectivity" and distancing within the interactional moment permitted in vernacular narrative.

NOTES

We would like to acknowledge especially Livia Polanyi for her assistance in parsing Mrs. Patricio's text, as well as the many useful comments by the anonymous referees of the present volume, and Judith T. Irvine. Of course we are responsible for errors and infelicities that remain.
1 "Molly Patricio" is a fictitious name, as are all others in the narrative. We have also changed the names of schools except for Pima College (the local community college), the "University", the University of Arizona, and St. John's Indian School; the first two are unique in their context, and the last has been attended by so many O'odham students that mentioning it compromises nobody's privacy.

The second speaker in the narrative is Ofelia Zepeda, one of the present authors, who is a native speaker of O'odham. Certain aspects of Zepeda's identity, as known to Mrs. Patricio before the interview and as constructed locally during the interaction analyzed here, may partly motivate the way Mrs. Patricio develops her argument. We return to these below.

Also present during the interview was Molly DuFort, graduate research assistant, who is not a speaker of O'odham. Her presence may be a factor in Mrs. Patricio's tendency to speak mainly in English, but we note that Ms. DuFort was present at many other interviews which proceeded entirely in O'odham.

2 Hill (1988) has proposed that a "voice system" is a system in rhetorical structure (Woodbury, 1987) that organizes the representation of point of view through a variety of devices. These include the "lamination" of the speaker into animator, principal, protagonist, strategist, and "figure" (Goffman, 1974), which involves the use of constructed dialogue. It involves code choice in the interaction between authorial and reported speech (Bakhtin, 1981, 1983; Voloshinov, 1973; Hill, 1988a, to appear a). It involves also the direct representation of point of view as, for instance, in "evaluation" (Labov, 1972a) or through deictic devices such as those of free indirect style (Banfield, 1982).

3 We have used minimal diacritical notation. Underlines mean that the syllable received especially heavy stress. Material in parentheses was uttered on a pulmonary ingressive airstream, a device common in the speech of O'odham women. O'odham words appearing in code-switched passages are glossed interlinearly. Each line is an "intonation unit" (Chafe, 1987). Conversational contributions by the interviewer are not given line numbers, but are indicated in the appropriate location in brackets; if they are on the line below the narrative speech, it means they were simultaneous with speech by the narrator (this is indicated by square brackets). In one case where the interviewer makes a rather long contribution it is indented without line numbers. In O'odham, the symbols /ḍ/ and /ṣ/ stand for retroflex consonants. /e/ is a central vowel.

4 This study was funded by the National Science Foundation under Grant BNS 8608009.

5 Zepeda grew up in a "cotton field" O'odham community, not on the reservation itself; we do not know whether Mrs. Patricio knew that or not.

6 We were anxious to consult speakers like Mrs. Patricio, since we felt that our dialect sample should include usage of people who have lived in O'odham communities off the reservation. While we have not conducted a complete analysis of variation in O'odham speaking skills, we tentatively classify Mrs. Patricio as a "semi-speaker" of her native language (Dorian, 1978). Her English is "Indian English" (Leap, 1977).

7 O'odham-dominant bilinguals also code-switch. We have not studied code-switching in the O'odham community carefully, but Zepeda believes that Mrs. Patricio may be rather extreme in her switching pattern.

8 The tribal entity now known as "Pima" is often called *Akimel O'odham* "river people." The language of this group is mutually intelligible with that of the Tohono O'odham; the boundaries between "Pima" and the northernmost Tohono O'odham dialects are quite uncertain.

9 Being "from the other side" is potentially a serious problem because of US immigration laws. Unlike Indians along the US–Canadian border in the north-east, the Tohono O'odham enjoy no special treaty guarantees of free movement, even though everybody recognizes that people were irrationally split up by the artificial border, right down to the level of nuclear families. Generally, Tohono O'odham districts have been willing to enroll people "from the other side," giving such immigrants *de facto* US citizenship. The Tohono O'odham Nation has also concerned itself with the plight of Mexican O'odham, who have little legal protection for their lands. But people are

understandably cautious about revealing an identity as *aigo amjeḏkam* to outsiders.

10 The fact that Zepeda is a highly educated person and a member of the faculty of the University of Arizona was known to Mrs. Patricio, since Patricio children have been in Zepeda's classes. Thus it seems likely that the development of the argument that Mrs. Patricio is a parent who supports her children's education serves not only her desire to "place" her children in the most advantageous position, but to achieve complicity with Zepeda in an opinion, the desirability of educational success for O'odham children, that Mrs. Patricio might safely assume Zepeda holds.

11 We believe that narrative sentences are complex in terms of world assignment. Some narrative sentences have their illocutionary effect as assertions in the interactional world, but their "referentiality" is rooted in the story world. Various rhetorical devices are used by vernacular narrators to exploit this ambiguous position of narrative sentences.

12 Note that anaphoric presupposition which somehow appeals to the wider narrative is possible within the world-line of conversations in constructed dialogue. This is seen, for instance, in line 112. There the "it" of "You can't do nothing about it" clearly implies that the speaking figure knows what we know about Mrs. Patricio's son's school problems, even though the conversation does not represent the reported speaker's acquisition of this information. Obviously, the anaphoric interrelationships between constructed dialogue and other discourse structures are very complex and require further research.

13 In the present analysis, we have taken direct-discourse sentences to be subordinated to locutionary verbs when these are present, as, for instance, at 108–9. Polanyi and Martin (1989) analyze locutionary verbs not as dcus but as discourse operators, a category that includes discourse particles such as "Yes" and "Well" that do not have propositional content. Since locutionary verbs can differ semantically along several dimensions, including what speech act they represent and their tenses, since their presence vs. absence (as in "dramatic" dialogue) seems to be significant, and since sequences of turns in dialogue seem to be able to constitute an event line (see Hill, 1989), we prefer to consider them as having propositional content, and represent them conventionally as matrix-clause DCUs with direct and indirect discourse subordinated to them.

14 Polanyi has borrowed the terms "PUSH" and "POP" from the computational metaphor of a stack. PUSH elements push discourse components in a stack (for example, a sequence of embeddings in a topic chain), while POP elements return to the top of a stack.

15 Interestingly, the narratives by upper-middle-class whites collected by Polanyi (1989) exhibit less representation of metaphorical social distribution in the form of a variety of supportive figurative voices, although they do exhibit local interactional distribution through the representation of the constructed dialogue of the teller in the story world. This raises the tempting possibility that relative "individuality" in English vernacular narrative may be associated with class (Hill, 1989).

THE GRAMMATICALIZATION OF RESPONSIBILITY AND EVIDENCE: INTERACTIONAL POTENTIAL OF EVIDENTIAL CATEGORIES IN NEWARI

EDWARD H. BENDIX

Introduction

In the study of discourse we look not only for the contribution of the whole – of the shared background and the developing speech record – to the interpretation of the part, but also for the contribution of the part to the creation of the whole. This chapter will examine some parts – some discourse fragments – for their contextual and strategic potentials. The fragments take surface forms interpretable as assertions and questions, and in Newari[1] they carry obligatory evidential verb morphology which can convey evidence and, by extension, responsibility for reported states of affairs or projections into the future, both when the information is asserted and when it is requested.

In other words, in the study of responsibility and evidence in oral discourse I shall start at the grammatical end. I shall analyze one language's system of grammaticalized evidential categories and illustrate how it can be manipulated in oral interaction in the belief that a rigorous theory of discourse cannot just assume the precise semantic contribution of grammar, but must analyze the parts if it is to show how they fit together to form the larger whole. Although concerned with the theme of the present volume, this chapter will thus stand out among the other contributions for the extent to which it deals with grammar.

The strategic potentials illustrated here in the use of the evidentials were generated by two established elicitation techniques. First, speakers were asked to construct pairs of contrasting discourse contexts to match with presented minimal pair sentences differing only in their evidential morphemes. Second, they were asked to construct contexts as well for marked use of the evidentials, including violations in the Gricean sense (Grice, 1975); that is, they were urged to interpret in a context, usually successfully, even sentences that, out of context, at first struck them as strange or unacceptable, a task given to them because speakers' reasons for initially rejecting elicitation sentences are not easily controlled.

Again, the use of techniques typically lumped together with many others into a category called "elicitation" will stand out in the context of the present volume. Elicitation is often seen as problematic in contrast to something considered to be naturally occurring speech or narrative. However, dividing speaker utterances into reliable natural ones and unreliable, presumably artificial ones is itself problematic, and so this issue will be addressed again in the concluding discussion section.

Finally, the use here of a pragmatic mode of reasoning seems to be part of a speech-act theory that has come under attack (see, e.g., DuBois and Duranti, this volume). Thus this issue as well will have to be addressed in the discussion section since a major objection is to the intentionality component, which the pragmatic mode I apply does not require in the sense of intention to communicate or communicated intention.

Unmarked usages of the evidentials

The finite verb endings of Newari may be divided into hypothetical and nonhypothetical ones.[2] These could also be called future and nonfuture or, as they have been, nonpast and past. There are two hypotheticals distinguishable as "internal" and "external." I shall discuss the three nonhypotheticals. These will be labeled the INT(ernal) evidential, the EXT(ernal) evidential, which is also perfective, and the CHAR(acterizing). These labels are used for reasons which will become clearer below although the more commonly encountered designations are "conjunct" for the internal category and "disjunct" for the external. The characterizing is often simply called the "long" form (Hale, 1980; Hargreaves, 1983; Genetti, 1986).

Loosely, INT expresses intentional performance of the action, EXT indicates observed evidence of the action, and CHAR depicts the subject referent as characterized by the predicate. Sentences (1)–(5) illustrate unmarked usages of the three nonhypotheticals in assertions. The morpheme-by-morpheme glosses are given above the Newari forms.[3] Note the co-occurrences of pronouns with evidential endings:

(1)   I   go-INT   I go, I used to go, I went, I have gone
       ji   *won-a*

(2)   you   go-EXT   You went, you have gone
       cho   *won-o*

(3)   s/he   go-EXT   S/he went, s/he has gone
       wo   *won-o*

(4)   you   go-CHAR   You go, you used to go, you went
       cho   *won-v̇*

(5)   s/he   go-CHAR   S/he goes, s/he used to go, s/he went
       wo   *won-v̇*

The glosses offered in this first section bring together the actual English words used by the speakers consulted, with minor editorial changes, such as using "s/he" to indicate the gender-neutral third-person pronoun of Newari.

The usages above are called "unmarked" in the extended sense[4] to mean that these are the usages of the evidentials one is most likely to encounter, they are the ones provided as translation equivalents of English sentences, or they are the ones often interpreted simply by translation into English. If contexts of use are requested for them, speakers often approach the task as though it is really unnecessary: the utterances are too general, too unmarked. These reactions contrast with those reported in the second section below in connection with marked usages where the need for contextualization is accepted.

When someone is said to go somewhere, our first expectation is that the person is represented as performing the action with conscious intention. Thus in (1) I am the reporter of my own action, and, from the paradigm of mutually opposed, obligatory evidentials, I expectedly select INT as the indicator of evidence for my assertion.[5] Not that I don't have other evidence for my going, but my own involvement in my action is what I am expected to express in the sense that using a non-INT can be interpreted as my choice to exclude my involvement, at least for present purposes. Inferentially, then, by using INT I can also be interpreted as taking responsibility for my action. In (2)–(5) I am reporting someone else's actions and must select EXT or CHAR since I cannot represent myself as having your or a third person's intention. Although CHAR, as in (4) and (5), is also in a sense external, it indicates that the subject is characterized by the predicate. It can be used to report single events, but evidence is vaguer than for EXT. As detailed below, EXT indicates incontrovertible, external evidence for the truth of the assertion, most saliently direct observation of the event.

The use of evidentials in questions is illustrated in (6)–(10):

(6) I   go-EXT QUES Did I go, (have I gone)?
    ji   won-o la

(7) you go-INT QUES Did you go, do you go, etc.
    cho won-a la

(8) s/he go-EXT QUES Did s/he go, etc.?
    wo won-o la

(9) you go-CHAR QUES Do you go, did you (used to) go?
    cho won-v́ la

(10) s/he go-CHAR QUES Does s/he go, did s/he (used to) go?
    wo won-v́ la

Note that the co-occurrence of pronouns with EXT and INT in questions in (6) and (7) is the reverse of what it is in (1) and (2). In past work on Newari, what is here called INT was commonly considered a first-person ending. The flip-flop with second person in the interrogative, when noticed, was considered an aberration although comparison with other evidential languages would have shown comparable phenomena. Evidentials are not, of course, personal endings. Still, how do we account for the flip-flop? An attempt can be made borrowing from speech-act practice without, however, adopting its theory as well.

In a question, I request you to make an assertion and give you the basic propositional content that I want you to put into your assertion (at least in the underlying form of your response when it is a simple "Yes" or "No"). Since, in Newari, the evidential endings remain grammatically obligatory in the interrogative, I must also select the kind and specificity of evidence that I indicate to you I hope you will base your answer on. In (6), I cannot tell you to experience my intention and therefore do not signal INT as the evidence I hope you will use to report whether I went. You can only be expected to report on the basis of what you know about me from your perspective, and I signal EXT as the hoped for kind of evidence. Such externals as CHAR or a quotative particle (discussed below) could also have been used. In (7), the unmarked case is that I expect you to answer from the perspective of your own involvement in your action, and so signal INT as the evidence you should use in reporting whether you went. Expectably, (8) and (10) about a third party do not change from (3) and (4). CHAR with the second person in a question as in (9), in contrast to INT as in (7), will be discussed below.

Analysis of INT, EXT, and CHAR

The following specifications may be offered summarizing how the three evidentials are interpreted:

(11) INT: The speaker expresses: the proposition being true (at least once), the predicate of the proposition referring to an action, and having direct experience of intention to perform the action.

In (11), it follows from "direct experience of intention," that the speaker or reporter of the action must be the actor (logical subject). "... At least once" covers one or more occurrences of the action although one might better leave the evidentials unmarked for frequency of the action. The word "true" is not used in a strict truth-conditional sense but more generally for labelling the evidentials as expressing that the state of affairs "is the case," "is so," etc.:

(12) EXT: The speaker expresses: the proposition coming to be true (at
           least once), and having experience of observing
           incontrovertible evidence.

In (12), direct observation of the event is only the most usual
or salient kind of incontrovertible evidence. Included is circumstantial
evidence that is seen as incontrovertible. Less certain circumstantial
evidence is expressed with some other form, such as adding the particle
khoni "it seems that" after EXT. Thus circumstantial evidence, which
some evidential languages appear to treat as a single category, is divided
by degree of certainty. "Comes to be true" is intended to encapsulate two
elements. As a perfective in the more general sense, EXT expresses an
event at a particular time and covers completive of an action or process,
inchoative of a state, inceptive of repeated occurrence of an action or
process, or establishment of the truth of the state of affairs (i.e. "it turned
out that ..."). "Establishment of the truth" requires some explanation
and two illustrations will be offered. As just said, "truth" or "true" is a
more general label:

(13) I heavy-EXT   I became/have become heavy/heavier
      ji jhyatul-o

In (13), EXT rather than INT is used on the verb "to be heavy" with
the first person since this is a report of a state or change of state rather
than of an intentionally performable action (on which more below).
Although I would use (13) to report that I have become heavier, it can
also be used where there has been no actual change in weight. Thus, in a
context of comparison with someone else, (13) could report that I
turned out to be heavier at the time we were both weighed. EXT on the
verb "to be small" could be used to describe a pair of shoes at the time
they were tried on for size. The shoes did not suddenly change their size
but only turned out to be too small when tried on. Thus EXT also
expresses inchoative, at the time of observation, of the state of knowing
something to be true. Hence, in (12), the wording "comes to be true" in
detailing this evidential covers establishing that something is the case by
observing it at the time it comes to be so or later. We could add that the
perfective here has variable scope, either covering the whole event or
only my coming to know its truth.

The specification in (14) is better seen as a typical inference rather than
as a semantic content, as explained below:

(14) CHAR: The speaker depicts the participant (logical subject) as
            characterized by the proposition, i.e. the speaker says the
            participant is/was such that ...

CHAR emphasizes characterization of something rather than the occurrence of events and is interpretable as expressing a strength of assertion weaker or vaguer than that of INT or EXT. Used on a state verb, such as "to be heavy" in (13), CHAR reports the existence of the state where EXT expresses the inchoative of the state. CHAR can also cover iterative inchoativity of the state. With event verbs, CHAR can be used to report a single event as well as habitual action. Evidential conditions for CHAR are weaker and could include hearsay.

In fact, it is best to see CHAR as the morphologically and semantically unmarked category. The transcription symbol -$\hat{v}$, then, is not morphemic but still only morphophonemic, indicating stem-final consonant deletion and compensatory vowel lengthening. (The antecedent of CHAR in earlier Newari texts was the bare stem with final consonant still on the surface.) I shall continue to use -$\hat{v}$ and CHAR to represent this unmarked category, but only as dummy symbols, not as standing for a morpheme.

As a morphologically and semantically unmarked category in a grammatical system of forced choices, CHAR stands in opposition to the semantic contents of the marked evidentials. In opposition to the "eventhood" of EXT, CHAR is interpretable as expressing a state, including characterization, as a kind of state, of the logical subject. In opposition to the express evidentiality of EXT, CHAR is open to interpretability for vaguer evidence. Against INT, CHAR takes on an external perspective, and opposed to the two hypotheticals, CHAR becomes more definite and nonfuture.

In general, these categories should not be seen as marking a sentence for a feature of assertion. There is no express assertive morpheme. A sentence is interpretable as an assertion. Thus unmarked morphologically, it is the unmarked category in opposition to sentences or clauses marked with the interrogative morpheme, the imperative, the nominalizer (which marks nonassertion), etc. This would seem to be not just a language-specific analysis, but apply more generally at the level of universals.

Affirmative/negative answers to questions with EXT and CHAR

As formulated, the specifications for EXT and CHAR are intended in part to account for the unmarked (i.e., usual and expected) ways of responding affirmatively and negatively to sentences with EXT and CHAR interpreted as questions. For the question in (15) with CHAR, here used to ask about a single event, (16) shows the unmarked yes/no answers to be simple repetitions of the verb with CHAR:

(15) s/he go-CHAR QUES Did s/he go?
     wo   *won-v́*   *la*

(16) (a)   yes   = go-CHAR
                     won-v́
     (b)   no   = not-go-CHAR
                     mo-won-v́

In (18) we see the unmarked possibilities for the EXT question in (17):

(17) s/he go-EXT QUES Did s/he go?
     wo   *won-o* *la*

(18) (a)   yes   = true-CHAR (It) is, (it) is so
                     kho-v́
     (b)   no   = not-true-CHAR (It) is not, (it) is not so
                     mo-kh-u

     or

     (c)   yes   = go-EXT
                     won-o
     (d)   no   = not-go-CHAR [!]
                     mo-won-v́
     (e)   no   = not-go-EXT [more marked than (d)]
                     mo-won-o

First of all we note that, in unmarked usage, the yes/no answers to a question in the CHAR mode, as in (16), are repetitions of the verb, not the truth asserters "(it) is so" or "(it) is not so" of (18a,b). The latter are, however, answers to a question in the EXT mode. This supports the analysis that, from its opposition to EXT and INT, CHAR derives interpretability as characterizing the subject participant rather than asserting "truths."[6]

A question with EXT such as (17) may also be answered by repetitions of the verb as in (18c,d). However, the unmarked negative answer to (17) that uses repetition of the verb, (18d), has the CHAR suffix. That is, with EXT the question requests a more strongly supported reply, but there was no event to witness and thus assert with the EXT evidential.[7] The negative answer with EXT, (18e), is possible, but (18d) with CHAR is the unmarked answer speakers will give for usual contexts, including contextless elicitation. When pressed for a context in which (18e) might indeed be a natural answer, the consultant goes from the paradigmatic mode of structural discourse for contextualizing unmarked utterances to narrative discourse when contextualizing marked utterances. Thus answer (18e) requires a more marked context in which an *expected* event is observed not to materialize at the expected time. For example:

> She says she has to leave. You and I ask her to stay a day or so longer. I leave the house on an errand. Then I phone you at the house and ask (17). Now you can reply [with the EXT in] (18e) since you stayed with her and saw her not go.

With its stronger requirements for evidence, EXT in a question is often interpretable as a request for confirmation of what is already suspected or believed. The following are examples of contrasting background contexts offered by one speaker for asking the questions (17) vs. (15):

For (17) EXT: I know he has to leave the house for the office at 10 o'clock. A little after 10 I phone the house and am told he is not there. So, I ask (17), whether he went (to the office).

For (15) CHAR: I know he has to leave the house for the office at 10 o'clock and also that he did not want to go. Later I phone back and ask (15) to find out whether he actually did go [i.e. was such as, or in the frame of mind as, to go].

The hearsay evidential and reported speech

The following are examples of unmarked usage with the quotative evidential particle:

(19) I   go-EXT QUOT   It is said, someone said, etc. that   I went
    ji   *won-o*   *hõ*

(20) you   go-EXT QUOT   "   "   "   you went
    cho   *won-o*   *hõ*

(21) s/he   go-EXT QUOT   "   "   "   s/he went
    wo   *won-o*   *hõ*

But:

(22) s/he   go-INT   QUOT   S/he$_i$ says that s/he$_i$ went   (she/he = s/he)
    wo   *won-a*   *hõ*

In (19) I report my going as asserted by some unnamed person, i.e. I cite hearsay as my evidence. This unnamed person, being other than the performer of the action, cannot use the INT evidential but must report my going from an external perspective. Likewise for (20) and (21). However, (22) has INT on the verb. Here it is inferentially clear that the source of the information must be the actor.

(23) x-ERG [y go-EXT] say-EXT/say-INT   x$_i$ said y$_j$ went   (x ≠ y)
    x-ń   [y *won-o*]   *dhal-o/dhoy-a*

(24) x-ERG [y go-INT] say-EXT/say-INT x$_i$ said y$_i$ went (x = y)
    x-*ṅ*   [y *won-a*]   *dhal-o/dhoy-a*

As with the quotative evidential particle, the use of EXT and INT in the embedded sentence of reported speech follows logically from their descriptions above. Thus in (23) it is inferred, in the unmarked case, that embedded EXT indicates that the reporting participant *x* and the embedded actor *y* are not the same person, i.e. the two NPs *x* and *y* are not co-referential ("ERG" = ergative case marking, described further below). On the other hand, in (24) embedded INT indicates that the two NPs *are* co-referential. Newari syntax does not require that NPs, including pronouns, occur overtly. If the NPs *x* and *y* are absent from the surface form of a sentence that follows the schema of (23) or (24), the particular combination of EXT and INT on both the embedded verb and the matrix verb together still allow tracking of the participants, specifically whether or not *x* and *y* are the same. The illustrations of (23) and (24) given in (25) and (26) also show sample equivalents of direct and indirect speech. Since (25) and (26) only give examples, not all combinations of person and EXT/INT are shown. To show them all would require a digression, but, as said, their outputs follow logically. Treatment of marked, or questionable, outputs might be extrapolated in part from the discussion of marked usages below:

(25) (a) s/he-Erg [(s/he   go-INT)] say-EXT S/he$_i$ said that s/he$_i$ went
        wo-ṅ   [(*wo*) *won -a*] *dhal-o*   (s/he = s/he)

   (b)   "   [I   go-INT]   "   S/he$_i$ said, "I$_i$ went"
         "   [*ji*   *won-a*]   "   (s/he = "I")

   (c)   "   [I   go-EXT]   "   S/he$_i$ said, that I$_j$ went
         "   [*ji*   *won-o*]   "   (s/he ≠ I)

   (d) you-ERG [(you) go-INT] say-EXT You$_i$ said that you$_i$ went
        cho-ṅ [(*cho*) *won -a*] *dhal-o*   (you = you)

   (e)   "   [I   go-INT]   "   You$_i$ said, "I$_i$ went"
         "   [*ji*   *won-a*]   "   (you = "I")

   (f)   "   [I   go-EXT]   "   You$_i$ said, that I$_j$ went
         "   [*ji*   *won-o*]   "   (you ≠ I)

   (g)   "   [you go-EXT]   "   You$_i$ said, that "you$_j$ went"
         "   [*cho* *won-o*]   "   (you ≠ "you")

(26)   (I-ERG) [(I)   go-INT] say-INT I$_i$ said that I$_i$ went
       ji-ṅ   [(*ji*) *won -a*] *dhoy-a*   (I = I)

In (26) the first-person pronoun need not appear in the surface form of the sentence in either the embedded or the matrix clause, but first-person reference is still clearly recoverable from the combination of the two instances of INT. The subjects of the two clauses are co-referential, as indicated by the two occurrences of "I_i." However, attribution of the responsible self (see Hill and Irvine's introduction to this volume) in the utterance of (26) is only to the "I_i" in the matrix clause, namely the utterer taking responsibility for the action of saying reported in the matrix clause. Such taking of responsibility is derived from the occurrence of the INT in the matrix clause, but it is not necessarily signaled by the embedded INT since the latter is in a clause embedded as object of the verb "say." If responsibility were necessarily signaled by all occurrences of INT, it would also be signaled by the embedded INT, which is not the case. Thus conveying or interpreting responsibility is only a potential use of INT.[8]

The interaction of INT/EXT with "Control"

Not all of the events we are participants in are expected to involve our intentional action. Verbs may be divided into three classes on the basis of how they interact with INT/EXT in the first person. Sentences with verbs of the first class and first-person logical subject are judged as "natural" or unmarked usage when the verb has the INT ending but as marked usage with EXT on the verb. Since Newari is ergative, the term "logical subject" is used here so as to include both the "subject" of an intransitive verb and the agent role of a transitive verb. This reflects the fact that INT/EXT interact in the same way with a logical subject whether or not it is the agent of a transitive verb. In the glosses here, "ERG(ative)" labels the "Source" suffix when it marks the agent.[9] Verbs of the second class produce sentences in the first person that are judged as natural or unmarked usage when either INT or EXT appears on the verb. INT/EXT simply lead to different interpretations. Verbs of the third class with the first person are unmarked when with EXT but are marked when with INT usually to the point of being judged, at least initially, as unacceptable.

Verbs of the first class, such as "do," "eat," "say," "take," "give," "wash," "fry," "bite," are illustrated in (27) and (28):

(27) I-ERG   do-INT   I did, do (it)
      ji-ń   *yan-a*

(28) I-ERG   eat-INT   I ate, eat (it)
      ji-ń   *noy-a*

The second class, including "be ashamed," "hear," "see," "touch," "go to sleep," "look at," "be afraid," etc., is exemplified in (29)–(32):

(29) (a) I ashamed-   INT   I felt shame (taking responsibility for what I did)
         jimochal-   *a*

(b) I   ashamed-EXT I felt shame ("Shame happened to me")
     ji   *mochal-o*

(30) (a) I -ERG   hear-INT   I heard, listened to (it)
          ji-ṅ   *nyon-a*

     (b) I -ERG   hear-EXT   I heard, happened to hear (it)
          ji-ṅ   *nyon-o*

(31) (a) I -ERG touch-INT   I touched (it)
          ji-ṅ   *thiy-a*
     (b) I -ERG touch-EXT   I touched, happened to touch (it)
          ji-ṅ   *thil-o*

(32) (a) I   gotosleep-INT I went to bed/sleep
          ji   *dyon-a*

     (b) I   gotosleep-EXT I fell asleep
          ji   *dyon-o*

The third class includes "fall," "get lost," "know," "be small," "be
stout," etc., as in (33)–(35):

(33)   I   fall-EXT   I fell (down)
        ji   *kutũwol-o*

(34)   I   getlost-EXT   I got lost
        ji   *ton-o*

(35) (a) I-Erg   know-EXT   I found out about (it)
          ji-ṅ   *sil-o*

     (b) I-Erg   know-CHAR I know (it)
          ji-ṅ   *syu-v̇*

From an inspection and comparison of the three lexical classes of verbs
above, one can generalize that verbs of the first class share the feature
[+ Control], verbs of the second class are unmarked for [Control], and
those of the third are [− Control]. The compatibility and incompatibility
of INT with [+ Control] and [− Control] respectively can thus be used to
account for the way verbs fall into three classes of unmarked usage. I shall
not here argue the relative merits of considering this binary feature a
semantic one for these verbs, i.e. to be included in their definitions, versus
deriving it pragmatically from beliefs about the kinds of actions and states
they represent. I shall also not digress to give consideration to arguments
for and against the alternative analysis of INT as signaling [+ Control]
rather than [+ Intentional]. This is, at least in part, a problem of defining
these terms in the metalanguage. In either case the factor of (in)compati-
bility remains.

The material in parentheses in (29a) and (29b) was supplied by one speaker to clarify the distinction between them. It illustrates the potential of INT for expressing responsibility in appropriate contexts, including such a context as finds (29a) and (29b) contrasted.

The verb "know," found in the third class in (35), is a state verb. The change of state, inchoative, is expressed separately by the perfective EXT. A state or a change in the state, as in many other languages, is inherently [−Control], as opposed to the action, which can be [+Control], which causes the change. The verb "know " is thus understandably rejected by speakers when suffixed with INT and, to express the intentional "find out" or "learn" with INT, is typically replaced by them with a sentence in which the derivational causative suffix is attached to the verb stem "know." The causative morpheme in Newari does not necessarily add a participant to the valences of a verb but may simply add the feature of action.

Marked usages and the strategic potential of INT/EXT

Following the criteria above, the verb "fall" is put in the third lexical class based on the naturalness of sentences such as (33) with EXT and on the initial rejection by speakers of sentences such as (36) below with INT. The rejection of such sentences is accounted for by identifying the contradiction [−Control] [+Intentional] in their "Verb-INT" segment, e.g. in (36) "fall-INT." In other terms, the event in (36) cannot have started out as a case of true falling if it was performed intentionally:

(36) (?) I fall-INT
     ji kutũwoy-a

Although a sentence might initially be rejected, pressing speakers to imagine, nevertheless, what interpretation might be given to an utterance of the sentence or to create a context into which the sentence might fit has often led to productive results. It can help establish whether the rejection is based on an inherent contradiction between the co-occurring items in the sentence, thus supporting such an account as that which identifies the features [−Control] and [+Intentional] in the respective definitions of the co-occurring items in initially rejected (36). Or it can help reveal whether the sentence simply does not fit into unmarked hypothetical contexts but requires a more unusual context to bring it to life. In other words, an initial rejection should not deter the investigator from exploring the fuller power of the language since we cannot easily control for the reasons for rejection.

Thus pressed after rejecting (36), one speaker said, "That would mean I fell down and was conscious of it all the way down." This initial rejection

and subsequent reply taken together can be shown to be consistent with
the [− Control] [+ Intentional] analysis by identifying it with one common
way of resolving initial contradictions, often used for making sense of
apparent errors in an utterance, namely ignoring part of the meaning of
one of the offending items and reinterpreting the sentence in a way that
makes sense. Thus we say that the speaker in this instance ignored part of
the meaning of "intentionally performed action" in INT and factored the
element of "consciousness" out of [+ Intentional]. This mode of elicitation is known to be useful for generating more incisive data to arrive at
definitions in the elusive semantics of abstract grammatical items.

The previous speaker did not, however, construct a context in which
(36) might occur. Similarly pressed for a reinterpretation or unusual
context after rejecting (36), another speaker created a narrative scenario.
A young bride who is having quarrels with her husband feigns falling out
the window to frighten him and goes home to her mother. She tells her
mother about the events, saying (36), i.e. "I 'quotes' fell down." Here we
see another typical resolution of an initial contradiction. The second
speaker has reinterpreted the utterance as representing a case of dissimu-
lation or lying. However, accounting precisely for why this particular
resolution of the initial contradiction was selected by the second speaker
in the context narrated falls into the province of discursive and dialogic
theories, such as of discursive participant frames (see Irvine, this volume).

In (37) and (38) we see two more initially rejected sentences as reinterpreted by speakers:

(37) (?) I   go-INT QUOT I say I *went*! or I *went*, I tell you!
          ji won-a   hõ   (an emphatic repetition of a previous
                                     assertion with fist pounding on table)

(38) (?) you-Erg   do-INT You did (it) (talking to oneself)
          cho-ṅ   yan-a

In (37), INT identifies the source of the hearsay (QUOT) information as
the actor, as explained for (22) above, but the pronoun identifies the actor
as the person uttering the sentence. Why would I indicate that my
evidence for the assertion is INT and then, in an apparent contradiction,
indicate it is hearsay? The speaker thought of the kind of context in which
one has just had one's assertion about one's own action (INT without
QUOT) doubted. That is, the assertion with INT has already been made.
One can then repeat the assertion with the quotative particle added to
insist on the assertion having been authoritative enough the first time to
be quotable as evidence. In general, QUOT can be used when repeating
an assertion just made by someone else in that person's presence. Not to
do so could imply claiming (also) one's own authority or ownership of the

assertion. The English equivalent in the translation of (37) above, like QUOT, is an expression of verbal informing, "say" or "tell." Again, an initial contradiction has been resolved by reinterpreting an item for only part of its meaning and ignoring the rest. QUOT now only indicates repetition of a previous assertion without evidentiality. An alternative analysis is possible, namely one in which QUOT is defined in the first place as indicating only repetition and evidentiality is its most salient pragmatically derived meaning or use.

When I assert that you did something, I cannot represent myself as having the internal experience of intentional performance as my evidence. Only you can do that, as said above for (2). Thus (38) with the INT evidential for asserting your action is initially rejected. Seen as a different aspect of the same whole, INT seems to imply that I am the actor, but the pronoun "you" indicates otherwise. The speaker resolves the apparent contradiction by reinterpreting the utterance for a context of talking to oneself, where "you" and "I" can refer to the same person. I am, then, one individual playing two simultaneous roles. This way of resolving a contradiction of referent identity is also a common one: the interpreter creates one individual split into two personae so that the referent is and is not two people, as in "I see me in the mirror" contrasting with "I see myself in the mirror."

In comparison with the preceding examples, reporting my own actions with EXT rather than the expected INT may also be a marked usage, but it is not a contradiction. Thus speakers, while not typically rejecting a sentence like (39), judge that it requires a context:

(39) I-ERG   do-EXT In context: I seem to have done it, I was seen to
      ji-ṅ   *yat-o*   do it, I saw myself do it (in a dream), I did it
                          (drunk, hypnotized, by some outside force)

(40) I go-EXT
      ji won-o

Since this evidential indicates an external perspective, it can also serve the strategy of shifting my empathy or viewpoint to your perspective on me. Thus (40) might be uttered upon leaving a group of people: "I'm off, you see me gone," as one speaker translated it.

In (41), (a) is a question to which (b) and (c), among others, are alternative affirmative answers:

(41) (a) you-ERG   do-INT QUES Did you do (it)?
        cho-ṅ   *yan-a*   *la*

     (b) (I-ERG)   do-INT   (I) did (it)   (the expected answer)
          (ji-ṅ)   *yan-a*

(c)   (I-ERG)   do-EXT   (I) did (it)   (marked)
      (ji-n̊)   *yat-o*

As opposed to the unmarked usage (41b), (41c) demands an interpretation. What the various interpretations might be requires a broader discursive and contextual theory. For example, it might account for why, if I am
believed to remember my personal involvement and yet utter (41c) in
reply to (41a) asked of me by a person who is my senior, I am interpreted
as being distant, flippant, and insulting towards that person. Am I not
taking responsibility for my action, not co-operating in my use of the
evidential since INT was requested as explained above in connection with
(7)? To a junior, if not also to a senior, (41c) might have the force of
"Yeah, I did it; what's it to you?"

In the case of reporting my actions with EXT when INT is believed to
represent correctly my remembering my intentional performance, note
that I am not necessarily expressing misleading information by using
EXT: it is, of course, expected that I have some sort of sensory or other
feedback experience of my own actions together with my experience of
intention. But the evidential opposition gives me the unmarked option of
providing the fuller information of my personal involvement. In Gricean
terms, I am not being as fully informative as I am believed capable of
being. Not selecting the INT option is a marked usage and, as said,
demands an interpretation. What that interpretation might be must be
derived from the frame the hearer perceives as the context in which the
utterance is produced:

(42) you-ERG do-EXT QUES So you did (it), eh? *or* Did you do (it)
     cho-n̊   *yat-o*   *la*   indeed?

What if I utter to *you* what looks like a question about *your* own action
using EXT, as in (42), rather than the usual INT in (7) or (41a)? A
consultant created a context in which you may have said something like
(27) with INT asserting that you did it, and I reply with (42). First of all, I
am making an apparent request for information which you have already
supplied. So, this would not seem to be a real question. How then is my
utterance to be interpreted? At this point theoretical approaches such as
presented elsewhere in this volume would have to step in. Furthermore, as
explained in connection with (6) and (7), my forced choice of an evidential
in questions indicates the kind of evidence I hope you will use for your
answer. But I am using EXT rather than asking for the expected closer
INT evidence of personal involvement in your report of your action.
Don't I really care to know? (Compare Searle's (1969) sincerity condition
for a question.) Also, a question is a request to the hearer to make an
assertion, but by not using INT I seem not to be asking you to indicate the

stronger evidence you could give in support of this assertion. Do I believe you don't have the evidence? The speaker interpretation paraphrased in (42) was that it is not a straightforward question but belongs in a context in which I express skepticism or an indirect accusation that you did not do it (see DuBois' duplex speech acts, this volume).

(43) (a) you-ERG   work   do-INT   QUES   Do you work?
          cho-ṅ   jya   yan-a   la

     (b) you-ERG   work   do-CHAR   QUES   Do you work?
          cho-ṅ   jya   ya-v̇   la

In (43b) I am asking you a question using CHAR, which is also a kind of external: that is, I am requesting that you give an answer which uses, and thus is appropriate to, CHAR, whereas in (43a) I want INT. Presented with the contrast (43a) vs. (43b), one speaker gave them the same translation above, but for two different scenarios contextualizing the subtle differences. With (43a) I want to check whether you are obeying doctor's orders, according to which you are not supposed to be working yet, because I see you spending money like anything, supposedly without a job, and suspect you may be working after all. For (43b) I want to place you in a job, and I have to know: do you know how to work, are you a worker, are you a person who does not malinger? As a partial account, we can say that the contrast (43a,b) emphasizes the intention in INT by contrast with the more external CHAR, favoring a scenario for (43a) where possible willful ignoring of doctor's orders is at issue. The inference from INT of responsibility may also be involved, given the further issue, here, of possible irresponsibility. Likewise, the external aspect of CHAR seems emphasized in the contrast, leading to a scenario for (43b) in which I am indeed using CHAR to ask you to step back and give a characterization of yourself.

(44) (a) I-ERG   unknowingly   down-Caus-INT   I accidentally knocked
          ji-ṅ   mosisse   kur-k-a   (it) down

     (b) I-ERG   (*unknowingly)   down-Caus-EXT   I seem to have knocked
          ji-ṅ   (*mosisse)   kur-kol-o   (it) down

Another example of manipulation of INT/EXT for taking responsibility is found in (44). One easy interpretation given for (44a) in this contrast is that I accept responsibility or blame for the whole event, derived from INT, but apologize, derived from the adverbial "unknowingly, accidentally." The apparent contradiction between this adverbial and the element "intentional" in INT was not felt by the speaker. For this we can offer the analysis that the causative morpheme expresses that there was an action causing a consequent event or state, here the object's falling down.[10] Further, INT has flexible scope, which is here interpreted to

cover only whatever my causing action was, leaving the resulting event as
the accidental part. In other words, I performed an intentional action but
with an unintended result.

With EXT in (44b) I distance myself more from involvement in the
event, as described for (39)–(41), and thereby from responsibility for it. By
inference, then, EXT here also conveys unintentionality. A speaker interpretation was that only later when the action was complete did I notice
what I had done. The speaker rejected inclusion of the adverbial "unknowingly, accidentally" in (44b), claiming that this was already
expressed by the EXT ending. The approximate effect of incoherence of
including the adverbial in (44b) can be created with the English equivalent
"I unintentionally knocked it down unknowingly," or perhaps "I unknowingly knocked it down unintentionally." In such a sentence structure, the two items "unintentionally" and "unknowingly" are both
logical predicates and do not reinforce each other additively; rather, one
falls within the scope of the other as part of the latter's argument. For
example, in prose, "My unintentionally knocking it down was (performed) unknowingly" with propositional structure indicates that the
"unknowingness" is the information. But it seems not to be new information since its content is not seen as providing information not already
present in "unintentionally," as the speaker said. This presents an unin-
terpretable contradiction.[11]

A final example manipulates the causative in addition to INT/EXT for
expressing degrees of involvement in, and perhaps responsibility for,
one's own getting angry:[12]

(45) (a)   I angryget-EXT
           ji   tomwol-o

     (b)   I angryget-INT
           ji   tomwoy-a

     (c)   I angryget-Caus-INT
           ji   tomwoe-k-a

     (d)   I-Erg self-Dat angryget-Caus-INT
           ji-ṅ   thov-to   tomwoe-k-a

With EXT in (45a) I can imply that the anger happened to me due to
external circumstances beyond my control. More of a decision to get
angry can be inferred from INT in (45b). With the causative in (45c) my
action of involvement in my getting angry is made explicit. The verb is still
intransitive: as noted above, the causative morpheme does not necessarily add a participant. The event expressed by the verb in (45c) is completely internal to the actor–experiencer, and this is an example of a verb

plus causative morpheme which does not require the ergative marking on its logical subject.[13] Finally, in (45d) with an overt reflexive and ergative marking, I can be imagined as really doing things to myself to work up a good anger.[14]

Discussion

We have been looking at one system of grammaticalized evidential categories and some examples of its potential for manipulation in discourse. The discussion has, I hope, shown that such systems should not just be left at the stage of analysis of establishing their epistemological categories, but that they are a fertile corner of research within the larger study of responsibility and evidence in strategic interaction. A valid direction for further inquiry would be the inferential potential of manipulating certain evidential suffixes for claiming or disclaiming ownership of their containing discourse fragments, for example with the quotative (compare Shuman, this volume).

In the work some of whose results are presented here, the consultants were asked to construct contexts since so-called context-less sentences are not in fact without context. Typically, sentences presented in isolation are interpreted for the most unmarked contexts but also for any context the person might think of, and these can remain unknown to the fieldworker. Thus one way to determine what context speakers are using as the frame for interpretation is to ask them to make the context explicit.

One of the features to be aware of when eliciting from contrasts between minimal pair sentences is that responses, even those that create contrasting scripts as contexts, are still given within the broader frame of the eliciting situation with its contrast task. Thus potential information from one or the other of the sentences can be made more salient in the contrast than might be the case if a given sentence is uttered without contrast in a more usual speaking situation. These minimal pair sentences, however, involve contrasts of grammaticalized units that stand in opposition to each other; that is, they implicitly involve forced choices. Thus selection of one such unit for use at a certain point in a discourse is an implicit rejection of a paradigmatically opposed unit. A contrast task is thus not unlike such an inherent choice and can be seen as making the choice explicit. Also, when we ask a language consultant to create contrasting meanings and contexts, we do not expect them to be created out of thin air, although the unreliable informant is a known problem to watch out for in any language work; rather, we are asking the person to perform the familiar task of creating meaning out of familiar linguistic material.

Each of the methods used to investigate a language has its problematic and also a contribution that it can make better than some other method. They are complementary. The established elicitation techniques applied in this study stand in contrast to the observational methods used elsewhere in this volume and could not generate the kind of knowledge the latter can, but they more easily flush out rare but insight-giving material than a method, for example, which scans transcriptions and other texts and may never meet such rare instances of language use. I shall leave it to the reader to form a judgment about these elicitation techniques from the material presented here.

The use of an analytic approach that would seem to be clearly in the pragmatic tradition of Grice and Searle needs some clarification since it does not use the appeal to communicative intentionality whose validity is attacked in this collection and other work. Pragmatic analyses of language use have produced many plausible and insightful observations, and theories using the concept of intentionality have been built upon such plausibility. However, the plausibility of the observations themselves still remains even if a theory built upon them is found faulty. If a theory is found to be ethnocentric, then such a finding only destroys its universality. As so often happens in the accumulation of knowledge, a theory thought to be universal turns out to be a special case of a more comprehensive theory.

Much hinges on differences in implicit goals of the theory. Concern with intentions may be culturally variable, but a theory dealing with fictional narrative, in which authors get into their characters' heads by in fact creating them and their intentions, must include the role of intentions if its goal is the analysis of language use in such fiction. Philosophers, like fiction writers, also introspect and create the insides of people's heads in their study of language. However, an approach which has as its goal understanding how real people use language may consider getting into their heads and at their intentions an unresearchable part of the enterprise, and therefore restrict its theory to what is researchable: for example, how hearers can construct meaning out of speakers' utterances in context. Giving informants the task of constructing meaning out of utterances need not involve asking them to impute intentions to the real or hypothetical speakers of those utterances. Even asking a speaker what s/he meant by a given utterance is most likely to involve turning that speaker into a hearer of an utterance presented for interpretation, albeit an utterance repeating what was originally the speaker's utterance. The speaker's intentions may change or even be forgotten by the time s/he is asked to construct meaning out of the repetition. Attacks on theories of intentions and counterattacks against interpretivist stances (Nuyts, 1989) must be careful not to confuse the goals of one theory with those of another in their overall evaluations.

The analytic approach used here borrows from speech-act theory the idea of preparatory conditions, for example. For assertives one preparatory condition is that the speaker have sufficient evidence for the truth of the assertion. Evidentials are then said to be further specification of the nature of this evidence. However, these conditions are not taken as performing their usual function of gauging the felicity of a given speech act; rather, they are seen from a communicative perspective as information extractable out of an utterance. If a hearer interprets a given utterance as an assertion (rather than as some other speech act or rather than as part of a performance of a fixed text, for example), then the hearer will also interpret the utterance as conveying the information that the speaker has evidence and, if an evidential is present, something about the nature of that evidence. Such a communicative perspective has no need for a concept of intentionality.

In much study of narratives and other discourse wholes, the particular semantic roles of given grammatical units must often be assumed. For the question of evidential categories, this article has tried to start at the other end with an analysis of grammatical units, since there is no need for their precise semantic roles in the discourse whole to be assumed, and to project outward from them into discourse.

The goal of the approach exemplified in this article, then, is to contribute to an understanding of how meaning can be constructed. It uses a pragmatic mode of reasoning without necessarily imputing intention. The goal of the grammatical and semantic analysis is to identify the meanings that are necessarily signaled by the forms that appear in an utterance. Pragmatic reasoning identifies what is further signaled by the interactions of these primary meanings, including identifying when something is wrong that thus demands further inferencing, such as the violations exemplified in the section on "marked usages." What needs to be interpreted further is identified, but the contribution of the approach stops there. What that further inferencing may be, how the violations are reinterpreted, and other further creation of meaning, fall within the domain of approaches presented by other contributors in this volume.

ABBREVIATIONS

CAUS:	causative
CHAR:	characterizing evidential
DAT:	dative
ERG:	ergative
EXT:	external evidential

INT: internal evidential
QUES: question
QUOT: quotative

NOTES

Among the Newari speakers who provided informant material, I wish to thank in particular my major consultants, Thakurlal Manandhar and Yogendra Singha, for the many patient hours they spent helping me fathom the workings of their language. The material presented here was collected in Kathmandu in 1965–6 and in the New York area in the 1970s.

1 Newari refers to a Tibeto–Burman family of dialects spoken in the Himalaya Mountains, primarily in Nepal. Largely, it coexists with Nepali, the Indo–Aryan official language of the country. The speech presented here is the modern prestige variety of Kathmandu.

2 Other work on Newari evidential categories may be found in Bendix, 1974; Hale, 1980; and Hargreaves, 1983. Evidential systems bearing similarities to that of Newari are found in other related languages, such as Tibetan (DeLancey, 1986; Agha, 1989) and Sherpa (Schottelndreyer, 1980; Woodbury, 1986).

3 Transcription note: $a = $ [a]; $o = $ [ə ~ ɔ];
                        $wo = $ [wə ~ wɔ ~ wo ~ o];
                        $yo = $ [yɔ ~ (y)ɛ ~ e];
    $\acute{v}$ and $\acute{n}$ are morphophonemic cover symbols:
    V-$\acute{v}$/Vv = [V:];   Vn-$\acute{v}$ = [Ṽ:];   V-$\acute{n}$ = [Ṽ:];
    –marks a morpheme boundary.

4 There are, for better or worse, several different relations all designated with the same term "(un)marked" (Moravcsik and Wirth, 1986). I shall be using at least four of them but shall identify them as they occur.

5 After experimenting with "A" and "B" and other notations for identifying hypothetical participants and finding them difficult to follow, I decided to use impersonal "I" and "you" since these make tracking of participants much easier. However, this purely expository device is to be read as "A" and "B" since what "I" says and "you" interprets is not what I say and you may interpret. As explained in the concluding discussion, communicated intentions are not a part of this analysis, and the aura of subjective intentionality that is likely to emanate from "I" and "you" is a chimera.

6 Further support is that the nominalizer -*gu* is not added to a verb in the CHAR mode. When -*gu* is suffixed after one of the other endings, the clause can then function to express a presupposition, in the sense of presuppositions being about "truths," not about characterizations. To render the presuppositional equivalent with -*gu* of a sentence (clause) in the CHAR mode, the verb of the sentence ends in the external hypothetical plus -*gu* for a propositional content that represents iterativity of an event or state, or in EXT plus -*gu* for the other

kinds of propositional content that can be said, with the CHAR ending, to characterize the subject. Before *-gu*, EXT undergoes a morphophonemic change of syllable loss and compensatory lengthening of preceding vowel that makes it look, misleadingly, like CHAR.

7 Note the parallel to languages with fewer tenses in the negative than in the affirmative.

8 The title of this chapter is therefore somewhat misleading. Responsibility is not claimed to be grammaticalized but can follow from the kind of evidentiality that *is* grammaticalized.

9 Thus, strictly speaking, there is no separate ergative or agentive case marking morpheme in Newari. The same suffix is used for agentive, instrumental, ablative of place, and for "because" on a nominalized clause. Which particular case is interpreted is derived most saliently from the nature of the NP suffixed. The underlying common denominator of these cases has been identified as "Source" in the literature (e.g. Genetti, 1991 [for Newari]; Gruber, 1976; DeLancey, 1981; Clark and Carpenter, 1989).

10 On such "bisentential" analysis of the causative, see Wojcik, 1976; Bendix, 1984.

11 An anonymous reviewer made a suggestion roughly along the lines that saying that an unknowing action was unintentional could imply that there are unknowing actions that are intentional. This observation would have to be expanded by pointing out that now the problem is the apparently contradictory meanings of "unknowing" and "intentional."

12 Compare Givón, 1985a on transitivity gradients in Newari.

13 We can offer an account of the lack of ergative marking in (45c), despite the presence of the causative morpheme, as follows. As said above, (n. 9), ergative is only one use of the case marker here. This suffix morpheme is best identified as signaling "Source." In localist theory then (Anderson, 1971), "Source," either literally or metaphorically, includes "movement" from the source to some goal, experiencer, etc. (see Gruber, 1976, for wordings alternative to "movement"). In such a case as (45c) we see the actor and experiencer depicted as one and the same. There can be no movement in such a representation and thus no source, and it is absence of the source morpheme which permits this depiction. Presence of the source morpheme would signal movement and thus represent separation of the actor and experiencer, as is the case in (45d).

14 I thank an anonymous reviewer for pointing out that there are "quite similar phenomena in the Australian context (right down to the ... case marking pattern of (45c)) in other morphologically "ergative" languages, such as Yidiny and Guugu Yimidhirr."

II

EVIDENTIARY STANDARDS FOR AMERICAN TRIALS: JUST THE FACTS

SUSAN U. PHILIPS

The basic exclusionary rule confines evidence to "fact." The law's present method of seeking truth is empirical. Ordinarily a witness may not give opinion or inference of deduction, or supposition however plausible. It is not coincidence that our rules of evidence began to take shape in the same century – the seventeenth – as did modern scientific method.

(Rembar, 1980:326)

Introduction

In this chapter I shall describe some of the key ways in which evidence law constitutes a legal sub-system specialization and distortion of more pervasive everyday and common-sensical evidentiary standards in American society. There are a number of instances of descriptions of evidentiary distinctions that are held to be language-specific (Chafe and Nichols, 1986) and a few that have been held to be culture-specific (e.g. Ochs and Schieffelin, 1984; Witherspoon, 1977). In contrast to such whole-language and whole-culture characterizations of evidentiary frameworks, this paper makes the point that evidentiary standards also vary within societies, depending on the domain, institutional sub-system or context with which one is dealing.

At the same time that this is true, there can also be interesting ways in which the specialized evidentiary standards associated with a particular domain or institutional sub-system are related to the evidentiary standards of other present or past sub-systems within the same society. Thus I shall argue here that, while evidence law applied in American court trials is in some ways quite distinctive and specific to the American legal sub-system, it nevertheless draws upon, or is influenced by, earlier Christian moral and evidentiary concern with truth, scientific evidentiary concerns with factuality or facticity and proof, and a particularly American political evidentiary commitment to achieving quality in decision-making through open head-on conflict between identifiable "parties" whose mutually debated views are then voted upon by an evaluating audience.

The chapter is divided into sections that consider first, some of the

248

salient general properties of evidence law from the point of view of the legal profession; second, the specific constraints of evidence law intended to enhance or increase the reliability of evidence through limitations placed on *how* evidence is presented, *what* evidence can be presented (content), *who* can present evidence, and how evidence can be *interpreted*; and finally, a brief discussion of the preceding section.

General legal constraints on evidence

Evidence law is conceived of as enabling "fact-finders" (a jury or a judge) to decide what really happened in an event or series of events involving a defendant being charged with a statutorily defined offense growing out of those events. Fact-finders decide (vote on) whether or not those events entailed the defendant's doing something that falls within the statutory description of the offense. "Facts" are presented and called into question by the prosecution and the defense. The fact-finders must decide who among the witnesses is "telling the truth" and who is "lying." If the accumulation of truths on the side of the prosecution is sufficient – if the prosecution has, in the minds of the fact-finders, met its burden of proof – then the defendant should be found guilty.

Factuality, a concept heavily influenced by scientific ideology, and *truth*, a concept heavily influenced by Christian notions of moral worth, become inextricably linked in evidence law, so linked that it is difficult for Americans to disentangle them when thinking about legal cases. Psychologists (e.g. Loftus and Palmer, 1974), and lawyers (e.g. Cleary, 1972) are aware that inconsistencies in a given witness' testimony are as likely if not more likely to be due to "perceptual failures" as to deliberate and knowing lying. But during trials, and in ways built into evidence law (for example, through conditions under which "character witnesses" may testify and through the regulation of "impeachment" of witnesses), inconsistencies are constantly treated as lies, which in turn are framed as, and associated with, other acts of moral reprehensibility, with the potential to stigmatize pervasively, in Goffman's sense (1963), anyone bold enough to assume the role of witness.

It is quite taken for granted that deciding "what really happened" is the overriding task of the American trial, and when anthropologists encounter management of conflicts in other societies in which there is not a primary obsession with and contestation of what really happened, we find it worth noting, documenting, and explaining. Indeed, during the several decades since Gluckman's (1955) publication of *The Judicial Process among the Barotse*, a primary concern among anthropological students of the conflict management process has been the emphasis in non-Western societies on the reintegration of social relationships ruptured by conflict, but there has not typically been an attendant focus in this literature on what then happens to the issues of facticity and truth. It is encouraging to note that more attention is now being given to this and other issues in non-Western dispute managements, such as the use of public dispute management forums to present interpretive or ideological stances that otherwise go unrecognized (Briggs, 1989; Hirsch, 1989), and to reinforce or renegotiate (Just, 1989) dominant value-systems.

American evidence law, then, is conceptualized as organized around facilitating the presentation and contestation of what really happened, of "facts" and "the truth." To this end, evidence law is also concerned, in a principled way, with *relevance* and with *reliability*. Again, the influence of scientific notions of information gathering is apparent. As in science, so in law, truth and factuality must be decided in a principled and rule-governed way, involving recognition that some forms of evidence are more reliable than others. Relevance and reliability will now be considered in turn.

Within the American legal framework of evidence law, not all facts are considered to be equally *relevant*. Evidence law is presented as intending to eliminate the irrelevant. That which is relevant is determined by the nature of the charge against a defendant. In criminal cases, for example, evidence law and criminal law interact. Each crime as statutorily defined has elements, and for each of these elements evidence must be presented in a trial. There must be a certain amount of evidence for each element of the charge for the judge to allow fact-finders to decide guilt or innocence. And once this decision has been given to the fact-finders, they must find evidence of guilt on each and every one of these elements in order to return a verdict of guilty. Only evidence relevant to proving or disproving the elements of a specific charge is permitted in a trial; all else is irrelevant.

Within this charge-specific framework, relevance is then weighed or balanced against prejudice, so that some forms of evidence are considered to be relevant – e.g. the character of one accused of a crime – but considered so prejudicial that their relevance is outweighed by the potential prejudice to the point of exclusion, except under highly circumscribed conditions (Cleary, 1972).

Evidence law is also conceptualized as enhancing the *reliability* of evidence presented during a trial. Evidence presented during a trial is viewed as more reliable than evidence about violations of law talked about outside the courtroom trial by virtue of the evidentiary constraints that are the focus of the rest of this paper. Such constraints are viewed as having filtered out evidence we use all the time every day, but probably shouldn't if we are being "fair" and "unbiased" in deciding which among competing accounts of events are "true" (Cleary, 1972; Conley, 1982). Historical accounts of the development of evidence law (e.g. Rembar,

1980) trace its origin to a mistrust of the jury – to the view that the jury was not capable of filtering out the reliable from the unreliable, the biased and the biasing from that which was not biased, and so this had to be done for them, by the judge.

The idea that forms of evidence differ in their reliability is recognized and treated as central (though its centrality is often assumed rather than carefully documented) to the linguistic concept of "evidentials," morphological markers found in many languages that distinguish different sources of evidence (see Chafe and Nichols, 1986; Bendix, this volume). The distinction that emerges most often in the documented examples of evidentials concerns information which the speaker acquired through a direct experience as opposed to some other source, while other distinctions regarding source of knowledge, such as that of commonly shared knowledge, or mythical knowledge seem more variable (e.g. Chafe and Nichols, 1986; Palmer, 1986). As we shall see below, this most salient distinction is also important in evidence law, and I believe that both the study of evidentials and the growing study of evidentiality have been very much influenced by American legal and non-legal evidential concerns such as those treated in this paper.

Linguistic and cultural studies of evidence and evidentiality have expanded to include a range of linguistic forms and epistemological concerns not necessarily limited to evidential morphology, so that they now overlap with other areas of linguistic and sociolinguistic interest such as the study of mood and mode and of politeness, and of more culturally constructed concepts such as responsibility and authority.

Because of this expansion, and its attendant proliferation of concepts and terms, it may be useful for me to explain here how I conceptualize the issue of reliability both in understanding evidence law and linguistic studies of evidentiality. In examining presentations of information by speakers in speech, it is necessary to distinguish between the *encoding of the speaker's attitude* toward the information she is presenting (which in English we find in hedges and intensifiers that are also confounded in English as in other languages with politeness and affect) and the *encoding of the sources* of the information she is presenting (which in English are enormously variable). Such sources can be analytically distinguished in a variety of ways, and I mean "sources" to cover a *range* of phenomena, including, for example, such encodings in English as reported speech and the animate human nouns to whom such speech is attributed.

Evidence law purports to improve reliability by controlling and constraining *sources* of evidence; it does not control the expression of speakers' attitudes toward the information they provide. Expressions of witnesses' attitudes toward the information they provide certainly affect the fact-finders' assessment of reliability in American trials, particularly where the salient-to-Americans phenomenological awareness of degrees of certainty is at issue (O'Barr, 1982; O'Barr and Atkins, 1980). Lawyers play upon fact-finders by making witnesses' certainty an issue. They manipulate this dimension of reliability as it is experienced by Americans, by choosing to put on the witness-stand witnesses who are more certain over witnesses who are less certain when possible. But assessments of relative reliability of testimony derived from the encoding of the witnesses' attitudes toward their own information is left to fact-finders and is not controlled by evidence law.

In the next section we shall consider the ways in which evidence law constrains *sources* of evidence with the purported intention of enhancing reliability, identifying by subsection the analytical dimensions of *sources* I consider salient in evidence law.

Constraints on evidence to enhance reliability

How *is evidence presented?*

The presentation of evidence in American trials is often characterized as adversarial (Thibaut and Walker, 1975), in that each side, prosecution and defense, presents its version of the events at issue. Thibaut and Walker (1975) contrast the adversarial approach to the establishment of facts within an inquisitorial approach, which they associate with European continental legal traditions, as opposed to the common-law traditions of Great Britain and her colonies. With inquisitorial treatment, a single judge listens to accounts from both sides and questions parties, rather than the adversarial lawyers carrying out the questioning.

In the adversarial tradition, the two sides of an issue are presented independently not once, but over and over again. The overall sequential organization of a trial dictates repeated alternations of opposing realities. Thus there are two opening statements which take two general positions on what will be found, then evidence for each of the two opposing positions is presented through the testimony of witnesses, first the prosecution's case and then the defense's case. Within each single witness' testimony, she is first questioned by the lawyer representing the "side" for which she has been called on direct examination, and then can be questioned by the other "side's" lawyer on cross-examination. Finally, both the prosecution and the defense offer closing statements. Thus, within the overall structure of opposition, oppositions are nested within oppositions.

Much is made of the virtues of this adversarial structure by the legal profession. It is viewed as a more reliable way to present evidence than presentations encountered in other contexts in American life, because of

the built-in and obligatory challenge to factual accounts and their interpretations. Common-sensically, it indeed appears to be the case that in
other contexts it is often considered rude or situationally inappropriate to
challenge the accounts others give us of events, regardless of the doubts
we may consciously register.

It is within the framework of direct examination, cross-examination
and re-direct examination of witnesses that considerable time and attention are given to efforts to elicit inconsistencies in testimony that will
undermine the overall credibility of a witness as either lying or failing to
perceive accurately (factually) what was witnessed. While Americans may
assume that the confrontational and bullying style associated with this
"conflict about a conflict" seen in American courtrooms and in televised
representations of courtroom trials is characteristic of all common-law
adversarial trial courts, it is not. After all, cross-examination is the choice
of the potentially cross-examining lawyer. The British lawyers with whom
I have discussed this dimension of evidence law uniformly express distaste
for the combativeness of American trial court practice. They deny it is
characteristic of British trial court practice, consistent with my observations of both Tongan and British lawyers in Tongan courts. Some non-
American lawyers in common-law-derived legal systems view American
practices in this area as inconsistent with, i.e. in violation of, the shared
common-law principle that witnesses must not be led (i.e. bullied) in their
testimony.

While it can be argued that this confrontation of testimonies is consistent with scientific notions that evidence be gathered and presented in ways
that allow it to be challenged, the American faith in oppositionally
organized elicitations of evidence is more obviously part and parcel of the
American commitment to oppositional party politics, embedded in every
level of political structure, but most evident in the discourse phenomenon
of "debate."

Who *can present* what *kind of evidence?*

Who and what are very closely interconnected in evidence law. There are
two main kinds of witnesses, the ordinary witness and the expert witness.
In order for their testimony to be admissible, ordinary witnesses must
have directly experienced what they testify about or report on. Other ways
of putting this are to say that the ordinary witness must have firsthand
knowledge of what she is testifying about, or have had sensory experience
of it. For this reason lawyers always begin direct examination of their
witnesses by laying a foundation in which the circumstances that placed
the witness in a position to experience directly relevant events are elicited
from her.

Ordinary witnesses are not supposed to make inferences or interpretations on the basis of what they have directly experienced, i.e. they are not supposed to express opinions about it. This is a particularly salient issue with regard to motive or intent, characteristically an element of a charge to be proved. Opinions from ordinary witnesses are excluded in part because they are considered less reliable than facts, but also because it is the fact-finders who are to make their own inferences as to the implications for guilt of what the witness experienced.

Expert witnesses, in contrast, are called in precisely to offer opinions that interpret evidence, specifically only in relevant areas about which, it has been agreed by law-makers, fact-finders (juries and judges) cannot readily draw conclusions on the basis of their knowledge. For example, a doctor might express the opinion that a particular type of wound could cause death. Expert witnesses, then, must have specialized knowledge that fact-finders lack, so when they are first introduced as witnesses in direct examination, they must be "qualified" or give evidence of training and experience that provides the basis of this specialized knowledge.

I have already noted that ordinary witnesses must base their testimony on direct sensory experiences. In selecting the sensorily experienced as more reliable than that which is acquired through other means, evidence law distinguishes among sources of evidence in practice that are morphologically distinguished in many languages by evidentials, suggesting both that such a distinction is widespread, and that it can be sustained in interaction in more than one way. But what is striking about evidence law is that it further distinguishes between that which has been heard and that which has been seen. Basically there are few evidentiary constraints placed on that which is seen, but a number of very obscurely differentiated constraints placed on that which has been heard by the witness, associated with the famous but often misunderstood hearsay exclusion.

Many people apparently think the hearsay exclusion prevents witnesses from reporting speech that others reported to them, i.e. speech that the witness did not herself hear. But this is actually considered double hearsay.

Hearsay in fact is anything said by another that the witness heard said, when that speech is used in a trial to prove the truth of what was said; for example if Mary had told the witness at some time in the past, "I changed my will to exclude my daughter," that utterance could not be used to prove that Mary did in fact change her will.

One justification for the exclusion of hearsay is that memory of what we heard said is less reliable than memory of what we saw done. Loftus and Palmer (1974), however, have provided interesting information suggesting that "eye witness" testimony is unreliable too.

But this argument is secondary in evidence law to the idea that hearsay is unreliable because two witnesses are involved in the hearsay, and the *truthfulness* of the original utterer cannot be assessed by the fact-finder because the following requirements imposed on witnesses cannot be met: the original utterer is not under oath; the original utterer is not present in the courtroom so that her demeanor is not available and fact-finders are expected to use demeanor to assess truthfulness; and finally there can be no opportunity to cross-examine the original utterer.

Interestingly enough, this means a witness *can* testify regarding her own previous utterances, since all these requirements can be met for her, often yielding very curious testimony in which the witness can present her side of a conversation, but not what her co-interactants said.

Within this framework there are many interesting forms of speech not considered hearsay because, it is argued, they are not being used to prove the truth of what was said. For example, utterances by others used to show the feelings or knowledge of the original speaker at a given point in time, or to show the effect of the words on their hearer, are not hearsay. Verbal acts at issue in trials involving concerns such as verbal contract violation or slander are also considered not hearsay when admitted as proof of oral utterances rather than as proof of what was asserted in them. Here we begin to be so removed from everyday phenomenological experience that a search for the "logic" of such positions becomes quite burdensome.

Finally, there are also many exceptions to the hearsay exclusion, and here the issue of reliability emerges again as central, since such exceptions exist because they are considered more reliable than most forms of hearsay. These include dying declarations, declarations against interest, and admissions of a party opponent.

As I have already noted, it is this area of evidence law that most readily lends itself to comparison with linguistic and cultural accounts of evidential distinctions in other societies. In the linguistic literature on evidentials, it is often *assumed* that reliability is the central issue in the distinction between information derived from direct experience and information derived from other sources (e.g. Chafe, 1986). But in more culturally oriented accounts that invoke the interpretive perspectives of members of a given society, this is less clearly the case.

For example, one of the more commonly noted differences between American culture and that of other societies for which there can be an evidentiary dimension is the reluctance of people in other societies to inquire into (K. Basso, 1979), and/or make inferences about, the intentions and motivations or internal states (Witherspoon, 1977; Ochs & Schieffelin, 1984) of others. If reliability is the central concern, one might think that this reluctance is due to the fact that it is difficult to be certain about what goes on in the minds of others. And this would then be a

comment on American society where people readily assume the plausibility of seeking and making such inferences about internal mental states of
everyday life, and in court, even though doing so in court is far more
elaborately controlled.

But such restraint in verbally speculating about, or committing oneself
to, the intentions or mental states of others is most commonly identified
as a way of showing respect or politeness, rather than as a reflection of
doubts people in other societies have about the ability to know what is in
others' minds. Thus Basso discusses the way in which among the Apache
the common American greeting, "How are you?" is taken as an imper-
tinent violation of personal privacy (K. Basso, 1979:49). Witherspoon
talks about how the Navajo generally refrain from taking positions on the
intentions of others as a way of avoiding exerting control over them.
When talking about the states and actions of others while they are
present, the Navajo use a fourth-person verb conjugation, which in other
contexts conveys a hypothetical sense (Witherspoon, 1977:83–4). Ochs
and Schieffelin discuss the general reluctance of both Kaluli and Samoans
to make statements about the internal states of others. They also consider
the ways in which Samoan social hierarchy affects who is responsible,
speaker or hearer, for clarifying speakers' meanings (Ochs and Schieffelin, 1984:298).

It is worth mentioning here too that in many societies evidential
distinctions are associated with greater or lesser value or persuasiveness,
not because of greater or lesser reliability, but because of greater or lesser
wisdom, beauty, or traditionalism, as is true, for example, of *matapule*
(talking chief) speech in Tonga (Philips, 1990).

The point then is that reliability is "our thing." By saying this I do not
necessarily mean to exclude everyone other than Americans from this
concern with reliability. This fascination with reliability in the American
courts is in scientistic imitation of a broader European scientific tradition
that has asserted its superior reliability in data collection standards of fact
and proof over those of not only Christianity but also common sense over
the last several hundred years. Concerns with reliability are no doubt
widespread cross-culturally, but these concerns are being assumed and
assumed to take a particular form, rather than that it is determined and
demonstrated that such assumptions are valid.

What are the constraints on the 'interpretation' of evidence?

I have already discussed some of the constraints on both regular and
expert witnesses regarding the kinds of interpretations they are allowed to
make so that here attention will focus on constraints on the jury, and on
fact-finders more generally.

First of all, jurors are instructed that they are to use *all* and *only* the information offered during the trial to decide whether a defendant did indeed do what he or she has been charged with. The concern that jurors use only what they learn in the courtroom is a confusing one to the layperson, and to the social scientist in some ways. It runs counter to common-sense expectations, and to phenomenological accounts of the way in which knowledge is indexed in making sense of speech.

The legal intent of such an instruction is not coherent. On the one hand, the idea that a defendant is evaluated by peers with the same knowledge and values as he or she has is basic to the jury system. On the other hand, it is standard practice to strike from juries prospective jurors who might be biased because of strong views about the issues at hand. Such views are often assumed to stem from significant personal involvement with issues similar to those with which the defendant is involved. For example, a person who has been injured in an accident and then proceeded to sue those she believed injured her, will be removed from the jury pool for a personal injury suit arising out of similar circumstances. Prospective jurors who are not necessarily biased, but simply knowledgeable in relevant areas, are also often considered undesirable as jurors, because of the belief that they will bring information from their own experience into jury deliberations, and exert undue and inappropriate influence on the jury's decision.

The legal profession conceives of the jury as using *all* information presented in that they are expected to draw upon not just what is said, but how it is said, or on the nonverbal and paralinguistic behavior that lawyers call demeanor. Demeanor is part of what a jury must use to decide whether the truth is being told, and it is the unavailability of demeanor when a witness reports on knowledge obtained from others, knowledge not owned by the witness, that partially justifies its exclusion from evidence.

An additional interpretive constraint on the jury that is distinctive to trial evidence is the instruction to the jury by the judge to ignore whatever he tells them to ignore in situations where evidence has come in that should not have been allowed in.

A final interpretive constraint upon the jury is that, in making their decision about the guilt or innocence of a party (which often entails deciding whether the facts presented, if believed, fit the description of the charge or crime), they are to follow the judge's interpretation to them of the law and its relation to the facts that fall within particular statutory definitions of violations of the law.

Both evidential and interpretive constraints imposed by evidence law place jurors, the officers of the court (judge, lawyers, clerks, and bailiff), and trial audiences in very different positions regarding the evidence they have available to them, and the interpretive principles they use in arriving at a judgment of guilt or innocence.

In criminal cases, for example, jurors often do not know, as officers of the court do, what former crimes a defendant has committed, or what happened to other defendants involved in the same events and charged with crimes in separate proceedings. Jurors also do not hear motions in court to exclude various forms of evidence that officers of the court and the audience hear.

Sometimes, then, the fact-finders do arrive at rather different decisions regarding guilt from those reached by others who have access to different information and who are unconstrained by the interpretive principles imposed on the jury. This is one basis for occasionally well publicized cries of outrage from "the public" when a defendant deeply believed by many to be guilty is found innocent. I believe this is also the most important reason why, in my experience, those who work in courts regularly believe that criminal defendants are guilty if they come to trial at all.

So in spite of the vaunted evidential superiority of what jurors are exposed to, court officials and trial audiences regularly give more credence to that which is excluded from trial court evidence than to that which is included.

Concluding discussion

This chapter has presented two ways to think about domain or institutional sub-system specializations in evidentiary standards. First, we can think of domain-specific evidentiary specializations as variants of everyday common-sensical evidentiary standards and interpretive procedures. For example, while we may normally consider second-hand information to be less reliable than first hand information, evidence law not only heightens our awareness of the distinction, but actively excludes the second-hand information we hear outside of trials, and also distinguishes between the seen and the heard through the hearsay exclusion in ways rather difficult for most of us to grasp, let alone apply in ongoing interaction.

Second, we can think of domain or institutional sub-system special-izations as related to, and mutually influencing, one another. Here I have suggested that evidence law has been very much influenced by scientific models of evidence, apparent in the concern with principled empiricism (facts are what is directly experienced), by political models of decision-making (oppositional parties in debate whose positions are voted on), and more covertly and implicitly by residual Christian models of morality and truth (inconsistency is lying and the liar is immoral/criminal).

These two constructs for conceptualizing intra-societal evidential variability are not entirely compatible, since the first suggests we are either in or out of an institution, while the second implies we are always in an institution, raising questions about how we shift among evidential frameworks in ongoing interaction.

Finally, evidentiality is recognized to be linguistically and culturally variable, even though we may still be carrying over our own evidential framework into comparative work by assuming that relative reliability is always central to evidentiality. But we need now to go further in this relativity, and recognize that there is intra-societal variability in both linguistic and cultural framings of evidentiality in all societies, rather than equating language structure with language use and culture with practice, particularly in societies other than our own.

12

RECOLLECTIONS OF FIELDWORK CONVERSATIONS, OR AUTHORIAL DIFFICULTIES IN ANTHROPOLOGICAL WRITING

TULLIO MARANHÃO

In 1974 I was doing fieldwork in Icaraí,[1] an isolated and small fishermen's village in the north-east of Brazil, studying the natives' fish classification, and the cognitive plans they employed in their dead-reckoning sailing and fishing strategies. My research project stemmed from the field of cognitive anthropology, and my general assumption was that the people of Icaraí had a "folk ichthyology" and a "folk nautics" constituting prominent parts of their "ethnoscience." I was, consequently, researching a variety of "science" which was different from "our science." This questioned whether only our sciences were different, or whether "I" and "they" also were. From a national point of view, there were no differences between them and me; we even shared a common mother tongue.[2] I did not think we were different, only that our "sciences" were, but they did not feel quite the same about me, for, in the first months of my stay in Icaraí, I was called the "Spaniard," or the "Foreigner." Naturally, this was rather annoying for me, because I did not think that our differences ran that "deep"; I thought that by virtue of our different historical backgrounds and modes of living we were exotic to each other, and although my anthropological ideology tempted me to construe them as radically different others, my political ideology watered these impulses down, forcing me to think of my hosts, at least partially, as "us," Brazilians like myself, therefore confronted with the same political challenge. To my eyes, certainly, the people of Icaraí were exploited, but somehow removed from the class exploitation of the Brazilian society at large, because of their geographical, political, social, and cultural isolation. Their "society," on the other hand, was hierarchical and unjust, but these realizations struck my political rage less forcefully, because they were diluted with my anthropological ideology which described them as "different" rather than "exploited." Undoubtedly, the fieldwork situation prodded my ethnographic curiosity and desire to describe, and left dormant my political indignation and desire to act. However, as it now seems clear, I was unwilling to embrace fully either an anthropological ideology of absolute difference or a political ideology of absolute exploitation. Furthermore, I had no desire to integrate the two contradictory pictures; like most anthropologists, I probably felt that I was a politically sensitive ethnographer in the same way that a political activist would think he was sensitive to the cultural differences of his proselytes.

There was one obvious difference between the people of Icaraí and myself: we seemed to have different views about how we should communicate with each other. At the time of my fieldwork I used to explain this difference with my iridescent rainbow of ideologies (anthropological or political), but now I understand it as a consequence of our choices of discourse. I should, therefore, like to remember the kind of problem I had during my fieldwork interviews without the explanations which satisfied me at the time, and which I shall summarize in the following reminiscence.

In such a study in cognitive anthropology, I had to elicit precise information about the defining characteristics by means of which the fishermen classified the approximately four hundred kinds of fish they identified. My hypothesis was that they organized these categories (fish) in a taxonomy, as the canon of ethnoscience recommended,[3] and indeed there was persuasive evidence that their ichthyological vocabulary presented relations of inclusion (e.g. *viola* is a type of *atabuado* ["flattened shark"], which is a type of *cação* ["shark"] which is a type of *peixe-de-couro* ["skin-fish"]). At first I asked general questions such as, "What is fish such-and-such like?," and later on more specific questions, such as those recommended in the literature in cognitive anthropology, leading to comparisons, "What is the difference between A and B?," as well as to a minute elicitation of distinctive features, "Among A, B, and C, which one is the farthest apart and why?" The fishermen's answers were often puzzling to me; after each question they would tell long stories that on the one hand, might mention something which could stand as an answer to my question (e.g. the color "red"), but on the other hand, often added a great deal more than I was interested in finding out at that point. A fisherman whom I had asked merely if he had been to sea in the past few days told me a forty-five-minute long story about a stormy trip he had had months ago; another one, whom I asked to explain the nautical operation of *botar-na-orsa* ("to let the sail go aloof") told me an equally long story. Situations like these repeated themselves day after day for the entire duration of my stay in Icaraí, even after I had joined a fishing crew and found myself at home living there.

The people of Icaraí were different indeed, and it had taken me some time to realize a few manifestations of this difference, and further adapt myself to their mode of living. I learned, for example, that I was being extremely rude in the way I approached their houses and asked to interview them. I would walk straight to the front door, knock, introduce myself, and ask for the interview. I should, instead, approach the house indirectly and squat under a near-by coconut tree (the village's thatched houses are scattered among sand dunes covered with coconut palms). After my presence had been noticed by an adult living in that household, I could approach the house, squat by the window, and a casual conversation, generally about the weather, could ensue. The next step would be an invitation for me to come in. Then the visit might last a whole morning, or a whole day; the conversation could become rather animated, many stories being told by the different speakers; I would usually leave when I felt tired, without ever knowing if my departure had been precipitous or unduly delayed. My opinion at the time was that these were characteristics of the Icaraí people: they like a male visitor to approach their houses in a roundabout way so that if no men were at home, his presence could pass unacknowledged and he should leave; and they liked to tell long stories and were not accustomed to dialogues with short questions and answers. These habits were of course disturbingly incompatible with the needs of an ethnographer unravelling the natives' "folk science."

I remember the difficulty I had in trying to obtain a straightforward and coherent system of color identification. Color was a criterion of the utmost importance in the fish classification, but there were enormous discrepancies from the answers of one informant to the next, and even in the answers of the same informant at different times. One day someone would say that a certain fish I exhibited to him was "black," the next day he would say the same fish was "white." After a while I learned that the "black/white" dichotomy was used to classify fish along at least three different dimensions: (1) in commercial terms, "black fish" is cheap fish, while "white" is more valuable independently of the actual color of the fish; (2) fish have "black" or "white meat," phrases which refer neither to the meat, nor to the color, but to certain properties such as having more or less blood, or living on the bottom or at the surface of the sea, characteristics with important implications for the dietary habits of the people of Icaraí;[4] (3) finally, fish can have "white" or "black" skin or scale, amongst several other colors; but in order to simplify matters the fishermen used to refer to all light-colored fish as "white" and all dark as "black," because the precision I was looking for was irrelevant for them. I concluded that what I needed was to contextualize my questions: "What is the color of the skin or scale of this fish?" Naturally, this specification improved the quality of the answers I obtained, but it did not entirely resolve my problems, since I continued to get long stories. Furthermore, many fishermen could not understand why I needed to ask for the color of a fish I had in my hands and could see for myself, as one of them once cautiously commented, careful not to offend me. I thought that they certainly had a "folk science" but was beginning to doubt their awareness of it. However, this constituted no checkmate for my anthropological armory: their "science" was "unconscious," or (to use a less loaded term) it was not verbalized. Mine, however, was, and the reason for my presence in Icaraí was to put theirs into words. But whose words, theirs or mine?

I had joined a fishing crew which included the ten-year-old son of the skipper; the two of us were apprentices on board. While the boy moved freely on the boat, and after the first trip was already able to take the tiller and maintain a course, I could barely keep myself inside the small rocking boat. Nevertheless, there were virtually no verbal exchanges between father and son, while I was constantly asking questions of the skipper, writing things down, looking out, figuring things out, and checking back with my teacher what I had learned. He struck me as precise and swift in his actions, but discouragingly sloppy in his answers. We joked about my slowness to learn in contrast to his son's cleverness. Every time the boy made a mistake his father would hit him with a stick, or yell at him. The skipper joked that perhaps that was the missing ingredient in my apprenticeship. I was often bewildered by my teacher's "evident" nautical competence and by his tottering explanatory skills, and torn in my confidence. How could I have entrusted myself to this man, thirty miles from the coast, in a rickety, sixteen-foot vessel, a man who could sail well, but could not talk? What I doubted, of course, was the soundness of his knowledge. He did not carry a compass and yet seemed to be able to tell me the direction of the wind, the movement of the tide, and the boat's course even upon waking up from under the stern, and before he had had a chance to stick out his head and look around. I checked the information he gave me on my compass, which he did not know how to read and disdainfully called the "man's watch," and it was always right.

My most immediate problem was how to stand and walk on the boat when the sea was choppy. One day, on another boat, a fisherman gave me the decisive clue: I could not keep my balance if I looked at the boat, I had to keep my eyes on the sea. Suddenly I realized that the fishermen had a "compass" in their minds which never stopped indicating the directions of the winds and the running of the tide. Even when on land, they were constantly aware of these two movements. Then it did not take long for me to realize that the noise of the water against the hull, which the fishermen referred to through a variety of onomatopoeic words, was all an experienced skipper needed to know in order to realize in which direction the boat was going, which wind was blowing and at what point was the movement of the tide. That "pah-pah-pah" or "shhhhhhhh" on the hull was the code which gave them their direction.[5]

I was thrilled with my discovery and checked it with my teacher, Zé Paula, but he was undaunted, acknowledging that the sound of the waves against the hull helped his orientation, but not always, and he told me stories on end which contained references to *areação* (to become lost at

sea "when the skipper's reason turns around"), but which did not answer
my fundamental question: "Is the noise on the hull the main orientation
sign when you cannot see the waves or feel the winds?" For me, evidently,
knowledge needed explanatory eloquence in order to be respectable.
Nevertheless, apparently I was equally convinced that "evidence" was
sufficient to bestow authority upon knowledge. If my political and
anthropological ideologies were a source of ambiguity, my epistemology
was no less so.

I wished to cover the fishermen's knowledge with the mantle of my
words which I assumed was to be the decisive validity test. My interlocutors also covered their knowledge with verbal explanations, and trusted
the evidence of facts. In the ethnographic dialogue between us, while they
relied on practical evidence, I looked for persuasive ("descriptive"?)
explanations. Evidence presupposed an ostensive reference capable of
generating agreement, while in our communication, employing different
discourse strategies to construe ostensive reference, the evidence that
precedes consensus was split into the texts of practical fishing and of
intellectual explanation. They could not "understand" my project of
writing a monograph about their sailing and fishing knowledge. I would
not explain it to them, and am afraid that had I tried, they would have felt
extremely bored. All they had from me in the way of explanation was my
questions, addressing an area of life which was irrelevant from their point
of view for the purpose of presentation in a book. They preferred me to
extol their moral worth in my monograph. I, in turn, could not "understand" their nautical knowledge. Notice that the two uses of the words
"understanding" are different; theirs was a question of accepting my
reasons or not, while mine was a matter of being able to put their actions
into words.

The explanations about the "fuzziness" in color identification, about
how to approach a house, and about how the Icaraí fishermen oriented
themselves at sea, were my own constructs, and in spite of the fact that my
"groundbreaking" explanations did not command my interlocutors' full
acquiescence, I concluded, in the respectable company of Jean Piaget,
Claude Lévi-Strauss and Noam Chomsky, that they bore "psychological
reality." Indeed, in structural anthropology, the ethnographer could not
expect to obtain the native's agreement to his structuralist explanations
based, for example, on binary oppositions. Likewise, in generative
grammar, although the linguist believed that his transformational rules
were precisely those employed by the speakers of the language to generate
sentences, he could not expect them to be aware of these rules, or
sometimes even to understand them. The implication of these scientific
assumptions in anthropology and in linguistics is this: there is a knowledge to which not every form of discourse has access. The problem with

which the fishermen and I were confronted was one of mutually incommensurable modes of discourse.

In this reminiscence of my fieldwork conversations it has become clear to me what the reasons were for the fishermen to tell me their stories as responses to my questions. When I asked for color specification, looking for word nuances in order to complete my dimensions of distinctive features, they felt affronted by questions with such obvious answers, and thought that I doubted their knowledge – an absolutely correct assumption, because if I had no doubts, there should be no reason for me to inquire. After all, matters such as the color of a fish were assumed to be rather self-evident for normal intelligence, and my insistence upon those questions sounded suspicious.

I wished my communication with them could have fallen into the practical give-and-take of everyday situations, but most of the time they chose to tell me stories rather than to answer with short speech acts, even when the context seemed to be appropriate for a short and immediate response. It was not unusual for me to ask a question about a technical operation while we were out at sea, and receive as a reply "I'll tell you later," when only a few words would have been sufficient to satisfy my curiosity. My interlocutor obviously felt it appropriate to answer me in an elaborate manner incompatible with the operational urgency of the occasion. It did not take long before I realized that they used their stories as answers to my questions rather than as an evocative, solidarity-exercising mode of discourse. Of course, they also told narratives as evocation, that is, neither as an answer to a question nor as a verbal intervention calling for a response. Their narrative responses to my questions were retrieved from their repertoire of stories told in more narrative contexts to an audience which already knew the story but took delight in hearing a good performance.

The population of Icaraí descends from the literate European Portuguese, and, although familiar with the characteristics of literacy and writing, the majority of the villagers are illiterate. They speak, however, in a marvelously "literary" genre sometimes reminiscent of the Portuguese national epic poem, *Os Lusíadas* by Luis de Camões ([1572] 1950), which takes after the model of rhetoric in classical antiquity as epitomized in the *Aeneid*. In this sense the Icaraí narratives obviously perform the mnemonic function of storing information of cultural value, although it would be wrong to assume that they replace written texts, *ipsis verbis*, as an ersatz of the literate information-retrieval system. The Icaraí narratives are a Jack-of-all-trades in their communicative procedures, as poetry, speech acts, texts or riddles are in other cultural contexts, and thus they are employed to achieve all kinds of illocutionary effects. I noticed that stories about tragic voyages were told with the purpose of teaching the secrets of sailing and fishing on the high seas. Narratives were also told for the exercise of consensus and social solidarity, as in conversations about the weather with a stranger upon a casual and brief encounter. Narratives were told for therapeutic purposes, selecting stories which had a soothing effect. The fishermen did not like to dream because for them it meant *fraqueza do juízo* (a certain "weakness of the mind"), and from time to time I saw a man refrain from going out to sea because he remembered a dream he had had the previous night. On those occasions the fisherman would spend the day off at home, generally in the company of an elder who told stories on end, stories which were tranquil and relaxing. The narratives also bore a strong epic aspect generally extolling the fisherman's identity as a quiet, peaceful, and humble man, but also courageous, altruistic, and tenacious.

The fishermen who told me long fishing stories were demonstrating their knowledge to an ethnographer whose "scientific" curiosity was interpreted as skepticism. At times they made poignant efforts to persuade me that they knew what they were talking about by building narratives which were truly gems, illustrating all aspects of their nautical and ichthyological knowledge, as well as the forms of social etiquette which were important within their social milieu. In one single narrative, the knowledge of the sea by the identification of its spectrum of colors was opposed to the orientation in sailing by fathoming the depth: lowering the lead sink could be misleading in case the weight should land on top of a rock instead of on the bottom of the sea, which might deceive the skipper into believing he was moving towards the land, while he could well be moving farther and farther away from it. The knowledge of the colors of the sea was more subtle, more difficult to acquire, but also more reliable. A true *mestre* ("skipper"), however, was not expected to boast about his experience, but to keep his skills secret until the opportunity presented itself for him to show them, not for the sake of exhibition, but for the noble purpose of saving his comrades from a dangerous situation. Once the experience had been lived through, it could enter the realm of stories and be told with full bravado. It was important for the speaker to abstain from talking about facts which had not taken place, because these inevitably led to an evaluation of the possibilities for action available to him under circumstances which had not occurred; that is, to a speculative assessment of his capabilities against which he could measure poorly.

At times, the narrative would address issues which were not ostensively present in the context of conversation, but which hovered over the speaker's mind. I once asked a married fisherman, who had taken my cook as his mistress, if his wife would not become suspicious of his frequent visits to my house during the late hours. His response was a story of how he had saved another fisherman who was drowning. His extra-marital affair tarnished his reputation, and so he was telling me what a man of valor he was. A woman, whom I was asking to identify and describe some fish, told me a story about how her husband had taught her about each of those fish. In spite of the fact that she was giving me the information I sought, she was also effacing herself as a speaker and invoking the character who should more properly be my interlocutor in that interview, her husband. The fisherman who told me the long story about the stormy fishing trip thought that my question (whether he had been fishing in the past few days) betrayed my suspicion that he was lazy, and consequently told me that he would not miss one day of fishing or even return earlier because of a storm. His forty-five-minute long narrative had the meaning of a speech act such as, "If your question implies that I am lazy, let me tell you that I am not, and the fact that even during severe storms, while most fishermen sail back, I stay out there doing my job goes to prove it."

Evidently, these examples underscore the difference between the form and the use of a mode of discourse. The fishermen's interventions in our verbal interactions took the form of narratives, but they were used as turns in a dialogue, as responses, reactions or corrections to something that I had said. The form of my questions and comments was dialogical – short and intended to produce a response – but I employed them precisely as the author of a text eliciting information in order to compose an essay. I was not interested, for instance, in persuading my interlocutors of anything, and even less so in disagreeing with them. My only goal was to build a picture representing their nautical and ichthyological knowledge, and my interactions with the Icaraí people were by and large guided by this authorial interest. I wanted to produce a text *as if* my interlocutors had written it, that is, as perfect as possible a copy of their knowledge. Obviously, the underlying assumption of such a project is that the discourse with which the fishermen "copied" their knowledge was not good enough, or was not comprehensible, at least not to the audiences I had in mind – my fellow anthropologists – and therefore I needed to bring into play the ethnographer's oracular services. But notice that, if all were a mere matter of translation, I did not need to learn their knowledge; it would be enough to translate their words to my discourse. The nub of the matter resided in the fact that, if my ultimate goal was clearly to compose a text, the procedures to achieve that were ambiguous: sometimes I acted as translator, taking for granted the mimetic faculty of my interlocutors' discourse; at other times I acted as oracle, assuming that I needed to tap the source of their knowledge. In the end, my text resulted from the hybrid combination among my descriptions of what I observed and experienced, their narratives, and my efforts to bridge the discrepancies between the two.

If I was ensnared in textual motives, my interlocutors also dabbled in textuality, but for very different motives. While knowledge for me could be defined by its potentiality to be congealed in a text, for them the text was a mere frame capable of celebrating virtue. For them men were not knowledgeable, but good, or courageous. My ten-year-old apprentice companion was a glaring witness to this discrepancy of hermeneutical standpoints. Since he had grown up within that cultural milieu, I imagine that already at the beginning of our initiation he knew a great deal more about fishing than I was ever going to learn. He was hit or admonished by his father for failing to do what he was expected to do. Perhaps, on occasions, the punishment was unfair, because he could not possibly know what was expected of him at that age, and with the amount of exposure he had had to sailing and fishing. Nevertheless, the poking functioned as a reminder that he should move quickly and succeed in his practice, or he would not grow up to be a man of quality. Ironically, as an ethnographer, I was not supposed to learn in the same way as my co-apprentice, but to cull the knowledge I wished to acquire out of my informants' discourse. Indeed, what he was learning from their point of understanding was not how to sail and fish, but how to become a good man, someone capable of providing for his family, and responsible for his comrades at sea with courage and self-sacrifice.

I remember that at the end of my stay in Icaraí, during an emotionally charged good-bye dinner, I thanked Zé Paula for all he had "taught" me. His reply, to my astonishment, was that he had never "taught" me anything; as a matter of fact I had learned nothing, because one only learned with the aim of doing, he proceeded, and when that was the case no teacher was necessary. He knew all along I did not intend to become a fisherman, although I talked about "learning," I mentioned that I wanted to write about them, and Zé Paula knew that in order to write I did not need to know. We further discussed the meaning of "learn," and he thought I had been using the word in a very loose way, *maneira de falar* ("way of speaking"); that is, as in the imprecise metaphors we use in our everyday speech, conveying expressionist complexes in a testimony of our common-sense wisdom to mistrust the exactness of language.

I used to think of myself as being in a dialogue with my interlocutors, when in fact I was merely composing a literary text. My art of composition was ambiguous at heart, because if on the one hand it praised self-evidential reality as every literary text must, on the other hand it reaped its knowledge from the fields of speech. The people of Icaraí immediately understood that I wished to compose a text about them. However, they wanted the text to extol their honor and valor, while I insisted that it should verse their nautical and ichthyological "knowledge." Their ultimate interlocutor was myself; my interlocutors, however, were not those informants, but the academic community of colleagues for whom I was writing.

It was probably the anthropological tradition of fieldwork which induced me/revealed to me this bricolage between discourses of a different pedigree in order to produce the ethnographic text.[6] Some anthropologists like Malinowski ([1935] 1978) attributed great importance to the natives' "true words," but no-one has entirely conducted his or her research exclusively with the informants' discourse in spite of groundbreaking efforts by Crapanzano (1980), Dwyer (1982), and D. Tedlock (1983). The ethnography of speaking singled out this topic as its subject matter, but instead of treating it as what it is – discourse – transformed it into another exotic object to be described by the ethnographer's metadiscursive procedures. To study discourse means to engage in a certain mode of discourse with others, and if the "others" of anthropology's speakers are their own academic peers, then there is no need to talk to the natives, as used to be the unquestioned case in the beginnings of the discipline with Edward Tylor, Henry Lewis Morgan, James Frazer, or Lucien Lévy-Bruhl. Anthropological fieldwork, however, forced ethnographers into this antinomic effort to combine the act of writing with the act of falling in dialogue with native interlocutors, and thanks to it/ in spite of it, I can separate the wheat from the chaff and remember the muddled picture I portrayed of my "others," and realize how the jumble still lurks in my memories, as in writing this report I struggle once again to domesticate the unbridled voices which constitute the cacophony of experience as represented in discourse.

The task of a writer/speaker is to move away from the muddle of experience, and perhaps I should open a parenthesis in my recollections of fieldwork conversations, and digress about the meanings of the word "text" in criticism and in hermeneutics. Until now I have employed the word loosely, referring to my research design in cognitive anthropology, to the natives' folk knowledge, to my efforts to elicit data for my study, to their endeavor to persuade me of their valor, and finally to the sum of these communicative experiences which would be encompassed by the phrase "fieldwork conversations" and which – according to the anthropological ideal – should be adequately and accurately represented in the ethnographic text.

In this connection, the question of central concern to us is whether the notion of text is inextricably associated with the technologies of literacy and writing. Ricoeur extends the concept to a wide variety of meaningful situations and writes:

... from the outset the notion of text incorporated features which freed it partially from the relation to writing as opposed to oral discourse. Text implies texture, that is, complexity of composition. Text also implies work, that is, labor in

forming language. Finally, text implies inscription, in a durable monument of
language, of an experience to which it bears testimony. By all of these features, the
notion of the text prepares itself for an analogical extension to phenomena not
specifically limited to writing, nor even to discourse.

(1981:37)

Gadamer would not disagree with Ricoeur's statement, for although
stressing the prominence of the literary text as the model of text par
excellence, he uses the concept "in the widest sense" (1989:111), including
a picture, an architectural work, and a natural event. Therefore the
question cannot be confined to orality and literacy. Within the hermeneutic tradition, the idea of interpretation, which initially had a liberating
ring when opposed to method, has become a limiting concept by emphasizing the autonomy of the text and the authority of the subject interpreter. The resulting notion of text relies more on "texture" and on
"inscription" – to stay with Ricoeur's words – than on "work." Hence the
monumental character of text on its way to scripturality (*Schriftlichkeit*)
has come to prevail over the work of construing a text. Thinking from the
point of view of criticism, it is inevitable to recast the question of
interpretation as something pursuing an always deferred goal, and as a
consequence the horizons of meaning look more like a construction site
than a garden of monuments. Interpretation and explanation cannot be
kept apart, for the answer that every text is to a question already contains
the seed of a spellbinding question. In interpreting/explaining a text the
subject struggles to come into being, but since neither the text nor the
subject's identity are complete, reading/writing is unbounded (*débordé*),
according to Derrida (1981:59).

 If interpreting is writing and writing is interpreting in the always
deferred task of finding/attributing meaning to landmarks of relevance,
that is, texts, and if furthermore the subject's identity comes to him in that
activity and is consequently always tentative and precarious, the best
metaphor to refer to textual work is Penelope's weaving during the day
and unweaving at night the shroud she prepared for her father-in-law
Laertes and the completion of which would signal the time for her to
choose one of the suitors as husband. But unlike Penelope, the text
worker's weaving and unweaving is not a matter of choice: it is a weaving
that never stabilizes in a durable structure between warp and weft.

 Jacques Derrida deconstructs the historical tale of literacy, and shows
that there is already a problem in the phonocentric description of language, for the relationship attributed to sound and thought is mysterious.
The analysis of language into minimal units – phonemes, words, sentences, or ideograms – is a creation of literacy itself, and it is writing
(*écriture*) which gives birth to our notion of the oral. Derrida argues that
speech has been given precedence over writing under the assumption that

it was closer to the essence it expressed. Hence the history of Western metaphysics is by and large reflected in the assumption that being is presence (speaking as opposed to writing) of a subject who legitimizes meaning by virtue of his identity. Thus the meaning of the said is rendered explicit in the act of disclosing the speaker's identity. Derrida contends that speech already implies difference and distantiation to the point that no speaker can be identified as unique behind a given utterance. Writing precedes speaking not only in time but in space, in the burgeoning it undergoes when compared to orality, creating a difference from whose space it towers up. He claims that there is an "arche-writing" more fundamental than writing as a medium of which technical writing is a repetition, however delayed or deferred. The "arche-writing" is an *écriture naturelle* and closer to *logos* than either speech or writing. Plato railed against the text, among other reasons, because it is a counterfeit of thought, pretending to be a copy or representation of speech, when in reality it removes from the writer the need to defend his ideas. For Plato, the text is external and artificial. Derrida, on the contrary, argues that the text is the *parole soufflée* ("whispered discourse"), and that, while speaking is a writing technology of the body, writing is a technology of the soul, more intimate and private, closer to *logos* (Derrida, 1974). Thus, if the main concern for Plato is the text as the final product of writing, for Derrida the nub of the matter is the very act of producing texts, that is, writing, something marking the beginning and the end of all we can talk about, and it is within this territory, commanding rhetorical moves intrinsic to text composition, that he creates the space necessary for his thought. One cannot help but note the similarity between his position and Gadamer's contention that the text is merely a between-product (*Zwischenprodukt*) in the process of understanding (1989).

Derrida's grammatology uproots the conceptual dichotomies of Western thought, singles out the marked categories in each pair (speech, for example, in the pair with writing), and steers away from those poles of knowledge, in a constant process of deconstruction which must also be of self-deconstruction, otherwise it becomes invalidated by claiming for itself a scaffolding for deconstruction which it denies to the objects of its criticism. This claim, however, becomes unsubstantiated when Derrida disposes of one horn of Western conceptual dilemmas only to grasp the other. This is obviously the case with oral and written discourse, as he criticizes the hegemony attained by the former in the Euro–American heritage, and hastens to adopt the latter which he erects as the scaffolding from which to deconstruct the logocentric enthrallment with speech. Indeed, he debunks the centrality of oral discourse but only for the purpose of enthroning written discourse.

The testimonial of anthropological fieldwork, leading ethnographers to the tearing pull between interview (and perhaps dialogue with natives) and writing for the academic community, in principle prevents this fall into the logocentrism of writing. Many anthropologists have come to the conclusion that the presence of being native was more pronounced than that of being alien. Some attributed this difference to the "essence" of the natives – primitive, tribal, kinship-based, illiterate, etc. – others, to the refraction created by the polarization of dialogue into observers and observed. Written anthropological discourse, however, blunts the nuances of self and other in dialogue, stressing the importance of the presence of anthropological discourse itself as well as of its authors. Thus we have Malinowski's Trobrianders or Evans-Pritchard's Nuer. Theories of society, culture, kinship or religion can be regarded as invented, and as bearing the imprint of their inventors. As a result, we are left with this crossbreed between the claims of presence of the "other" in anthropological fieldwork and the testimonial of presence of the "writing self" in anthropological literature. The co-existence with this dilemma of communication between the ethnographer who writes to his fellow anthropologists and the native who talks to the ethnographer creates a difference which in part prevents anthropologists from falling outright into the illusion that anthropology is a dialogue with another fellow anthropologist or with another as native. The speaking–writing at cross purposes of anthropological discourse is troubling for positive science, but very salutary for criticism. Nevertheless, the pressure to bestow respectability on anthropological "findings" forces a choice of discourse which entails pictures of emboldened presence of self and other. Indeed, in this light anthropology is a discourse constituting identities of ethnographer and of native which cannot be upheld in the world of difference and of experience, because, in spite of the anthropological claim for relativism, the difference it can shelter in its bosom is a drop of rain in the world of difference. From today's vantage-point, with the tradition of criticism we have had, it is clear that in its effort to encompass the cultural dimension of difference, anthropological discourse has produced the opposite effect, that is, it has restricted the possibilities of differentiating in its own talk.

Before I go further in my reflection about the act of writing and the product of writing, I must summarize my empirical or experiential arguments. In the foregoing recollection of my fieldwork conversations in Icaraí, I concluded that there was a great difference between "knowledge" and "discourse" for them and for me. From my interlocutors' point of view the validity of knowledge resided in successful practice; for me, on the happy match between observation and evidence whose success was measured by the degree of verbalization. They could not see how talking (or writing for that matter) could be related to sailing and fishing. Talking was about the quality of men and women in society. However, if we consider "knowledge" as just another sphere of "discourse," what the fishermen of Icaraí and I could have done was to choose one type of discourse and "speak within" it. In a way we could not do it, however, because they and I were talking at cross purposes, trying to embrace both worlds of discourse, the fishermen, self-conscious of their knowledge, struggling to persuade me of their character, and I in turn, self-conscious of my discourse, struggling to make them talk in order to match my discursive assumptions. Had there not been such a difference of intentions, my fieldwork would not have concluded on the happy note that it did. I imagine that if we had "spoken" my "discourse," or "manifested" "knowledge" as I assumed it to be, I would have experienced my fieldwork as the act of opening a book about bio-systematics and copying from its pages a fish taxonomy. The communicative difficulties/differences led me in the direction of refining my theoretical apparatus in order to account for the diversity of experiences and situations I found in the field. If my informants did not hold consistently either a criterion of identification or one of classification of fish in a conversation, a taxonomy represented in a diagram was unfitting for description, because there was no graphic solution to the problem of criss-crossing lines when two different sets of dimensions were simultaneously and competitively applied to the same domain of terms. In analyzing my data, back at home in Brasília, I discovered the notion of numerical taxonomy which allowed me to overcome the discrepancy and to criticize the naivety of ethnoscientists who assumed that a graphic model of taxonomy, conditioned by the two-dimensional constraint of a sheet of paper, could replicate a cognitive structure of the human mind. Likewise, the decision-making models used at the time to explain fishing strategies and, in my own application, nautical plans, were too narrow to do justice to a situation in which improvisation was more salient than the pattern of following a rule. Again, I felt myself compelled to work on the theoretical models I had at hand which were based on the language of computer programming of the 1960s, and expanded them with notations and theorems drawn from symbolic logic. The confusion between "discourse'" and "knowledge" and the discrepancy between "theory" and "reality" turned out to be productive in the end but, instead of heeding those differences, as a dutiful student of science I struggled to overcome them, to domesticate them in my final product of a coherent text.

These reflections inevitably present the game of knowing as something very similar to looking through a kaleidoscope. Once a kaleidoscopic tube opens and the pieces of colored glass are sorted out, the mosaics lose a great deal of their esthetic value; they lose their charm. Evidently, even after "knowing" the interior of the kaleidoscope I may still enjoy looking through the tube and observing the different patterns of reflection, but when I am doing that I proceed *as if* I did not know how it works. I think that the conversational fuzziness of my fieldwork interviews is more the consequence of my interlocutors' and of my choice to act as if we did not know, or we did not care, about what was going on in the here-and-now of our encounter, each party carrying through its pre-text, its programmed strategy which stemmed from my and their respective world-views and immediate interests. We could not heed this fact that I realize so many years later, because we never focused on the communicative situation which bonded us, and kept referring to the pre-textual circumstances prompting the discourse of each party.

In another step towards disassembling the kaleidoscopic tube, I realized that the form of the modes of discourse told me nothing about their employment. There were the natives of Icaraí using their epic narratives to persuade me that I should write about their honor rather than about their nautical and ichthyological knowledge. And there I was, absolutely convinced that I entertained a dialogue with them, while all I was doing was to compose a text for another questionable dialogue contrived with my fellow anthropologists. The composition of the text itself was ambiguous because it stemmed from the combined but irreconcilable efforts on my part to *grasp* and, at the same time, to allow myself to *be persuaded.*

Finally, both their and my distinction between orality and literacy was equally muddled because it was based on the techno–empirical difference. Icaraí appeared to be an "oral culture" since its population was illiterate, and fieldwork struck me as an essentially oral activity. I did not have the faintest suspicion that the fishermen's nautical and ichthyological knowledge, organized through a "folk" logic, appealing to the suasive force of evidence in practical accomplishments, and compelled by the survival imperatives of right or wrong (if they were "wrong" they could lose themselves at sea, or fail to find the fish which constituted their staple), could not be equated with my notion of self-evident referents and encompassed in my text. The fishermen's moral self-portrayal, in turn, was textual in a literary sense, so much so that they wanted to have it framed in my book about them. But while the text for me was regarded as a vehicle for discovery, for them it was an instrument of celebration.

They saw me writing and never showed any curiosity about that activity. What was puzzling for them was my tape-recorder which, in addition to recording our voices, could, they believed, speak by itself, dauntingly reproducing our voices, giving me whichever answers I wished to obtain.[7] Despite the fact that they did not know how to read or write, they belonged unquestionably to a literature culture. In such a culture the oral is obviously as bizarre a picture as the electronic, and although they and I were at odds in our respective representations of the tape-recorder, we could not agree more in our veiled conception of oral speech. I can then say, paraphrasing Derrida, that while I "wrote" the fishermen's "knowledge" and "discourse," they "wrote" their moral self-portrayal, albeit only I used the actual technology of drawing signs on paper pads. The writing technology, however, was not the main procedure in that writing endeavor which included interviews, narratives, teaching, fishing and sailing work, and tape-recordings, in addition to taking notes, and later on organizing all these efforts into a text. This fundamental writing akin to text is based on the technique of composition (a systematic/logic/coherent/linear picture), on the mimetic technique (a "copy" of "speech" or of "thought"), and on a technique of communication (the presentation of the text as a discovery/revelation or celebration during a scientific/persuasive undertaking).

Along these lines of reflection it could be said that my informants and I were competing for the authorship of the text we wished to produce. Composing a text is naturally a different activity from engaging in a dialogue or telling a story, although it may comprise these other procedures, but what matters in order to characterize the writing action is its teleology, that is, the production of text. In any world of text construction, in addition to the productive action the author must fasten the text in writing, in memory or in any other medium, and further stabilize it in a genre or style such as narrative, satire, essay, aphorisms, or puns. Once the text is fastened, it can be used in a variety of illocutionary ways, as a reflexive or assertorial narrative, as a narrative dialogue and so on. Furthermore, and as an extension of this foregoing possibility, the text can be used in a perlocutionary connection, that is, with the aim of producing a certain effect on the audience of its performer, independently of the text's illocutionary force acquired in the stages of its fastening.

The characteristics of the text determine a distantiation between the author and his product.[8] First, its fixation in a certain technical writing, alphabetical or mnemonic, for example, thrusts a wedge between the worker and his text. The following complementary fastening into a genre or style accentuates the separation. Secondly, the possibility of using the text in many illocutionary keys and for a variety of perlocutionary effects steals the text away from its author, entrusting it to the care of any performer. If at the moment of production the text reflected its author's intentions, once it becomes fastened under certain conventions, the author can no longer change, stress or withdraw his intention. He will often experience his product as if it were beginning a life of its own, interpreted by others and attributed intentions foreign to the author's wishes. Thirdly, texts are addressed to "universal" or unspecified audiences who increase the potential for multiple interpretations, underscoring the impression that the text has a life of its own, and can therefore conjure intentions unforeseen by its author. What happens under these circumstances is that texts, after being passed on from authors to performers, wind up in the possession of audiences, undergoing a fragmentation set into motion by the conflict of interpretations. Once this happens, the fastened aspect of texts becomes preposterous and they look like a mere linguistic asset open to any use. Finally, texts break the link between discourse and ostensive reference, that is, the reference shared by speaker and hearer, raising the claim that that to which the text refers is self-evident. In this connection, in the roots of the literary text we find together the embryos of science and fiction, both relying on the self-evidence of the entities constituted by their respective discourses. Appealing to the self-evidence of that about which it "talks," the text becomes a fantasy, in Freudian parlance, severing the bonds with the desire which was the original impulse towards its creation, but which once repressed underwent sublimation, replacing the fulfillment of pleasure by a fantasy or a symptom. This cultural product opposed to desire is alien to its producer's intention, and therefore can be repossessed by anyone.

My interviews in Icaraí were characterized not only by the competition between my informants and me for the authorship of the text we were trying to produce, but also by the alienation of the author inherent in every text. The text, or the texts, in this sense, had been produced before our encounter, the Icaraí text about honor, my text about cognitive anthropology. My interlocutors and I were in the role of performers, actors not authors, and indeed were experiencing enormous difficulties in authoring our respective scripts because we were unaware of our removal from our pre-given texts. Moreover, I was in command of the writing technology, and hence my interlocutors' writing efforts were all directed at me and filtered through me. While I tried to obtain more thorough responses from my interlocutors, they further endeavored to persuade me that I should write about their valor, by telling me more stories about honor. In this struggle, I increased the fragmentation of the text of ethnoscience, and it was inevitable that the resulting essay I wrote constituted an indictment against the principles of cognitive anthropology: taxonomies were a graphic bias rather than cognitive structures, classifications were artificial reconstructions of practical identifications, and so on.[9]

Ironically, as it seems to me from today's vantage-ground, I was making ropes out of sand, further splintering the scientific text of cognitive anthropology in my own effort to build it, because I was constructing something already built, trying to become the original owner of something which is new and unexpected, but to create such an impression without actually disrupting the existing texts. In a certain way, I succeeded in that effort as I encompassed my "discoveries" about ichthyological classification and nautical operations in formal systems surpassing in complexity the formalisms with which I had begun: that is, replacing taxonomies by numerical taxonomies and decision-making models by symbolic logic.

Now the nature of my dialogue with the Icaraí fishermen is clear. Their tradition, as expressed to me, had one text which versed their valor. This text was imparted to me through their narratives, both those which recurred in their repertoire of stories and those composed *ad hoc* in order to persuade me. The nautical and ichthyological knowledge was a practical matter, an aspect of humdrum everyday life, and as such discouraged either description or celebration. I was pursuing the dialogue of questions and answers with them, convinced that their discourse failed to do justice to their knowledge. I tried to remedy this lack by filling in my own discourse. But the tradition I expressed to them also had its pre-text, namely, cognitive anthropology, according to which the natives of Icaraí had a "folk science" which it was relevant to describe. They and I were so ensnared in our respective textual and discursive traditions that we could not address our difficulties in communicating with each other in the here-and-now of the dialogical situation. Ours was a dialogue of the deaf, which we found ourselves condemned to repeat as long as we ignored the nature of the stumbling-block of our communication difficulties.

Why could my interlocutors and I not stop our hyperbolic discourse by trying to find out what the other wanted? If anthropologists became scribes of the natives' wishes, they would certainly lose respectability in their scientific milieu, where authors have priority over typists, speakers over shorthand writers, and writers over translators, because they would be giving up their author-ity. However, the authority only exists as long as the text is being composed and it is possible to imagine an author in full presence; the moment the writing is fastened into a text, the imagination of presence dwindles and authority becomes a controversial issue. This, nevertheless, is not a subject for hard and fast conclusion, for it is uncertain where one text ends and the next begins, and there is no authority in the construction of meaning capable of claiming absolute presence. As Derrida puts it, all we have are traces of traces of traces . . .[10] It would be difficult to take the argument about the limitation of authority to its ultimate conclusions without procuring a metaphysics of authorship, but this, at any rate, is what we find ourselves constantly doing, and I re-enact it right here as I write these lines. What then is the purpose of these reflections?

The narrative transcribed in the Appendix was told to me by Zé Horácio in response to questions I was asking about the tarpon. The story begins with Zé Horácio's premonition that he should follow Chico Primo on his way to get the fish out of the *curral* (see the Appendix for a description of this fishing trap). He saw Chico Primo go in, but after a long time had elapsed and the sun was already setting, he still did not come out. Zé Horácio went in to find out what was going on, and found his fellow "cowboy" (see the Appendix) knocked down and blacked out. First he thought that Chico Primo was dead. The idea that he could be accused of killing him chilled Zé Horácio, but brave and altruistic, he carried his fellow "cowboy" out. Then he returned to the *curral* and killed the tarpon which had knocked Chico Primo down, thus avenging his comrade. Finally, he carried Chico Primo and the load of fish caught in the *curral*, stressing that the effort required to carry all that weight was beyond human power. In addition to illustrating the aggressive nature of the tarpon in answer to my question as to whether that kind of fish could cause harm to a man, Zé Horácio told a tale of his moral worth, presenting himself as someone endowed with the special powers of pre-monition and superhuman strength, altruistic, courageous, and in solidarity with his fellow fishermen. I recorded the story, but in writing my monograph I culled out of it only the description of the tarpon. The rest, although interesting, was just noise cluttering up the message of most interest to me at the time. But this fact hardly constitutes an anthropological problem for other ethnographers go to the field without having definite research projects, and just record whatever they witness, which presumably is the natives' stories in the way in which they wish them presented. But is this "spontaneous" anthropological work better than the work unfolding from a project?

The desire to be faithful to the native's voice has run a stiff competition to anthropological theory, from Malinowski's minute transcriptions of the Trobrianders' utterances ([1935] 1978) to D. Tedlock's recording of the Quiché Maya's *Popol Vuh* or "Council Book" (1983). Tedlock remembers Malinowski's images of the missionary as someone who translates "the white man's point of view to the native," and of the anthropologist as the translator of the natives' "point of view to the European" (1983:334). It seems as though the ethnographer's work is oracular, and his or her great gift for undertaking that work lies in the capacity to restrain one's own point of view, thereby allowing the natives' to flow. What seems to be implied in this image is the fact that, in order to let the other talk, the self has to be restrained or even effaced. While the flow of the native's voice depends on the ethnographer's self-restraint, the white man's voice flows only in the wake of repression of the native's. But this is a particularly dogmatic generalization of the encounter between the Western European and the others. Anthropological encounters contain a greater variety of situations, including those of cacophony, with the two voices struggling to stifle each other. Tedlock's lesson on "learning to listen" (1983: chapter 3) is steeped in intertextuality. Every story is preceded by a triggering story which can be the silent but inquisitive presence of the ethnographer, or any purpose for the narrative to be told. Tyler argues that translation is not an adequate trope for anthropological work because, by interspersing the native's text with the ethnographer's (a rendition of the native's point of view *in terms of* the ethnographer's language, categories of knowledge, interests, etc.), the anthropologist claims the right to *represent* the interlocutor (1987:95–6). In Tyler's opinion dialogue is a far better trope for anthropological work, but not "dialogue rendered as text," "for dialogue is the source of the text" (1987:66). The ethnography is a sign of a dialogue which took place.

The subject in dialogue is constituted in the ballet danced by self and other. The other is only established as native by the ethnographer's act of christening as native. The ethnographer, in turn, is also christened in that act. However, that christening is not extended to the anthropologist's activities as a scribe, for the role of subject in an interview is no kin to the role of author of a text. The awareness that the language game of fieldwork cannot be carried on to the language game of writing an ethnography makes us more tolerant of all the discrepancies cropping up between the two games. The ethnography is always a recollection and as such it is an intervention in a dialogue different from that one which took place in the field. From this vantage-point of reflection in the tradition of American anthropology, and informed by the discussions in hermeneutics and in the postmodern debate, it seems inevitable to conclude that anthropological discourse hardly completes the caricatures of responsible subjects – ethnographer and native – and that it does not refer to anything evident, because its staple resides precisely in the negotiation of ostensiveness between self and other. But the way out of the quandary is neither in the reformation of the style for writing ethnographies nor in any scientific and methodological revolution capable of improving the persuasiveness of anthropological discourse. What has changed is the mode in which an anthropologist recollects his fieldwork adventures and misadventures. The evocative mode, however, is hardly at ease with the anthropological tradition. We evoke the turning-points of life such as birth, marriage, and death with pictures and other kinds of mementos, but it would be odious to naturalize the primordiality of evocation, and give birth, get married, and die for the purpose of future remembrance.

APPENDIX

The following narrative is about fishing in *currais*. A *curral* "corral" is a fishing trap approximately 70 meters long and 20 meters wide. It consists of three circles coupled through openings displayed in sequence. In front of the opening of the first circle there stretches a fence (a barrier) which forces the fish to go through this opening, entering the first circle. The openings are built in such a way that the fish only see them when they are outside. Once inside the first circle, the fish will only see the opening to get into the second circle, but never the opening to go out. The fish keep moving in circles within the fenced circles, until they finally fall in the third circle, where the chances of escape are practically nil. The walls of the *curral* are made up of a fence of wooden poles 2 to 3 meters high, woven by vines. The fence is fixed to logs thrust in the stone on top of the reefs near the coast. When the tide is high, the walls of the *curral* disappear under the surface of the water. As the tide lowers, the tips of the fences emerge and surface; on full moon tides, even the reefs are uncovered. The fisherman who works with this kind of trap is called a *vaqueiro* "cowboy". His work consists in going to the *curral* during the two low tides of the day, and collecting the trapped fish. On quarterly tides, the level of the water only lowers a little. As the *curral* may trap big and dangerous fish such as sharks, quarter-tide fishings make the work of the *vaqueiro* quite adventurous and dangerous.

The tarpon can weigh up to 60 kilos. It is a very fierce fish and has a prominent and hard lower jaw that the fishermen call *colher* "spoon". It jumps over the man within the *curral* and the collision can be fatal to the *vaqueiro*. This story was prompted by a series of questions I was asking about the tarpon. When I asked if it could cause harm to a man, my interlocutor told me this story in which his courage and altruism are exalted and the tarpon's aggressiveness is illustrated. I use some symbols in the transcription as follows:

[...] omitted passage.
— sudden interruption of the flow of the sentence.
(– – –) clause accompanied by a gesture.
( ) pause.
: extended duration of sound.

eu vi um – aquele Chico	I saw one – that Chico Primo there
Primo ali (– – –)	(– – –)
num sei se você conhece ele . . .	I don't know if you know him . . .
é o sogro do Luis Cabo	he is the father-in-law of Luis Cabo
interessante – será no	interesting – would it be in
mês de agosto?	the month of August?
mês de trumenta . . .	the month of the storm
num tava dando nada	weren't catching anything
eu saí daqui uma tarde	I left here one afternoon
e fui pra rua	and went to the street
mas eu não ia atrás de	but I wasn't going after fish

peixe não	
só ia pra ir pra rua	I was only going to go out
porque eu gosto de andar	because I like to walk around
por lá	
eu saí	I left
quando eu cheguei bem	when I arrived right there (– – –)
ali (– – –)	
[...]	
Cheguei acolá (– – –)	I arrived there (– – –)
ele ia passando assim (– – –)	he was going by like this (– – –)
... maré de quarto ...	tide was of the quarter moon
faltava – negócio de qua	it was almost – around four p.m.
tro horas	
aí eu também – ele ia	then I also – he was passing by
passando ali (– – –)	there (– – –)
mas eu não cheguei a falar	but I didn't get to talk with him
com ele não	at all
passei	I went by
quando eu cheguei lá na	when I arrived there at the edge
beira da praia	of the beach
me deu aquele palpite de	I got that feeling of going out to
ir pra maré ... sabe, mais	sea ... you know, with him
ele	
chegue ali (– – –) *do*	I arrived there (– – –) on that site
Calá pra lá	of Calá
ele já ia indo acolá em	he was already going there below
baixo (– – –), *na beira da*	(– – –) by the edge of the beach
praia	
mais na frente —	further ahead – –
"sabe que eu vô"	"you know, I'm going"
aquela vontade de ir ...	that desire to go ...
aí só fiz descer	then all I did was go down
[...]	
cheguei lá naquela pedra	I arrived there at that rock (– – –)
(– – –), *que tem na rumada*	that there is in that grove of
acolá (– – –)	coconut trees there (– – –)
... aquelas pedras – ele	those rocks – he arrived in the
chegou no curral	*curral*
e eu cheguei só nas pedras	and I only reached the rocks
aí de lá ele tirou a roupa	then from there he took off his clothes
e entrou	and went in
entrou ... aí eu desci	he went in ... then I went down

cheguei na casinha   I arrived there at the shack
[...]   [...]
cheguei na casinha   I reached the shack
e me pus de pé lá   and I stood up there
esperando que ele voltasse   waiting for him to return
e o sol se pos   and the sun went down
e ele ainda não chegou   and he still hasn't arrived
eu digo   I say
"vô atrás do Chico Primo.   "I'll go after Chico Primo. That's
Aquilo é peixe que tem   fish that's inside and he can't kill
dentro e ele tá aperreado   them"
pra mater e num pode"
aí tirei a roupa   then I took off my clothes
e entrei   and I went into the *curral*
cheguei ali na boca do   I arrived there at the entrance of
chiqueiro   the pigsty (the smallest circle)
cacei ele entro do chiqueiro ...   I looked for him inside the pigsty...
nada   nothing
aí eu vi o uru boiando   then I saw his straw basket floating
dentro do curral   in the *curral*
subia e descia, o mar mar com   going up and down, the waves with
                                        it there
                                        in the corner of the *curral*
ele, num canto do corral lá (– – –)   there (– – –)
que o mar lá é bravo   because the sea there is rough
o mar faz é medo   the sea is frightening
aí eu entrei pro chiqueirinho   then I went into the little pigsty
eu chego assim (– – –) *cacei*   I arrived like this (– – –) I looked
ele   for him
num achei   I didn't find him
[...]
aí eu olho assim (– – –) *pro*   then I look like this (– – –)
lado de baixo ...   underneath ...
ele tava ... recostado   he was ... leaned like this (– – –)
assim (– – –) *no canto*   in the corner
o mar – pá:::pá:::, batendo   the surf – pa:::pa:::, breaking
todo tempo nos peito   constantly on his chest
dele
eu calculei comigo   I thought to myself
"tá morto"   "he is dead"
[...]
sozinho, sem nada, eu digo   alone, without anything, I say
"tá morto"   "he is dead"

eu imaginei logo comigo, né	I immediately thought to myself, right
eu digo	I say
"agora sim! o hômi tá morto.	"Now right! the man is dead. I need to
Precisa eu levar esse	take this man, then they will say that
hômi, aí uão dizer que fui eu que matei esse hômi"	it was I who killed this man"
[...]	
aí também eu só fiz passar pro lado de dentro	then also all I did was to go inside
cheguei lá	I arrived there
peguei ele assim (−−−) na mão	I took his hand like this (−−−)
e chamei	and called
ele num respondeu	he didn't answer
eu chamei de novo	I called again
aí ( ) quando eu chamei de novo ele respondeu	then ( ) when I called again he answered
mas quase num sai fala	but speech almost didn't come out
fez gemer dentro	it was like a groan inside
digo	I say
"o quê que você tem, Seu	"how are you feeling Seu Chico? what
Chico? o que foi que houve − aconteceu com você aqui?"	was it − that happened with you here?"
aí ele num pôde falar	then he couldn't talk
só fiz mesmo pegá ele aqui (−−−) na mão	all I really did was to grab him here (−−−) by his hand
[...]	
botei ele nas costas	I put him on my back
[...]	
saí no seco	I went back to dry land
vim deixá ele cá na casinha	I came and left him here in the shack
cheguei na casinha	I arrived at the shack
aí ele num se sigurava	then he couldn't hold still shaking
[...]	
na tremura num se sigurava	he couldn't hold still
e perguntando a ele	and asking him
inté que ele dixe	until he said

tinha sido – . . . um camurupim	it was – . . . a tarpon had jumped on
tinha dado um salto em riba dele	top of him
tinha pegado nos peito dele	had caught him in the chest
e ele tinha ficado sem fala	and he had lost his voice
e tava pra morrer	and was about to die
eu digo	I say
"pois fique aí que eu vô	"well, stay there, I'm going to kill the
matá o peixe"	fish"
"você fica aí?"	"will you stay there?"
bateu a cabeca que ficava	he nodded his head that he would stay
aí eu voltei	then I went back
[. . .]	
eu chegei lá, rapaz	I arrived there, man,
o peixe tava era dentro	the fish was inside
[. . .]	
e o peixe era do tamanho	and the fish was about the size
desse que eu matei hoje	of this one I killed today
eu já ia sabendo que o	I went already knowing that the
peixe tava dentro	fish was inside

[. . .]
(In a long sequence he describes his fight with two big fish, one of which was the tarpon, and then continues:)

mas aí eu soltei a curimã	but then I released the striped mullet
e me agarrei com a pema	and I grabbed the tarpon
a minha vontade era nele sabe	I wanted to get him, you know
me enlinhei com ele	I grappled with him
ora, tinha um bom cacete . . .	well, I had a good club . . .
meti-lhe o pau	I clubbed him
matei	I killed him
aí enfiei no cipó	then I threaded him on the vine
passei pro lado de fora	I passed him to the outside
[. . .]	
bom, aí eu vim	well, then I came back
cheguei no seco	I arrived on dry land
ele tava	he was there
[. . .]	
eu digo	I say

"vamo simbora"
ele não podia ir não
não podia vim não
que não butava
digo
"agora sim! como é que eu

vô levá esse hômi e esse
peixe?"
era um pema bem de 6kg, uma
curimã bem de 5 kg, e um uru

chei-inho de peixe"
talvez vinhesse ali uns 200
barbudos
[...]
digo
"num posso levar"
[...]
mas o homem é pra tudo
aí eu peguei no braço dele
peguei assim (– – –) no braço

dele
"rambora!"
ora, ele não andou nadinha
andou nadinha, sentou-se
peguei dixi
"sabe de uma coisa, vô butá

exe danado nas costas junto
com esse peixe"
[...]
me levantei
taquei
saía candeia de fogo pra
todos os cantos dos ôio,
do peso
"mas eu levo, num deixo!"
eu truxe até a rumada

"na rumada eu desço"
desceu

"let's go"
he couldn't go at all
he couldn't come at all
because he couldn't make it
I say
"now right! how am I going to carry
this man this fish?"

it was a tarpon of a good 6 kilos, a
striped mullet of a good 5 kilos, and a
basket filled to the top with fish
perhaps there were about 200
barbudos

I say
"I can't carry it"

but a man is for everything
then I grabbed his arm
I grabbed like this (– – –) on his arm

"let's go!"
well he didn't walk at all
didn't walk at all, sat himself down
I said
"you know something, I'll put this damned
guy on my back together with this fish"

I stood up
I went on
I felt flashes in every corner of
my eyes, because of the weight
"but I take him, I don't leave him!"
I brought him up to the coconut grove
"at the grove I get down"
he got down

tirou ali um pedacinho ...	he walked for a short while ... again
de novo	
aí eu vim inté perto do	then I came up close to Calá
Calá	
chegou ali	when we arrived there
eu dixi	I said
"agora eu vô vê se eu vô"	"now let me see if I can go"
"rambora!"	"let's go"
aí saímo ... trombando pra-	then we left,... staggering here
qui e pracolá ...	and there ...
vim deixá ele na casa dele	I left him in his home
chegamo a umas hora da noite	we arrived late at night
era um dia de domingo, umas	it was Sunday, late at night.
hora da noite.	

NOTES

This chapter was originally prepared as a paper for the session on "Responsibility and Evidence in Oral Discourse," organized by Joel Sherzer and Judith Irvine in 1983, during the Annual Meeting of the American Anthropological Association. I have made several presentations of the paper's argument in Germany, at the Universities of Cologne, Heidelberg, Maine, Siegen, Mannheim, and Munich. In addition to Professors Hill and Irvine, I would like to thank Professors Ulla Johansen, Thomas Hauschild, Richard Burghart, Ivo Strecker, Karl-Heinz Kohl, Ludwig Pfeiffer, Vittoria Borso, and Matthias Laubscher for the stimulating contexts of discussion.

1 The village of Icaraí is a small enclave of Portuguese colonial days. It was formed in the eighteenth century, in the wake of the destruction of Tupinambá society, probably by Portuguese settlers and children of whites and indians (*caboclos*) who would not be accepted into a white slavist society. The communal memory of this village evinces historical facts of the period of its original settlement. Foreigners to the Icaraí dwellers are Dutch or French, two nations who had encroachments in the north-east of Brazil during the sixteenth and seventeenth centuries, Spaniards who visited the area throughout the colonial era and still do as missionaries, and Germans, since shipwrecked sailors of a German submarine came ashore during the Second World War. They also talk about indians, although there has not been a single indian in the region for two hundred years. A few villages like Icaraí remained stranded from the rest of the country for centuries, aided in their isolation by geographical factors. The communications between Icaraí and the capital of the Município of Itapipoca are interrupted six months of the year, during the rains. The village does not have electricity or running water, and is forgotten at the fringes of that part of the Brazilian coastline which is still too underdeveloped for tourism, and is not rich enough in lobster to attract the fishing industry.

2 The inhabitants of Icaraí speak Portuguese like all Brazilians, but in a dialect combining both regional influences (the dialect of the north-east of Brazil) and the historical background of an eighteenth-century Portuguese colonial settlement. Despite the dialectal differences, my dialect of Portuguese being that of Rio, the people of Icaraí and I could communicate without any difficulties insofar as language was concerned.

3 See S. A. Tyler, 1969.

4 Fish with "black meat" falls under the category of *peixe reimoso* together with shell-fish, fish inhabiting the bottom of the sea, and those species falling within the ambiguous or grey areas of classification, such as the *Beijupirá*, a shark which nevertheless has scales (all other sharks are "skin-fish"). *Peixe reimoso* must be avoided by all those who are ill, and by women during menstruation.

5 The fishermen sail as far as 30 miles away from the coast, dead-reckoning by means of the direction of the waves, the tide, and the winds, by fathoming the depths with a lead sinker, and by observing the stars and the kind of fish they catch as they sail along. In this village of 400 people, there are 12 boats, each belonging to one family traditionally involved in fishing. Each boat carries 3 or 4 fishermen including the skipper, and may undertake short fishing trips or longer journeys in which they can stay between 3 and 7 days on the ocean. Fishing from a boat is not the only method of catch they practice in Icaraí, nor is it the most lucrative, but it is surrounded by an aura of tradition and heroism. The Icaraí fishermen say that fishing is not work, nor is it leisure. It requires courage and endurance. The skippers are generally respected and feared. They are the characters of many tales told by the other fishermen, but they themselves are too reserved and reticent to talk about themselves. They remind me of Odysseus in Homer's epic, and live by a code of honor reminiscent of the Japanese samurai. Each family of fishermen "owns" a rock somewhere in the sea which is generally a good fishing spot. Some rocks are close to the coast, and when the boat is fishing over them it can be seen from the beach. Some others lie out in the ocean and require complex navigational plans to be reached. To sail to one of these distant rocks, the fishermen carry out a series of triangulating maneuvers. The time of the year and the wind that is blowing determine the direction of the first tack. Coconut trees, sand dunes, and other outstanding marks on land constitute two points of the triangle, while the boat is the third. When he departs for a certain rock several miles away from the coast, leaving land in January, on a morning in which the north-east wind is blowing, the skipper knows exactly how big his triangle will be, and after he loses sight of the shore, he tacks and sails on a straight line which is one side of the triangle until he reaches his fishing spot.

6 As S. A. Tyler (1987:172) writes, "In its positive aspect, postmodern anthropology seeks to atone for the original sin of LANGUAGE, that separation of speech and world we know as the disjunction of words and things, and to make that atonement by means of a return to the commonsense, plurivocal world of the speaking subject. In its negative aspect, it seeks to incarnate the transcendental object called LANGUAGE, and to cast out the doxology of 'signs' and 'signification' which is the means of transcendence and false objectification."

7 Like the Nambīcuará studied by Lévi-Strauss, the villagers of Icaraí noticed that the mode of communication (of registering) employed by the ethnographer was a source of control and therefore of power, but unlike the Brazilian indians, the fishermen did not try to appropriate the medium and use it by themselves; instead, guessing the power of the tape-recorder to disseminate their message, they wanted to record their voices and sometimes even merely to dictate their names to the tape-recorder. (see Lévi-Strauss, 1978:294–304.)

8 Here I turn to terminology introduced by speech-act theory, as well as to Paul Ricoeur's model of the text as meaningful action amenable to the interpretive work of critical hermeneutics. (see also Austin, 1962, and Ricoeur, 1981).

9 See T. Maranhão, 1975, and 1977.

10 See J. Derrida, 1974.

REFERENCES

Abrahams, Roger. 1970. A performance-centered approach to gossip. *Man* (n.s.) 5:290–301.

Agha, Asif. 1989. Epistemic mode and cognitive perspective in Lhasa Tibetan. Paper presented at the 88th Annual Meeting of the American Anthropological Association, Washington, DC, November 1989.

Ahern, Emily M. 1979. The problem of efficacy: Strong and weak illocutionary acts. *Man* (n.s.) 14:1–17.

Anderson, John M. 1971. *The Grammar of Case: Towards a Localistic Theory*. Cambridge University Press.

Anderson, Lloyd B. 1986. Evidentials, paths of change, and mental maps: Typologically regular asymmetries. In Chafe and Nichols, eds., pp. 273–312.

Aune, Michael B. n.d. Liturgy as communication and performance of the gospel. MS, Pacific Lutheran Theological Seminary, Berkeley. (To appear in an anthology edited by Patrick Keifert).

Austin, John L. 1962. *How to Do Things with Words*. Cambridge, MA: Harvard University Press.

Bach, Kent. 1990. Communicative intentions, plan recognition, and pragmatics: Comments on Thomason and on Litman and Allen. In Cohen, Morgan, and Pollack, eds., pp. 389–400.

Bach, Kent and Robert Harnish. 1979. *Linguistic Communication and Speech Acts*. Cambridge, MA: MIT Press.

Bakhtin, Mikhail M. [1929] 1984. *Problems of Dostoevsky's Poetics*. Trans. Caryl Emerson. Minneapolis: University of Minnesota Press.

[1934] 1981. *The Dialogic Imagination*. Caryl Emerson and Michael Holquist, eds. and trans. Austin: University of Texas Press.

Banfield, Ann. 1973. Narrative style and the grammar of direct and indirect speech. *Foundations of Language* 10:1–39.

1982. *Unspeakable Sentences: Narration and Representation in the Language of Fiction*. Boston: Routledge and Kegan Paul.

Barber, Benjamin R. 1990. The most sublime event. *The Nation*, March 12, p. 351.

Bascom, William. 1969. *Ifa divination: Communication between gods and men in West Africa*. Bloomington: Indiana University Press.

1980. *Sixteen cowries: Yoruba divination from Africa to the New World*. Bloomington: Indiana University Press.

Başgöz, Ilhan. 1975. The tale-singer and his audience. In Ben-Amos and Goldstein, eds., pp. 140–203.

Basso, Ellen. 1987. *In Favor of Deceit*. Tucson: University of Arizona Press.

1990. The trickster's scattered self. *Anthropological Linguistics* 30 (3/4):292–318.

Basso, Keith. 1979. *Portraits of "The Whiteman": Linguistic Play and Cultural Symbols among the Western Apache*. New York: Cambridge University Press.

289

Bateson, Gregory. 1972. *Steps to an Ecology of Mind.* New York: Ballantine Books.
1979. *Mind and Nature: A Necessary Unity.* New York: E. P. Dutton.
Bauman, Richard. 1972. The La Have Island general store: Sociability and verbal art in a Nova Scotia community. *Journal of American Folklore* 85:330–43.
1977a. Settlement patterns on the frontiers of folklore. In William R. Bascon, ed., *Frontiers of Folklore,* pp. 121–31. Boulder, CO: Westview Press.
1977b. *Verbal Art as Performance.* Reprint edition 1984, Prospect Heights, IL: Waveland.
1983. The field study of folklore in context. In Richard M. Dorson, ed., *Handbook of American Folklore,* pp. 362–68. Bloomington: Indiana University Press.
1986. *Story, Performance, and Event: Contextual Studies of Oral Narrative.* Cambridge University Press.
1987a. The role of performance in the ethnography of speaking. *Working Papers and Proceedings of the Center for Psychosocial Studies* (Chicago, IL), No. 11:3–12.
1987b. De-centered discourse. Paper delivered at the 86th Annual Meeting of the American Anthropological Association, Chicago, IL, November 1987.
Bauman, Richard and Charles L. Briggs. 1990. Poetics and performance as critical perspectives on language and social life. *Annual Review of Anthropology* 19:59–88.
Bauman, Richard and Joel Sherzer, eds. 1974. *Explorations in the Ethnography of Communication.* Cambridge University Press.
Beardsley, Monroe C. and W. K. Wimsatt, Jr. 1953. Intention. In Joseph T. Shipley, ed., *Dictionary of World Literature,* pp. 229–32. Revised edition. New York: Philosophical Library.
Beattie, John. 1967. Divination in Bunyoro, Uganda. In Middleton, ed., pp. 211–31.
Becker, Alton L. 1979. Text-building, epistemology, and aesthetics in Javanese shadow theatre. In Alton L. Becker and Aram A. Yengoyan, eds. *The Imagination of Reality: Essays in Southeast Asian Coherence Systems,* pp. 211–43. Norwood, NJ: Ablex.
Beckett, Samuel, 1974. *Texts for Nothing.* Trans. Samuel Beckett. London: Calder and Boyars.
Ben-Amos, Dan and Kenneth S. Goldstein, eds. 1975. *Folklore: Performance and Communication.* The Hague: Mouton.
Bendix, Edward H. 1974. Indo–Aryan and Tibeto–Burman contact as seen through Nepali and Newari verb tenses. In Franklin C. Southworth and Mahadev L. Apte, eds. *Contact and Convergence in South Asian Languages,* Special Issue of *International Journal of Dravidian Linguistics* 3(1):42–59.
1984. The metaterm "cause": Exploring a definition in Newari and English. In Lawrence J. Raphael, C. B. Raphael, and M. R. Valdovinos, eds. *Language and Cognition: Essays in Honor of Arthur J. Bronstein,* pp. 11–27. New York: Plenum Press.
Benveniste, Emile. 1971. Subjectivity in language. In *Problems in General Linguistics,* 233–30. Coral Gables, FL: University of Miami Press.
Besnier, Niko. 1990a. Language and affect. *Annual Review of Anthropology* 19:419–51.
1990b. Conflict management, gossip, and affective meaning on Nukulaelae. In Karen A. Watson-Gegeo and Geoffrey White, eds. *Disentangling: Conflict Discourse in Pacific Societies,* pp. 290–334. Stanford, CA: Stanford University Press.

Bloch, Maurice. 1975. Introduction. In Maurice Bloch, ed. *Political Language and Oratory in Traditional Society*, pp. 1–28. London: Academic Press.

1989. *Ritual, History and Power: Selected Papers in Anthropology*. London: Athlone.

Bohannan, Paul. 1975. Tiv divination. In John Beattie and Geoffrey Lienhardt, eds. *Essays in Social Anthropology*, pp. 150–66. Oxford University Press.

Bolinger, Dwight. 1982. Intonation and Its Parts. *Language* 58:505–33.

Bourdieu, Pierre. 1975. Le langage autorisé: Note sur les conditions sociales de l'efficacité du discours rituel. *Actes de la Recherche en Sciences Sociales*, No. 5/6:183–90.

1977. *Outline of a Theory of Practice*. Cambridge University Press.

Boyer, Pascal. 1990. *Tradition as Truth and Communication: A Cognitive Description of Traditional Discourse*. Cambridge University Press.

Brenneis, Donald N. 1986. Shared territory: Audience, indirection, and meaning. In Duranti and Brenneis, eds., pp. 339–47.

1987. Talk and transformation. *Man*, (n.s.), 22:499–510.

Brenneis, Donald N. and R. Padarath. 1975. "About those scoundrels I'll let everyone know": Challenge singing in a Fiji Indian community. *Journal of American Folklore* 88:283–91.

Briggs, Charles L. 1986. *Learning How to Ask: A Sociolinguistic Appraisal of the Role of the Interview in Social Science Research*. Studies in the Social and Cultural Foundations of Language, 1. Cambridge University Press.

1988. *Competence in Performance: The Creativity of Tradition in Mexicano Verbal Art*. Philadelphia: University of Pennsylvania Press.

1989. Personal expression and social criticism in Warao ritual wailing: Notes toward a reconsideration of language and gender. MS.

Brown, Penelope and Stephen Levinson. 1978. Universals in language usage: politeness phenomena. In Esther Goody, ed. *Questions and Politeness*, pp. 56–289. Cambridge University Press.

1987. *Politeness: Some Universals in Language Usage*. Cambridge University Press.

Bunzel, Ruth. 1952. *Chichicastenango: A Guatemalan Village*. Locust Valley, NY: J. J. Augustin.

Burke, Kenneth. 1935. Permanence and change. *New Republic* (1935):223–26.

1969. *A Rhetoric of Motives. A Grammar of Motives*. Berkeley: University of California Press.

Butor, Michel. 1965. The second case. *New Left Review* 34:60–8.

Camones, Luis de. [1572] 1950. *The Lusiads*. Trans. Leonard Bacom. New York: Hispanic Society of America.

Caton, Steven C. 1985. The poetic construction of self. *Anthropological Quarterly* 4:141–51.

Cerquiglini, Bernard. 1984. Le style indirect libre et la modernité. *Langages* 19:7–16.

Chafe, Wallace L. 1961. *Seneca Thanksgiving Rituals*. Bureau of American Ethnology Bulletin 183. Washington, DC: Smithsonian Institution.

1967. *Seneca Morphology and Dictionary*. Smithsonian Contributions to Anthropology 4. Washington, DC: Smithsonian Institution.

1976. Givenness, contrastiveness, definiteness, subjects, topics, and point of view. In Charles N. Li, ed., *Subject and Topic*, pp. 25–56. New York, Academic Press.

1980. The deployment of consciousness in the production of a narrative. In Wallace L. Chafe, ed. *The Pear Stories*, pp. 9–50. Norwood, NJ: Ablex.

1985. Information flow in Seneca and English. In Mary Niepokiy *et al.*, eds. *Proceedings of the Eleventh Annual Meeting of the Berkeley Linguistics Society*, pp. 14–24. Berkeley, CA: Berkeley Linguistics Society.

1986. Introduction. In Chafe and Nichols, eds., pp. vii–xi.

1987. Cognitive constraints on information flow. In Russell S. Tomlin, ed. *Coherence and Grounding in Discourse*, pp. 21–52. Philadelphia: John Benjamins.

Chafe, Wallace L. and Johanna Nichols, eds., 1986. *Evidentiality: The Linguistic Coding of Epistemology*. Norwood, NJ: Ablex.

Cicourel, Aaron V. 1974. *Cognitive Sociology: Language and Meaning in Social Interaction*. New York: Free Press.

Clancy, Patricia. 1980. Referential choice in English and Japanese narrative discourse. In Wallace L. Chafe, ed. *The Pear Stories*, pp. 127–202. Norwood, NJ: Ablex.

Clark, Eve V. and Kathie L. Carpenter. 1989. The notion of source in language acquisition. *Language* 65:1–30.

Clark, Herbert H. and Thomas B. Carlson. 1982a. Hearers and speech acts. *Language* 58:332–73.

1982b. Speech acts and hearer's belief. In Neel V. Smith, ed. *Mutual Knowledge*, pp. 1–36. New York: Academic Press.

Clark, Katerina and Michael Holquist. 1984. *Mikhail Bakhtin*. Cambridge, MA and London: The Belknap Press of Harvard University Press.

Cleary, Edward W., ed. 1972. *McCormick's Handbook of the Law of Evidence*. St. Paul, MN: West Publishing Co.

Clifford, James. 1988. *The Predicament of Culture: Twentieth-Century Ethnography, Literature, and Art*. Cambridge, MA, and London: Harvard University Press.

Clifford, James, and George Marcus. 1986. *Writing Culture: The Poetics and Politics of Ethnography*. Berkeley: University of California Press.

Cohen, Philip R., Jerry Morgan, and Martha E. Pollack, eds. 1990. *Intentions in Communication*. Cambridge, MA: MIT Press.

Colby, Benjamin N. and Lore M. Colby. 1981. *The Daykeeper: The Life and Discourse of an Ixil Diviner*. Cambridge, MA: Harvard University Press.

Cole, Peter and Jerry Morgan, eds. 1975. *Syntax and Semantics 3: Speech Acts*. New York: Academic Press.

Comaroff, John L. and Simon Roberts. 1981. *Rules and Processes: The Cultural Logic of Dispute in an African Context*. University of Chicago Press.

Comrie, Bernard. 1986. Tense in indirect speech. *Folia Linguistica* 20:265–96.

Conley, John. 1982. The law. In William O'Barr, ed. *Linguistic Evidence*, pp. 41–9. New York: Academic Press.

Crapanzano, Vincent. 1980. *Tuhami: Portrait of a Moroccan*. University of Chicago Press.

Davidson, Donald. 1984. *Inquiries into Truth and Interpretation*. Oxford: Clarendon Press.

Davitz, Joel R. 1964. *The Communication of Emotional Meaning*. New York: McGraw-Hill.

Delancey, Scott. 1981. An interpretation of split ergativity and related patterns. *Language* 57:626–57.

1986. Evidentiality and volitionality in Tibetan. In Chafe and Nichols, eds., pp. 203–13.

Derrida, Jacques. 1973. *Speech Phenomena, and Other Essays on Husserl's Theory of Signs.* Trans. David B. Allison. Evanston, IL: Northwestern University Press.

1974. *Of Grammatology.* Trans. Gayatri Chakravorty Spivak. Baltimore: Johns Hopkins University Press.

1978. *Writing and Difference.* Trans. Alan Bass. University of Chicago Press.

1981. *Positions.* Trans. Alan Bass. University of Chicago Press.

Dorian, Nancy. 1977. The problem of the semi-speaker in language death. *International Journal of the Sociology of Language* 12:23–32.

Dowling, William C. 1983. Intentionless meaning. *Critical Inquiry.* 9:784–9.

Du Bois, John W. 1986. Self-evidence and ritual speech. In Chafe and Nichols, eds., 1986. pp. 313–36.

1987. Meaning without intention: Lessons from divination. *IPrA Papers in Pragmatics* 1:80–122.

1989. Protodialogue: constituting the speech event precedent. Paper presented at the 88th Annual Meeting of the American Anthropological Association, Washington, DC, November 1989.

Forthcoming, a. Mechanical meaning in the semiotics of divination. MS, UC Santa Barbara.

Forthcoming, b. Words without speakers: The language of magic and ritual in traditional societies. MS, UC Santa Barbara.

Duranti, Alessandro. 1981a. *The Samoan 'Fono': A Sociolinguistic Study.* Pacific Linguistics, series B, vol. 80. Canberra: The Australian National University, Department of Linguistics, Research School of Pacific Studies.

1981b. Speechmaking and the organization of discourse in a Samoan *fono.* *Journal of the Polynesian Society* 90:357–400.

1983a. Samoan speechmaking across social events: One genre in and out of a *fono. Language in Society* 12:1–22.

1983b. Intentions, self, and local theories of meaning: Words and social action in a Samoan context. *Center for Human Information Processing Technical Reports* 122. San Diego, CA: Center for Human Information Processing.

1990. Politics and grammar: Agency in Samoan political discourse. *American Ethnologist* 17:646–66.

Duranti, Alessandro and Donald Brenneis, eds. 1986. *The Audience as Co-Author.* *Text* 6(3) (Special Issue).

Duranti, Alessandro and Elinor Ochs. 1986. Literacy instruction in a Samoan village. In Bambi B. Schieffelin and Perry Gilmore, eds. *Acquisition of Literacy: The Ethnographic Perspective,* pp. 213–32. Norwood, NJ: Ablex.

Durkheim, Emile. [1915] 1965. *The Elementary Forms of the Religious Life.* Trans. Joseph Ward Swain. New York: Free Press.

Dwyer, Kevin. 1982. *Moroccan Dialogues.* Baltimore: Johns Hopkins University Press.

Evans-Pritchard, Edward E. 1937. *Witchcraft, Oracles, and Magic among the Azande.* Oxford: Clarendon Press.

[1956] 1962. *Sanza,* a characteristic feature of Zande language and thought. In *Social Anthropology and Other Essays,* pp. 330–54. New York: Free Press.

Finnegan, Ruth. 1969. How to do things with words: Performative utterance among the Limba of Sierra Leone. *Man* (n.s.) 4:537–52.

1977. *Oral Poetry: Its Nature, Significance, and Social Context.* Cambridge University Press.

Firth, Raymond. 1975. Speech making and authority in Tikopia. In Maurice Bloch, ed. *Political Language and Oratory in Traditional Society*, pp. 29–43. London: Academic Press.

Fisher, Lawrence. 1976. Dropping remarks and the Barbadian audience. *American Ethnologist* 3:227–42.

Fontenrose, Joseph. 1978. *The Delphic Oracle: Its Responses and Operations, with a Catalogue of Responses*. Berkeley: University of California Press.

Fortes, Meyer. 1966. Religious premises and logical technique in divinatory ritual. *Philosophical Transactions of the Royal Society of London*, series B, 251:409–22.

Foster, Michael K. 1974a. When words become deeds: An analysis of three Iroquois Longhouse speech events. In Bauman and Sherzer, eds., pp. 354–67.

1974b. *From the Earth to Beyond the Sky: An Ethnographic Approach to Four Longhouse Iroquois Speech Events*. Canadian Ethnology Service Paper No. 20. Ottawa: National Museums of Canada.

Foucault, Michel. 1977. What is an author? In Donald F. Bouchard, ed. *Language, Countermemory, Practice: Selected Essays and Interviews*, pp. 113–38. Ithaca, NY: Cornell University Press.

Friedrich, Paul. 1979. *Language, Context, and the Imagination*. Stanford University Press.

1986. *The Language Parallax: Linguistic Relativism and Poetic Indeterminacy*. Austin: University of Texas Press.

Friedrich, Paul and James Redfield. 1978. Speech as a personality symbol: The case of Achilles. *Language* 54:263–88.

Gadamer, Hans-Georg. 1975. *Truth and Method*. Garrett Barden and John Cumming, eds. New York: Seabury Press.

1976. *Philosophical Hermeneutics*. D. E. Linge, ed. and trans. Berkeley: University of California Press.

1981. *Reason in the Age of Science*. Trans. G. Lawrence. Cambridge, MA: MIT Press.

1989. Text and interpretation. In Diane P. Michelfelder and Richard E. Palmer, eds. *Dialogue and Deconstruction*, pp. 21–51. Albany: State University of New York Press.

Geertz, Clifford. 1973. *The Interpretation of Cultures*. New York: Basic Books.

1983. *Local Knowledge: Further Essays in Interpretive Anthropology*. New York: Basic Books.

Genetti, Carol. 1986. The grammaticalization of the Newari verb *tol*. *Linguistics of the Tibeto–Burman Area* 9(2):53–70.

1991. From postposition to subordinator in Newari. In Bernd Heine and Elizabeth C. Traugott, eds. *Approaches to Grammaticalization*. Volume II, pp. 227–56. Amsterdam: John Benjamins.

Gilbert, Margaret. 1983. Notes on the concept of social convention. *New Literary History* 14:225–51.

Gill, Sam D. 1977. Prayer as person: The performative force in Navaho prayer acts. *History of Religions* 17:143–57.

1987. *Native American Religious Action: A Performance Approach to Religion*. Columbia: University of South Carolina Press.

Givón, Talmy. 1980. *On Understanding Grammar*. Perspectives in Neurolinguistics and Psycholinguistics Series. New York: Academic Press.

1985. Ergative morphology and transitivity gradients in Newari. In Franz Plank, ed. *Relational Typology*, pp. 89–108. Berlin: Mouton de Gruyter.

ed. 1985. *Topic Continuity in Discourse*. Philadelphia: John Benjamins.

Gluckman, Max. 1955. *The Judicial Process among the Barotse*. Manchester University Press.

1965. *The Ideas in Barotse Jurisprudence*. New Haven: Yale University Press.

1972. Moral crises: Magical and secular solutions. In Max Gluckman, ed. *The Allocation of Responsibility*, pp. 1–50. Manchester University Press.

Goffman, Erving. 1963. *Stigma: Notes on the Management of Spoiled Identity*. Englewood Cliffs, NJ: Prentice-Hall.

1974. *Frame Analysis: An Essay on the Organization of Experience*. New York: Harper and Row.

1979. Footing. *Semiotica* 25:1–29. Reprinted in *Forms of Talk*, pp. 124–59. Philadelphia: University of Pennsylvania Press, 1981.

1983. Felicity's condition. *American Journal of Sociology* 89:1–51.

Goodwin, Charles. 1981. *Conversational Organization: Interaction between Speakers and Hearers*. New York: Academic Press.

1986. Audience diversity, participation, and interpretation. In Duranti and Brenneis, eds., pp. 283–316.

Goodwin, Marjorie H. 1978. *Conversational Practices in a Peer Group of Urban Black Children*. University of Pennsylvania Ph.D. Dissertation.

1982. Instigating: Storytelling as a social process. *American Ethnologist* 9:799–819.

1990. *He-Said-She-Said: Talk as Social Organization among Black Children*. Bloomington, IN: Indiana University Press.

Gossen, Gary. 1974. *Chamulas in the World of the Sun: Time and Space in a Maya Oral Tradition*. Prospect Heights, IL: Waveland Press.

Granger, Byrd H. 1977. *A Motif Index for Lost Mines and Treasures*. Tucson: University of Arizona Press.

Grice, H. Paul. 1957. Meaning. *The Philosophical Review* 66:377–88. Reprinted in Jay F. Rosenberg and Charles Travis, eds. *Readings in the Philosophy of Language*, pp. 436–44. Englewood Cliffs, NJ: Prentice-Hall.

1968. Utterer's meaning, sentence-meaning, and word-meaning. *Foundations of Language* 4:225–42.

1969. Utterer's meaning and intentions. *Philosophical Review* 78:147–77.

1975. Logic and conversation. In Peter Cole and Jerry L. Morgan, eds. *Syntax and Semantics 3: Speech Acts*, pp. 41–58. New York: Academic Press.

1989a. Meaning revisited. In *Studies in the Way of Words*, pp. 283–303. Cambridge, MA: Harvard University Press.

1989b. Retrospective epilogue. In *Studies in the Way of Words*, pp. 339–85. Cambridge, MA: Harvard University Press.

Griffin, Peg and Hugh Mehan. 1981. Sense and ritual in classroom discourse. In Florian Coulmas, ed. *Conversational Routine: Explorations in Standardized Communication Situations and Prepatterned Speech*, pp. 187–213. The Hague: Mouton.

Grosz, Barbara. 1977. *The Representation and Use of Focus in Dialogue Understanding*. Artificial Intelligence Center Technical Report No. 151. Menlo Park, CA: SRI International.

Gruber, Jeffrey S. 1976. *Lexical Structure in Syntax and Semantics*. North-Holland Linguistic Series 25. Amsterdam: North-Holland.

Gumperz, John. 1982. *Discourse Strategies*. Cambridge University Press.

Haiman, John and Sandra A. Thompson. 1984. "Subordination" in universal grammar. In Claudia Brugman *et al.*, eds. *Proceedings of the Tenth Annual Meeting of the Berkeley Linguistics Society*, pp. 510–23. Berkeley, CA: Berkeley Linguistics Society.

Hale, Austin. 1980. Person markers: Finite conjunct and disjunct verb forms in Newari. In Ronald L. Train *et al.*, eds. *Papers in South-East Asian Linguistics*, no. 7, pp. 95–106. Canberra: Australian National University.

Hargreaves, David. 1983. *Evidentiality in Newari*. MA Thesis, University of Oregon.

Haviland, John B. 1977. *Gossip, Reputation, and Knowledge in Zinacantan*. University of Chicago Press.

1986. "Con buenos chiles": Talk, targets, and teasing in Zinacantan. In Duranti and Brenneis, eds., pp. 249–82.

1988. "We want to borrow your mouth": Tzotzil marital squabbles. *Anthropological Linguistics* 30:395–447.

Herskovits, Melville J. 1938. *Dahomey: An Ancient West African Kingdom*, I–II. New York: J. J. Augustin.

Hewitt, John P. and Randall Stokes. 1975. Disclaimers. *American Sociological Review* 40:1–11.

Hickmann, Maya, ed. 1987. *Social and Functional Approaches to Language and Thought*. Orlando, FL: Academic Press.

Hill, Jane H. 1988. Operationalizing "voice" in the study of oral discourse. Paper presented to the 87th Annual Meeting of the American Anthropological Association, Phoenix, AZ, November 16–20, 1988.

1989. The cultural (?) context of narrative involvement. In Brad Music, Randolph Graczyk, and Caroline Wiltshire, eds. *Papers from the 25th Annual Regional Meeting of the Chicago Linguistic Society, Part Two: Parasession on Language in Context*, pp. 138–56. Chicago Linguistic Society.

1990. Weeping in a Mexicano woman's narrative. In Ellen Basso, ed. *Native Americans Through Their Discourse*, pp. 29–50. Bloomington IN: The Folklore Institute. (Also in *Journal of Folklore Research* 27 (1/2):29–50.)

Forthcoming. The voices of Don Gabriel: Responsibility and moral grounds in a modern Mexicano narrative. In Bruce Mannheim and Dennis Tedlock, eds. *The Dialogic Emergence of Culture*.

Hirsch, E. D., Jr. [1960] 1971. Objective interpretation. In Hazard Adams, ed. *Critical Theory Since Plato*, pp. 177–94. New York: Harcourt Brace Jovanovich.

1983. Beyond convention? *New Literary History* 14:389–98.

Hirsch, S. 1989. Asserting male authority, recreating female experience: Gendered discourse in Coastal Kenyan Muslim courts. Paper presented at the Law and Society Association Meetings, Madison, WI.

Hohepa, Patrick W. 1981. A look at Maori narrative structure. In Jim Hollyman and Andrew Pawley, eds. *Studies in Pacific Languages and Cultures in Honor of Bruce Biggs*, pp. 35–46. Auckland: Linguistic Society of New Zealand.

Holquist, Michael. 1983. The politics of representation. *The Quarterly Newsletter of the Laboratory of Comparative Human Cognition* 5(1):2–9.

Hopper, Paul and Sandra A. Thompson. 1980. Transitivity in grammar and discourse. *Language* 56:251–99.

Hymes, Dell H. 1962. The ethnography of speaking. In Thomas Gladwin and William C. Sturtevant, eds. *Anthropology and Human Behavior*, pp. 13–53. Washington, DC: Anthropological Society of Washington.

1971. Sociolinguistics and the ethnography of speaking. In Edwin Ardener, ed. *Social Anthropology and Language*, pp. 47–93. ASA Monographs no. 10. London: Tavistock.

1974a. Ways of speaking. In Bauman and Sherzer, eds., pp. 433–51.

1974b. *Foundations in Sociolinguistics*. Philadelphia: University of Pennsylvania Press.

[1975] 1981. Breakthrough into performance. In Ben-Amos and Goldstein, eds. pp. 11–74. Reprinted in *In Vain I Tried to Tell You: Essays in Native American Ethnopoetics*, pp. 79–141. Philadelphia: University of Pennsylvania Press.

Irvine, Judith T. 1973. *Caste and Communication in a Wolof Village*. Ph.D. Dissertation, University of Pennsylvania.

1978. When is genealogy history? Wolof genealogies in comparative perspective. *American Ethnologist* 5:651–674.

1979. Formality and informality in communicative events. *American Anthropologist* 81:773–90.

1980. How not to ask a favor in Wolof. *Papers in Linguistics* 13:3–50.

1982a. Language and affect: Some cross-cultural issues. In Heidi Byrnes, ed. *Contemporary Perceptions of Language: Interdisciplinary Dimensions, Georgetown University Round Table on Language and Linguistics 1982*, pp. 31–47. Washington, DC: Georgetown University Press.

1982b. The creation of identity in spirit mediumship and possession. In David Parkin, ed. *Semantic Anthropology*, pp. 251–60. London: Academic Press.

1989. When talk isn't cheap: Language and political economy. *American Ethnologist* 16:248–67.

1990. Registering affect: Heteroglossia in the linguistic expression of emotion. In Catherine Lutz and Lila Abu-Lughod, eds. *Language and the Politics of Emotion*, pp. 126–61. Cambridge University Press.

Isambert, François. 1979. *Rite et efficacité symbolique: Essai d'anthropologie sociologique*. Paris: Cerf.

Ito, Karen L. 1985. Affective bonds: Hawaiian interrelationships of self. In Geoffrey White and James Kirkpatrick, eds. *Person, Self, and Experience: Explaining Pacific Ethnopsychologies*, pp. 301–27. Berkeley: University of California Press.

Jakobson, Roman. 1960. Linguistics and poetics. In Thomas A. Sebeok, ed. *Style in Language*, pp. 350–77. Cambridge, MA: MIT Press.

1971. The dominant. In Ladislav Matejka and Krystyna Pomorska, eds. *Readings in Russian Poetics: Formalist and Structuralist Views*, pp. 82–93. Cambridge, MA: MIT Press.

Jakubinskij, Lev P. [1923] 1979. On verbal dialogue. Trans. Jane Knox. *Dispositio* 4(11–12):321–36.

Jarvik, Lawrence and Nancy Strickland. 1988. Anti-Semite and Jew? *Tikkun* 3(4):72–4.

Jones, Andrew J. I. 1990. Toward a formal theory of communication and speech acts. In Cohen, Morgan, and Pollack, eds., pp. 141–60.

Just, P. 1989. Making representations collective: Dispute and moral evaluations among the Dou Donggo. Paper presented at the 1989 Law and Society Association Meetings, Madison, Wisconsin.

Kitagawa, Chisato and Adrienne Lehrer. 1990. Impersonal uses of personal pronouns. *Journal of Pragmatics* 14:739–59.

Knapp, Steven and Walter Benn Michaels. 1982. Against theory. *Critical Inquiry* 8:723–42.

Kochman, Thomas. 1983. The boundary between play and nonplay in Black verbal dueling. *Language in Society* 12:329–37.

Kuipers, Joel C. 1989. "Medical discourse" in anthropological context: Views of language and power. *Medical Anthropology Quarterly* 3(2):99–123.

1990. *Power in Performance: The Creation of Textual Authority in Weyewa Ritual Speech.* Philadelphia: University of Pennsylvania Press.

Kuno, Susumu. 1976. Subject, theme, and the speaker's empathy: A reexamination of relativization phenomena. In Charles N. Li, ed. *Subject and Topic*, pp. 417–44. New York: Academic Press.

Kuroda, S.-Y. 1973. Where epistemology, style, and grammar meet: A case study from Japanese. In Stephen R. Anderson and Paul Kiparsky, eds. *A Festschrift for Morris Halle*, pp. 377–91. New York: Holt, Rinehart and Winston.

Laboratory of Comparative Human Cognition. 1983. Culture and cognitive development. In W. Kessen, ed. *L. Carmicael's Manual of Child Psychology: History, Theories, and Methods*, pp. 295–356. New York: John Wiley.

Labov, William. 1972a. The transformation of experience in narrative syntax. In *Language in the Inner City*, pp. 354–96. Philadelphia: University of Pennsylvania Press.

1972b. Rules for ritual insults. In David Sudnow, ed. *Studies in Social Interaction*, pp. 120–69. New York: Free Press.

Ladrière, Jean. 1973. The performativity of liturgical language. *Concilium* 82:50–62.

Lakoff, Robin T. 1974. What you can do with words: Politeness, pragmatics, and performatives. In *Berkeley Studies in Syntax and Semantics* 1,XVI:1-55. Berkeley, CA: University of California, Institute of Human Learning.

Langacker, Ronald. 1985. Some observations and speculations on subjectivity. In John Haiman, ed. *Iconicity in Language*, pp. 109–50. Philadelphia: John Benjamins.

Larkin, Fanaafi. 1971. Review of *The Social Organization of Manu'a*, second edition, by Margaret Mead. *Journal of the Polynesian Society* 6:219–22.

Leach, Edmund. 1964. Animal categories and verbal abuse. In Eric Lenneberg, ed. *New Directions in the Study of Language*, pp. 23–64. Cambridge, MA: MIT Press.

Leap, William. 1977. The study of American Indian English: An introduction to the issues. In William Leap, ed. *Studies in Southwestern Indian English*, pp. 3–20. San Antonio, TX: Trinity University Press.

Leech, Geoffrey N. 1978. Natural language as metalanguage: An approach to some problems in the semantic description of English. *Transactions of the Philological Society of London* 1976–7, D. pp. 1–31.

1980. Language and tact. In *Explorations in Semantics and Pragmatics*, pp. 79–118. Amsterdam: John Benjamins.

Leontyev, A. N. 1981. *Problems of the Development of the Mind.* Moscow: Progress Publishers.

Levelt, Willem J. M. 1989. *Speaking: From Intention to Articulation.* Cambridge, MA: MIT Press.

Levinson, Stephen C. 1983. *Pragmatics.* Cambridge University Press.

1988. Putting linguistics on a proper footing: Explorations in Goffman's concepts of participation. In Paul Drew and Anthony Wootton, eds. *Erving Goffman*, pp. 161–227. Oxford: Polity Press.

Lévi-Strauss, Claude. 1978. *Tristes Tropiques.* New York: Atheneum.

Linde, Charlotte. 1972. *On the Linguistic Encoding of Spatial Information.* Ph.D. Dissertation, Columbia University.

Loftus, Elizabeth F. and John C. Palmer. 1974. Reconstruction of automobile destruction: An example of the interaction between language and memory. *Journal of Verbal Learning and Verbal Behavior*, 13:585–9.

Longacre, Robert E. 1976. *An Anatomy of Speech Notions.* Lisse: Peter de Ridder Press.

Lutz, Catherine and Lila Abu-Lughod. 1990. Introduction: Emotion, discourse, and the politics of everyday life. In Catherine Lutz and Lila Abu-Lughod, eds. *Language and the Politics of Emotion*, pp. 1–23. Cambridge University Press.

Lyons, John. 1982. Deixis and subjectivity: Loquor, ergo sum? In R. J. Jarvella and W. Klein, eds. *Speech, Place, and Action*, pp. 101–24. New York: John Wiley.

McNeill, David. 1985. Language viewed as action. In James V. Wertsch, ed. *Culture, Communication, and Cognition: Vygotskian Perspectives*, pp. 258–70. Cambridge University Press.

Malinowski, Bronislaw. [1935] 1978. *Coral Gardens and Their Magic*, vol. II: *The Language of Magic and Gardening.* New York: Dover.

Maranhão, Tullio. 1975. Náutica e classificacao ictiológica em Icaraí, Ceará: Um estudio em anthropologia cognitiva. MA thesis, Department of Anthropology, Universidade de Brasilia, Junho 1975.

　　1977. The status of taxonomies in anthropology and in linguistics. *Anthropological Linguistics* 19(3):111–22.

Martinich, A. P. 1975. Sacraments and speech acts, II. *Heythrop Journal* 16:405–17.

Marx, Karl and Friedrich Engels. [1845–6] 1978. *The German Ideology.* In Robert C. Tucker, ed. *The Marx–Engels Reader*, second edition, pp. 146–200. New York: Norton.

Mauss, Marcel. [1950] 1972. *A General Theory of Magic.* London: Routledge and Kegan Paul.

Mead, Margaret, 1937. The Samoans. In Margaret Mead, ed. *Cooperation and Competition among Primitive People*, pp. 282–312. Boston: Beacon Press.

Medvedev, Pavel Nikolaevich. [1928] 1985. *The Formal Method in Literary Scholarship: A Critical Introduction to Sociological Poetics.* Trans. Albert J. Wehrle. Cambridge, MA: Harvard University Press.

Mehan, Hugh. 1981. Social constructivism in psychology and sociology. *The Quarterly Newsletter of the Laboratory of Comparative Human Cognition* 3(4): 71–7.

Mendonsa, Eugene L. 1982. *The Politics of Divination: A Processual View of Reactions to Illness and Deviance among the Sisala of Northern Ghana.* Berkeley: University of California Press.

　　ed. 1967. *Magic, Witchcraft, and Curing.* Austin: University of Texas Press.

Mills, C. Wright. 1940. Situated actions and vocabularies of motive. *American Sociological Review* 5:904–13.

Milner, G. B. 1966. *Samoan Dictionary.* Oxford: Oxford University Press.

Mitchell-Kernan, Claudia. 1972. Signifying and marking: Two Afro–American speech acts. In John J. Gumperz and Dell H. Hymes, eds. *Directions in Sociolinguistics: The Ethnography of Communication*, pp. 161–79. New York: Holt, Rinehart and Winston.

Moerman, Michael. 1988. *Talking Culture: Ethnography and Conversation Analysis.* Philadelphia: University of Pennsylvania Press.

Moore, Omar Khayyam. [1957] 1979. Divination – A new perspective. *American Anthropologist* 59:69–74. Reprinted in William A. Lessa and Evon Z. Vogt, eds. *Reader in Comparative Religion*, 4th edition, pp. 376–9. New York: Harper and Row.

Moore, Sally Falk. 1972. Legal liability and evolutionary interpretation: Some aspects of strict liability, self-help and collective responsibility. In Max Gluckman, ed. *The Allocation of Responsibility*, pp. 51–108. Manchester University Press.

Moravcsik, Edith and Jessica Wirth. 1986. Markedness – an overview. In Fred R. Ekman, Edith A. Moravcsik, and Jessica R. Wirth, eds. *Markedness*, pp. 1–11. New York: Plenum Press.

Morgan, Jerry. 1990. Comments on Jones and on Perrault. In Cohen, Morgan, and Pollack, eds., pp. 187–93.

Morgan, Marceliena H. 1991. Indirectness and interpretation in African-American women's discourse. *Pragmatics* 1:421–51.

Munro, Doug and Niko Besnier. 1986. The German plantation at Nukulaelae Atoll. *Oral History Association of Australia Journal* 7:84–92.

Munro, Pamela. 1982. On the transitivity of "say" verbs. In Paul J. Hopper and Sandra A. Thompson, eds. *Studies in Transitivity, Syntax and Semantics* 15, pp. 301–18. New York and London: Academic Press.

Myers, Fred and Donald Brenneis. 1984. Introduction. In Fred Myers and Donald Brenneis, eds. *Dangerous Words: Language and Politics in the Pacific*, pp. 1–29. New York: New York University Press.

Niebuhr, H. Richard. 1963. *The Responsible Self*. New York: Harper and Row.

Nuyts, Jan. 1989. On the functionality of language. *Papers in Pragmatics* 3(1):88–129.

O'Barr, William. 1982. *Linguistic Evidence: Language, Power, and Strategy in the Courtroom*. New York: Academic Press.

O'Barr, William and Bowman K. Atkins. 1980. "Women's language" or "power-less language"? In Sally McConnell-Ginet, Ruth Borker, and Nancy Furman, eds. *Women and Language in Literature and Society*, pp. 93–110. New York: Praeger.

Ochs-Keenan, Elinor. 1974. Norm-makers, norm-breakers: Uses of speech by men and women in a Malagasay community. In Bauman and Sherzer, eds., pp. 125–43.

Ochs, Elinor. 1979. Planned and unplanned discourse. In Talmy Givón, ed. *Discourse and Syntax, Syntax and Semantics* 12, pp. 51–80. New York and London: Academic Press.

1982. Talking to children in Western Samoa. *Language in Society* 11:77–104.

1984. Clarification and Culture. In Deborah Schiffrin, ed. *Meaning, Form, and Use in Context: Linguistic Applications, Georgetown University Round Table on Languages and Linguistics 1984*, pp. 325–41. Washington, DC: Georgetown University Press.

1986. From feelings to grammar: A Samoan case study. In Bambi B. Schieffelin and Elinor Ochs, eds. *Language Socialization Across Cultures*, pp. 251–72. Studies in the Social and Cultural Foundations of Language, 3. Cambridge University Press.

1988. *Culture and Language Development: Language Acquisition and Language Socialization in a Samoan Village*. Cambridge University Press.

Ochs, Elinor and Bambi Schieffelin. 1984. Language acquisition and socialization: Three developmental stories. In Richard A. Shweder and Robert A. Levine, eds. *Culture Theory: Essays on Mind, Self, and Emotion*, pp. 276–320. Cambridge University Press.

Ohmann, Richard. 1971. Speech acts and the definition of literature. *Philosophy and Rhetoric* 4:1–19.

Olson, David R. 1980. On the language and authority of textbooks. *Journal of Communication* 30:186–96.
Paine, Robert, ed. 1981. *Politically Speaking: Cross-Cultural Studies of Rhetoric.* Philadelphia: ISHI.
Palmer, F. R. 1986. *Mood and Modality.* New York: Cambridge University Press.
Paredes, Américo. 1977. On ethnographic work among minority groups: A folklorist's perspective. *New Scholar* 6:1–32.
Paredes, Américo and Richard Bauman, eds. 1972. *Toward New Perspectives in Folklore.* Austin: University of Texas Press.
Park, George K. 1967. Divination and its social contexts. In Middleton, ed., pp. 233–54.
Parker, Arthur C. 1913. *The Code of Handsome Lake, the Seneca Prophet.* New York State Museum Bulletin 163. Albany, NY.
Partee, Barbara H. 1973. The syntax and semantics of quotation. In Stephen R. Anderson and Paul Kiparsky, eds. *A Festschrift for Morris Halle,* pp. 410–18. New York: Holt, Rinehart and Winston.
Pascal, Roy. 1977. *The Dual Voice: Free Indirect Speech and Its Functioning in the Nineteenth-Century European Novel.* Manchester University Press; Totowa, NJ: Rowman and Littlefield.
Perrault, C. Raymond. 1990. An application of default logic to speech act theory. In Cohen, Morgan, and Pollack, ed., pp. 161–85.
Philips, Susan. 1990. Tongan speech levels: Practice and talk about practice in the cultural construction of social hierarchy. To appear in *Austronesian Linguistics.*
Pliskin, Z. *Guard Your Tongue.* New York: Moriah Offset.
Polanyi, Livia. 1985. A theory of discourse structure and discourse coherence. In W. H. Eilfort, P. D. Kroeber, and K. L. Peterson, eds. *Papers from the General Session at the 21st Regional Meeting of the Chicago Linguistic Society,* pp. 306–22. Chicago Linguistic Society.
[1985] 1989. *Telling the American Story.* Cambridge, MA: The MIT Press.
Polanyi, Livia and Laura Martin. 1990. On the formal treatment of discourse particles: The case of Mochó *la* and *-a.* Paper presented at the Annual Meeting of the Linguistic Society of America, New Orleans, LA, January, 1990.
Pratt, Mary Louise. 1977. *Toward a Speech Act Theory of Literary Discourse.* Bloomington: Indiana University Press.
1981. The ideology of speech act theory. *Centrum,* N.S. 1:5–18.
Psathas, George, ed. 1979. *Everyday Language: Studies in Ethnomethodology.* New York: Irvington.
Rajan, Rajeswari S. and Zakia Pathak. 1989. Shahbano. *Signs Spring 1989*:14(3):558–82.
Rappaport, Roy A. 1974. Obvious aspects of ritual. *Cambridge Anthropology* 2:3–69.
1976. Liturgies and lies. *Internationales Jahrbuch für Wissens- und Religionssoziologie* 10:75–104.
1979. *Ecology, Meaning, and Religion.* Richmond, CA: North Atlantic Books.
Ravenhill, P. L. 1972. Religious utterances and the theory of speech acts. Paper read at the Georgetown University Round Table on Languages and Linguistics, Washington, DC, 1972. (Mimeographed; cited in Foster (1974)).
Rembar, Charles. 1980. *The Law of the Land: The Evolution of Our Legal System.* New York: Simon and Schuster.

Retel-Laurentin, Anne. 1969. *Oracles et ordalies chez les Nzakara*. Paris: Mouton.
Reynolds, B. 1963. *Magic, Divination, and Witchcraft among the Barotse of Northern Rhodesia*. London: Chatto and Windus.
Ribeiro, René. 1956. Projective mechanisms and the structuralization of perception in Afro–Brazilian divination. *Revue Internationale d'Ethnopsychologie Normale et Pathologique* 1:3–23.
Ricoeur, Paul. 1971. The model of the text: Meaningful action considered as a text. *Social Research* 38:529–62.
      1976. *Interpretation Theory: Discourse and the Surplus of Meaning*. Fort Worth, TX: The Texan Christian University Press.
      1981. *Hermeneutics and the Social Sciences*. John B. Thomson, ed. and trans. Cambridge University Press.
Rosaldo, Michelle. 1982. The things we do with words: Ilongot speech acts and speech act theory in philosophy. *Language in Society* 11:203–37.
Rose, H. J. 1928. Divination (Introductory and primitive). In James Hastings, ed. *Encyclopedia of Religion and Ethics*, vol. 4, pp. 775–80. New York: Charles Scribner's Sons.
Ross, Andrew, ed. 1989. *Universal Abandon: The Politics of Postmodernism*. Minneapolis: University of Minnesota Press.
Ryan, M. L. 1981. When "je" is "un autro": Fiction, quotation, and the performative analysis. *Poetics Today* 2:127–55.
Sacks, Harvey. 1970. Unpublished lecture notes.
      1974. An analysis of the course of a joke's telling in conversation. In Bauman and Sherzer, eds., pp. 337–53.
Said, Edward. 1978. *Orientalism*. New York: Pantheon.
Sapir, Edward. 1921. *Language*. New York: Harcourt, Brace and World.
      1927. Speech as a personality trait. *American Journal of Sociology* 32:892–905.
Scha, Remko and Livia Polanyi. 1988. An augmented context – free grammar for discourse. Proceedings of COLIN688, Budapest, Hungary.
Schegloff, Emanuel. 1982. Discourse as an interactional achievement: Some uses of "Uh Huh" and other things that come between sentences. In Deborah Tannen, ed. *Analyzing Discourse: Text and Talk, Georgetown University Round Table on Languages and Linguistics 1981*, pp. 71–93. Washington, DC: Georgetown University Press.
Schegloff, Emanuel, Gail Jefferson, and Harvey Sacks. 1977. The preference for self-correction in the organization of repair in conversation. *Language* 53:361–82.
Schenkein, Jim, ed. 1978. *Studies in the Organization of Conversational Interaction*. New York: Academic Press.
Schiffrin, Deborah. 1984. How a story says what it means and does. *Text* 4:313–46.
Schottelndreyer, B. 1980. Person markers in Sherpa. In Ronald L. Trail, ed. *Papers in South-East Asian Linguistics*, no. 7, pp. 125–36. Canberra: Australian National University.
Searle, John. 1969. *Speech Acts: An Essay in the Philosophy of Language*. Cambridge University Press.
      1976. The classification of illocutionary acts. *Language in Society* 5:1–23.
      1979. *Expression and Meaning*. Cambridge University Press.
      1983. *Intentionality: An Essay in the Philosophy of Mind*. Cambridge University Press.
      1990. Collective intentions and actions. In Cohen, Morgan, and Pollack, eds., pp. 401–15.

Sebeok, Thomas A. 1964. The structure and content of Cheremis charms. In Dell H. Hymes, eds. *Language in Culture and Society*, pp. 356–71. New York: Harper and Row.

Seitel, Peter. 1969. Proverbs: A social use of metaphor. *Genre* 2:143–61.

Sherzer, Joel. 1983. *Kuna Ways of Speaking: An Ethnographic Perspective*. Austin: University of Texas Press.

Shore, Bradd. 1982. *Sala'ilua: A Samoan Mystery*. New York: Columbia University Press.

Shuman, Amy. 1986. *Storytelling Rights: The Uses of Oral and Written Texts by Urban Adolescents*. Cambridge University Press.

Shuman, Amy, D. Schaffer, and S. Webber. 1992. Rethinking "think globally, act locally". In Marilyn Waldman, Muge Galin, and Artemis Leontis, eds *Changing Tradition: Cross-cultural perspectives on women*. Papers in Comparative Studies 7.

Silverstein, Michael. 1976. Shifters, linguistic categories, and cultural description. In Keith Basso and Henry Selby, eds. *Meaning in Anthropology*, pp. 11–56. Albuquerque: University of New Mexico Press.

1977. Cultural prerequisites to grammatical analysis. In Muriel Saville-Troike, ed. *Linguistics and Anthropology: Georgetown University Round Table on Languages and Linguistics 1977*, pp. 139–51. Washington, DC: Georgetown University Press.

1979. Language structure and linguistic ideology. In Paul R. Clyne, William F. Hanks, and Carol L. Hofbauer, eds. *The Elements: A Parasession on Linguistic Units and Levels*, pp. 193–247. Chicago Linguistic Society.

1981. The limits of awareness. *Sociolinguistic Working Papers* 84. Austin, TX: Southwest Educational Development Laboratory.

1984. On the pragmatic "poetry" of prose: Parallelism, repetition, and cohesive structure in the time course of dyadic conversation. In Deborah Schiffrin, ed. *Meaning, Form and Use in Context: Linguistic Applications, Georgetown University Round Table 1984*, pp. 181–99. Washington, DC: Georgetown University Press.

1985. The culture of language in Chinook narrative texts: or, on saying that ... in Chinook. In Johanna Nichols and Anthony C. Woodbury, eds. *Grammar Inside and Outside the Clause: Some Approaches to Theory from the Field*, pp. 132–71. Cambridge University Press.

Smith, Paul. 1988. *Discerning the Subject*. Minneapolis: University of Minnesota Press.

Sperber, Dan and Deirdre Wilson. 1981. Irony and the use-mention distinction. In Peter Cole, ed. *Radical Pragmatics*, pp. 295–318. New York: Academic Press.

1988. *Relevance: Communication and Cognition*. Cambridge, MA: Harvard University Press.

Stallman, Robert W. E. 1974. Intentions [problem of]. *Princeton Encyclopedia of Poetry and Poetics*, pp. 398–400. Princeton University Press.

Sternberg, Meir. 1982. Proteus in quotation-land: Mimesis and the forms of reported discourse. *Poetics Today* 3(2):107–56.

Stoeltje, Beverly and Richard Bauman. 1988. The semiotics of performance. In Jean Umiker-Sebeok and Thomas A. Sebeok, eds. *The Semiotic Web*, pp. 585–99. Berlin: De Gruyter.

Stokes, Randall and John P. Hewitt. 1976. Aligning actions. *American Sociological Review* 41:838–49.

Strawson, P. F. [1964] 1971. Intention and convention in speech acts. *Philosophical Review* 73:439–60. Reprinted in Jay F. Rosenberg and Charles Travis, eds. *Readings in the Philosophy of Language*, pp. 599–614. Englewood Cliffs, NJ: Prentice-Hall.

Streeck, Jürgen. 1980. Speech acts in interaction: A critique of Searle. *Discourse Processes* 3:133–54.

Tambiah, Stanley J. 1973. Form and meaning of magical acts: A point of view. In Robin Horton and Ruth Finnegan, eds. *Modes of Thought: Essays on Thinking in Western and Non-Western Societies*, pp. 199–229. London: Faber and Faber.

   1985. A performance approach to ritual. In *Culture, Thought, and Social Action: An Anthropological Perspective*, pp. 123–66. Cambridge, MA: Harvard University Press.

Tannen, Deborah. 1986. Introducing constructed dialogue in Greek and American conversational and literary narrative. In Florian Coulmas, ed. *Direct and Indirect Speech*, pp. 311–32. Trends in Linguistics, Studies and Monographs, 31. Berlin: Mouton de Gruyter.

   1988. Hearing voices in conversation, fiction, and mixed genres. In Deborah Tannen, ed. *Linguistics in Context: Connecting Observation and Understanding*, pp. 89–113. Advances in Discourse Processes, 29. Norwood, NJ: Ablex.

Tedlock, Barbara. 1982. *Time and the Highland Maya*. Albuquerque: University of New Mexico Press.

Tedlock, Dennis. 1972. On the translation of style in oral narrative. In Paredes and Bauman, eds., pp. 114–33.

   1983. *The Spoken Word and the Work of Interpretation*. Philadelphia: University of Pennsylvania Press.

Thibaut, John W. and Laurens Walker. 1975. *Procedural Justice*. Hillsdale, NJ: Lawrence Erlbaum.

Thompson, Stith. 1955–8. *Motif-Index of Folk Literature*. 6 vols. Bloomington: Indiana University Press.

Trawick, Margaret. 1988. Spirits and voices in Tamil songs. *American Ethnologist* 15:193–215.

Turner, Victor. 1974. *Dramas, Fields, and Metaphors: Symbolic Action in Human Society*. Ithaca, NY: Cornell University Press.

   1975. *Revelation and Divination in Ndembu Ritual*. Ithaca, NY: Cornell University Press.

Turner, Victor, and Edward M. Bruner, eds. 1986. *The Anthropology of Experience*. Urbana: University of Illinois Press.

Tyler, Stephen A., ed. 1969. *Cognitive Anthropology*. New York: Holt, Rinehart and Winston.

   1987. *The Unspeakable: Discourse, Dialogue, and Rhetoric in the Postmodern World*. Madison: Wisconsin University Press.

Urban, Greg. 1989. The "I" of discourse. In Benjamin Lee and Greg Urban, eds. *Semiotics, Self, and Society*, pp. 27–52. Berlin: Mouton.

Verschueren, Jef. 1983. On Buguslawski on promise. *Journal of Pragmatics* 7:629–32.

   1984. Some methodological reflections of the comparative study of basic linguistic action verbs, illustrated with reference to the Polynesian languages. In F. Daems and L. Goossens, eds. *Een Spyeghel voor G. Jo Steenbergen: Huldealbum Agneboden bij zijn emeritaat*, pp. 393–411. Leuven: Acco.

Voloshinov, Valentin Nikolaevich. [1929] 1978. Reported speech. In Ladislav Matejka and Krystyna Pomorska, eds. *Readings in Russian Poetics: Formalist and Structuralist Views*, pp. 176–96. Michigan Slavic Contributions Series, 8. Ann Arbor, MI: Michigan Slavic Publications.

[1929–30] 1973. *Marxism and the Philosophy of Language.* Trans. Ladislav Matejka and I. R. Titunik. New York: Seminar Press.

Vygotsky, Lev Semonovich. [1934] 1986. *Thought and Language.* Cambridge, MA: MIT Press.

1978. *Mind in Society: The Development of Higher Psychological Processes.* Michael Cole, Vera John-Steiner, Sylvia Scribner, and Ellen Souberman, eds. Cambridge, MA: Harvard University Press.

Wallace, Anthony F. C. 1970. *The Death and Rebirth of the Seneca.* New York: Knopf.

Watt, Ian. [1957] 1964. *The Rise of the Novel.* Berkeley: University of California Press.

Wertsch, James V. 1985. *Vygotsky and the Social Formation of Mind.* Cambridge, MA: Harvard University Press.

Wetterström, Thomas. 1977. *Intention and Communication: An Essay in the Phenomenology of Language.* Doxa.

Wheelock, Wade T. 1982. The problem of ritual language: From information to situation. *Journal of the American Academy of Religion.*

Whorf, Benjamin Lee. 1956. Some verbal categories in Hopi. In John Carroll, ed. *Language, Thought, and Reality,* pp. 112–24. Cambridge, MA: MIT Press.

Wierzbicka, Anna. 1974. The semantics of direct and indirect discourse. *Papers in Linguistics* 7:267–307.

1985. A semantic metalanguage for a cross-cultural comparison of speech acts and speech genres. *Language in Society* 14:491–514.

1987. *English Speech Act Verbs: A Semantic Dictionary.* Sydney: Academic Press.

Wimsatt, W. K., Jr. and Monroe C. Beardsley. 1946. The intentional fallacy. *Sewanee Review* 54:468–88. Reprinted in Lambropoulos, V. and P. N. Miller, eds. *Twentieth-Century Literary Theory: An Introductory Anthology.* Albany, S.U.N.Y. Press, 1987.

Witherspoon, Gary. 1977. *Language and Art in the Navajo Universe.* Ann Arbor: University of Michigan Press.

Wojcik, R. H. 1976. Where do instrumental NPs come from? In Masayoshi Shibatani, ed. *Syntax and Semantics 6: The Grammar of Causative Constructions,* pp. 165–80. New York: Academic Press.

Wolfson, Nessa. 1978. A feature of performed narrative: the conversational historical present. *Language in Society* 7:215–37.

Woodbury, Anthony C. 1986. Interactions of tense and evidentiality: A study of Sherpa and English. In Chafe and Nichols, eds., pp. 188–202.

1987. Rhetorical structure in a Central Alaskan Yupik traditional narrative. In Joel Sherzer and Anthony C. Woodbury, eds. *Native American Discourse,* pp. 176–239. Cambridge University Press.

Young, Katherine. 1977. Indirection in storytelling. *Western Folklore* 37:46–55.

1987. *Taleworlds and Storyrealms.* Dordrecht: Martinus Nijhoff.

Zuesse, Evan M. 1987. Divination. In Mircea Eliade, ed. *The Encyclopedia of Religion,* pp. 375–82. New York: Macmillan.

INDEXES

Index of subjects

abuse, and circumlocution 105–106; constructed in interaction 109–110; discourse frames in 106, 109–110, 123, 128; embedded in specific moral systems 109; indigenous categories 110–111; in Barbados 127; in Mexicano 13; in Wolof 12, 105–134; in Wolof conversation 124–128; in Wolof *xaxaar* 114–123; in Zande 105–106; linguistic forms of 106, 107–110, 120, 128; pragmatic vs. referential dimension of abuse 105; semantic content 107–110, 128
accountability 5, 164; *see also* responsibility
accuracy, challenges to 136, 137, 140, 141, 144, 148; in service of reputation 144–145; relation to experience 137, 149–150; vs. authority 135; vs. entitlement 148; *see also* authenticity, fidelity, truth
accusations 3, in Samoa 34–36, 38–39; 141
addressing self, in Goffman 11
addressor, vs. sender 33, 40
adolescent narrative 135–160
adversarial, vs. inquisitorial approach 252
adversarial system, and American ideology 253
affect 6, 163–164; in divination 64–65; in involvement 220; in Nukulaelae reported speech 15, 161–179; in Weyewa women's songs 103–104; in Wolof *xaxaar* 12; neglected by linguists 163
African-American, indirectness 26; narrative 222; participants in fight stories 137; ritual insult 26, 110; speech 26, 33; *see also* Barbados
agency 1, 2, 3, 4, 9, 23 n. 4, 209; attribution as interpretive process 4; and Samoan ergative 22
ambiguity, in abuse 111, 114, 129; in discourse structure 215; in English modals 17; in protodialogic context 62; in responsibility for speech 113–114

anaphora, in world shift 212–214
anaphoric inaccessibility, of reported speech 212–214, 225 n. 12; and discourse hierarchy 214–215
animator 11, 13, 198, 224 n. 2
antipersonalist critique, 8, 40, 51, 67; and politeness theory 20; *see also* speech act theory, personalism
Apache 256
apersonality, in divination 10, 59–65
argument, moves in 206–210
assertion, in novel 53; in Newari 226, 227–228, 231, 232
audience 9, 25, 26, 45, 111, 115, 119, 138–139, 162, 183, 195–196, 212, 225 n. 10, 248, 257, 276; inference by 18, 198, 208–209, 220, 221, 240; *see also* jury, participant roles
authenticity 6, 154; in reported speech in Nukulaelae 162, 168, 169, 173, 177; *see also* accuracy, truth
author, for Goffman 11; intention of 52; oracle as 10
authoritative discourse 150; and entitlement 157
authoritativeness of discourse 6, 10, 11, 157
authority, and evidence 264; appropriation of in reported speech 135, 152, 157; challenges to 136, 152, 157; for Bakhtin 152–153, 157–158; in adolescent world 151; in Chamula 102; in divination 68; in Mexicano (New Mexico) 102; in Nukulaelae 15, 164, 167; in Seneca 86–87; in Weyewa 91, 97–98, 99–100; vs. accuracy 135, 136
authorship 4; in anthropological writing 267, 269, 271–273, 275–276; in Newari 238–239; in Nukulaelae ideology 164; in Wolof *xaxaar* 123; negotiation for in fieldwork 275
Azande, *see* Zande

306

Indexes 307

Bali 40
Barbados "dropping remarks" 127
Barotse law 2–3, 19, 249
Brazil 19–20, 260–279
Chamula 102
children, and responsibility 21; and Wolof
 abuse 124–126; on Nukulaelae 166; on
 Samoa 43, 166
Chinookan 184
code-switching 204, 224 n. 7
cognition, as sociohistorical 45
commissive, shift to declaration 140
communicative event 4; as social
 accomplishment 182; participation
 frameworks in 11
communicative competence 187–188
consciousness 14, 223; Marx's view of 45;
 in Newari 238
consequences, 6; for participant 138, 153;
 of speech acts in Nukulaelae 167; of
 speech acts in Samoa 9, 24–38, 52, 67
constructed dialogue, see reported speech
Control, in Newari 235–237
control, of diviner 59; over quoted speech
 176
courts, American vs. British 253
deixis 14; adverbial, in Nukulaelae
 Tuvaluan 171–172; in subjectivity 221;
 shift in indirect discourse 163, 210
demeanor, in evidence 257
deontic modality 17
dialogicality 1–2, 5, 20, 66, 158; in
 anthropological fieldwork 260, 268–269,
 271–273, 277, 279; in evidentiality 18; in
 Weyewa 88, 92–95
direct discourse, see reported speech
directness, in speech 31, 106, 129–130; see
 also indirection
discours, for Benveniste 14
discourse structure 16
displacement 157, 221
dispute 2–3, 4, 6, 19, 250; among
 adolescents 136
distribution, of responsibility 7, 12–13, 16,
 21, 197–198, 208–212, 221–222
divination 3, 5, 9, 53–71; as projective
 technique 71 nn. 15, 16; Ixil Maya 61;
 mechanical vs. mental 53–54, 70 n. 8;
 Naskapi scapulimancy 65; Nzakara 64;
 Quiche Maya 61; Sisala symbol-spinning
 58–59, 61; Tiv 60, 62; Weyewa 90, 92–95;
 Yoruba Ifa 56, 61–62, 70 n. 15, 70 n. 16;
 Yoruba Sixteen Cowrie 54–56; Zande
 poison oracle 56–58
dramaturgical persona 6
dramaturgical theory of Goffman 11

duplex speech event 70 n. 9, 241; see also
 voice split
elicitation method 7, 18, 226–227, 232,
 237–238, 243–244, 261, 261–265, 267
emotion, see affect
empathy 172; see also involvement
English 14, 15, 17, 18–19, 23 n. 4, 51, 70
 n. 13, 168, 181 n. 9, 213, 214, 221, 225
 n. 15; intonation unit length in 74
English, Indian 224 n. 6
entertained vs. asserted propositions in
 divination 65
entextualization 11, 88, 102–103
entitlement 12, 135–159; challenges to 140,
 142–144, 148, 152, 155; dimensions of
 151; for Sacks 140; levels of negotiation
 for 137, 141; to involvement 138; to
 ownership of experience 136, 140–141,
 156–157; to recontextualize 151; to use
 reported speech 148, 151
epistemic modality 4, 17
epistemological stance, in Seneca 85–86
ergative case, in Newari 234, 235, 243, 247
 n. 9, 247 n. 13; in Samoan 22
ergative languages 247 n. 14
ethics, Samoan 42
ethnographic, experience 178; practice 196;
 writing 6, 20, 269–275
ethnography, as essential to pragmatic
 analysis 25
ethnography of speaking 2, 182, 269
ethnopragmatics 24–25, 40, 44–45
ethnoscience 20, 260, 261, 273
evaluation (narrative) 224 n. 2; external
 211; internal 211
event, account vs. experience of 137–138,
 149; on narrative main line 215; see also
 speech event, communicative event
evidence 2, 4, 5, 17; and affect 163–164;
 and discourse genre 19–20; and
 institutional context 248, 258; and
 knowledge 264, 272; and responsibility 6,
 136; as cultural construction 258–259;
 circumstantial 230; hearsay (English)
 233, (Newari), 238, 254–255; in English
 19, 251; in adversarial proceeding
 252–253; in US court proceedings 19,
 248–259; practical 264
evidentials 5, 7, 17, 22, 164, 251; in Newari
 17–18, 226–245; in Seneca particles 85–86
experience, and discourse 269; and
 evidence 251, 254–255; and narrative
 account 137–140, 149, 185, 193–194,
 197–223, 266; as sociocentric 198,
 211–212; firsthand, as negotiated 141,
 150; ownership of 140, 142, 144–155

Index of names